AN INSIDER'S GUIDE TO THE UN

AN INSIDER'S GUIDE

TO

THE UN

LINDA FASULO

Yale University Press / New Haven and London

Set in Scala type by Keystone Typesetting, Inc. Printed in the United States of America by Vail-Ballou Press.

Library of Congress Cataloging-in-Publication Data
Fasulo, Linda M.
An insider's guide to the UN / Linda Fasulo.
    p.   cm.
Includes bibliographical references and index.
ISBN 0-300-10155-4 (cloth : alk. paper)
ISBN 0-300-10762-5 (pbk. : alk. paper)
1. United Nations—Popular works. I. Title.
JZ4984.6.F37 2003
341.23—dc21   2003010668

A catalogue record for this book is available from the British Library.

The paper in this book meets the guidelines for permanence and durability of the Committee on Production Guidelines for Book Longevity of the Council on Library Resources.

10 9 8 7 6

For my son, Alex, my husband, Rob, and my mother, Mary

CONTENTS

CONTENTS

For my son, Alex, my husband, Rob, and my mother, Mary

ACKNOWLEDGMENTS

This book would not have been possible without the encouragement, advice, and support of many people. To all the diplomats, UN officials, analysts, and observers whom I have interviewed, I express my thanks for their interest in this project. This especially includes Secretary of State Madeline Albright; ambassadors John C. Danforth, Richard Holbrooke, John Negroponte, David Malone, Nancy Soderberg, and Danilo Turk; and Shepard Forman, Mark Malloch Brown, Michael Sheehan, and Shashi Tharoor, who all graciously shared their unique and invaluable personal insights.

For their generous financial support, I'm very grateful to the UN Foundation, in particular Tim Wirth, Melinda Kimble and Phyllis Cuttino. I also thank the Rockefeller Brothers Fund, specifically its president Stephen Heintz, for helping to fund the project. In addition, I thank the World Affairs Council of Philadelphia, especially its president, Buntzie Ellis Churchill, and Claudia McBride and Margaret Lonzetta for their enthusiastic sponsorship.

Warm thanks go to Kirsten Plonner, my researcher, for her devoted day-to-day work in seeing this book to completion, and to longtime friend and colleague Bill Zeisel of QED Associates for his discerning eye in the preparation of the manuscript. I thank my son Alex for his technical savvy and research assistance, and my friend Esther Margolis for introducing me to Yale University Press. I'm grateful to have had the opportunity to work with the wonderful staff at Yale University Press, particularly senior editor John Kulka and manuscript editor Nancy Moore.

I also express appreciation to my friends and colleagues at the UN, NBC News, and National Public Radio who gave encouragement along the way. And throughout this experience, my family has been remarkably patient and supportive. For this I am extremely grateful.

Working as a news correspondent at the United Nations has given me a first-hand perspective on one of the world's finest and most important governing bodies. Nowhere else in the world can you watch an international group of luminaries discuss the great issues of our day and make decisions that can define our lives for years to come. Curbing international terrorism, combating diseases like malaria and AIDS, and trying to bring rogue nations like North Korea to account are only a few of the big problems the UN can address in a year.

At the UN, before the proceedings begin the agenda has been set, the members have prepared themselves, confrontations have played out in relative privacy, and the public sees a polished performance. Many onlookers will accept this performance at face value and never give it another thought. For those who want to know more, who ask how the proceedings are conceived, prepared, and paid for, and about their chances for a lasting impact, I have written this book, relying on my personal observations as well as the experiences and insights of other insiders. Just as I was about to start writing, however, the world changed forever.

President George W. Bush speaks at a luncheon hosted by UN Secretary General Kofi Annan for world leaders attending a General Assembly meeting on terrorism, Nov. 10, 2001. UN/DPI photo by Eskinder Debebe.

The book would have been different if I had written it before 9/11. It would have devoted much more space to discussing the effectiveness of the UN and whether it serves American interests. It would have argued more extensively for the importance of globalization as a force that has woven the United States into the world fabric so tightly and in so many ways that we can no longer fantasize about "going it alone." It might even have dwelled on the need to keep the UN based in New York City rather than move it to another world capital as some have suggested. All these points are now moot.

The terrorist attacks in New York City and Washington, D.C., have changed many things, not least how the United States sees the United Nations. The media have begun to focus on the UN as a key ally in the fight against international terrorism. The UN has become more favored as a partner of the world's sole superpower. Americans have begun regarding the UN with renewed hope and interest, asking if it can transcend its old reputation for shortcomings. The insiders who

The UN was officially established on Oct. 24, 1945, when the UN Charter was ratified. Thus October 24 is celebrated every year as UN Day. President Franklin D. Roosevelt coined the name "United Nations," first used in the "Declaration by United Nations" on January 1, 1942.

run the UN and its associated agencies, and the diplomats who represent its member nations, have been asking similar questions. Most believe it will step up to the new challenges, but that is by no means the unanimous view.

More than half a century ago, the United States and its allies in World War II created an international body that they hoped would enable nations to prosper and live peacefully with one another. When the war ended in 1945, the new organization began with enormous goodwill, moral support from all sides, and strong US leadership. The world waited to see if the UN could rectify the shortcomings of the League of Nations, its predecessor organization, which dissolved in the late 1930s, victim of totalitarian regimes and US indifference. Could it be the uniting force among the victorious nations, whose ideologies and political interests often seemed at odds?

The cold war soon replaced idealistic collaboration with power politics between the West and the East. From the late 1940s until the breakup of the Soviet Union in 1991, confrontation among the blocs defined most UN relationships, discussions, debates, programs, and activities. A whole generation grew up with an East–West mindset, whose ghost still surfaces at the UN and elsewhere, even though the old blocs are gone and a new world is gradually emerging. During these many decades, expectations about the UN changed, becoming either more realistic or more cynical, depending on the viewpoint.

Today, although Americans do not expect the UN to solve all the world's problems, at the least we would like it to be a more effective partner in dealing with the forces that are transforming our world. These forces include international terrorism and much more. Economic forces are spinning new webs of relations among nations.

> "People [at the UN] acknowledge and recognize our importance and want to find ways to work more closely with us. They don't necessarily want to write us a blank check or do something that they perceive to be writing the United States a blank check, but they go to considerable lengths to work with us."—John Negroponte, US Ambassador to the UN

Public opinion is becoming something that many governments have to reckon with, as citizens connect with the world and become more affluent, educated, and willing to stand up for their rights. Changes in the natural environment are presenting challenges that can be solved only through international cooperation. Even the notion of human rights has changed, largely owing to the successful efforts of bodies like the UN to create and publicize international standards of behavior. What constitutes a threat to peace and security has broadened, to include dangers as diverse as AIDS, rights abuses, drug trafficking, and money laundering. We are less willing than before to let cultural difference excuse rights abuses, if only because nearly all nations have signed treaties that outlaw such abuses.

In the face of such rapid and wrenching change, we have to wonder how an organization created nearly sixty years ago, in a very different world, could possibly be relevant today, let alone in the future. That is the UN's greatest challenge—one it is addressing by trying to focus more on "the people" than on governments. Although the UN was created and still functions largely as an organization composed of government representatives, it is reaching out directly to the people in various ways. If this effort succeeds, the UN will become quite a different kind of organization.

This new emphasis on the people highlights the importance of the human factor in institutions like the United Nations. As one of my "insiders" says, people really do matter at the UN, and they act in a context full of illusion, opinion, perception, and emotion. In order to provide some understanding of that context, this book begins by exploring some basic aspects of the UN, such as how it came into existence and the governing principles that guide its operation.

ACABQ—Advisory Committee on Administrative and Budgetary
   Questions
ACUNS—Academic Council on the United Nations System
ASIL—American Society for International Law
BCUN—Business Council for the United Nations
CEDAW—Convention on the Elimination of All Forms of
   Discrimination Against Women
CND—Commission on Narcotic Drugs
CONGO—Conference on Non-Governmental Organizations in
   Consultative Status
CRC—Convention on the Rights of the Child
CTBTO—Preparatory Commission for the Comprehensive Nuclear-
   Test-Ban Treaty Organization
DPA—Department of Political Affairs
DPI—Department of Public Information
DPKO—Department of Peacekeeping Operations
E-10—Elected 10 members of the Security Council
ECOSOC—Economic and Social Council
ECOWAS—Economic Council of West African States

ETTA—East Timor Transitional Administration
EU—European Union
FAO—Food and Agriculture Organization
G-77—A coalition of developing countries
GA—General Assembly
GAO—General Accounting Office
GATT—General Agreement on Tariffs and Trade
HCHR—High Commissioner for Human Rights
IAEA—International Atomic Energy Agency
ICAO—International Civil Aviation Organization
ICC—International Criminal Court
ICCPR—International Covenant on Civil and Political Rights
ICJ—International Court of Justice
ICTR—International Criminal Tribunal for Rwanda
ICTY—International Criminal Tribunal for (the former) Yugoslavia
IDA—International Development Association
IFAD—International Fund for Agricultural Development
ILO—International Labor Organization
IMF—International Monetary Fund
IMO—International Maritime Organization
INSTRAW—International Research and Training Institute for the
    Advancement of Women
IPCC—Intergovernmental Panel on Climate Change
ISA—International Studies Association
ITU—International Telecommunications Union
NAM—Nonaligned Movement
NATO—North Atlantic Treaty Organization
NGO—nongovernmental organization
OAU—Organization of African Unity
OEWG—Open-Ended Working Group on the Question of Equitable
    Representation on and Increase in the Membership of the Security
    Council
OHCHR—Office of the High Commissioner for Human Rights
OIOS—Office of Internal Oversight Services
OPCW—Organization for the Prohibition of Chemical Weapons

P5—Permanent 5 members of the Security Council
PCT—Patent Cooperation Treaty
PR—A Nation's Permanent Representative or Perm Rep
SC—Security Council
SG—Secretary General
UN—United Nations
UNA-USA—United Nations Association of the United States of
    America
UNAIDS—Joint United Nations Program on HIV/AIDS
UNCTAD—UN Conference on Trade and Development
UNDCP—UN International Drug Control Program
UNDP—United Nations Development Program
UNEP—United Nations Environment Program
UNESCO—United Nations Educational, Scientific, and Cultural
    Organization
UNF—United Nations Foundation
UNFPA—United Nations Population Fund
UNHCR—Office of the United Nations High Commissioner for
    Refugees
UNICEF—United Nations Children's Fund
UNIDO—UN Industrial Development Organization
UNIFEM—UN Development Fund for Women
UNMEE—UN Mission in Ethiopia and Eritrea
UNMOVIC—United Nations Monitoring, Verification, and
    Inspection Commission on Iraq
UNODC—United Nations Office on Drugs and Crime
UNOPS—UN Office for Project Services
UPU—Universal Postal Union
UNRWA—United Nations Relief and Works Agency for Palestine
    Refugees in the Near East
UNSCOM—United Nations Special Commission on Iraq
UNTAET—UN Transitional Administration in East Timor
UNTSO—United Nations Truce Supervision Organization
UNV—UN Volunteers
UPU—Universal Postal Union

WEOG—Western Europe and Others bloc
WFP—World Food Program
WHO—World Health Organization
WIPO—World Intellectual Property Organization
WMO—World Meteorological Organization

AN INSIDER'S GUIDE TO THE UN

CHAPTER 1

An Overview

As the Charter makes clear, the United Nations was intended to introduce new principles into international relations, making a qualitative difference to their day-to-day conduct. The Charter's very first Article defines our purposes: resolving disputes by peaceful means; devising cooperative solutions to economic, social, cultural and humanitarian problems; and broadly encouraging behavior in conformity with the principles of justice and international law.

— Kofi Annan, Secretary General of the United Nations

The UN came into existence as a result of the most terrible war in history. During World War II, American President Franklin Roosevelt, British Prime Minister Winston Churchill, and the leaders of several other major combatant nations agreed that it was necessary to create a world organization that would help ensure the peace in future years. Their ideas are enshrined in the Preamble to the UN's Charter, which is one of its fundamental documents:

We the peoples of the United Nations determined
to save succeeding generations from the scourge of war, which twice in our lifetime has brought untold sorrow to mankind, and

Josef Stalin, Franklin Roosevelt, and Winston Churchill meet at the Yalta Conference in Yalta, USSR, Feb. 12, 1945. UN/DPI photo.

to reaffirm faith in fundamental human rights, in the dignity and worth of the human person, in the equal rights of men and women and of nations large and small, and

to establish conditions under which justice and respect for the obligations arising from treaties and other sources of international law can be maintained, and

to promote social progress and better standards of life in larger freedom,

and for these ends

to practice tolerance and live together in peace with one another as good neighbors, and

to unite our strength to maintain international peace and security, and

to ensure, by the acceptance of principles and the institution of methods, that armed force shall not be used, save in the common interest, and

to employ international machinery for the promotion of the economic and social advancement of all peoples,

have resolved to combine our efforts to accomplish these aims
Accordingly, our respective Governments, through representatives
assembled in the city of San Francisco, who have exhibited their
full powers found to be in good and due form, have agreed to the
present Charter of the United Nations and do hereby establish an
international organization to be known as the United Nations.

As the Preamble declares, the world's peoples, acting through their
representatives, seek to create a just and prosperous world through
common action. It could hardly be simpler, and yet during more than
half a century of trying we still live amid global insecurity and, in
many places, injustice and suffering. And the UN itself is far from
simple. It straddles the globe, operating in almost every nation on
earth, and has a bewildering variety of offices, programs, and personnel. Let's begin, then, with some basic points and language that will
appear throughout the book.

What Is the United Nations?

One of the points is that the UN is not always what it seems to be.
Consider the following: many people, if asked to define the UN, would
probably respond that it is a large organization devoted to world peace,
and that it has several main bodies, such as the General Assembly and
the Security Council, and an executive leader, the Secretary General. It
is headquartered in New York City, they would say, but has operations
all over the world.

A look at the UN's organizational flowchart largely confirms this
general picture. At the top are the six principal organs (see Appendix
A), some of which are household names: the International Court of
Justice (better known as the World Court), the Security Council (where
five selected countries have the right to veto any resolution they don't
like), the General Assembly (which consists of delegates from all
member nations of the UN), the Economic and Social Council, the
Trusteeship Council (which did its job so well it has lost its reason for
being), and the Secretariat (whose director, Kofi Annan, is a global

diplomat-superstar). With the exception of the Trusteeship Council, these principal organs get the most media coverage and are, in some ways, the most significant movers and shakers within the UN (see Appendix A for a breakdown of UN groups).

When we move to the second tier of organizations, the scene is more complicated. Here we find an amazing collection of entities and organizations, some of which are actually older than the UN itself and operate with almost complete independence from it. Best known to the public are the "Specialized Agencies," such as the United Nations Educational, Scientific, and Cultural Organization (UNESCO), the World Health Organization (WHO), the World Bank, and the International Monetary Fund (IMF). Another group, called "Programs and Funds," includes one very well known body, the United Nations Children's Fund (UNICEF), and several others that appear frequently in the news, like the United Nations Environment Program (which considers global warming and other environmental issues) and the United Nations High Commissioner for Refugees (UNHCR). Below them on the chart are "Other UN Entities," featuring one standout, the Human Rights Commission, which meets in Geneva and receives enormous press coverage, and three others that play important but less publicized roles. The five research institutes likewise keep a low public profile.

The "related organizations" are a unique group because they contain two entities with the same acronym (bad planning!): the World Trade Organization, which almost everyone has heard of, and the World Tourism Organization, which almost no one has heard of except tourism professionals. Above them are two sets of commissions. The "Functional Commissions" include some that on first glance seem to poach on the ground of other entities. For example, the Commission on Narcotic Drugs seems to overlap the UN Drug Control Program, on the left side of the chart. Similarly, the Commission on the Status of Women seems to overlap the UN Development Fund for Women. However, the overlap is more apparent than real in these two cases, because the Functional Commissions concentrate on policy while the agencies are oriented more toward implementation. Now, if there are "Functional Commissions," you might expect to find "Dysfunctional Commissions" too (and their existence has been asserted by some critics). Instead we find the "Regional Commissions," which are among the least known of UN bodies. They set policy about economic development in the regions of Africa, Europe, Latin America and the Caribbean, Asia and the Pacific, and Western Asia.

The position of the supporting organizations on the flowchart does not make them merely adjuncts of the entities above them. To the contrary, many of them run their own affairs with little interference and, as critics have complained, with not much communication with the peer agencies, programs, or commissions with which they share interests.

We now have a good schematic picture of the UN's structure. But this is only a beginning. When we think about these organizations in action, flowcharts aren't very helpful. They don't answer simple questions like whether the UN has a military establishment or whether it can raise taxes. Nor does it help to ask the people around you, because polls have revealed that while most Americans have a pretty friendly view of the UN, they know little about even its basic workings, and often attribute to it powers and authority it doesn't have. Richard Holbrooke, the US Ambassador to the UN during the last two years of the Clinton administration, has a reputation for toughness and a penchant for aggressively pushing the American viewpoint. He tells a story about a recent speaking engagement in Odessa, Texas—"George Bush country," as he puts it—when "some guy asked 'What do you think about this world government thing?' I said there was no such thing, and he said, 'What about the UN, that's a world government, they are trying to take away our liberties.' And I said, 'Well, Sir, that is just not true.' There are people out there who think the UN has that kind of power and insidious influence, and the truth is the exact opposite, the UN is too weak, not too strong. You start with a certain percentage of people completely misunderstanding the UN, criticizing it from the wrong point of view. Too strong is their fear when in fact too weak to be effective is the truth."

THE UNITED NATIONS SYSTEM

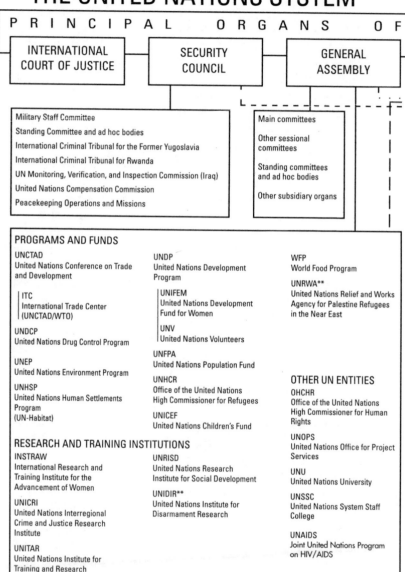

P R I N C I P A L   O R G A N S   O F

| INTERNATIONAL COURT OF JUSTICE | SECURITY COUNCIL | GENERAL ASSEMBLY |

Military Staff Committee

Standing Committee and ad hoc bodies

International Criminal Tribunal for the Former Yugoslavia

International Criminal Tribunal for Rwanda

UN Monitoring, Verification, and Inspection Commission (Iraq)

United Nations Compensation Commission

Peacekeeping Operations and Missions

Main committees

Other sessional committees

Standing committees and ad hoc bodies

Other subsidiary organs

PROGRAMS AND FUNDS

UNCTAD
United Nations Conference on Trade and Development

ITC
International Trade Center (UNCTAD/WTO)

UNDCP
United Nations Drug Control Program

UNEP
United Nations Environment Program

UNHSP
United Nations Human Settlements Program
(UN-Habitat)

UNDP
United Nations Development Program

UNIFEM
United Nations Development Fund for Women

UNV
United Nations Volunteers

UNFPA
United Nations Population Fund

UNHCR
Office of the United Nations High Commissioner for Refugees

UNICEF
United Nations Children's Fund

WFP
World Food Program

UNRWA**
United Nations Relief and Works Agency for Palestine Refugees in the Near East

RESEARCH AND TRAINING INSTITUTIONS

INSTRAW
International Research and Training Institute for the Advancement of Women

UNICRI
United Nations Interregional Crime and Justice Research Institute

UNITAR
United Nations Institute for Training and Research

UNRISD
United Nations Research Institute for Social Development

UNIDIR**
United Nations Institute for Disarmament Research

OTHER UN ENTITIES

OHCHR
Office of the United Nations High Commissioner for Human Rights

UNOPS
United Nations Office for Project Services

UNU
United Nations University

UNSSC
United Nations System Staff College

UNAIDS
Joint United Nations Program on HIV/AIDS

* Autonomous organizations working with the United Nations and each other through the coordinating machinery of the Economic and Social Council.

** Report only to the General Assembly.

Published by the United Nations Department of Public Information
DPI/2299–February 2003.

THE UNITED NATIONS

ECONOMIC AND SOCIAL COUNCIL	TRUSTEESHIP COUNCIL	SECRETARIAT

FUNCTIONAL COMMISSIONS

Commission for Social
Development
Commission on Human Rights
Commission on Narcotic Drugs
Commission on Crime Prevention
and Criminal Justice
Commission on Science and
Technology for Development
Commission on Sustainable
Development
Commission on the Status of
Women
Commission on Population and
Development
Statistical Commission

REGIONAL COMMISSIONS

Economic Commission for Africa
(ECA)
Economic Commission for
Europe (ECE)
Economic Commission for Latin
America and the Caribbean
(ECLAC)
Economic Commission for Asia
and the Pacific (ESCAP)
Economic Commission for
Western Asia (ESCWA)
United Nations Forum on Forestry
Sessional and Standing
Committees Expert, ad hoc, and
related bodies

RELATED ORGANIZATIONS

IAEA
International Atomic Energy Agency

WTO (trade)
World Trade Organization

WTO (tourism)
World Tourism Organization

CTBTO
Preparatory Commission for the
Comprehensive Nuclear-Test-Ban-
Treaty Organization

OPCW
Organization for the Prohibition of
Chemical Weapons

SPECIALIZED AGENCIES*

ILO
International Labor Organization

FAO
Food and Agriculture
Organization of the United
Nations

UNESCO
United Nations Educational,
Scientific, and Cultural
Organization

WHO
World Health Organization

WORLD BANK GROUP

IBRD	International Bank for Reconstruction and Development
IDA	International Development Association
IFC	International Finance Corporation
MIG	Multilateral Investment Guarantee Agency
ICSID	International Center for Settlement of Investment Disputes

IMF
International Monetary Fund

ICAO
International Civil Aviation
Organization

IMO
International Maritime
Organization

ITU
International Telecommunications Union

UPU
Universal Postal Union

WMO
World Meteorological
Organization

WIPO
World Intellectual Property
Organization

IFAD
International Fund for
Agricultural Development

UNIDO
United Nations Industrial
Development Organization

OSG
Office of the Secretary-General

OIOS
Office of Internal Oversight
Services

OLA
Office of Legal Affairs

DPA
Department of Political Affairs

DDA
Department for Disarmament
Affairs

DPKO
Department of Peacekeeping
Operations

OCHA
Office for the Coordination of
Humanitarian Affairs

DESA
Department of Economic and
Social Affairs

DGAACS
Department of General
Assembly Affairs and
Conference Services

DPI
Department of Public
Information

DM
Department of Management

OIP
Office of the Iraq Program

UNSECOORD
Office of the United Nations
Security Coordinator

ODC
Office on Drugs and Crime

UNOG
UN Office at Geneva

UNOV
UN Office at Vienna

UNON
UN Office at Nairobi

The Trusteeship Council

Of the six principal organs of the UN, the Trusteeship Council is easily the least well known, and for good reason. On Nov. 1, 1994, it suspended operations and ceased to exist except on paper. How can it be that one of the UN's original working parts should no longer be considered necessary? The demise of the council is part of the very successful role the UN has played in decolonization, the process by which some eighty nations have come into existence, since 1945. When decolonization began, most of Africa was controlled by a few Western nations, mainly the UK, France, and Belgium, while the Netherlands, UK, and France ruled large parts of Asia, including Indonesia, India, Pakistan, and Vietnam. Japan had ruled Korea for half a century, and the United States had just acquired, through military conquest, control of many Pacific islands such as the Marshalls. Many of the colonized peoples sought independence, and soon the world's colonial empires were being swept away or voluntarily relinquished. Sentiment against colonialism mounted quickly in the UN, which encouraged the move to independence.

Scattered around the world were territories, like Papua, New Guinea, and the Mariana Islands in the Pacific, that had been wards of the League of Nations and were now administered by Australia, the US, and other nations. Article 75 of the Charter states that "the United Nations shall establish under its authority an international trusteeship system for the administration and supervision of such territories as may be placed thereunder by subsequent individual agreements. These territories are hereinafter referred to as trust territories." The UN wanted to ensure that trustee nations would truly look after the best interests of their charges and help them secure self-government, either on their own or as parts of larger entities. To guarantee that they received adequate attention, the Trusteeship Council was composed of the five permanent members of the Security Council. Palau, an island group in the Pacific, was the last UN trust territory. During World War II, the US occupied Palau, which had been under the trusteeship of Japan through the League of Nations. Palau became a UN member on Dec. 15, 1994.

The UN Cast

The UN is made up of Six Principal Organs, all based [in New York] City except the ICJ, which is based in The Hague:

Secretariat
Security Council
General Assembly
International Court of Justice (ICJ)
Trusteeship Council (no longer meets)
Economic and Social Council

—Plus UN programs and funds, which are essential to working for development, humanitarian assistance, and human rights. They include the UN Children's Fund (UNICEF), the UN Development Program (UNDP), and the Office of the United Nations High Commissioner for Refugees (UNHCR).

—Plus the UN specialized agencies, which coordinate their work with the UN but are separate organizations. Agencies, such as the International Monetary Fund, the World Health Organization (WHO), and the International Civil Aviation Organization, focus on specific areas.

—Plus thousands of nongovernmental organizations (NGOs) that are independent citizens' organizations associated with the UN. They are concerned with many of the same issues as the UN, such as human rights, arms control, and the environment. NGOs are not part of the UN but have become important to its functioning in many key areas.

The UN's New York City headquarters is considered international territory.

One former US Ambassador to the UN, Nancy Soderberg, claims that "there is no such single thing as the UN." Rather, the UN "is 191 countries with different agendas and a whole collection of civil servants who work there, and it's all Jell-O. You can't say what the UN is because you touch one area and it comes out looking differently on the other side." According to Michael Sheehan, an American who

Michael Sheehan was UN Assistant Secretary General for Peacekeeping, 2001–3. A former US Army officer, he was Ambassador-at-Large and Coordinator for Counter Terrorism in the US State Department, and before that served in the Clinton White House on the staff of the National Security Council, as director of International Organizations and Peacekeeping. In 2003 Sheehan was appointed Deputy Commissioner of Counter Terrorism in the New York City Police Department.

served in the UN's peacekeeping department, "the UN is an organization that has enormous talent, but often its mandates are so obtuse that its actual ability to function is limited." It may be blamed for failing to meet goals for which its members—the world's nations—don't give it sufficient resources.

Yet, can we ignore it? The United States does not have the choice of acting "only through the UN or only alone," says former Secretary of State Madeleine Albright. "We want—and need—both options. So in diplomacy, an instrument like the UN will be useful in some situations, useless in others, and extremely valuable in getting the whole job done." The UN can help make the world a better place, which is to our advantage because we know that "desperation is a parent to violence, that democratic principles are often among the victims of poverty and that lawlessness is a contagious disease." Albright has stated it neatly: "We cannot be the world's policemen, though we're very good at it."

UN and US: Perfect Together?

Insiders agree that just as the United States needs the UN, the United Nations needs the US. "I need to underscore repeatedly that the UN is only as good as the US commitment," says Richard Holbrooke, who negotiated the Dayton Accords that ended the war in Bosnia in 1995. The United States is such a vast global presence that its support is essential for success: "The UN cannot succeed if the US does not support it."

In 1999 Mark Malloch Brown became the Administrator of the UN Development Program, a post to which he was reappointed in 2003 for a second four-year term. He chairs the UN Development Group, a committee of the heads of all UN development funds, programs, and departments. From 1994–99 he served at the World Bank. He founded the *Economist Development Report* and served as its editor from 1983–86. He is a British citizen, educated in Great Britain and the United States.

Unfortunately, many insiders say, the US has usually been unable to find and follow a clear, consistent policy toward the UN. Mark Malloch Brown, Administrator of the United Nations Development Program (UNDP) and highly regarded by his American peers, sees a "bewildered superpower, self-confident at home, uneasy abroad . . . and all of this comes together at the UN." One manifestation of the US government's ambivalence has been its reluctance to pay its dues to the general budget of the UN and some of the subbudgets. As described in more detail in Chapter 12, the accumulated arrears (almost $1 billion by September 2001) severely cramped the UN's ability to operate and was the source of much friction. To be fair, however, it should be noted that the US and some other nations have withheld dues in varying amounts for a variety of reasons, including allegations of mismanagement and poor allocation of funds.

Most insiders I've talked with believe that the US can generally have as much influence as it wants in the UN. David Malone, a former Canadian diplomat and now president of the International Peace Academy, argues that "a strong coherent US lead at the UN is nearly always followed by UN member states." But, "when Washington sends mixed signals, as it is too often wont to do owing to divergent views in Congress and the White House, then the UN may not know what is wanted."

Michael Sheehan speaks of a love-hate relationship between the US and the UN but doesn't see it as particularly unusual in the context of

A career Canadian Foreign Service officer, David Malone was from 1992–94 Ambassador and Deputy Permanent Representative of Canada to the UN, where he chaired the negotiations of the UN Special Committee on Peacekeeping Operations and the UN General Assembly consultations on peacekeeping issues. From 1990–92, he represented Canada on the UN's Economic and Social Council (ECOSOC). He is president of the International Peace Academy, a think-tank on UN issues, in New York City.

American political thought. "I think the US and the UN will always have this difficult relationship. It's inevitable because the UN is designed to be an organization where all nations have a chance to voice themselves."

Shepard Forman, of New York University's Center on International Cooperation, thinks the US needs to be more trusting of its partners. "We don't seem to trust anyone when it comes to US national security, and therefore we are fully prepared to go it alone, and presume others will come along and help as we need them, but we don't always need them. Then by extension where we think there are intersects between security and other things, narcotic trafficking, money laundering, where we don't think other countries may see the problem the same way or provide the degree of help to us, we will also go it alone. We've accepted our own hubris on being a superpower, the indispensable nation."

Shepard Forman is director of New York University's Center on International Cooperation, which he founded. Previously he was director of the Ford Foundation's Human Rights and Governance and International Affairs programs. Trained in anthropology and economic development, he was a faculty member at several major US universities before joining the Ford Foundation. He has written many papers, articles, and books on international affairs, development, and public policy.

What's in It for Me?

Putting aside international diplomacy, why should Americans care about the UN? Pressed to identify a specific UN-related item or service they have encountered recently, they might mention UNICEF holiday cards. But is that all? The UN sets standards that affect us every day. "You may think that you have never benefited personally from the UN," says Madeleine Albright, "but if you have ever traveled on an international airline or shipping line, or placed a phone call overseas, or received mail from outside the country, or been thankful for an accurate weather report—then you have been served directly or indirectly by one part or another of the UN system."

What It Means to You

"I'm struck by how relevant the work that I've had to do at the UN has been to the US national security and foreign policy agenda. Part of our debate here in the US has always turned around the issue of what does the UN mean to me? My answer to any American today is it means as much as national security and foreign policy should mean to you. It is certainly very much tied into all of that."
—John Negroponte, US Ambassador to the UN

CHAPTER 2

UN Founding Documents

Article 1
All human beings are born free and equal in dignity and rights. They are
endowed with reason and conscience and should act toward one another in
a spirit of brotherhood.

Article 2
Everyone is entitled to all the rights and freedoms set forth in this Declara-
tion, without distinction of any kind, such as race, color, sex, language,
religion, political or other opinion, national or social origin, property, birth
or other status.　　　　—Universal Declaration of Human Rights

As with any organization that exists in this ever-changing world, the
UN cannot act according to an unchanging set of rules. But it has
established two very specific annotated documents to guide its members. The UN is defined by its Charter, written in 1945, which functions as the Constitution does for the United States, and by a Universal Declaration of Human Rights, which is a manifesto of human
dignity and value that remains as fresh and radical now as it was when
adopted in 1948 (the entire Declaration appears in Appendix B).

The Charter lays out all the major components of the organization,

A close-up of the UN Charter, with the Egyptian delegation at the June 26, 1945, San Francisco Charter ceremony in the background. UN/DPI photo.

including its director (Secretary General), its lines of authority, and the responsibilities and rights of its members—that is, of governments that constitute UN membership. The Charter was signed on June 26, 1945, by fifty nations, and the chapters and articles constitute a treaty and are legally binding on the signatories. Article 103 of the Charter stipulates that if a member state finds that its obligations under the Charter conflict with duties under "any other international agreement," they must place their Charter obligations first.

The Universal Declaration of Human Rights is the product of the UN's Commission on Human Rights, founded in 1946, which was then led by former First Lady Eleanor Roosevelt, who had an international reputation as a crusader for human rights. Under her guidance the commission drafted the Universal Declaration as a fundamental statement about rights and freedom. Resting on Enlightenment ideals

Eleanor Roosevelt displays the Universal Declaration of Human Rights poster in November 1949. UN photo.

of human dignity, it is unique both in its breadth and in its success as an international standard by which to identify the basic rights that every person should enjoy. Most human rights law, and many national constitutions, reflect its provisions. It is an inspiration to people seeking freedom and to organizations that seek to advance the cause of freedom and justice. Unlike the Charter, the Universal Declaration is not a treaty and its provisions therefore are not law, but it has been largely incorporated into two international treaties that came into effect in 1976 and have been accepted by most member states: the International Covenant on Economic, Social, and Cultural Rights and the International Covenant on Civil and Political Rights. The UN refers to these covenants and the Universal Declaration as the International Bill of Rights.

18

CHAPTER 3

The Secretary General and the Secretariat

Article 97
The Secretariat shall comprise a Secretary-General and such staff as the Organization may require. The Secretary-General shall be appointed by the General Assembly upon the recommendation of the Security Council. He shall be the chief administrative officer of the Organization.
—UN Charter

According to many insiders the UN could not have appointed a better, more effective Secretary General than Kofi Annan, who will serve in that post until December 31, 2006. How he got the job, a fascinating story in its own right, will be recounted in Chapter 14. What he has accomplished since he began his first term, on January 1, 1997, is described here.

Many regard Kofi Annan as the best Secretary General ever appointed, the equal even of the legendary Dag Hammarskjöld (1953–61). As Mark Malloch Brown puts it, "We've had a series of Secretaries General since Hammarskjöld who were more secretaries than generals. This is the first time since then we have a Secretary General who dwarfs his institution."

Secretaries General

1. Kofi Annan (Ghana)	1997–Present
2. Boutros Boutros-Ghali (Egypt)	1992–96
3. Javier Perez de Cuellar (Peru)	1982–91
4. Kurt Waldheim (Austria)	1972–81
5. U Thant (Burma)	1961–71
6. Dag Hammarskjöld (Sweden)	1953–61
7. Trygve Lie (Norway)	1946–52

Annan is the first rank-and-file UN staffer to become SG, having held posts with several agencies, including the World Health Organization and the Office of the UN High Commissioner for Refugees, before becoming Undersecretary General for Peacekeeping from 1993 through 1996. Annan was born in Ghana in 1938, the son of a hereditary chief of the Fante people who was also the elected provincial governor. He grew up in an environment steeped in politics,

Secretary General Dag Hammarskjöld on a 1961 Peace Mission to the Congo, during which he was killed in a plane crash. UN photo.

which may explain his excellent interpersonal skills and his sensitivity to the views of others. As a child of the elite, the young man attended college both in his native country and in the United States (Macalester College in Minnesota), with postgraduate training at the Institute of Advanced International Studies in Geneva and also at Massachusetts Institute of Technology. Benefiting from the more activist stance the UN was able to take during the 1990s, he was soon regarded as a dynamic and resourceful leader.

Despite considerable personal modesty, and a reluctance to place himself at center stage, Annan has great presence in social settings and conveys intelligence and easy elegance. The media have covered him enthusiastically for both his charisma and his official position. His highly accomplished wife, Nane Lagergren, a Swedish lawyer and artist, is the niece of Raoul Wallenberg, who helped save many Jews from the Nazi death camps late in World War II, only to die in a Soviet prison.

Annan, Secretary General

Kofi Annan is both a media fixture and the UN official who is ultimately responsible for ensuring that members of the UN have the means and motivation to perform effectively. The Secretary General is in charge of the entire operation of the Secretariat, including policy, personnel, public relations, and long-range planning. Although the Secretariat's scope embraces almost all the significant activities of the world body, the most urgent challenges usually involve some aspect of national or international peace: making it, keeping it, or ensuring that it is not breached. In these efforts, the Secretary General works closely with the Security Council, advising the council about threats to international peace and assisting it through personal diplomacy.

In the post–cold war era, with the emergence of the United States as the dominant superpower and global peace enforcer, the Secretary General and the US President have become frequent allies in the effort to steer the world through the stresses of war, terrorism, and other threats.

The many, often conflicting responsibilities of the Secretary General

Secretary General Kofi Annan and his wife, Nane Annan, arriving in Eritrea on Dec. 8, 2000. UN/DPI photo by Jorge Aramburu.

make the post one of the most demanding imaginable. It requires intelligence and experience, certainly, but also drive, vision, and infinite tact and patience. The Secretary General must be able to communicate with the entire UN family as well as with all the nations of the world, while also administering a global array of programs and agencies.

The position of the Secretary General, only briefly described in the UN Charter, has evolved over time: "In the Charter of the UN," says Richard Holbrooke, "the role of Secretary General is only described with a single phrase, that the UN will have a chief administrative officer. It doesn't describe the authority of the Secretary General as the Constitution describes the powers for the President and Congress. It's all been done, like the British constitution, by precedent and strong Secretaries General, of whom we've had two, Dag Hammarskjöld and Kofi Annan."

Mark Malloch Brown adds that the Charter "doesn't envisage significant powers for the SG in international relations." Rather, he says, the internationally active Secretaries General have succeeded by "convincing genuinely important individuals, heads of government and so on, that they can be helpful." Michael Sheehan says that one of the Secretary General's roles is to "tell the Security Council what it has to know, not what it wants to hear. So the Secretariat is not just a puppet on a string of the member states; it has a role, and there's a dialogue between the Secretariat and the member states."

The Secretary General conducts operations through the Secretariat, consisting of approximately 8,900 staff members from about 160 countries. Most of them work in the New York City headquarters, but the Secretariat has other offices in Geneva, Vienna, and Nairobi. In keeping with the letter and spirit of the Charter, which aimed to create an international civil service, member states agree not to exert improper influence on the Secretariat's staff, and the staff, in turn, take an oath that they will be responsible solely to the United Nations and will not seek or take directions from any other authority.

Some insiders rate the staff's quality as mixed, with a few outstanding people, many good ones, and quite a few careerists who simply put in a day's work. David Malone estimates that "40 percent of the Secretariat staff are movers and shakers and carry the full burden of action. About 30 percent do no harm and do no good, and about 40 percent spend their time making trouble. Which means that the 30 percent who get work done are fairly heroic, and they exist at all levels of the system." One of the more generous evaluations comes from Nancy Soderberg, who thinks that Kofi Annan has tossed out a lot of the deadwood. "I would say that 90 percent are terrific. You have the young people who are very enthused about it and the senior people who have worked their life in the UN and loved it, and then you have a few people scattered around who are there for life. The Secretary General has very definitely moved them out over the past few years." David Malone, too, credits Annan with doing a good job of selecting first-rate people for important posts, which he rates "the most important aspect of his job" after peacekeeping.

Mark Malloch Brown makes a somewhat different criticism of the bureaucracy, citing a pervasive "disconnect between merit and

From the UN Charter, Chapter XV: The Secretariat

ARTICLE 99

The Secretary General may bring to the attention of the Security Council any matter which in his opinion may threaten the maintenance of international peace and security.

ARTICLE 100

1. In the performance of their duties the Secretary General and the staff shall not seek or receive instructions from any government or from any other authority external to the Organization. They shall refrain from any action which might reflect on their position as international officials responsible only to the Organization.
2. Each Member of the United Nations undertakes to respect the exclusively international character of the responsibilities of the Secretary General and the staff and not to seek to influence them in the discharge of their responsibilities.

ARTICLE 101

1. The staff shall be appointed by the Secretary General under regulations established by the General Assembly.
2. Appropriate staffs shall be permanently assigned to the Economic and Social Council, the Trusteeship Council, and, as required, to other organs of the United Nations. These staffs shall form a part of the Secretariat.
3. The paramount consideration in the employment of the staff and in the determination of the conditions of service shall be the necessity of securing the highest standards of efficiency, competence, and integrity. Due regard shall be paid to the importance of recruiting the staff on as wide a geographical basis as possible.

reward." He notes, "There's something rational that if you work hard and do well, you get promoted, and if you don't work hard you don't. In parts of the UN that doesn't happen." He advocates "reconnect[ing] merit to make the UN again an international meritocracy." To do this, however, Malloch Brown believes that the UN must stop promoting on the basis of political correctness that encourages hiring staff proportionately from certain regions of the world. At first glance, this might be interpreted to mean that Malloch Brown wants fewer staff from developing nations and more from the Europe–North American axis, but actually he wants just the opposite. Malloch Brown argues that Asia, Africa, and other so-called less developed regions now offer a large pool of talented, skilled, and highly motivated professionals that the UN ought to make more use of. These individuals are so highly qualified, he believes, that they will readily move up through the UN system without need of the traditional hiring quotas or the "cultural relativism which is used to promote incompetents."

Kofi Annan is ideally suited to do just what Malloch Brown urges. He knows the key UN personnel and is committed to promoting for merit. When he took office he continued and intensified an administrative overhaul begun by his predecessor, Boutros Boutros-Ghali. He has encouraged development of a corporate culture aimed at making results, not efforts, the test of effectiveness. An upshot was the creation of a new post, Deputy Secretary General of the UN, established in 1997 to help manage the Secretariat and coordinate UN programs and activities, especially those relating to economic and social development. Annan, who has sought to raise the status of women at the Secretariat, appointed Canadian Louise Fréchette to the new position.

Annan, Rights Advocate

Annan's reform efforts have generated mostly positive comment from experts, the public, and other interested observers, except in the controversial area of human rights. Everyone is "for" human rights, of course, which are enshrined in the Charter and in scores of

Louise Fréchette is the first Deputy Secretary General of the UN. A national of Canada, she assumed her duties on March 2, 1998, after having been appointed by Secretary General Kofi Annan. The Deputy Secretary General assists the Secretary General and also represents the UN at conferences and official functions. She chairs the Steering Committee on Reform and Management Policy and the Advisory Board of the UN Fund for International Partnerships (UNFIP), which handles relations with the foundation set up by Ted Turner in support of the UN (see Chapter 15). Before joining the UN, Fréchette was the Deputy Minister of National Defence of Canada. She served as Permanent Representative of Canada to the UN from 1992–95.

international treaties and conventions. The problem comes when these rights seem to conflict with national boundaries. If mass murder is committed within a nation, does the world community have the obligation or the right to intervene to stop it? The usual response over the decades has been that international law does not cross national borders. And yet, the spirit of the UN Charter clearly should lead member states to act when human rights are being grossly violated.

Annan has proposed to alter the historical approach radically by arguing that international human rights law must apply in each member state, and that certain acts like genocide cannot be allowed to occur with impunity. He has based his view, no doubt, on his own bitter experience with events in places like Bosnia and Rwanda, where the UN was accused of doing too little to prevent mass murders. In 1995, during the dissolution of Yugoslavia, Serb militia in the Bosnian town of Srebrenica killed thousands of Muslim civilians in a so-called safe haven protected by UN peacekeepers. A report issued in late 1999 condemned the peacekeeping force for not acting to prevent the tragedy. The blame might better have fallen on the UN itself, and the Security Council specifically, for providing too few peacekeepers to constitute an effective defense; nevertheless, the peacekeeping effort had clearly failed. In Africa, during the 1994 civil war in Rwanda

Deputy Secretary General Louise
Fréchette, Mar. 5, 2002. UN/DPI
photo by Eskinder Debebe.

between Tutsi and Hutu tribes, hundreds of thousands of civilians were murdered, sometimes in plain view of the international media. Some of those killed included ten Belgian members of the UN Assistance Mission for Rwanda (UNAMIR), established in 1993 to monitor a truce between the Hutu-dominated central government and Tutsi-led insurgents based in neighboring Uganda. The UNAMIR commander, General Romeo Dallaire of Canada, had warned about the possibility of ethnic violence and asked for more forces, which the Security Council finally authorized after the killing began, but member states were slow to contribute contingents. The genocide continued until the Tutsi-led insurgents reached the capital and installed a new government.

The Rwanda massacres occurred while Annan was UN Undersecretary General for Peacekeeping. After he became SG, Annan commissioned a report to examine what had happened and suggest remedies. When the report concluded that the sending of UN peacekeepers could have prevented most of the deaths—an analysis by no means universally accepted, since the massacres occurred so quickly that effective UN response might have been difficult—Annan accepted responsibility for failing to act more quickly.

Annan formally stated his new approach to intervention in an address at the General Assembly in September 1999, in which he asked member states "to unite in the pursuit of more effective policies to stop organized mass murder and egregious violations of human rights." Conceding that there were many ways to intervene, he asserted that not only diplomacy but even armed action was an acceptable option. This provoked debate around the world. Rights organizations generally supported Annan's comments. Human Rights Watch hailed his statement as a "highlight" of 1999, a year when "sovereignty gave way in places where crimes against humanity were being committed." Others were less happy. They feared that the concept of "humanitarian intervention" might disguise unjustified interference in a nation's affairs, or might encourage secessionist movements to provoke gross violations of human rights in order to bring on an international presence that might aid their cause. There was concern that weak states were probably more likely than strong ones to suffer such intervention.

Acknowledging the value of arguments put forth by critics and skeptics, Annan has posed a difficult question: "If humanitarian intervention is, indeed, an unacceptable assault on sovereignty, how should we respond to a Rwanda, to a Srebrenica—to gross and systematic violations of human rights that offend every precept of our common humanity?" He has laid out the issues very clearly:

> We confront a real dilemma. Few would disagree that both the defense of humanity and the defense of sovereignty are principles that must be supported. Alas, that does not tell us which principle should prevail when they are in conflict. Humanitarian intervention is a sensitive issue, fraught with political difficulty and not susceptible to easy answers. But surely no legal principle—not even sovereignty—can ever shield crimes against humanity. Where such

crimes occur and peaceful attempts to halt them have been exhausted, the Security Council has a moral duty to act on behalf of the international community. The fact that we cannot protect people everywhere is no reason for doing nothing when we can. Armed intervention must always remain the option of last resort, but in the face of mass murder it is an option that cannot be relinquished.

No one has yet provided a generally accepted answer to Annan's question or been able to articulate a consistent alternative approach.

Although Annan's ideas about intervention are surely influenced by the UN's failures in places like Srebrenica, another factor is also involved. Annan has spoken often and vigorously about the need for the UN to imagine itself as an organization composed both of nations and of individuals. The Charter, he reminds listeners, delimits many individual rights and speaks not only of the world's nations but of its people. If the need to protect individual rights requires bypassing a national government, so be it. "Once and for all," he has said, "we must make clear that the rights for which we fight are not the rights of states or factions, but the rights of the individual human being to live in dignity and freedom."

Annan sees individual rights as central to the world of the future. In his view they are key elements in economic and social development. Abandoning the traditional view that modern nations progress through education and capital investments, followed by greater personal rights, he has reversed the order: human rights are a precondition for national development. Such "rights-based" development is gaining attention at the UN and elsewhere, as analysts ponder the inability of some nations to raise their social and economic levels despite years of development efforts and big loans and grants from the World Bank and other donor agencies. The logic is very powerful, but also very threatening to some governments that fear they will lose control over their citizens.

It is not yet clear whether Annan's new approach to rights and national sovereignty will prevail. But the fact that someone in his position has raised the issue suggests it is an idea whose time has come. And it is significant that Annan's election to a second term as SG came after, not before, he made his most controversial statements on the subject.

A Cult of Personality?

It is hard to find anyone who can mount a serious criticism of Annan's performance as Secretary General. Mark Malloch Brown praises his unusual combination of tact and firmness. "There are plenty of people with tact that just give in to the lowest common denominator," he observes, and "plenty of people with firmness that fall at first hurdle because they don't understand the need for cultural sensitivity." Annan, however, has both qualities and has used them to assemble "a genuine, multicultural management team, which is more than a team, it's a force." In addition, says Malloch Brown, Annan has made his office important internationally by being helpful to heads of government and other leaders.

Secretary General Kofi Annan accepts the Nobel Peace Prize on Dec. 10, 2001, in Oslo, Norway. UN/DPI photo by Sergey Bermeniev.

Blame It on the Politicians

"An awful lot of us did graduate school in the US. . . . We feel comfortable with Americans because they are more multiculturally tolerant than other nationalities. The perverse thing is, the only one who doesn't like the UN is the American government. Washington is much more skeptical than the rest of America."
—Mark Malloch Brown, UNDP

So impressive has Annan been that the Security Council nominated him for a second term, ahead of schedule, and the General Assembly approved the choice by acclamation. He began his second and final term in 2001, the year he received the Nobel Peace Prize. He and US Secretary of State Colin Powell developed a close and strong working relationship—a rarity in UN–US relations during recent decades. He began to work amicably with the Bush administration, which was initially indifferent to the UN if not outright hostile.

The tough-minded Richard Holbrooke rates Annan "an astonishingly effective person considering the problems that he faces." Annan "combines a series of qualities that are inconceivable to find in one person: he's from Africa and has real stature in his native country; he is the first SG ever to know the bureaucracy from the inside; and he is married to a European who happens to be the niece of one of the great humanitarian figures [Raoul Wallenberg]. And he has great moral authority. You can't ever match that again."

If there is a downside to Annan's popularity, it comes from the very personal nature of his success. Malloch Brown argues that when Annan decides that something matters, like development or poverty reduction, the UN system and the world in general pay much more attention than if "the UN passes some dreary resolution." But Annan "doesn't seem to have coattails in terms of the UN system." Although he is esteemed by all, "even including Senator Helms, who considers Kofi his great friend," this admiration doesn't elevate the UN in general. "In that sense, Kofi has performed an extraordinary act of self-levitation. He hovers above the UN system, so to speak, in everybody's imagination, somehow personally not tainted by the shortcomings of the UN. But the corollary of that is that his extraordinary personal performance doesn't always seem to rub off in positive ways on the UN." The next Secretary General, Malloch Brown fears, will have to start from zero to build his or her credibility. A more charitable view might be that Annan's longest coattail is the cohort of smart and idealistic personnel he has appointed to important positions in the Secretariat.

Will Our Luck Hold?

Annan has a few years in which to strengthen his influence. The Secretary General is elected by the General Assembly for a renewable five-year term, and Annan will finish his tenure at the end of 2006. Possibly the main candidates are already drawing up their plans and preparing their campaign teams. The process of choosing the Secretary General involves two UN bodies: the Security Council, which recommends a candidate, and the General Assembly, which ratifies the choice. Candidates are unlikely to come from certain countries because they either raise too many animosities or complications, like

A Hostile Review

"I thought Kurt Waldheim was a terrible SG from the beginning. He didn't care about anything except his own political position. I remember the refugee conference in Geneva which he was supposed to chair, 1979, and how he went to Geneva but didn't appear. He said he had a sore throat. He wouldn't even come to sit quietly; he let someone else read his speech. People began to joke about it. We used to call him a Nazi, but we didn't realize he really was a Nazi."
—Richard Holbrooke

Secretary General Dag Hammarskjöld (left) and his successor, General Assembly President U Thant of Burma (right), listen to statements during the General Debate on Oct. 1, 1959. UN photo.

Libya, or are divided, like Korea. Political correctness often becomes an issue, because both the industrial and nonindustrial nations accept the notions, first, that no single nation or group of nations should dominate the world organization and, second, that the smaller and less developed countries should be guaranteed a strong voice.

For the past twenty years the unwritten agreement has been that the SG should rotate among regions of the world. Accordingly, Javier Perez de Cuellar, from South America, served two terms and was followed by Boutros Boutros-Ghali, from Africa, who served only one term. Kofi Annan succeeded him with the understanding that he would serve only one term. In fact, Annan will have served two terms, so Africa has contributed more than its "share" to the ranks of UN leaders. Because Europe has produced several Secretaries General, ending with Kurt Waldheim, the post ought to go next to Asia (which, in the UN system, includes the Arab states of the Middle East). But Asia is very big and diverse, so the number of potential donor countries would seem to be large. Not according to Richard Holbrooke, however. He points out that China is disqualified because the five permanent members of the Security Council are traditionally excluded from offering candidates. Japan is excluded, he argues, "because there is so much aversion to Japan and the Chinese won't want them." Holbrooke dismisses Korea because of the country's division between North and South, and asserts that India and Pakistan "cancel each other out." A candidate from an Arab state is not impossible but unlikely, he thinks. Among the other Asian nations, Holbrooke does not see an obvious choice. Burma provided one Secretary General, U Thant (1961–71), but then "disappeared into forty years of dictatorship." He discounts Indonesia's chances because of its recent political and social turmoil; Sri Lanka or Malaysia would be a stretch. "It's very limited," he concludes. "So your pool of countries is Philippines, Singapore, Thailand, Bangladesh. And that's probably it."

Or is it? The funny thing about election campaigns is that they don't always play out as the pollsters and pundits predict, as we know from our own national politics. It's hard to know what Asia will be like when it's time for the next Secretary General to be chosen, so even the most perceptive experts are making, at best, educated guesses.

CHAPTER 4

The American Ambassadors

But in the case of the American ambassador, there are multiple agencies within Washington involved. The State Department doesn't always have the last word. The President is sometimes in touch either directly or through the National Security Advisor. The Pentagon is never shy about being in touch. The American Ambassador at the UN has to sort through this and has to practice diplomacy with Washington even more than she or he practices diplomacy at the UN.
—David Malone, former Canadian diplomat and current
President of the International Peace Academy

Each member nation maintains a UN Mission in New York City, staffed by a head, known as the Permanent Representative, who also carries the title of Ambassador. The term of the Permanent Rep varies by nation, usually extending over several years. So the word "permanent" shouldn't be taken too literally, but it conveniently denotes the key person in a delegation of representatives. The current US Permanent Representative is John Negroponte, who succeeded Richard Holbrooke in 2001.

The US Permanent Rep has the highest-visibility job at the UN,

US Permanent Representatives to the UN, 1946–2002

Edward R. Stettinius Jr. (March 1946–June 1946)
Herschel V. Johnson (acting) (June 1946–January 1947)
Warren R. Austin (January 1947–January 1953)
Henry Cabot Lodge Jr. (January 1953–September 1960)
James J. Wadsworth (September 1960–January 1961)
Adlai E. Stevenson (January 1961–July 1965)
Arthur J. Goldberg (July 1965–June 1968)
George W. Ball (June 1968–September 1968)
James Russell Wiggins (October 1968–January 1969)
Charles W. Yost (January 1969–February 1971)
George H. W. Bush (February 1971–January 1973)
John P. Scali (February 1973–June 1975)
Daniel P. Moynihan (June 1975–February 1976)
William W. Scranton (March 1976–January 1977)
Andrew Young (January 1977–April 1979)
Donald McHenry (April 1979–January 1981)
Jeane J. Kirkpatrick (February 1981–April 1985)
Vernon A. Walters (May 1985–January 1989)
Thomas R. Pickering (March 1989–May 1992)
Edward J. Perkins (May 1992–January 1993)
Madeleine K. Albright (February 1993–January 1997)
Bill Richardson (February 1997–September 1998)
A. Peter Burleigh, Chargé d'Affaires (September 1998–August 1999)
Richard C. Holbrooke (August 1999–January 2001)
John Negroponte (September 2001–)

next to the Secretary General, and one of the most complicated owing to US geopolitical eminence and the Byzantine nature of US policy-making. "The job of an American ambassador at the UN is a particularly tough one," says David Malone. "Most ambassadors at the UN get one set of instructions that are channeled through the foreign minister and occasionally they will hear from their head of govern-

US Secretary of State Madeleine Albright and President of Mozambique Joaquim Alberto Chissano meet before the Security Council's session on the Congo on Jan. 24, 2000. UN/DPI photo by Eskinder Debebe.

ment or head of state. That's the case of France, for example, where the head of state plays quite an active role." The US Ambassador, however, has many bosses and many peers who feel free to make suggestions and intervene in other ways. The greatest diplomatic skill is required to manage such a complicated chain of command while still being able to accomplish something at the UN.

Personal ambition adds another level of complexity. Malone suggests, for example, that when Madeleine Albright was Permanent Rep she had "real influence" in Washington but preferred not to take risks because she was angling for an even bigger job, which she got when she became Secretary of State. She practiced "endless diplomacy," Malone claims, not so much in New York as in Washington, "in order not to make enemies." In contrast, Richard Holbrooke felt sufficiently strong in Washington to define a "Holbrooke policy" at the UN and expect others to follow it. Amazingly, says Malone, they generally did.

Born in Prague, Madeleine Korbel Albright was the US Permanent Representative to the UN from 1993–97 and served as America's first female secretary of state from 1997–2001. Albright was a staff member on the National Security Council and at the White House, where she was responsible for foreign policy legislation, from 1978–81.

Richard C. Holbrooke was the US Permanent Representative to the UN from 1999–2001. While US Ambassador to Germany from 1993–94, and later Assistant Secretary of State for European and Canadian Affairs, he was also chief negotiator for the historic 1995 Dayton Peace Accords, which ended the war in Bosnia. Holbrooke began his career as a Foreign Service Officer in 1962, in Vietnam. He is vice chairman of Perseus, a private equity firm.

Bill Richardson was US Permanent Rep from 1997–1998, after having been a congressional representative from New Mexico. He left his UN position to become Secretary of the US Department of Energy, and is now governor of New Mexico.

"Nobody really spoke back to him. He had the ear of the President. The Vice President liked and respected him. . . . He essentially made policy on every subject that he discussed at the UN, and he then advised Washington on what their policy was henceforth to be. It was a very interesting performance."

The Current Head of Mission

With John Negroponte, the current Permanent Rep, Malone believes we have "returned to a career diplomat who is very skilled in dealing with other ambassadors of the UN. He telegraphs to them a respect

John D. Negroponte became US Permanent Representative to the UN on Sept. 18, 2001. As a member of the Career Foreign Service from 1960 to 1997, he served at posts in Asia and Europe, and was ambassador to Honduras and then Mexico. For several years he was executive vice president for global markets of The McGraw-Hill Companies.

for their country's position. He also telegraphs very consistent, conservative Washington views on what the UN should be doing."

Few Permanent Reps have assumed office under more difficult conditions. Negroponte was sworn in as United States Representative to the United Nations on September 18, 2001, only one week after 9/11, when the UN was consumed with trying to respond constructively in the emerging international alliance against terrorism. "I arrived here the 19th of September," he noted in a recent interview, "and my experience has been very much shaped by the events of September 11th and our response to that. The first several months were pretty much absorbed with the issue of terrorism and Afghanistan."

Negroponte's first months gave new meaning to the concept of on-the-job-training. Fortunately, he's a fast learner. His background as a career diplomat, with some experience at the White House, helped, along with his corporate experience dealing with global markets. He is very much a team player and a listener. "You've got to meet face to face with people to get yourself comfortable, to get comfortable with the policy issues," he has said.

Negroponte has found that while he needs all his diplomatic skills as US Permanent Rep, he uses them very differently. In some of his former diplomatic posts, such as ambassador to Mexico and to the Philippines, he had time to become an expert on each nation and culture, but at the UN he has to deal with an endless variety of people and issues. "To be a representative here, you have to know a little bit about a lot of issues. And managing your own time so you make sure you know what you need to know in order to be effective is a challenge because some days on your agenda there are three or four various conflicts that come up." He has likened the UN post to being a member of a legislature, and it has helped him understand what it's like to be a member of Congress. "You don't have complete control over your schedule, things come up all of a sudden. It's a bit like a three-ring circus. You've got the General Assembly, the Security Council, the six [General Assembly] committees. Things can come up in those committees that need your attention. I've noticed that I don't have as much control over my schedule or my agenda as I did when I was a bilateral ambassador."

Negroponte has also become familiar with the UN penchant for debates and resolutions, especially relating to Israel and the Palestinians. "I've been a little bit distressed by how much time does get absorbed on what I consider to be a pretty sterile Middle Eastern debate," he states. Conceding that some discussion about the Middle East has been constructive—particularly one resolution, 1397, that affirmed the vision of a Palestinian state, which the US Mission initiated—he nevertheless has been forced to conclude that "the protagonists see the UN as a forum, just another public arena, rather than a way of really devising solutions to problems." He is bothered by the "blame game" in which some delegations try to score points for short-term gain. That game wastes everyone's time and isn't very good for the UN, he believes, because it can undermine the UN's credibility.

To remedy the situation, Negroponte has been urging delegations to be patient once a resolution has been passed by the Security Council, rather than immediately calling for yet another resolution. "I think we've made some success," he has said, but it has been "the most exhausting part of my job."

Often, however, Negroponte finds that his hardest job is managing the home base. In New York City the UN has great public visibility and strong political support. "There is a natural constituency," says Negroponte. "But outside of NY and outside the beltway, that's more of a challenge."

CHAPTER 5

The Security Council

Article 24
In order to ensure prompt and effective action by the United Nations,
its Members confer on the Security Council primary responsibility for
the maintenance of international peace and security, and agree that in
carrying out its duties under this responsibility the Security Council acts on
their behalf.   —UN Charter

The Security Council is the UN's enforcer, charged with making the
world a safer, more stable place by preventing or stopping armed
conflict among and even within nations. The council has the authority
to examine any conflict or dispute that might have international repercussions. It can identify aggressive action by states and call on UN
members to make an appropriate response, including application of
economic sanctions and even military action. Consequently, the council must be ready to deliberate at any time.

The SC is the only UN body whose resolutions are legally binding.
It has the authority to decide matters affecting the fate of governments, establish peacekeeping missions, create tribunals to try persons accused of war crimes, and in extreme cases declare a nation to

From the UN Charter

ARTICLE 41

The Security Council may decide what measures not involving the use of armed force are to be employed to give effect to its decisions, and it may call upon the Members of the United Nations to apply such measures. These may include complete or partial interruption of economic relations and of rail, sea, air, postal, telegraphic, radio and other means of communication, and the severance of diplomatic relations.

ARTICLE 42

Should the Security Council consider that measures provided for in Article 41 would be inadequate or have proved to be inadequate, it may take such action by air, sea, or land forces as may be necessary to maintain or restore international peace and security. Such action may include demonstrations, blockades, and other operations by air, sea, or land forces of Members of the United Nations.

be fair game for corrective action by other member states. Richard Holbrooke has called the Security Council "the most important international body in the world. Countries give it a legitimacy because it can authorize the use of force for peacemaking or even a war, as in Korea, Kuwait, and Afghanistan."

Big Job, Big Tools

The council has tools to match this very big job. It has fifteen members, ten of them elected by the General Assembly to two-year terms. The other five—the Permanent 5, or P5, which have veto power over resolutions—are China, France, the Russian Federation, the United

Security Council Composition

Permanent Five (P5) members: China, France, Russia, UK, and US
Nonpermanent members: 3 Africans, 2 Latin Americans, 1 Arab, 1
Asian, 1 Eastern European, and 2 Western Europeans

Kingdom, and the United States. Acting as a sort of club, the permanent members usually play a leading role in deliberations. The council is presided over by the president, an office that rotates monthly, according to the English alphabetical listing of SC member states.

It takes nine votes to pass a resolution. A permanent member can abstain from voting if it does not want to take a public stand on the measure. However, if it objects to the measure but cannot find the votes to defeat it, it can exercise a veto as a last resort. Each member of the P5 has used the veto. Vetoes were more common during the cold war, when the world was divided into Communist and non-Communist blocs, but in recent years they have become rare (see Table 1). The most recent veto was by the US, on December 20, 2002, against a Syrian resolution that condemned Israel for destroying a UN facility on the West Bank and killing several staff.

Following the US Star

According to David Malone, "in the Security Council the US is very much the dominant power. Nothing can be done against its wishes. Its active support is required for major decisions. It is also prepared to accommodate other countries every now and then, but it's more used to being accommodated itself." The United States has become deeply engaged in the SC when it has seen advantages for its own international interests and policies. As Madeleine Albright has commented, the UN's ability to intervene in certain emergencies often reduces the job of the United States: "This serves our interest because when the US

The Security Council holds its first summit-level meeting on Jan. 31, 1992.
UN/DPI photo by M. Grant.

intervenes alone, we pay all of the costs and run all of the risks. When
the UN acts, we pay a quarter of the costs and others provide the vast
majority of troops."

The United Kingdom and France also play leading roles in the
council. Malone says they "work much harder than any of the other
permanent members to come up with initiatives in areas far and wide.
They send people of extraordinary skill to the council. If one looks at
the current ambassadors of Britain and France they are both superb
operators with good staffs. They have hit the ground running faster
than anyone else. The British are notorious for always having a draft

An Important Distinction

"You have to make a distinction between the UN as an institution and an organization, on the one hand, and the member states, particularly the Permanent 5, on the other. It's axiomatic that the solid achievements of the Security Council have tended to be when the P5 can act in harmony or consensus. If there is either strong disagreement or reluctance on the part of one or more of the P5 members, that's when you start getting into difficulties."
—John Negroponte, US Ambassador to the UN

in their back pocket. For these countries, their permanent membership really matters to their international identity precisely because their role in the world has shrunk. They're working very hard to stay permanent members of the Security Council."

The larger countries are usually more active on the council than the smaller ones because they have the staff time needed to keep up with the constantly increasing load. Recalls Richard Holbrooke, "Tom Pickering told me that when he was ambassador, the Security Council met two or three times a month. Now it meets almost every day. It's a nonstop forum for discussion, much of it useless."

Table 1 shows that the number of annual meetings has tripled since 1988, from 55 to 167, while the number of resolutions adopted has risen two and a half times, from 20 to 50.

The Need for Leadership

Although the council has a small membership compared with the General Assembly, and tries to operate by consensus, it works most efficiently and effectively when one of the P5 exercises leadership. Absent decisive guidance, it may dither and flounder, as it often did with Iraq during the late 1990s. The Iraq case shows not only the

Table 1 Security Council Meetings, Resolutions, and Vetoes, 1988–2000

Year	Meetings	Resolutions Considered	Resolutions Adopted	US Vetoes
2000	167	52	50	0
1999	124	67	65	0
1998	116	73	73	0
1997	117	57	54	2
1996	114	59	57	1
1995	130	67	66	1
1994	160	78	77	0
1993	171	95	93	0
1992	129	74	74	0
1991	53	42	42	0
1990	69	40	37	2
1989	69	25	20	5
1988	55	26	20	6

Source: Adapted from US Department of State, *18th Annual Report on Voting Practices in the UN, 2000*, p. 86.

importance of leadership but the need to have a consensus view of what constitutes leadership. When Iraq invaded Kuwait in 1990, the Security Council acted quickly to condemn the invasion and impose sanctions to encourage the world community to expel the attacker. The US took the leading role in acting as champion of the Kuwaiti people and representative of the world community in the UN forum. The US-led coalition defeated the Iraqi forces in 1991 and liberated Kuwait; however, the council's resolve began to drain away as the urgency of war became a memory and the battered Iraqi military seemed to pose little threat to neighboring countries.

The council's main concerns about Iraq after the war centered on the issue of disarmament. The cease-fire agreement ending the war stipulated that Iraq would surrender or destroy all its so-called weapons of mass destruction, meaning biological, chemical, and nuclear weapons. During the Gulf War the Iraqis shot off scores of SCUD missiles that were inaccurate but had considerable psychological impact on civilians. They would have been far more terrifying if they had carried chemical or nuclear warheads—not an outlandish notion considering the strong interest of the Saddam Hussein regime in acquiring such technology. The UN gained the right, under the cease-fire, to send inspectors to examine arms facilities to ensure Iraq's compliance. The job of finding any such weapons fell to the United Nations Special Commission (UNSCOM), assisted by the International Atomic Energy Agency (IAEA). During the next seven years, despite both passive and active resistance from Saddam's regime, UNSCOM supervised the destruction of thousands of weapons and chemical munitions.

When UNSCOM pulled out its inspectors in 1998, Saddam's regime banned their return, which prevented the UN from giving Iraq a clean bill of health and lifting sanctions. None of the members of the P5 took a strong enough stand to force Saddam's regime to comply with the terms of the cease-fire and admit inspectors. The best the Security Council could do was to replace UNSCOM in 1999 with a new entity, the UN Monitoring, Verification, and Inspection Commission (UNMOVIC), in the hope of making a fresh start and finally getting proof that Iraq no longer possessed weapons of mass destruction. The Security Council was divided about how to handle Saddam, until pressure from the US government brought clarity to the situation. At the General Assembly in September 2002, President Bush challenged the UN to enforce its own resolutions concerning Iraq. In November, the P5 hammered out a resolution that gave Iraq a final opportunity to disarm fully. Saddam, faced with a resolute Security Council and a very threatening United States, began slowly and grudgingly to comply during the early months of 2003. In the US view, the belated Iraqi response was inadequate and more apparent than real, while some Security Council members took the opposite view and declared that Iraq was finally responding forthrightly to the council's demands. In March the US and Great Britain invaded Iraq, despite the objections of the other members of the P5. When the brief war ended, efforts were made in the council and the General Assembly to condemn the invasion, but they failed. US Permanent Rep John Negroponte attributes the failure partly to the intense discussion among SC members, during which "countries became familiar enough with our position and had enough of their own discussion that the proponents of condemning us in the council and in the General Assembly were unable to muster sufficient votes to get that done. Or, at least countries gave the matter sufficient thought to conclude that whatever reservations they might have, it wasn't worth it for them politically, they didn't want to incur the political cost or the political friction of further disagreeing with the United States on this issue."

Other Ways of Thinking about Security

The Security Council has traditionally viewed security as an issue of physical assault. The Universal Declaration of Human Rights, however, lists an array of securities, such as freedom from hunger, the right to adequate housing and decent employment, and the right to live in a healthy environment (see Appendix B). Does the Security Council also oversee these forms of security? Historically the answer has been no. Rather, the council has left these matters to other parts of the UN system, especially the various agencies, programs, and commissions established to address issues like food supply, disaster relief, and health care. This has its logic, because the SC imagines itself as an executive body more than an administrative system. Recently, however, the council did formally address a health-related issue on the grounds that vital security interests were at stake. US Ambassador Richard Holbrooke set precedent by persuading the Security Council to discuss the impact of the AIDS crisis in Africa in January 2000 at a meeting chaired by US Vice President Al Gore. A State Department report noted that while the discussion was "controversial at the time," it set the stage for a later council meeting and resolution about AIDS and caused language about HIV/AIDS to be included in peacekeeping resolutions.

Reforming the Council

In recent years, many UN member states have begun urging a change of the Security Council to make it more reflective of today's international realities. Since the council was created in 1945, more than a hundred nations have come into existence, and former pariah states like Japan, Germany, and South Africa have rejoined the world community, while many developing nations have become economic and trade dynamos. Yet the council still operates on the same basic principles and with the same P5. Formal debates about reform have occurred in the General Assembly, and informal discussions occur everywhere in the UN system as participants advance their particular agendas and seek allies. "Reform" is always a loaded word because its meaning is often so subjective and because any significant change will affect power relationships and the status of particular member states.

One suggested change is to expand the number of council members. The Japanese, who would like to gain a permanent seat, have suggested raising the number from fifteen to twenty-four members and possibly restricting the veto. The current arrangement gives the P5 the right to veto any resolution and to exercise the veto as often as they like. If the veto power is curbed, that might profoundly change the ways in which the P5 view the council, because they would no longer be assured of protecting their own interests. Kofi Annan has gone on record supporting additional permanent seats and increasing the core group to a P7 or P8. This might be less threatening to the P5 because it slightly waters down their individual impact without diminishing the ability to cast the veto. It would, however, complicate relations among veto holders by increasing the number of parties who need to be engaged in the kind of consensus-building that gives the P5 so much power in the UN.

Some insiders wonder if the reform advocates fully understand the impact of their proposed changes. "Any expansion risks making the council unworkable because it would become so big," claims Nancy Soderberg. "If you expand it you will just have more side groups to

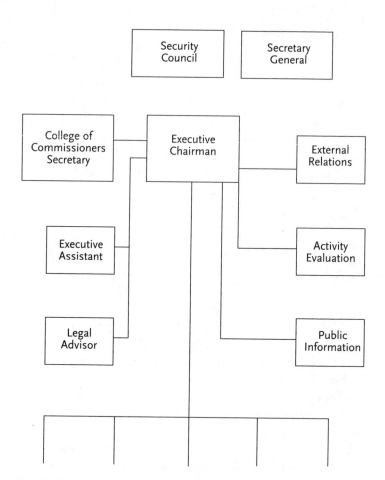

Organizational chart of the UN Monitoring, Verification, and Inspection Commission (UNMOVIC). This commission was created by Security Council resolution 1284 of December 17, 1999, with the task of disarming Iraq of weapons of mass destruction. Hans Blix of Sweden was the commission's Executive Chairman until 2003. BW = biological weapons; CW = chemical weapons; M = missiles.

Administrative Service	Division of Technical Support and Training	Division of Planning and Operations	Division of Analysis and Assessment	Division of Information
Budget and Finance	Equipment, analytical services, procurement	Baghdad BW Ongoing Monitoring and CW Verification Center	BW	Export/import joint unit
			CW	Imagery
Personnel, recruitment, health and safety	Communications, transportation, security		M	
				Outside information sources
	Training	Multidisciplinary inspections (including export/import and IAEA)	Multidisciplinary inspections (analysis)	
Translation and interpretation	Bahrain field office			Data Processing and archives

Team Players at Last

"If something really matters to the US, Britain, or France, or indeed to some of the nonpermanent members of the council, Russia rarely stands in the way. China never stands in the way. China and Russia don't play the wrecker role that they used to during the cold war. The Russians and Chinese have become genuinely post–cold war players in the Security Council."   —David Malone

work out things. You can't have an efficient body and negotiate with 26 people on it." She agrees that the Europeans shouldn't have so many seats, especially with the European Union: "How can you argue for four European countries on the council when Africa and Asia get one? It's just not going to fly. . . . You're not going to have meaningful council expansion until you have a rotating EU seat with a veto." She plausibly argues that such changes won't happen soon, because the member states that must agree on it "are not going to put themselves out of power, nor will the US work to get rid of its two best allies, France and the UK, in the council."

To members like France, Great Britain, and the United States, which have enjoyed a preeminent role in the council, calls for change may seem like gratuitous tinkering—but they cannot be ignored. Recently, the US suggested it could support an expanded council including consideration of three new permanent seats for representatives from the developing countries of Asia, Africa, and Latin America and the Caribbean. The US wanted no change in the status or privileges of the existing permanent members as outlined in the UN Charter, including any limitations on the veto. Even if the US were to embrace reform of the council enthusiastically, reform might still not happen soon owing to the sharp differences of opinion among member states about which of them should be admitted to an enlarged council. Members of major regional groupings, such as Africa or Asia, have been unable to agree on which of them should be selected for a permanent council seat.

The locus for formal discussion is in the General Assembly, in a committee with the catchy name of the Open-Ended Working Group on the Question of Equitable Representation on and Increase in the Membership of the Security Council (OEWG). It has met for nearly a decade without being able to reach a consensus on a "framework resolution" for consideration by the full assembly, so the process of Security Council reform remains ongoing.

CHAPTER 6

Peace Operations

Article 43

All Members of the United Nations, in order to contribute to the mainte-
nance of international peace and security, undertake to make available to
the Security Council, on its call and in accordance with a special agreement
or agreements, armed forces, assistance, and facilities, including rights of
passage, necessary for the purpose of maintaining international peace and
security. —UN Charter

Although peacekeeping is one of the quintessential UN functions,
it is mentioned only briefly in the Charter. Its full scope and nature
have gradually emerged, through need, as a middle ground between
mere arbitration of disputes, on the one hand, and use of armed force,
on the other. The Security Council's first peacekeeping resolution set
important precedents, establishing the United Nations Truce Supervision Organization (UNTSO) in 1948 to oversee the truce between
Arabs and Jews when the United Kingdom left Palestine. Like peacekeepers today, the UNTSO troops were provided by member states.
The troopers wore the blue helmets that have marked UN peacekeepers ever since. UNTSO also set the model for nomenclature: it is

invariably referred to by its acronym rather than its full name. That decades-old practice has led to a roster of past and current operations that read like a chapter out of Genesis, with names that sound like the biblical Gog and Magog—actually, MOONUC and UNOMIG. UNTSO is still in operation, with an expanded mandate that includes supervising the implementation and observance of the general agreements between Israel and its four Arab neighbors.

Once the Security Council authorizes the deployment of an operation, defines its mission, and recommends how it should be carried out, the Secretary General appoints a Force Commander and through the Secretariat's Department of Peacekeeping Operations (DPKO) arranges for management and logistics. Member states are asked to provide personnel, equipment, and logistics. The UN pays member states at the rate of $1,100 per peacekeeper per month, and the governments pay the troops according to their own scales. Member states retain control over their units. Peacekeeping personnel rely less on their arms than on their international authority and their reputation for impartiality. They wear their country's uniform and are identified as peacekeepers by a UN blue helmet or a beret and a badge.

Some UN peacekeeping operations consist of military observers charged with monitoring truces, troop withdrawals, and borders or demilitarized zones. Other operations involve military formations capable of acting as buffers between hostile forces. More recently, some peacekeeping operations have combined military and police or civilian functions and personnel, with the aim of creating or strengthening political institutions, providing emergency aid, clearing land mines, or administering and monitoring free elections.

Peace-related issues have always been central to Security Council deliberations, but in the past decade they have become especially numerous and demanding of time and resources. The decade of the 1990s saw the UN launch more peace-related operations than in all the previous four decades. During the year ending June 2003 there were 14 peacekeeping missions, employing 45,000 personnel at a cost of $2.6 billion.

And the nature of the disputes has largely changed. The norm used

A Peace Glossary

Just as Eskimos have many words to describe the various kinds of snow, the UN has developed words and phrases for the making and keeping of peace. Here are just a few.

preventive diplomacy
As its name suggests, preventive diplomacy seeks to head off disputes before they become full-blown conflicts. The UN prefers this kind of diplomacy but is able to apply it in only some instances. The UN employs its extensive contacts and offices around the world to detect early signs of potential threats to international peace and security.

peacemaking
Peacemaking involves the use of diplomacy to persuade belligerents to stop fighting and negotiate an end to their dispute.

peace enforcement
Peace enforcement involves the use of force against one of the belligerents to enforce an end to the fighting.

peace-building
Peace-building involves helping nations promote peace before, during, or after a conflict. Broadly defined, it employs a wide range of political, humanitarian, and human rights activities and programs.

to be that wars occurred between nation-states, which fought with field armies that were supposed to target combatants and not civilians—that was the theory, anyway. But these days nation-states have been remarkably well behaved toward one another, and in some places, like Europe, they have even forged close political ties. Instead, conflicts tend to occur within nations, in the form of civil wars (as in Rwanda, Congo, and the former Yugoslavia) or national resistance

Many parts of the UN system may join in a peace-building effort, as well as private bodies like nongovernmental organizations (NGOs). The Secretary General often appoints representatives to coordinate the activities through special peace-building support offices, such as those established in Liberia, Guinea-Bissau, and the Central African Republic.

the responsibility to protect
The Charter gives the UN the right to intervene in a nation's affairs to prevent egregious human rights violations, but in recent years there has been talk about a variant on this, called the responsibility to protect. A recent international commission stated in its report that "the responsibility to protect implies an evaluation of the issues from the point of view of those seeking or needing support, rather than those who may be considering intervention."

movements (like the East Timorese against Indonesian occupation, the Islamic separatists in the Philippines, the independence fighters in Kosovo, or the Palestinians against the Israelis).

The Talking Cure

Today, the council has to address so many requests for making or keeping peace that it usually begins by looking for a solution that does not involve a UN deployment. It starts with behind-the-scenes diplomacy, escalating to open diplomacy as needed.

A good example is the conflict between Ethiopia and its breakaway province of Eritrea, which began in the 1990s and has only recently been resolved, largely through UN and regional efforts. During the early 1980s, Ethiopia, a landlocked country, unilaterally annexed Eritrea, which gave it a port on the Red Sea; but the Eritreans resisted and finally secured their independence after a long war. Then, on May 6,

1998, the Eritrean government ordered its armed forces to occupy a slice of disputed territory on the border with Ethiopia. A regional body, the Organization of African Unity (OAU), worked out an agreement for settling the dispute, but neither side would commit to it.

In February 1999, the Security Council stepped in and urged the disputants to accept the OAU's plan. When they refused and began fighting, the council moved to its next stage of action, which was to tell the combatants to stop fighting, start talking, and arrange a cease-fire. The US also joined the cease-fire efforts, and in February and March OAU special envoy Ahmed Ouyahia (of Algeria) and former US National Security Advisor Anthony Lake visited Asmara and Addis Ababa. Algeria then brought the two parties together for talks, which broke down.

The fighting had by then stopped but seemed on the verge of resuming when, in April, the council reiterated its demand for a cease-fire and implementation of the OAU's plan. In June, the council again asked the two parties to negotiate, citing a looming humanitarian crisis as drought and unrest threatened massive starvation. The US sent more than 700,000 metric tons of food assistance to Ethiopia and 100,000 to Eritrea. A UN Security Council mission to Congo, led by US Permanent Representative Richard Holbrooke, began shuttle diplomacy during several days early in May, with Holbrooke leaning on both sides not to renew the fighting.

The shuttle talks failed, the mission left, and on May 12, 2000, Ethiopia sent its forces deep into Eritrea. The Security Council passed a resolution demanding an end to military action, but the next day Ethiopia's forces made a major breakthrough and eventually advanced to within a hundred kilometers of the Eritrean capital. Then the Ethiopian government, apparently satisfied it had acquired a good bargaining position, stated it was ending the war. Meanwhile, the Security Council passed another resolution, 1298, requiring that member states enforce an arms sales embargo on both combatants. Eritrea then declared that it would move its troops back to the border that existed in May 1998.

As each combatant backed off, the OAU, UN, and other parties arranged for new talks in Algiers, which led to an agreement on June 18 for a cease-fire. Once the fighting ended, the council created the UN Mission in Ethiopia and Eritrea (UNMEE), charged with monitoring the border and ensuring that the provisions of the cease-fire were honored. The council authorized the mission at a strength of more than 4,200 military and other personnel.

By then, Ethiopia and Eritrea had been fighting or at least glaring at each other for more than two years. Why did the council wait so long? The answer is that UN peacekeepers maintain peace once it is agreed to by the combatants, but they do not create peace through military action. The main purpose of peacekeeping is simply to help prevent fighting from erupting and to give negotiators a chance to find a permanent resolution to the dispute.

A resolution seems to have been found in the Ethiopia–Eritrea border dispute. In fall 2000, the OAU envoy and Anthony Lake pursued shuttle diplomacy while members of the Security Council urged the disputants to negotiate a complete solution. At Algiers in December 2000 the two nations signed a final accord in the presence of Secretary General Kofi Annan and US Secretary of State Madeleine Albright. The end is in sight but not quite achieved. UNMEE is expected to remain deployed until the final border between the two nations is demarcated, and until the two governments establish sufficient dialogue to ensure that they can peacefully resolve any disagreements or misunderstandings that might arise between them.

UN Sanctions

Sanctions are nonlethal, noninvasive mechanisms aimed at preventing a state from interacting with the outside world in certain ways, such as engaging in trade or acquiring arms. Travel bans and financial or diplomatic restrictions are also types of sanction. Although sanctions are intended to pressure governments, they may also unintentionally harm civilians too. Sometimes it is the poorest or most vulnerable

Fourteen countries had been subject to UN sanctions as of June 2003:

Afghanistan	Rwanda
Angola (lifted)	Sierra Leone
Ethiopia and Eritrea (lifted)	Somalia
Haiti (lifted)	South Africa (lifted)
Iraq (mostly lifted)	Southern Rhodesia (lifted)
Liberia	Sudan (lifted)
Libya (suspended)	The former Yugoslavia (lifted)

members of society who are most harmed when their nation is placed under a sanction, especially one that affects trade and commerce. Consider the case of Saddam Hussein's regime in Iraq, after the Gulf War.

When Iraq invaded Kuwait in 1990, the UN imposed sweeping sanctions intended to bar the aggressor from all trade and financial dealings, except for humanitarian purposes, with the rest of the world. After the US and its allies, with the blessing of the UN, routed the Iraqi armed forces and arranged a cease-fire (which the UN monitored) in 1991, the UN left the sanctions in place while stipulating that Iraq divest itself of weapons of mass destruction. Because the Iraqi government was not fully cooperating with inspections, the UN continued the sanctions throughout the years of the Saddam Hussein regime.

The Iraqi government, meanwhile, was able to partly evade the sanctions while complaining noisily that its citizens were being deprived of access to vital medicines, food, and other necessities. This effective campaign influenced the Security Council to create the Oil for Food program, which permitted the Iraqi government the option of exporting specified amounts of crude oil, under UN scrutiny, in order to pay for "humanitarian goods." Terms of the program were liberalized in 1998 and 1999, and finally in 2002, to give Iraq access to most civilian goods. The last liberalization was done through a Security Council resolution offered by the US in May 2002. The idea behind the resolution was to replace typical UN sanctions with "smart sanctions" that would enable Iraqi citizens to get necessities more easily while making it more difficult for Saddam Hussein's regime to use trade in order to obtain arms and other forbidden items. On May 22, 2003, two months after the US-led invasion of Iraq, the Security Council lifted sanctions, except for the sale of weapons and related materiel.

Rethinking Peacekeeping

Although traditional peacekeeping remains important, it is increasingly regarded as merely the first step in a process of moving from armed conflict to political dialogue and engagement. The new approach tries to engage all stakeholders in dialogue, which means governments, of course, but also nongovernmental organizations (which represent civil society and will be discussed in Chapter 18) and other groups. Among the pioneers of the new approach is Kofi Annan, who spent four years in charge of peacekeeping operations when he was Undersecretary General, and one of his top aides, Shashi Tharoor. As Tharoor says of his experiences during the 1990s, when the new approach emerged, in addition to doing the usual peacekeeping tasks they were experimenting with "all sorts of new things, everything from delivering humanitarian aid under fire, hunting down warlords, and of course monitoring no-fly zones. It was very much like fixing the engine of a moving car."

One of the places where the UN has applied its new thinking about peacekeeping is East Timor, which recently gained national independence from Indonesia. The Security Council hosted the negotiations that led in 1999 to a popular referendum in which the Timorese rejected autonomy within Indonesia and opted for complete independence. But the council had to authorize a multinational security force after Indonesian-backed militants unleashed a campaign of system-

East Timor independence leader Xanana Gusmao greets Secretary General Kofi Annan during his trip to East Timor in February 2000. UN/DPI photo by Eskinder Debebe.

atic destruction and violence in response to the Timorese referendum. Many East Timorese were killed and more than 200,000 were forced to flee, most of them to West Timor.

In October 1999, acting under Chapter VII of the UN Charter, the Security Council established the UN Transitional Administration in East Timor (UNTAET) to restore order and provide administrative services as East Timor prepared for independence. The SC appointed Sergio Vieira de Mello of Brazil as the Transitional Administrator for East Timor. UNTAET began a program of "Timorization" of key government posts to prepare for transition to full independence. In July UNTAET established the East Timor Transitional Administration (ETTA), with a cabinet of nine ministries, five headed by East Timorese. Then UNTAET appointed a thirty-six-member National Council representing a wide spectrum of Timorese society. UNTAET began preparations for elections in late summer 2001 for a national assembly, which drew up and adopted a constitution. In 2002 the Timorese elected a president and became a new nation.

The UN's nation-building has succeeded in launching East Timor on its new path, but interestingly the effort has gotten mixed reviews. David Malone praises its director: "To make good things happen at the UN requires particular skills and qualities that may not be required in running a major corporation or running a major government. They are particular skills of endurance and determination that I think find expression in Sergio Vieira de Mello, who pulled off the East Timor operation in spite of tremendous problems on the ground and enormous bureaucratic inertia within the UN. He just has the sheer determination to get things done and they did get done." Shepard Forman concedes that the effort went fairly well but questions whether it was appropriate: "The UN as a government in Kosovo and East Timor is questionable. Few of the people that went out to govern had any more experience than any of the East Timorese. That's an example of where it [the UN] took on a role to prove itself, and it did an all right job, but we lost a year or so in terms of the Timoreses' own capacity to develop, to reconstruct."

Good, bad, or inappropriate, the UN's mission to East Timor shows that new ideas are floating about and being acted on, which is crucial if the world body is going to adapt and remain vital. Which opens up another area of change: the faces under those blue helmets.

New Peacekeepers, New Faces

A relic of the colonial era, which didn't end until the 1970s, is that the Western media tend to present the European-American nations as militarily superior. This is increasingly an outdated notion. David Malone says, "It's just assumed that the West, because it is so well equipped when it goes into the peacekeeping field, is the only region providing qualified peacekeepers." Not so, he asserts. The Indians and the Pakistanis are "excellent peacekeepers," and the Bangladeshis and the Kenyans "have proved very good in the field." As proof he cites the case of the UN peacekeeping mission established in Rwanda in 1993, the same mission that was unable to stop the genocide between Hutus and Tutsis. The commander, Canadian general Romeo Dallaire, led a mixed force of Europeans and Ghanaians, who were outnumbered by the killers and suffered casualties as they tried to protect specific groups of victims. The Ghanaian peacekeepers saved the most lives, according to Malone, under their own brigadier general, Dallaire's deputy. "About 500 of them stayed behind and they saved at least 25,000 lives in the Kigali stadium and elsewhere," he says. "They never received any attention at all, and this tells us something about the way that peacekeeping is covered by the media. Dallaire has constantly tried to draw attention to the heroic behavior of the Ghanaians, but never with any success whatsoever."

Malone's own solution is to combine the technical prowess of the West with the commitment and courage of the Africans and other peacekeepers. "What is important in peacekeeping is that some of the Western militaries have the high-tech capacities that, say, the Ghanaian army doesn't have. So ideally a peacekeeping force in Africa will be composed of a mix of developing-country contingents and Western contingents."

Equally needed, as Malone and other insiders would agree, is a basic overhaul of how the UN constitutes and funds its peacekeeping missions. Imagine having to conduct potentially risky and difficult military operations when you don't have a standing army and lack the right to levy taxes. Understandably, the attempt to enlarge the peacekeeping concept along lines described above has stretched the peacekeeping effort sometimes beyond what it can handle. Some have likened UN peacekeeping to a volunteer fire department—but it's not that well organized, according to Kofi Annan, because for every mission it is necessary to scrounge up the fire engines and the money to pay for them "before we can start dousing any flames."

The Security Council commissioned a study led by Lakhdar Brahimi, the former Foreign Minister of Algeria, to examine the main shortcomings of the current operation and offer solutions for change. This so-called Brahimi report, submitted in August 2000, has become

The Size and Cost of Peacekeeping

Current Operations, as of June 2003

personnel

Military personnel and civilian police serving in missions on May 31, 2003   34,941

Countries contributing military personnel and civilian police on May 31, 2003   89

International civilian personnel on May 31, 2003   3,215

Local civilian personnel on May 31, 2003   6,665

Total number of fatalities in peacekeeping operations since 1948 as of May 31, 2003   1,797

financial aspects

Approved budgets for the period from July 1, 2002–June 30, 2003   About $2.63 billion

Estimated total cost of operations from 1948 to June 30, 2003   About $28.73 billion

Outstanding contributions to peacekeeping on May 31, 2003   About $1.15 billion

Note: The term "military personnel" refers to military observers and troops, as applicable. Fatality figures include military, civilian police, and civilian international and local personnel. Prepared by the United Nations Department of Public Information, Peace, and Security Section, in consultation with the Department of Peacekeeping Operations and the Peacekeeping Financing Division, Office of Program Planning, Budget and Accounts.

untso since june 1948
UN Truce Supervision Organization
Strength: military 154; international civilian 102; local civilian 113
Fatalities: 38
Appropriation for year 2003: $25.9 million

unmogip since january 1949
UN Military Observer Group in India and Pakistan
Strength: military 45; int'l civilian 24; local civilian 47
Fatalities: 9
Appropriation for year 2003: $9.2 million

unficyp since march 1964
UN Peacekeeping Force in Cyprus
Strength: military 1,248; civilian police 35; int'l civilian 44; local civilian 105
Fatalities: 170
Approved budget 07/03–06/04: $45.77 million (gross)
including voluntary contributions of $14.57 million from Cyprus and
    $6.5 million from Greece

undof since june 1974
UN Disengagement Observer Force
Strength: military 1,043; int'l civilian 37; local civilian 87
Fatalities: 40
Approved budget 07/03–06/04: $41.81 million (gross)

unifil since march 1978
UN Interim Force in Lebanon
Strength: military 2,029; int'l civilian 114; local civilian 302
Fatalities: 246
Approved budget 07/03–06/04: $94.06 million (gross)

unikom since april 1991
UN Iraq-Kuwait Observation Mission
Strength: military 13; int'l civilian 56; local civilian 162
Fatalities: 17
Commitment authority 07/03–10/03: $12 million

minurso since april 1991
UN Mission for the Referendum in Western Sahara
Strength: military 229; civilian police 25; int'l civilian 167; local civilian
   120
Fatalities: 10
Approved budget 07/03–06/04: $43.4 million (gross)

unomig since august 1993
UN Observer Mission in Georgia
Strength: military 116; int'l civilian 99; local civilian 176
Fatalities: 7
Approved budget 07/03–06/04: $32.10 million (gross)

unmik since june 1999
UN Interim Administration Mission in Kosovo
Strength: civilian police 4,097; military 38; int'l civilian 1,005; local
   civilian 3,184
Fatalities: 22
Approved budget 07/03–06/04: $329.74 million (gross)

unamsil since october 1999
UN Mission in Sierra Leone
Strength: military 13,804; civilian police 119; int'l civilian 310; local
   civilian 577
Fatalities: 109
Approved budget 07/03–06/04: $543.49 million (gross)

monuc since december 1999
UN Organization Mission in the Democratic Republic of the Congo
Strength: military 4,515; civilian police 60; int'l civilian 603; local
   civilian 708
Fatalities: 17
Approved budget 07/03–06/04: $608.23 million (gross)

unmee since july 2000
UN Mission in Ethiopia and Eritrea
Strength: military 4,077; int'l civilian 236; local civilian 260
Fatalities: 3
Approved budget 07/03–06/04: $196.89 million (gross)

unmiset since may 20, 2002
UN Mission of Support in East Timor
Strength: military 3,497; civilian police 517; int'l civilian 418; local civilian 824
Fatalities: 11
Approved budget 07/03–06/04: $193.34 million (gross)

minuci since may 2003
UN Mission in Côte d'Ivoire
Maximum authorized strength: 26 military liaison officers in the initial period and up to 50 additional officers as needed, and a small civilian staff
Estimated financial implications for a one-year period: $26.9 million (gross)
Adapted from "United Nations Peacekeeping Operations,"
http: //www.un.org/Depts/dpko/home.shtml

a blueprint for such efforts. The report recommends that the UN make fundamental changes in its policies and practices of peacekeeping and that it provide more financial backing. It urges an updating of the concept of peacekeeping to address modern situations where the combatants may be heavily armed and not always obedient to commanders or political leaders. In such highly charged scenarios the peacekeepers may have to choose sides, at least temporarily, in order to protect the innocent. The Security Council must therefore provide peacekeeping missions with precise instructions on how to act in a variety of possible circumstances. Equally important, according to the report, is the integration of military functions with historically civil concerns such as human rights, policing, and food, shelter, and medical services. The UN has begun acting on the report, beginning with the Security Council's acceptance of the report's recommendations. Questions now are whether the General Assembly will deliver adequate financial support and whether the council and the Secretariat have the will to follow through on the report over the long term.

CHAPTER 7

The General Assembly

Article 9
1. The General Assembly shall consist of all the Members of the United Nations
2. Each Member shall have not more than five representatives in the General Assembly —UN Charter

The General Assembly is both more and less than it seems to be. Although modeled on national parliaments, it has a global purview and visibility that no national legislature can match. It is a center for discussion and debate among all the world's governments. Every member state, no matter how big or small, has a seat and one vote. The GA starts its official year with opening sessions, usually on the third Tuesday of each September. A week later, at the General Debate, heads of state address the opening sessions, which bring together representatives of nearly 200 nations (for a list of member states see Appendix C), many wearing national garb. Then the members get down to the substantive work, which lasts until mid-December.

The UN Charter assigns the General Assembly responsibility for considering any issue that relates to a UN body or agency. The assembly commissions studies about international law, human rights, and all forms of international social, economic, cultural, and educational cooperation. It controls the purse strings, approves budgets, and decides how much each member state should contribute. It also elects the rotating members of the Security Council, as well as the members of the Economic and Social Council (ECOSOC) and the Trusteeship Council. In collaboration with the Security Council, it elects the judges of the International Court of Justice and appoints the Secretary General. Under some conditions the Security Council may ask the GA to meet in special session, and such sessions can also be requested by a majority of member states. Issues deemed more pressing may warrant an emergency special session of the assembly, convened on twenty-four hours' notice at the request of the Security Council or a majority of member states.

Despite these weighty responsibilities, the GA's resolutions have no legally binding force and derive their authority solely as acts of the world community.

Procedures

A two-tier system governs voting. Important matters like budgets and admission of new members require a two-thirds majority vote to pass, whereas others need only a simple majority. If, as often happens, the leadership can establish a consensus on a given matter, a formal vote may not even be needed.

General Assembly affairs are marked by a consuming passion for giving every member state some part of the action. There is a strong feeling that everyone should participate in as many decisions, committees, and issues as possible. The parliamentary and administrative structure of the assembly reflects and embodies this need.

At the beginning of each new General Assembly session, the members elect a president, twenty-one vice presidents (yes, twenty-one!), and the heads of the six Main Committees that run most of the assembly. Regional and national rivalries feed the politically charged voting for these positions. To keep peace among members, formal and

From the UN Charter

ARTICLE 11

1. The General Assembly may consider the general principles of co-operation in the maintenance of international peace and security, including the principles governing disarmament and the regulation of armaments, and may make recommendations with regard to such principles to the Members or to the Security Council or to both.

2. The General Assembly may discuss any questions relating to the maintenance of international peace and security brought before it by any Member of the United Nations, or by the Security Council, or by a state which is not a Member of the United Nations in accordance with Article 35, paragraph 2, and, except as provided in Article 12, may make recommendations with regard to any such questions to the state or states concerned or to the Security Council or to both. Any such question on which action is necessary shall be referred to the Security Council by the General Assembly either before or after discussion. . . .

informal mechanisms ensure that the prerogatives and rewards of office are spread around. The presidency, for example, is rotated annually according to geographical region. If an Eastern European member state has the presidency one year, it must go to another region the next year. Because no one can be president of the GA two years in succession, it is impossible to have continuity in the office. This produces a certain inefficiency that is tolerated because of a perceived greater good.

Main Committees

The speeches and debates of the full General Assembly often make good media events and excellent political theater, but they are not

ARTICLE 13

1. The General Assembly shall initiate studies and make recommendations for the purpose of:
   a. promoting international co-operation in the political field and
      encouraging the progressive development of international law
      and its codification;
   b. promoting international co-operation in the economic, social,
      cultural, educational, and health fields, and assisting in the
      realization of human rights and fundamental freedoms for all
      without distinction as to race, sex, language, or religion. . . .

ARTICLE 17

1. The General Assembly shall consider and approve the budget of
   the Organization.
2. The expenses of the Organization shall be borne by the Members
   as apportioned by the General Assembly.
3. The General Assembly shall consider and approve any financial
   and budgetary arrangements with specialized agencies referred to
   in Article 57 and shall examine the administrative budgets of such
   specialized agencies with a view to making recommendations to
   the agencies concerned.

necessarily effective means of examining issues in depth and arriving
at solutions. For that, the GA relies heavily on a clutch of committees:
a General Committee, a Credentials Committee, and six Main Committees. Committees are common in legislatures worldwide because
they enable many issues to be carefully examined simultaneously.
In the US Congress, committees consider legislation in the form of
"bills," which become "laws" when passed by the full House and
Senate and signed by the President. General Assembly committees
call their bills "resolutions." Each committee deliberates during the
assembly session, votes on issues by simple majority, and sends its

Symbolic Logic

"The General Assembly unfortunately has become a fairly useless body. At the symbolic level, it represents universality at the UN. All countries of the world virtually, even Switzerland now, are members of it. But the way it works has meant that it rarely takes meaningful decisions, and it takes so many un-meaningful decisions that it has been largely written off by the media. There's one significant function of the General Assembly. It serves as the umbrella for treaty negotiations on everything from the International Criminal Court to treaties on climate change, biodiversity, you name it. The treaties matter tremendously in the conduct of international relations."
—David Malone

draft resolutions to the full GA for a final vote. General Assembly resolutions, even when passed by vote, remain "resolutions" and, unlike laws, are not legally binding.

The General Committee consists of the GA president, the twenty-one vice presidents, and the heads of the other committees. The Credentials Committee is responsible for deciding who are the proper, accredited GA representatives of each member state. This is usually a pro forma matter except when a nation is divided by civil war and two delegations claim the same seat. Then this normally unobtrusive committee becomes the scene of intense politicking and high emotions. A recent example of a disputed delegation involved Afghanistan, where the sitting delegation was challenged by the Taliban regime when it seized power. The Credentials Committee listened to presentations by both sides and then "deferred consideration," effectively confirming the old delegation without explicitly rejecting the claim of the other one. Such sidestepping, or action through inaction, is a classic political ploy.

Each of the six Main Committees has both a number and a name, and either may be used to describe it, but insiders usually use only the number. First Committee (Disarmament and International Security) considers resolutions about global security and weapons of mass destruction, as well as more conventional weapons. Second Committee (Economic and Financial) is responsible for examining economic and social development and international trade, including the reduction of barriers that prevent developing nations from reaching their full export potential. Third Committee (Social, Humanitarian, and Cultural) is concerned with a hodgepodge of issues ranging from disaster relief to human rights. It also deals with international crime, including drugs, human trafficking, and money-laundering, as well as government and business corruption. Fourth Committee (Special Political and Decolonization), despite its name, no longer addresses decolonization because there are no more colonies. Instead, it has made peacekeeping its primary mission. The committee also has oversight of the United Nations Relief and Works Agency for Palestine Refugees in the Near East (UNRWA). Fifth Committee (Administrative and Budgetary) oversees the UN's fiscal affairs, and it drafts the resolutions for the general budget that the GA votes on. Sixth Committee (Legal) oversees important legal issues, such as human cloning, international terrorism, and war crimes.

The World's Conference Host

The General Assembly also hosts conferences, many of which have played a key role in guiding the work of the UN since its inception (which occurred at a conference in San Francisco in 1945). Since 1994, the UN has held thirty-four conferences (as of May 2002) around the world on a variety of issues. Recent high-profile meetings on development issues have put long-term, difficult problems like poverty and environmental degradation at the top of the global agenda. In an effort to make the meetings into global forums that will shape the future of major issues, the UN has encouraged participation of thousands of nongovernmental organizations (NGOs), experts, and others not formally associated with the UN.

A landmark conference that is continuing to redefine the UN's mission is the Millennium Summit in September 2000 and its

Annual Days and Weeks

The UN year is marked by nearly sixty days and weeks that call attention to important world issues and provide the occasion for educational and public events both inside and outside the United Nations.

21 February—International Mother Language Day

8 March—United Nations Day for Women's Rights and International Peace

21 March—International Day for the Elimination of Racial Discrimination

21 March—Beginning Week of Solidarity with the Peoples Struggling Against Racism and Racial Discrimination

22 March—World Day for Water

23 March—World Meteorological Day

7 April—World Health Day

23 April—World Book and Copyright Day

3 May—World Press Freedom Day

15 May—International Day of Families

17 May—World Telecommunication Day

22 May—International Day for Biological Diversity

25 May—Beginning Week of Solidarity with the Peoples of Non-Self-Governing Territories

31 May—World No-Tobacco Day

4 June—International Day of Innocent Children Victims of Aggression

5 June—World Environment Day

17 June—World Day to Combat Desertification and Drought

20 June—World Refugee Day

23 June—United Nations Public Service Day

26 June—International Day Against Drug Abuse and Illicit Trafficking

26 June—International Day in Support of Victims of Torture

July—International Day of Cooperatives (first Saturday of July)

11 July—World Population Day

9 August—International Day of the World's Indigenous People

12 August—International Youth Day

23 August—International Day for the Remembrance of the Slave Trade and Its Abolition

8 September—International Literacy Day

16 September—International Day for the Preservation of the Ozone Layer

21 September—International Day of Peace

September—World Maritime Day (during last week of September)

1 October—International Day of Older Persons

4–10 October—World Space Week

5 October—World Teachers' Day

October—World Habitat Day (first Monday of October)

October—International Day for Natural Disaster Reduction (second Wednesday of October)

9 October—World Post Day

10 October—World Mental Health Day

16 October—World Food Day

17 October—International Day for the Eradication of Poverty

24 October—United Nations Day

24 October—World Development Information Day

24–30 October—Disarmament Week

6 November—International Day for Preventing the Exploitation of the Environment in War and Armed Conflict

16 November—International Day for Tolerance

20 November—Africa Industrialization Day

20 November—Universal Children's Day

21 November—World Television Day

25 November—International Day for the Elimination of Violence Against Women

29 November—International Day of Solidarity with the Palestinian People

1 December—World AIDS Day

2 December—International Day for the Abolition of Slavery

3 December—International Day of Disabled Persons

5 December—International Volunteer Day for Economic and Social Development

7 December—International Civil Aviation Day

10 December—Human Rights Day

18 December—International Migrants Day

World leaders attending the UN Millennium Summit held Sept. 6–8, 2000.
United Nations photo by Terry J. Deglau/Eastman Kodak.

accompanying Millennium Assembly (Sept. 12–Dec. 23, 2000). The
lofty Millennium Development Goals, which all member states have
agreed to meet by 2015, include:

Eradicate extreme poverty and hunger
Achieve universal primary education
Promote gender equality and empower women
Reduce child mortality
Improve maternal health
Combat HIV/AIDS, malaria, and other diseases
Ensure environmental sustainability
Develop a global partnership for development

Millennium Assembly delegates also took a special look at the problems in Africa, particularly the HIV/AIDS crisis.

Although the Millennium Summit was a landmark event for the
UN, it has attracted less press attention than the so-called Monterey
Conference held in March 2002. Monterey's official name, the Inter-
national Conference on Financing for Development, holds a clue to

The General Assembly Hall, September 1990. UN photo 176114 by John Isaac.

the meeting's high public visibility, because it addressed fundamental issues of globalization that raise strong emotions among governments, the business community, and NGOs concerned about perceived inequities in the internationalized economy of the past decade. Some 50 government heads joined business leaders, agency directors, and representatives of civil society to examine ways of achieving a new global approach to financing development. A series of roundtables enabled more than 800 members of various stakeholder constituencies to express their views while heads of government and of key organizations like the World Bank and the World Trade Organization listened. It was quite a show.

Some Criticism

The assembly's culture favors moving through consensus, which takes time when nearly 200 delegates are involved. Nancy Soderberg and other insiders accustomed to the relative speed and decisiveness of the Security Council chafe at the inefficient and polarized approach in the GA: "It's very difficult to be in the General Assembly because everything is done by consensus so it's the lowest common denominator of 191 different countries, which is a pretty low standard." This means that the assembly effectively cedes decisive action to the Security Council. As Soderberg says: "Everyone pretends that they don't want to be run by the Security Council, but the key agenda is run by the council. The assembly can put out resolutions on laudatory, amorphous goals, but if you're really going to have an impact and do things, do it through the Security Council."

Critics also complain about the GA's tendency to form cliques and blocs and stay with them even after they have outlived their purposes. Soderberg accuses the blocs of being out of step with current realities. "Look at the Nonaligned Movement," she says, referring to a coalition established during the cold war. "What are they nonaligned against now? There is no alignment, which means that they are really trying to oppose the US more often than not, which makes no sense." Richard Holbrooke shares her exasperation. The Nonaligned Movement and the G-77 (a group of third-world nations) do tremendous damage because they "just don't serve the interests of most of their members. They are two groups which are pulled by old-school politics." Compounding the problem is the passion for making speeches. Holbrooke describes the GA as "a forum for people to make speeches. It started off as a wonderful dream for people to exchange ideas. There is nothing that the GA does that is important," he claims, except for some of the speeches in the annual fall session.

CHAPTER 8

Coordinating to Fight International Terrorism

The spread of terrorism is a threat to the very foundations of the United Nations, and to the spirit of its Charter. Over the years, the organization has played an important role in establishing a legal framework for the eradication of terrorism through one of its basic roles: the codification of international law—more specifically through twelve United Nations anti-terrorist conventions and protocols. These conventions must be strictly observed and effectively implemented if terrorism is to be defeated.

—Kofi Annan, Secretary General of the United Nations

After the September 11 attacks in the US, the General Assembly held a five-day debate on what to do about international terrorism. Not that this was a new issue for the delegates. Dealing with international terrorism has been on the UN's agenda for many years, but it did not claim major attention until the 1990s. Terrorist attacks have long been a part of life for the citizens in some nations, notably the Israelis, Spanish (Basques), British (Northern Ireland), Filipinos (Muslim separatists), and others. The attacks became more frequent and bloody during the 1990s, after the end of the cold war saw the outbreak of conflicts—in Chechnya, for example—that fanned hatreds. Meanwhile, the intensification of economic globalization made national borders more porous

Secretary General Kofi Annan speaks at the UN Peace Bell Ceremony, which was postponed for three days out of respect for the victims of the September 11 terrorist attacks against the United States. UN/DPI photo by Eskinder Debebe.

while hugely increasing people's mobility, so that it was easier for terrorists to move both money and weapons. The attacks of September 11 placed the United States at the head of terror-afflicted nations and helped raise international awareness about the urgency of the threat.

An Emerging Consensus

A striking aspect of recent anti-terrorist deliberations is that the major powers all seem to be generally on the same page. The Security Council's P5 publicly and officially agree that only through joint efforts can they hope to stop or reduce terrorism. The US anti-terrorist position became especially visible several years ago, once Osama bin Laden emerged as leader of his Al Qaeda network and began targeting American government and military facilities. Late in 1999, at US urging, the Security Council passed a resolution requiring the Taliban government in Afghanistan to give up bin Laden. It also imposed limited sanctions as a goad to the Taliban, but to no avail. Soon after, the council passed Resolution 1269, which pledged a "common fight against terrorists everywhere" and specified that member states should share information and refuse to provide a safe haven to terrorists. Since then the pace has quickened. At the end of 1999, the General Assembly voted to adopt the International Convention for the Suppression of the Financing of Terrorism. This convention makes it a crime to participate in raising funds for terrorist activity, even if no terrorist act ensues. One day after 9/11, the Security Council officially decreed, for the first time, that acts of international terrorism are threats to international peace and security.

The events of September 11 pushed the council to act quickly in creating a broad resolution aimed at cutting off all support to international terrorists. Resolution 1373, approved on September 28, 2001, requires that all member states prevent their citizens and banking institutions from providing money to terrorists or give terrorists safe haven, and it requires each member state to report steps it has taken to the Security Council's new Counterterrorism Committee. The US has submitted a detailed report, which it hopes will become a blueprint for other nations in fighting terrorism.

Meanwhile, the General Assembly has been deliberating on its own anti-terrorism measure, a comprehensive resolution designed to augment the dozen international anti-terrorism conventions now on the books. As you might expect, the assembly's diverse membership has struggled to find consensus. One area of dispute is how to define terrorism. Delegates from some Middle Eastern and Asian states argue the need to distinguish between terrorism, which they agreed is an evil, and acts done in the name of ethnic or national self-determination, which they view as legitimate. The US and its friends, however, have branded such distinctions as unacceptable.

Security Council Resolution 1373 (2001)

Adopted by the Security Council at its 4385th meeting, on 28 September 2001

The Security Council,

Reaffirming its resolutions 1269 (1999) of 19 October 1999 and 1368 (2001) of 12 September 2001,

Reaffirming also its unequivocal condemnation of the terrorist attacks which took place in New York, Washington, D.C. and Pennsylvania on 11 September 2001, and expressing its determination to prevent all such acts,

Reaffirming further that such acts, like any act of international terrorism, constitute a threat to international peace and security,

Reaffirming the inherent right of individual or collective self-defence as recognized by the Charter of the United Nations as reiterated in resolution 1368 (2001),

Reaffirming the need to combat by all means, in accordance with the Charter of the United Nations, threats to international peace and security caused by terrorist acts,

Deeply concerned by the increase, in various regions of the world, of acts of terrorism motivated by intolerance or extremism,

Calling on States to work together urgently to prevent and suppress terrorist acts, including through increased cooperation and full implementation of the relevant international conventions relating to terrorism,

Recognizing the need for States to complement international cooperation by taking additional measures to prevent and suppress, in their territories through all lawful means, the financing and preparation of any acts of terrorism,

Reaffirming the principle established by the General Assembly in its declaration of October 1970 (resolution 2625 (XXV)) and reiterated by the Security Council in its resolution 1189 (1998) of 13 August 1998, namely that every State has the duty to refrain from organizing, instigating, assisting or participating in terrorist acts in another State or acquiescing in organized activities within its territory directed towards the commission of such acts,

Acting under Chapter VII of the Charter of the United Nations,

1. Decides that all States shall:

(a) Prevent and suppress the financing of terrorist acts;

(b) Criminalize the wilful provision or collection, by any means, directly or indirectly, of funds by their nationals or in their territories with the intention that the funds should be used, or in the knowledge that they are to be used, in order to carry out terrorist acts;

(c) Freeze without delay funds and other financial assets or economic resources of persons who commit, or attempt to commit, terrorist acts or participate in or facilitate the commission of terrorist acts; of entities owned or controlled directly or indirectly by such persons; and of persons and entities acting on behalf of, or at the direction of such persons and entities, including funds derived or generated from property owned or controlled directly or indirectly by such persons and associated persons and entities;

(d) Prohibit their nationals or any persons and entities within their territories from making any funds, financial assets or economic resources or financial or other related services available, directly or indirectly, for the benefit of persons who commit or attempt to commit or facilitate or participate in the commission of terrorist acts, of entities owned or controlled, directly or indirectly, by such persons and of persons and entities acting on behalf of or at the direction of such persons;

2. Decides also that all States shall:

(a) Refrain from providing any form of support, active or passive, to entities or persons involved in terrorist acts, including by suppressing recruitment of members of terrorist groups and eliminating the supply of weapons to terrorists;

(b) Take the necessary steps to prevent the commission of terrorist acts, including by provision of early warning to other States by exchange of information;

(c) Deny safe haven to those who finance, plan, support, or commit terrorist acts, or provide safe havens;

(d) Prevent those who finance, plan, facilitate or commit terrorist acts from using their respective territories for those purposes against other States or their citizens;

(e) Ensure that any person who participates in the financing, planning, preparation or perpetration of terrorist acts or in supporting terrorist acts is brought to justice and ensure that, in addition to any other measures against them, such terrorist acts are established as serious criminal offences in domestic laws and regulations and that the punishment duly reflects the seriousness of such terrorist acts;

(f) Afford one another the greatest measure of assistance in connection with criminal investigations or criminal proceedings relating to the financing or support of terrorist acts, including assistance in obtaining evidence in their possession necessary for the proceedings;

(g) Prevent the movement of terrorists or terrorist groups by effective border controls and controls on issuance of identity papers and travel documents, and through measures for preventing counterfeiting, forgery or fraudulent use of identity papers and travel documents;

3. Calls upon all States to:

(a) Find ways of intensifying and accelerating the exchange of operational information, especially regarding actions or movements of terrorist persons or networks; forged or falsified travel documents; traffic in arms, explosives or sensitive materials; use of communications technologies by terrorist groups; and the threat posed by the possession of weapons of mass destruction by terrorist groups;

(b) Exchange information in accordance with international and domestic law and cooperate on administrative and judicial matters to prevent the commission of terrorist acts;

(c) Cooperate, particularly through bilateral and multilateral arrangements and agreements, to prevent and suppress terrorist attacks and take action against perpetrators of such acts;

(d) Become parties as soon as possible to the relevant international conventions and protocols relating to terrorism, including the International Convention for the Suppression of the Financing of Terrorism of 9 December 1999;

(e) Increase cooperation and fully implement the relevant international conventions and protocols relating to terrorism and Security Council resolutions 1269 (1999) and 1368 (2001);

(f) Take appropriate measures in conformity with the relevant provisions of national and international law, including international standards of human rights, before granting refugee status, for the purpose of ensuring that the asylum-seeker has not planned, facilitated or participated in the commission of terrorist acts;

(g) Ensure, in conformity with international law, that refugee status is not abused by the perpetrators, organizers or facilitators of terrorist acts, and that claims of political motivation are not recognized as grounds for refusing requests for the extradition of alleged terrorists;

4. Notes with concern the close connection between international terrorism and transnational organized crime, illicit drugs, money-laundering, illegal arms-trafficking, and illegal movement of nuclear, chemical, biological and other potentially deadly materials, and in this regard emphasizes the need to enhance coordination of efforts on national, subregional, regional and international levels in order to strengthen a global response to this serious challenge and threat to international security;

5. Declares that acts, methods, and practices of terrorism are contrary to the purposes and principles of the United Nations and that knowingly financing, planning and inciting terrorist acts are also contrary to the purposes and principles of the United Nations;

6. Decides to establish, in accordance with rule 28 of its provisional rules of procedure, a Committee of the Security Council, consisting of all the members of the Council, to monitor implementation of this resolution, with the assistance of appropriate expertise, and calls upon all States to report to the Committee, no later than 90 days from the date of adoption of this resolution and thereafter according to a timetable to be proposed by the Committee, on the steps they have taken to implement this resolution;

7. Directs the Committee to delineate its tasks, submit a work programme within 30 days of the adoption of this resolution, and to consider the support it requires, in consultation with the Secretary-General;

8. Expresses its determination to take all necessary steps in order to ensure the full implementation of this resolution, in accordance with its responsibilities under the Charter;

9. Decides to remain seized of this matter.

The UN System at Work

Although the Security Council and the General Assembly lead in defining and addressing the threat of international terrorism through debates and resolutions, they receive assistance from a variety of UN bodies. One of them is the UN Office on Drugs and Crime (UNODC), an umbrella office for programs and entities directed at all aspects of international criminal activity, including terrorism.

The Vienna-based UNODC has two broad program centers—the Drug Program and the Crime Program. (The Drug Program is discussed in Chapter 26.) The Crime Program directs the Global Program Against Terrorism, established in 2002, which works closely with the Security Council's Counter-Terrorism Committee, to encourage international cooperation against terrorism. The Crime Program also helps member states ratify and implement UN conventions relating to crimes, narcotics, and terrorism, such as the Convention against Transnational Crime. Adopted by the General Assembly at the Millennium Summit in November 2000, the convention went into force in September 2003.

In the aftermath of September 11, the International Atomic Energy Agency (IAEA) has led the conversation about preventing terrorists from using nuclear weapons. It is the world's forum for discussing, debating, and regulating the peaceful, and sometimes not so peaceful, use of atomic energy. The IAEA's director, Mohamed El Baradei, noted in a recent press account that because terrorists were willing to take their own lives when committing their violence, the nuclear threat was very serious. Since 1993, the IAEA has identified 175 cases of trafficking in nuclear material, but only a handful have involved weapons-grade uranium or plutonium. The IAEA operates the Emergency Response Center, the world's only international response system capable of reacting quickly to the effects of a nuclear terrorist attack.

Terrorists have other weapons available should they lack enriched uranium or plutonium. In 1995, for example, members of a Japanese

As of December 2001, the US had signed and enacted legislation to implement 10 of the 12 UN anti-terrorism conventions and protocols:

1. Convention on Offenses and Certain Other Acts Committed On Board Aircraft, 1963 (Tokyo Convention)
2. Convention for the Suppression of the Unlawful Seizure of Aircraft, 1970 (Hague Convention)
3. Convention for the Suppression of Unlawful Acts Against the Safety of Civil Aviation, 1971 (Montreal Convention)
4. Convention on the Prevention and Punishment of Crimes Against Internationally Protected Persons, 1973
5. International Convention Against the Taking of Hostages, 1979 (Hostages Convention)
6. Convention on the Physical Protection of Nuclear Material, 1980
7. Protocol for the Suppression of Unlawful Acts of Violence at Airports Serving International Civil Aviation, 1988, supplementary to the Convention for the Suppression of Unlawful Acts Against the Safety of Civil Aviation
8. Convention for the Suppression of Unlawful Acts Against the Safety of Maritime Navigation, 1988
9. Protocol for the Suppression of Unlawful Acts Against the Safety of Fixed Platforms Located on the Continental Shelf, 1988
10. Convention on the Marking of Plastic Explosives for the Purpose of Detection, 1991

The government hoped soon to ratify the International Convention for the Suppression of Terrorist Bombings and the International Convention for the Suppression of the Financing of Terrorism. (*Source:* US Department of State, *US Report to the UN Counterterrorism Committee*, 2001, 14–15.)

cult killed a dozen people by releasing the deadly nerve gas Sarin in the Tokyo subway. Information about chemical weapons—like nerve gases—and countermeasures is available from the Organization for the Prohibition of Chemical Weapons (OPCW). Established to implement the Chemical Weapons Convention, which entered into force in 1997, the OPCW tracks the international movement of materials that can be used to make these weapons. The convention prohibits states from using chemical weapons and makes it a crime for citizens to do anything that violates the convention.

It is illegal to use a biological agent like anthrax in war, according to the 1972 Convention on the Prohibition of the Development, Production, and Stockpiling of Bacteriological (Biological) and Toxin Weapons and on Their Destruction. But all nations have not yet signed the convention, which in any case does not include enforcement mechanisms. This is an area of great concern to UN officials. Meanwhile, the World Health Organization (WHO), a UN specialized agency, can provide information about the identification and treatment of most biologically induced illnesses.

For many years, terrorists have used commercial airliners as targets for destruction or as pawns in blackmail efforts. The International Civil Aviation Organization (ICAO) is the world's leader in setting policies to prevent such attacks. Created in 1944, the ICAO does this as part of its general mandate to develop international standards for aviation safety and efficiency. An ICAO ministerial conference in 2002 that looked at the effectiveness of anti-terrorism airline regulations drew representatives from 154 governments and approved a new security plan that includes regular audits of airport security.

Protection of people and goods at sea is the concern of the International Maritime Organization (IMO), created in 1958 to help governments more safely and effectively control ships engaged in international trade. Most UN members have ratified the United Nations Convention for the Suppression of Unlawful Acts Against the Safety of Maritime Navigation and its Protocol for the Suppression of Unlawful Acts Against the Safety of Fixed Platforms Located on the Continental Shelf.

The vulnerability of the mails to terrorism was demonstrated vividly in fall 2001, when members of Congress and others received letters purposely contaminated with anthrax spores. As long ago as 1989, a UN specialized agency, the Universal Postal Union (UPU), created a Postal Security Action Group to examine and publicize mail-related security issues. The UPU helps national postal systems collaborate with one another to ensure that mail travels efficiently and reliably across the globe. Out of sight and mind of most of us, it sets the rules that govern what kind of mail we can send abroad and how the letters and packages will be handled. Its world postal security network offers postal authorities advice and training about preventing dangerous materials from being sent through the mails. And, although the network was originally aimed at drug-trafficking, money-laundering, fraud, and child pornography, it has obvious relevance to acts of terrorism.

Terrorism and Failed States

"An area where we do spend a lot of our time is the issue of failed states. The breeding ground for terrorism or proliferation or any other manner of ills of this world, whether it's narcotics trafficking or other forms of antisocial behavior, is more likely to develop in a country whose institutions have broken down. My speechwriter, Bob Earle, invented a wonderful phrase when we first spoke of Afghanistan. He said Afghanistan wasn't promoting state-sponsored terrorism; rather, Afghanistan was a terrorist-sponsored state. You break down law and order, you destroy the economic system and existing institutions, and then a criminal enterprise moves in and takes the place over and uses the country for its own purposes. That's what Osama bin Laden did when he moved in on the Taliban and used Afghanistan for his own purposes. We at the UN have an interest in states not failing and we spend a lot of time dealing with states that are threatened in that way."
—John Negroponte, US Ambassador to the UN

CHAPTER 9

The UN Village

The amount of psychology in diplomacy is remarkable. States behave very much as human beings. It is very ego driven, I would say. We want to be there, we want to be where decisions are taken.

—Danilo Türk, Former Slovenian Ambassador to the UN and Assistant Secretary General for Political Affairs

The United Nations is known for operating in ways that often seem complicated and convoluted. The Secretariat's administrators have their intricate procedures and protocols and their proper, not always straight and narrow, channels. The same is true in the General Assembly, where red tape decorates resolutions, studies, reports, and memoranda. In the many related bodies like the World Bank or agencies like UNESCO, a passion for creating and filing paper does occasionally obscure the central point of the organization.

But just as often the UN is as simple and straightforward a place as can be imagined, because, as David Malone notes, "people really matter at the UN." Many experts who look at the UN's structure, procedures, and resolutions don't realize that "anything that happens at the UN happens because of certain individuals."

Malone calculates that "at any given time, out of a hundred and ninety ambassadors, about thirty-five control the game. Within the Security Council four or five ambassadors at any given time are dominant, perhaps a few more counting the nonpermanent ones. This is also true in each of the General Assembly committees. In the Secretariat it's true." So, if you know those thirty-five key people, you can do anything. And if you don't, forget it.

When trying to understand the UN, it's also important not to confuse administrative problems with issues of governance and decision-making. When talk turns into decision and action, the procedures can be very different from what bureaucrats are accustomed to, and often that difference is the reason things get done. Governance and decision-making often involve levels of persuasion, guile, and gall that one would find in a novel or movie about Wall Street.

The Village

Think of a small town, where decisions are made by groups of key people who know one another and often socialize while standing at street corners or sipping coffee at a café. In fact, this is exactly how Richard Holbrooke describes his experience as US Permanent Rep under President Clinton. Looking back on those sixteen months in New York City, he remembers a place that he calls the UN Village, located on the Upper East Side, "with its own language and time zone, where 'demand' means 'ask,' 'strong' means 'not so strong' and 'severe' means 'not so severe' and 'urges' means 'begs.' All a different lingo. Thousands of people live here who have very little interaction with the rest of the city." The village works through small groups, formal or informal, endless meetings, caucuses, speeches, and meals. "Food is probably the thing that holds the UN together," notes Holbrooke. "Boy, do those guys like to eat!"

The current US Permanent Rep, John Negroponte, also operates in the UN Village. "I've called on a hundred and fourteen delegates," he remarked recently when asked about his first few months at the UN. "I'm going to call on everyone that I'm allowed to call on. The diplomatic practice is that if you arrived after another delegate, then you go and call on them. If they've arrived after you have, then they go and see you. The new kid on the block comes around to see you."

Negroponte tries even harder to meet with regional groups "because the regional groups are where a lot of the business of the UN is done." He visits with the European Union "once every six or eight weeks" and with the South African Development Group, the Economic Council of West African States (ECOWAS), and others. "Meeting with" can often mean drinks or dinner, sometimes at the Waldorf Astoria.

As a suave and skilled professional diplomat, Negroponte tries to avoid ruffling feathers. "We're diplomats, so whatever feelings people may have they're going to be muted, guarded, and careful," he says. "I think most diplomats feel that you can disagree without being disagreeable. I think that's part of our work ethic, because otherwise you could live in quite unbearable circumstances." Even when one must take an unpopular position, he argues, one can try to do it respectfully and courteously, and that's appreciated by the others.

Within the UN Village are "neighborhoods," some of them pretty exclusive. Negroponte lives in one of the toniest, the Security Council. "Most of my dealings are in the Security Council, which is a fairly small and tight-knit group and we meet each other one way or another every day. We get to know each other pretty well. And so there is a certain camaraderie in the Security Council." He also has to spend some time in that other part of town, the General Assembly, where crowds of ordinary nations mill about, shouting and waving their hands. "I think where the nerves sometimes get a little frayed around the edges is in some of these big General Assembly special sessions, particularly when you have to reach consensus on a document. Nerves can get frayed and you have these marathon meetings that go on until eight in the morning, and you have NGOs in the bleachers which are pushing single-minded positions. But even there, particularly if you can succeed in achieving consensus, if you can reach consensus on a document, I think there's always a huge sense of relief even amongst

Nancy E. Soderberg was alternate US representative to the UN, with the rank of Ambassador, from 1997–2000. Previously she was deputy assistant to President Clinton for national security affairs. She is currently Vice President of the International Crisis Group.

those who were opposed to positions we had. They can say to themselves, at least we produced something at the end of this."

Like all villages, this one has its cliques and factions. For one thing, the population is very male, a sort of diplomatic stag party of political incorrectness. (By contrast, women do very well in many other parts of the UN: in 2000, American women represented over 53 percent of all Americans in professional and senior positions in the UN Secretariat and 44 percent of Americans in all UN agencies.)

The few women who crash the party have described the experience in various ways. Madeleine Albright, who was US Permanent Representative, remembers the thrill of being not just a woman in that environment but "the woman who represents the United States," the dominant power.

Other women representatives may not feel the power rush yet recall the special quality of life at a men's club. Nancy Soderberg remembers old-fashioned gallantry. "Being a woman there is interesting, particularly if you are on the Security Council, because there are no women on the Security Council." She enjoyed the men's attention. "One of the things that I just loved, being a young woman on the council, is that chivalry really does live there. They are so gentlemanly and just wonderful. At times they come up and kiss your hand and everyone stands up for you." Try that in the US Senate!

Security Council Politics

The UN Village is especially visible on the Security Council, which is a small body that constitutes an elite club within the UN system. Most member states regard participation on the council as an honor, but not everyone sees it that way.

John Negroponte recalls that it took a while for Mexico to make up its mind about seeking a council seat because of concerns among many Mexicans about a no-win situation: "If we agree with the US, then that will be taken for granted, and if we disagree with the US, that will hurt us in our bilateral relationship with the US." Newly elected president Vicente Fox and others took the opposite tack, maintaining that Mexico needed to be more visible on the world stage and not worry about how the audience would react. Mexicans at the UN constantly asked Negroponte, "Will you hold it against Mexico if we take positions against the US or at odds with the US?" Negroponte replied with diplomatic aplomb, "Everything we do is going to be in the context of an excellent bilateral relationship . . . we may have our differences, but it's a crucial relationship to us and it's going to remain that and we're going to deal with Mexico accordingly."

Mexico has by no means been the only nation to hesitate before deciding whether to run for election to the Security Council. When the newly minted nation of Slovenia, once part of Yugoslavia, took stock of its diplomatic situation, one of the first matters considered was possible candidacy for the Security Council. Danilo Türk was Slovenia's Ambassador to the UN during the 1990s (and Security Council President in August 1998). "I thought Slovenia would make a good show in the Security Council," he says, but that was not the universal opinion either in the UN or in Slovenia itself. "There was a debate whether or not we need that. Membership in the Security Council brings exposure to have to deal with issues which are very politically contested. It was not an easy decision, and I presented pluses and minuses." One of the pluses was that membership would strengthen the new nation's profile in the world community.

Finally Slovenia decided to throw its hat in the ring for the elections scheduled in 1997. But first the government had to decide which voting bloc it should run in. As always in the UN, a quota system ensures that each world region will have representation. In any given year, a certain number of places will open up for the "Western Europe

Danilo Türk is UN Assistant Secretary General for Political Affairs and was Slovenia's first Ambassador to the UN (1992–2000). In addition he served on the Security Council from 1998 to 1999. He is a lawyer and a former academic.

and Others" bloc (WEOG) or for the "Latin American" bloc, for example, and countries in those regions will compete with one another for a seat. Sometimes the countries of a region will agree who should be elected to the open slots. Other times the countries will engage in a genuine political campaign involving arm-twisting, alliances, and occasional back-stabbing.

The politics can get especially nasty if one nation finds the candidacy of another obnoxious. For example, in fall 2000, three Western European countries were fighting for two slots. According to news reports, Norway and Italy were "wining and dining decision-makers in New York and elsewhere," while the third candidate, Ireland, was appealing to developing countries in the General Assembly, "stressing its poor, former-colonial roots as proof that it understands their needs." The United States was not taking sides but was concentrating instead on backing an African nation, Mauritius, in order to prevent Sudan, which was under Security Council sanctions, from becoming a Security Council member. The US accused Sudan of massive human rights abuses and of having links with terrorists. African diplomats, however, were said to resent US strong-arm tactics, while European diplomats were claiming that the US could have persuaded Sudan to withdraw its candidacy by offering to lift its own sanctions against Sudan. But the US persisted and was rewarded when the General Assembly elected Mauritius, in the fourth round of voting, as one of five new Security Council members to serve in 2001 and 2002.

Danilo Türk did not face quite such high-powered politics when he guided Slovenia through its Security Council candidacy, but he did have to decide whether to campaign for the slot of "Western Europe and Others" or "Eastern Europe." "Initially we didn't want to be a member of the eastern European group. We said we are geographically west of Vienna, we didn't think automatically that there should be any linkage between the former Yugoslavia membership in the east European group and Slovenian membership in the same group." Later the Slovenians changed their minds, "because we thought, it is important to get elected." They decided in 1996 to join the Eastern European group, "where it is easier to get elected than the western because the competition is not as tough." Valuable time had passed, however, and there were two other candidates for the seat, Belarus and Macedonia. "Usually member states announce their candidature five years in advance, in some cases, ten or fifteen years in advance, and they campaign gradually. The last two years they campaign very intensely. Of course if the seat is not contested, there is no campaign but even then they have to talk to other members because they have to get two-thirds of the entire membership. We came very late and there were two other candidates, but I had to do it. Because if I didn't, I would be asked, Where were you, what were you doing? Belarus withdrew at last minute, a couple of days before elections because they had no chance. We defeated the remaining candidate. So that's how Slovenia became a member of the Security Council."

And it was worth it, says Türk, if only for all the international publicity. "We discovered that half of what was important internationally about Slovenia related to the Security Council in those two years [1998–99]. For a small country, this is an incredible exposure."

Türk makes a bigger, more interesting argument when he observes that smaller nations may not be as bound by rigid policies and positions as larger ones, giving them the opportunity to orchestrate some creative diplomacy where otherwise there might be conflict or confrontation. "If a country like Slovenia fails, it is no problem, but if a big country fails with a proposal, that usually has political repercussions. So small countries, nonpermanent members, can be constructive and genuinely helpful members of the Security Council. They can afford some imagination and experimentation. I always believed that. I never thought that only permanent members count." David Malone largely agrees. Although nonpermanent members vary enormously in qual-

A Diplomat Rates the Media

"The professionalism among the reporters at the UN is one of my big discoveries at the Security Council. They knew the background, knew what to quote, and they also knew how to formulate an opinion. It was always very clear what is quotation, what is opinion, so I could rely on the reports from the local press. Sometimes things got tricky, on Iraq, on Kosovo. We had questions: What do you mean? Did you say that? And sometimes the one who comes to you with an accusation or interpretation can be trumped by the original report. So I took the reports from the newspaper or the press agency and said, 'Look that is what was reported, that is absolutely correct. It is your understanding or your explanation which creates a problem.' My respect for reporters grew exponentially as a result of such experiences. People who work here are very knowledgeable and are good reporters, so it's something that has to be respected."   —Danilo Türk

ity, "at any given time you have a number of high-quality delegations or ambassadors" who may function at a high level on the council.

Formally Informal or Informally Formal?

Once a member state becomes a player in a clique or faction, it needs to know the rules and procedures. One of the basic principles is that the most important business is done ostensibly in the open but actually in private. There's a reason why so many decisions, not just at the UN but in organizations all over the world, are made by a few people in a back room. Chances are that if the terms of the agreement were discussed in public, with all the constraints of touchy issues, no one would agree to anything significant. So a common arrangement at the UN is to begin a debate or discussion in a large public setting, like the Security Council chamber, and then, as the individual points become defined, break up into smaller, less public groups. Finally, a few

Between Acts

"You see another side of these guys when you get them out of the formal setting. Wang is very interesting. He's very quiet, but if you get him alone, he's very curious and down to earth and more open than other Chinese reps I've seen. You can actually have an argument with him about Tibet."

—Nancy Soderberg

people sitting at a table resolve the most contentious points, with no media presence and sometimes not even anyone taking notes.

In the Security Council, the opening discussions are referred to as the formals, and the subsequent less public ones as the informals. Nancy Soderberg came to regard the formal meetings as "just a staged show, there is just nothing that happens in them." Rather, the serious negotiations happen at the informals, "because you can't negotiate in a formal setting, you can't talk to people." Occasionally the formal setting is good for sending signals to another member, but nothing happens there. "For the most part, you go in, there's a briefing that nobody pays attention to, and everyone reads prepared statements and nothing happens."

Sometimes, though, even the informals are too formal for serious talk. "The informals are not so informal," says Soderberg. "It still is pretty formal because you have a chair who does everyone in order. It's really hard to have negotiations when you have to wait your turn." The actual decision may already have been made anyway. But where? "In the back room," says Soderberg.

Quids for Quos

There are few secrets in the UN Village. Everyone knows everyone else—not just their strengths and weaknesses but their quirks too, and their sensitive places where you don't touch unless you're prepared for a strong reaction. Surprises are still possible, though, especially when one member state, or group of states, steps across one of the invisible annoyance lines that surround every member like the isobars on a weather map.

China, for example, is known to be very ticklish on the question of Taiwan. But some Central American countries have long championed membership for Taiwan in the UN. Every year they introduce a resolution in the General Assembly to admit Taiwan, and every year it is defeated. "But it never fails to irritate the hell out of China," remarks David Malone. A few years ago, when Guatemala was ending its civil war and needed a UN peacekeeping operation, the Chinese vetoed it, "as a signal to Guatemala that they simply wouldn't stand for Guatemala continuing to participate in this effort to legitimize Taiwan at the UN." So the Guatemalans met privately with the Chinese, "negotiated a reformulation of the Guatemala position on Taiwan that satisfied the Chinese, and the Chinese veto was lifted about ten days later."

Malone recalls another awkward Taiwan moment that occurred when the UN was engaged in a "preventive" deployment in Macedonia. "After a change of government in Macedonia, this was in 1998, a new government cozied up to Taiwan and was alleged to have accepted significant financial aid from Taiwan. When the mandate renewal of the UN preventive deployment came up, China vetoed it. It was denounced by other members of the Security Council for doing so, but naturally the Macedonian government should have known this would be the outcome of its cozying up to Taiwan."

CHAPTER 10

Rights versus Sovereignty: The US and the International Criminal Court

Bush administration officials said today that the new International Criminal Court should expect no cooperation from the United States, and that its prosecutors would not be given any information from the United States to help them bring cases against any individuals.

—*New York Times*, May 7, 2002, report by Neil A. Lewis

To what degree can and should the UN infringe on national sovereignty in the pursuit of justice against those who grossly violate human rights? In Chapter 3 we saw Kofi Annan's strong endorsement of the claims of rights over sovereignty. Now we turn to another round in the debate, the establishment of the International Criminal Court (ICC), a permanent tribunal for trying cases involving military or government personnel accused of committing genocide, war crimes, and other crimes against humanity.

The UN is associated with two international courts that are easily conflated by the casual observer but in reality are so different that they seem to be operating in different worlds. The International Court of Justice, also known as the World Court, is one of the Six Principal Organs of the UN. It hears only those cases involving states, not individuals. It also gives advisory opinions on legal questions at the request of international organizations. Its fifteen judges, serving nine-year terms, are elected through a complicated procedure by the Security Council and the General Assembly. No two judges may be nationals of the same state. The World Court is a fixture of the UN system and hardly controversial.

The other court, the ICC, is not formally part of the UN (although it expresses values embedded in the UN Charter). This court has become very controversial, at least in the United States, where one Congressman actually introduced a bill that, if made into law, could have American troops invading Holland, our longtime partner in the North Atlantic Treaty Organization (NATO) and the seat of the court. The ICC is solely a criminal tribunal. Its prosecutors and eighteen judges are not part of the UN and are accountable only to the countries that ratify the Rome Statute (1998), which established the court. The contentious point is that the court has the authority to bring individuals to trial without needing permission from any individual or government.

The Need to End Impunity

The ICC is designed to end impunity, which means the ability to act illegally without worrying about being caught and prosecuted. This is a major concern because enforcement has not kept pace with the rapid growth of international human rights law during the past fifty years. Too many atrocities go unpunished.

The UN sees the ICC as a way of addressing a problem that, in a sense, the UN helped create through its decades of assisting in the writing and codification of international rights law. The Charter enjoins the UN to systematize international law as part of its goal of encouraging global peace, justice, and stability. Through conventions, treaties, and other documents, the UN has helped create a framework for civilized behavior in all aspects of life, including war and unrest. The International Law Commission is the body that does the actual drafting of text for international conventions.

Unfortunately, in recent decades a new wave of war crimes has appeared, as soldiers increasingly find themselves engaged in civil wars and other forms of internal conflict involving guerrillas, para-military groups, or civilians. An especially vicious situation appears when one ethnic group fights against another, and personal and group prejudices and hatreds take over. Genocide can result when the restraints of military training and moral limitations are forgotten. Until recently there were no international courts for trying persons accused of committing atrocities, except for special tribunals such as the one at Nuremberg after World War II. Most perpetrators of atrocities have been able to act with impunity, as long as they remain in power or can find exile or asylum in a friendly country.

During the past half century, however, world opinion has turned sharply against ignoring or protecting persons accused of atrocities. A good example is Chile's former strongman, General Augusto Pinochet, who negotiated an end to his rule with safeguards that enabled him to live in Chile with little fear of prosecution for complicity in committing state human rights crimes while he held power. But when he left the country for medical attention several years ago, he was arrested and brought to Spain, where he narrowly escaped a trial in a Spanish court for crimes against humanity. If there had existed a single, international body with acknowledged jurisdiction to try cases involving human rights abuses, it is possible Pinochet would have actually been brought to justice.

The ICC remedies this deficiency. If the country where the atrocity occurred cannot or will not conduct its own investigation and trial, as was the case with Chile's refusal to try Pinochet, the court can step in. The existence of the ICC means that the Security Council will no longer be the sole world body authorized to establish human rights tribunals. The council created the first such tribunal in 1993 to deal with massacres in the former Yugoslavia. Staffed by 1,200 employees and operating out of The Hague, it has taken into custody and is trying publicly indicted war criminals, including former Yugoslav president Slobodan Milosevic. In 1994 the Security Council established a tribunal to examine the genocide in Rwanda; it has a staff of approximately 900 and is based in Kigali, Rwanda. The two tribunals share a chief prosecutor, Carla del Ponte of Switzerland. In 2000, a special court was set up in Sierra Leone to try those accused of committing atrocities against civilians and attacking UN forces disarming and demobilizing the combatants after a civil war.

The US applauded the formation of the UN tribunals and has been their most generous donor. In 2000, for example, its assessed and voluntary contributions amounted to about $53 million.

A Permanent Court for Atrocities

The ICC institutionalizes the concept of the international tribunal for crimes against humanity. However, the court is not a venue of first resort. Instead, individuals accused of committing a crime against humanity must be tried by their own government, if that government has ratified the treaty. The accused would come before the ICC only if their home country was unable or unwilling to act. In order to prevent malicious or frivolous accusations, the statute requires prosecutors to justify their decisions according to generally recognized principles that would exclude politically motivated charges. The Security Council has the authority to halt an improper prosecution.

Because the US has been a staunch supporter of previous tribunals, we would expect an equally enthusiastic response to the ICC. The Clinton administration signed the treaty in its closing weeks, although with reservations, but the Bush administration stated that it would not send the treaty to Congress for ratification without major changes aimed at protecting US military and government personnel against "politically motivated war crimes prosecutions." The Bush administration substantially hardened its stance, removing the US signature from the treaty, to the delight of congressional conservatives who claim it violates US sovereignty. Friends of the treaty minimize the sovereignty issue by noting that the document includes language for "harmonizing" international law with domestic law.

The White House has declared that the United States government will offer no cooperation with the court and provide no information to its prosecutors. A friend of the treaty, Senator Russell Feingold

(D-Wisc.), questioned the government's sudden about-face, less than two years after the previous president had signed the treaty. Feingold claims that the turnabout may hinder the effort against international terrorism because the United States may find it hard to ask nations to honor international commitments against terror and violence while the United States itself shows "a lack of respect for multilateralism."

The issue is not totally or only the darling of conservatives. Some US journalists worry that international tribunals compromise the objectivity and effectiveness of the press by asking, and in some cases compelling, war correspondents to testify in court against alleged war criminals. Nina Bernstein examined the issue in a 2002 *New York Times* story about an American correspondent, Jonathan Randal, who had reported on the war in the Balkans and been subpoenaed to testify at the International Tribunal for the Former Yugoslavia. Instead of testifying, Randal filed an appeal and won. In a precedent-setting move, the court agreed that he should not be compelled to testify, and further ruled that "to subpoena a war correspondent the evidence sought must be 'of direct and important value in determining a core issue of the case' and cannot be reasonably obtained elsewhere." This decision is the first by any tribunal that offers legal protection to war correspondents, and it will probably be cited by other tribunals and the ICC, according to lawyers Bernstein interviewed for the article. Until the ICC makes a formal statement on the issue, however, the legal status of journalists in the court's proceedings remains ambiguous.

While the White House and Congress have stalled ratification, the rest of the world has been steadily moving toward making the ICC a reality. In March 2003, the court was officially inaugurated in The Hague. Its first chief prosecutor, Argentine lawyer Luis Moreno Ocampo, was elected a month later.

CHAPTER 11

The Call for Reform

Other than its membership, whom is the UN accountable to? Its member-ship is of state parties, many of which are authoritarian governments, who couldn't give a damn what their people think of it. There aren't checks and balances by public constituencies over what member states do at the UN, so it's undemocratic in that sense. It's also undemocratic in the sense that it is dominated by a few key members, particularly the P5, and the power of the veto.
—Shepard Forman, New York University's Center on
International Cooperation

The controversy we reviewed in Chapter 5 about "reforming" the Security Council to make it more relevant to modern times, echoes throughout the UN. Loud voices from many corners call for reforms, or at least improvements, in most of the bodies, agencies, and ac-tivities that constitute the UN. The calls are fed partly by concern that the Secretariat, the agencies, and other parts of the UN system could be much more effective, efficient, and accountable than they are, and partly by allegations that the bureaucracy has been a juicy career plum for a small group of administrators who put their interests ahead of those of the organization. As always with the UN, perception readily passes for reality, and the illusion of change can be just as much a goad to praise or criticism as actual change.

Richard Holbrooke argues that the UN "is the flawed but indispensable institution that we have two choices with: weaken it by undermining it or trying to strengthen it by getting it to correct its flaws." For him, the choice is obvious: "In America when we discern flaws we try to fix them. We should do the same with the UN because in the end, it's a highly leveraged organization that helps America and the nation's interest and world. But what a mess it is." He analyzes internal US politics this way: "The Congress, a critical variable, is divided into three types of people: the group that hates the UN is probably 20 percent; 40 percent supports the UN strongly, [which is] most of the Democrats; then you have the swing vote in the middle, the group that will support the UN if they reform, and that is the group that you need to bring on board. That takes real leadership on the part of the US executive branch as well as support from the UN leadership."

Others complain that the UN response to calls for reform has too often been knee-jerk and has not tried to address the significant problems that exist within the bureaucracy. Forman criticizes the UN for acting in so self-referencing a manner. He begins with the assumption that "it's a membership organization, and that most membership organizations' first order of business is to serve their membership." That is hard to do with such a diverse membership, however, and it places a lot of pressure on the Secretary General to act more as a mediator than a leader. But the ultimate problem, Forman believes, is the lack of accountability. Unlike the US government, the UN doesn't have an effective system of checks and balances.

The accountability issue surfaces also in comments by Michael Sheehan. If the UN is indeed like a membership organization, we would expect power to be decentralized among the members. That ought to encourage executives and staffers to avoid making any decision to which a member might take exception. Sheehan complains that at the UN this tendency is evident, as some staff try to "push decision-making upward." "Recommendations made are buried in

> ## Talent Wrapped in Red Tape
>
> "I do want to debunk the notion that the UN has nothing but dead wood. That is completely wrong. The UN has a number of very good people. But the UN is bound up in rules, most of them imposed by the member states. The red tape at the UN is, I don't need to tell you, completely dysfunctional."   —David Malone

nuance in page 3 of a memo. No one takes a stand. And that's what grinds down this bureaucracy, this lack of clarity in options, lack of clarity in decision-making, kick decisions upstairs and then micromanaging." He sees a reluctance to make decisions and take risks, although he admits that "since I've been here I've been supported by those who've asked me to come here and work."

The UN's Response

One of the first substantive efforts by the UN to address the criticisms came in 1994 with the establishment of the Office of Internal Oversight Services (OIOS), charged with making the bureaucracy more effective and efficient. Creation of the office thrilled the US government, which described it as "one of the most significant management reforms adopted by the General Assembly in many years."

When Kofi Annan took office in 1997, he launched what he called his "quiet revolution," to streamline the organization and make it both more efficient and more effective without raising costs. The quiet revolution managed to stop the Secretariat's budget creep for a few years, beginning in 1998, and even reduced it a little. Although the UN claims that the total number of all staff in the UN system (about 52,000) is much smaller than the number of employees at many large corporations, it has nevertheless tried to keep the number from growing too fast. The Secretariat's staff fell from about 12,000 in 1984–85 to 8,900. The Secretariat gained a new reform tool in December

2000, when the General Assembly authorized it to start "results-based budgeting." Long urged by the US as a way of rationalizing the allocation and spending of funds, results-based budgeting establishes objectives for each department or program and develops "performance indicators" to measure progress in reaching them.

Most observers credit Annan's quiet revolution with making real improvements. Madeleine Albright remembers that when she became UN Rep, she was told that "the UN was too bureaucratic to change, and too big ever to achieve consensus on measures to improve its governance." She gleefully counters, "Those cynics were wrong. We have made impressive progress. UN headquarters and the entire UN system are better led than they have ever been. UN leaders and members can take pride in the gains made, but we all know there is much more work to be done." Nancy Soderberg rates the Secretariat as "a collection of really dynamic individuals who care deeply about the organization and really work their tails off, interspersed with incompetent people who are there for regional balance, who are just never going to get fired."

One of the most objective and carefully reasoned analyses of reform came in May 2000, after the US Congress asked its research arm, the General Accounting Office, to do an evaluation. The report was generally positive, much to everyone's surprise. It praised the restructuring of the UN's leadership and operations but warned that the main reform objectives had not yet been achieved, particularly the goal of holding the Secretariat accountable for "accomplishing missions" rather than merely "carrying out activities." The main barrier to change was the General Assembly, which insisted on passing excessive numbers of resolutions for the Secretariat to carry out. In the most recent two-year period, the GA had more than doubled the number of its resolutions, and fully one-fifth of them "had vague or open-ended expectations." The report further noted that while coordination among agencies in the field had improved, much remained to be done in that regard. Richard Holbrooke is blunter: "The field coordination is appalling, and the agencies in the field have no real single head. They have a coordinator system that doesn't work."

Turnaround at UNESCO

One agency in particular has demonstrated both the need for reform at the UN and the ability of a committed executive to make reform a reality. The US is a founding member of UNESCO, the UN Educational, Scientific, and Cultural Organization, but in 1984 withdrew from full membership (and payment of annual dues), citing as its reasons alleged politicization and mismanagement. During succeeding years, rumors persisted not only in the US but elsewhere that the organization was poorly run, and some observers claimed that it was losing its institutional focus and momentum. It was charged, for example, that UNESCO's important office in Brasilia could not account for a large portion of its funds. Things came to a head in 1999, when a leaked internal UNESCO document described favoritism, nepotism, corruption, and poor management throughout the organization. The Canadian government was so concerned that it conducted its own investigation, which largely confirmed the charges. Media coverage in the US and abroad gave the organization bad publicity and seemed to vindicate those US critics of UNESCO who had encouraged the American pullout fifteen years before. The very existence of the organization seemed to be at stake.

Change came with the election in 2000 of a new director, Koichiro Matsuura, who had been Japan's ambassador to France. After moving quickly to slash the number of field offices and upper-level administrators and make other cuts in staff and costs, he addressed the agency's accountability problem by proposing creation of a single internal oversight system that would replace an array of audit and evaluation departments and units. This reform began with an impartial investigation by a team from a private organization, the Institute of Internal Auditors, who in summer 2000 did a business-focused quality assurance review of the agency's auditing, evaluation, and investigative functions. Their draft report, presented in September 2000 (and available on UNESCO's website), mentioned, among other points, that "the current internal monitoring functions of UNESCO generally do not conform to the *Standards for the Professional Practice of*

Internal Auditing, which is a widely used approach for structuring an organization's mechanism of internal financial and management controls. Their proposed changes would bring UNESCO into harmony with this standard and give it new tools for managing its projects and funds.

The team's report provided a basis for implementing the kind of far-reaching changes that the director had been seeking. UNESCO's Executive Board approved the creation of a consolidated internal oversight system in September 2000. One of the new office's first assignments was to investigate the mismanagement allegations at the Brasilia office. It found "weaknesses in the control environment," while an external auditing group found problems that "were serious" and might call in question UNESCO's financial statements for the 2000–2001 fiscal year.

It is clear that Director Matsuura is pushing hard to give the organization a squeaky-clean look. Additionally, he has been refocusing the organization on issues of growing global importance, and has done it in such a way as to attract favorable US interest. One of UNESCO's projects, for example, involved reopening schools in Afghanistan after the US-led overthrow of the Taliban; another was to help preserve Iraq's cultural heritage after the US-led invasion against the regime of Saddam Hussein. In 2002, President Bush declared that the US would soon rejoin UNESCO, and subsequently Congress approved payment of American dues to the organization. In only a few years, the organization experienced a complete turnaround in its image and relationship with the US government.

An obvious way of reforming the UN would be to choose strong directors for the various agencies. If UNESCO has finally obtained an effective and reform-minded director, why not go the same route for all the other agencies, programs, and commissions? It is a reasonable thought that turns out to be difficult to implement. Some UN insiders have suggested that because running a nation requires many skills, former heads of government would make good UN directors. David Malone regards this "strange belief" as naïve. "UN agencies are much harder to run than governments, particularly in the western world,"

Answers to Common Questions

Understandably, most Americans know little about the inner workings of the UN administration and are therefore likely to take at face value complaints about excessively good pay and benefits and special perks like free parking. The following items, adapted from the UN's website, give the other side of the argument. Note, however, that they refer mainly to the Secretariat in New York City, not to the specialized agencies, which have their own procedures and pay scales.

STAFF SELECTION

To complaints that the UN hires by quota more than by merit, the UN replies that the Charter requires the Secretariat to be sure its staff reflects "the whole membership of the UN, so that it will be responsive to the diverse political, social and cultural systems in the world and so that all Member States will have confidence in it. To ensure such diversity, the UN employs qualified people from all over the world, and recruits globally. Tough competitive examinations are used to recruit the core professional staff at the junior and middle levels." In any case, nationals of developing countries compose only 44 percent of the "core" professional posts at the UN.

COMPENSATION

The UN bases its professional salaries "on a direct, net comparison with the pay of United States federal civil service employees, adjusted to reflect differences in cost-of-living expenses between New York City and Washington, D.C." If anything, says the UN, its pay is on the low side and is often a hindrance to recruiting the best people.

The UN operates on an internal merit system. "The pay of United Nations staff is regulated by the International Civil Service Commission, an independent, 15-member body of experts representing all regions of the world. The Commission reports to the United Nations General Assembly."

UN staff are not supposed to double-dip. "UN employees are not permitted, under staff regulations, to accept supplementary payments or subsidies from their Governments, in order not to compromise their independence as international civil servants."

The head of the UN, the Secretary General, receives an annual salary of about $227,000, which is "far below that of the chief executives of many businesses."

All UN staff pay income tax. A "staff assessment" is deducted from their gross salary at the rate of 30 to 34 percent, with no deductions allowed, so it is effectively a "flat tax." US citizens working for the UN pay the US Social Security tax. "UN employees (except for the very few with diplomatic status) pay the same sales, real estate and other taxes as anyone else."

BENEFITS AND PERKS

Most UN staff have no diplomatic status or other special standing, and must obey all local laws. Approximately 120 UN employees, including the Secretary General and the most senior officials of the UN system, have diplomatic status.

Diplomats (as distinct from staff) do not work for the UN but for their own governments. "All Member States maintain in New York 'permanent missions,' which in effect are their countries' embassies to the UN. Missions are headed by ambassadors, known as permanent representatives, who make up the core of the diplomatic community in New York."

And finally, there is no free parking. Employees must pay to park in the on-premises UN garage, "which has limited space."

he asserts. Whereas western democracies "pretty much run themselves," and the prime minister simply makes policy, UN agencies "are very resistant to direction from the top on policy even more than on administrative reform and are a much bigger challenge for a head."

Malone cites the case of Ruud Lubbers, one of the most successful prime ministers in recent Dutch history, who "presided over coalitions that were unstable that he held together, that brought about an economic miracle in the Netherlands—a highly successful guy." The Office of the UN High Commissioner for Refugees, however, may be more of a challenge. "The administrative problems of UNHCR, which he's tackled very bravely, are resisting the types of solutions he's proposing. Refugee problems of a very fundamental nature keep arising that aren't susceptible to the easy solutions that are often possible in government. How do you deal with Australia when it turns back refugees from Afghanistan on a ship, knowing Australia is the country that takes the most refugees per capita in the world other than Canada? Lubbers has to stand up for refugees, but Australians by and large do a fabulous job on refugees. So he doesn't want to completely alienate Australia."

Perhaps the final word on the reform question should go to Richard Holbrooke, who cautions against harping excessively on the bureaucracy's failings. "We've got to be very careful as Americans not to be holier than thou because we have an inefficient bureaucracy as well, and ours is much larger and better funded." Amen.

CHAPTER 12

UN Finances

With throats parched by a week of talks on the Middle East, U.N. Security Council members carried their own mineral water to meetings after the United Nations cut the budget for pitchers of iced tap water. A plan to balance the world body's $2.625 billion two-year administrative budget calls for about $75 million in cuts—including lowering heat, rationing air conditioning and eliminating pitchers and glasses of ice water at meetings.

—Reuters, Apr. 8, 2002

How the UN gets and manages its funds has been under fire, from critics both outside and inside the system. The debate about getting funds has focused on three big issues. First is the long-standing problem of US arrears to the UN (a matter largely settled, at least for now) and how much the organization's largest patron should pay. Second is how the UN can operate with less waste and more efficiency. And third is whether it is legitimate to expand the variety of income sources through relationships with the corporate world. These issues raise sensitive questions. If the United States pays less, doesn't everyone else have to pay more? Could the search for corporate-related income risk new dangers such as "selling out" to big business?

Many Budgets

Debates about UN finances require distinguishing among the major budgets of the world body. Most discussions in the media relate to the "regular budget," which pays for activities, staff, and basic infrastructure but not peacekeeping. In 2002, this was $1.149 billion. (The regular budget is for a two-year period, a biennium, so $1.149 is simply half of the $2.29 billion that the General Assembly approved when it voted on the budget.) Peacekeeping expenses are treated separately. Annual peacekeeping costs peaked at $3.5 billion in 1994, during the large-scale operations in the former Yugoslavia, dropped to $1.3 billion in 1997, and rose toward the $3 billion level in 2002. It is estimated that the total cost for the regular budget, peacekeeping, the UN agencies, funds, and programs, excluding the World Bank and the IMF, comes to some $11 billion each year.

Behind these big and round numbers lie the complexities that give the UN its unique flavor. When asked about the size of his agency's budget, Mark Malloch Brown of the United Nations Development Program (UNDP) replied: "I call it $1.2 billion, and there are two other numbers which others use. One is $750 million, which is core contributions. I call it $1.2 billion because that's core plus donor contributions to special trust funds for special issues. Some call it $2 billion because that includes what we call co-financing, where developed countries kick in a huge volume of resources because they like us, in many cases, to spend their money for them. I count that out because for various reasons not dealt with it's a little misleading. So I say $1.2 billion, pessimists say $750 million, the optimists say $2 billion or $2.1. And it's growing. Last year the core in dollar terms grew 4%." Is that perfectly clear?

As the UN constantly points out, its budgets are pretty small potatoes in today's world of trillion-dollar economies. For example, the UN's website notes that "the budget for UN worldwide human rights activities is smaller than that of the Zürich Opera House." And again: "The budget of the World Health Organization is equivalent to that of a medium-sized teaching hospital in an industrial country."

UN Budget 2002

Regular: $1.149 billion
Peacekeeping: $2.77 billion (July 2001–June 2002)

Money Talks

"The test of the American commitment to the UN, above all, is financial. That's what tests it, and whether we seek to strengthen the UN
through a combination of resources and reform or weaken it through
neglect and punishment. On that point this administration appears
to be conflicted internally. I have no doubt at all Colin Powell wants to
strengthen the UN, but it is not clear whether other members of the
administration share that view."   —Richard Holbrooke

Remarkably, the budgets have not increased appreciably during the
past decade. In fact, when adjusted for inflation and currency fluctua-
tions, the UN regular budget declined during several years, so that for
1998–99 it was actually 3 percent less than in 1996–97.

Sources of Income

The income to support the regular budget comes from assessments of
member states. Membership in the UN comes with the obligation to
help pay for its support—something that has never been questioned.
Instead, the focus has been on the size of the contribution a state has
to make. The formula for contributing is based largely on the nation's
share of the world economy. In other words, the rich pay more than
the poor. The United States, having the world's largest economy by a
wide margin, naturally pays the largest share, and very poor nations
pay a nominal amount.

Strictly speaking, the contributions don't follow economic size. For

> ### What's a Few Billion among Friends?
>
> "The remarkable thing about China and Russia, both of which nowadays have virtually no interest in most of the developing world, is that they have not sought to block rather expensive peacekeeping operations serving the interests of Africa or Eastern Europe. In that way the Russians and the Chinese are rather different from Americans. . . . Russia went to great lengths to pay its arrears to the UN. It knows that the US will always quibble over dollars and cents, so it leaves the dirty work to the US."   —David Malone

example, the Vatican, which ranks as an affluent organization, pays only $2,776 a year for its observer status (2002), which carries no vote but enables it to wield great influence in debates and meetings. Far poorer nations have to pay a minimum of about $11,104 annually for their UN dues (which, admittedly, includes the right to vote in the GA).

A few of the rich states have actually sought to get their assessments reduced. The United States has negotiated several reductions in its share of the general budget. For example, in 1974 the UN agreed to place a cap of 25 percent on the size of a member state's assessment, effectively lowering the United States' share in subsequent years. Another change came in 2000, when the General Assembly reduced the US share of the regular budget to a maximum of 22 percent, and its share of peacekeeping costs from 31 percent to about 27 percent. Both reductions came at the urging of the US government, based on the Helms-Biden Law, which stipulated that the US would pay nearly $1 billion in arrears over three years if the UN met certain conditions, such as a reduction in the assessment rate. Congress praised the rate reduction of 2001, and so did many others both at the UN and abroad, who felt that a major bone of contention between the US and the UN had finally been removed.

However, other nations were less enchanted with this reduction

Table 2 Fifteen Most Highly Assessed Member States for Regular Budget, 2002 (Total: $1.149 billion)

Country	Assessment in $ millions	% Share of UN General Budget
United States	$283.0	22.00%
Japan	218.4	19.67
Germany	109.3	9.9
France	72.3	6.5
United Kingdom	61.9	5.6
Italy	56.6	5.1
Canada	28.6	2.5
Spain	28.1	2.5
Brazil	23.2	2.1
South Korea	20.7	1.9
Netherlands	19.4	1.8
Australia	18.2	1.6
China	17.1	1.6
Russia	13.3	1.2
Argentina	12.8	1.2
Totals	$982.9	85.2%

Source: www.un.org

because they assumed that they were being asked to pick up the slack. To its credit, the US government responded to complaints. The State Department, in its annual report about the UN in 2000, announced that the US government had taken the unprecedented act of offering "to compensate countries in year 2001 in order to mitigate the impact of the reduction in ceiling rate from 25 to 22 percent." This meant that ninety-one countries would be spared raises in their assessment for one year. The compensation was the result of a gift from the Turner Foundation to the US State Department, which passed on the funds to the UN.

Despite the adjustment, the US and several other large developed nations remain major funders of the UN, contributing some 85 percent of the regular budget, as Table 2 shows.

Peacekeeping is treated separately from other budgets. The scale used to make peacekeeping assessments has ten levels of support, with the least developed countries paying 10 percent of what they would have owed according to the assessment scale for the regular budget and the five permanent Security Council members paying a surcharge of about 25 percent. In 2001, the US share of peacekeeping costs was reduced from 31 percent to about 27 percent.

Ideally, each member state accepts its assessment as being appropriate and immediately sends a check to the UN for the full amount. Reality is more complicated. Even for routine and predictable budgets, like the regular budget, the UN has a hard time getting everyone to pay fully and on time. By May 31, 2002, for example, only 80 members, some 40 percent of the membership, had paid their 2002 dues, leaving the UN having to wait for 110 countries. Many of the poor nations cannot afford to pay their full assessment and are in arrears. Still others have delayed their payments for various reasons, usually unrelated to their ability to pay. The Charter (Article 19) permits the UN to penalize a member that is two years in arrears by taking away its vote in the GA. This has been done quite a bit, as a last resort, and even the US has found itself in danger of penalization during years when it was withholding its dues or paying them slowly to express its unhappiness with the UN.

Fairness

A complaint, not specific to the United States, is that the many small nations can control the regular budget through their voting power in the General Assembly. The United States has long complained about being outvoted by blocs of members, such as the Group of 77 (a coalition of UN member states from Third World countries), and having little effective control over how the UN spends its money. The UN's general budget is the product of a complicated process designed to ensure that all interested parties have their say in how funds are obtained and spent. The Secretary General proposes a draft budget and gives it to the Advisory Committee on Administrative and Budgetary Questions (ACABQ) for review. The committee consists of sixteen

From the UN Charter, Chapter IV: The General Assembly

ARTICLE 19

A Member of the United Nations which is in arrears in the payment of its financial contributions to the Organization shall have no vote in the General Assembly if the amount of its arrears equals or exceeds the amount of the contributions due from it for the preceding two full years. The General Assembly may, nevertheless, permit such a Member to vote if it is satisfied that the failure to pay is due to conditions beyond the control of the Member.

In May 2002, 21 member states were without their vote in the General Assembly under Article 19:

Afghanistan	Kyrgyzstan
Burundi*	Liberia
Central African Republic	Mauritania
Chad	Republic of Moldova
Comoros*	Sao Tome and Principe
Democratic Republic of the Congo	Seychelles
Dominica	Somalia
Georgia	Tajikistan
Niger	Uzbekistan
Guinea-Bissau	Vanuatu
Iraq	

*The General Assembly, citing extenuating circumstances, permitted these countries to exercise their vote until June 30, 2002.

individuals nominated by their governments, usually including a US national, and elected by the General Assembly. The Committee for Program and Coordination, made up of thirty-four experts elected by the General Assembly, reviews the program aspects of the budget. Unlike the Advisory Committee, in which the experts serve in their personal capacity, the Program Committee experts represent the

Secretary General Kofi Annan meets with members of the US Senate Foreign Relations Committee on Jan. 21, 2000. Attending are US Ambassador
Richard Holbrooke (second on left); Committee Chairman and Senator
Jesse Helms (third on left), and ranking Democratic Senator Joseph Biden
(fourth on left). UN/DPI photo by Evan Schneider.

views of their governments. The revised draft is sent to the General
Assembly for approval, when it becomes the official UN general budget for the next biennium. Each country has the opportunity to suggest changes in the draft budget, but the changes may not necessarily
be adopted.

The UN replies to criticisms from affluent nations that a lot of the
money it spends eventually finds its way back to the major donors. For
example, the UN's headquarters is in New York City, where UN staff
and diplomats contribute to the city's economy. Additionally, developed countries supply a substantial share of UN employees and consultants. US citizens make up the greatest single national share of
Secretariat employees (not surprising, given that the Secretariat is in
New York City).

But other statistics tell a different story, according to a study just

Helms-Biden Law

The Helms-Biden Law put the US on course to pay nearly $1 billion in back dues over three years, providing the UN met certain benchmarks:

Year 1: Conditions were met: US paid $100 million toward arrears in 1999.
Year 2: UN agreed to new assessment rates for regular budget and peacekeeping:
US paid $582 million in 2001.
Year 3: US paid $244 million.

completed by the US General Accounting Office (GAO). It seems that both Japan and the United States are underrepresented among staff at the UN in relation to their financial contributions to the world body, while British, French, and Canadian citizens are overrepresented. The GAO examined the Secretariat and six agencies that had established hiring quotas, concluding that only the Secretariat met its own goals for hiring US citizens. Similarly, Japan, despite contributing 19.5 percent of the UN budget, held only 2 percent of senior positions, while twelve countries, including Russia, the Philippines, and Pakistan, were overrepresented in the Secretariat.

The US State Department came up with similar conclusions when it did its own estimate of national representation. It examined hiring patterns in the Secretariat and four agencies that have established a system of "described ranges," or quotas: the Food and Agriculture Organization (FAO), International Civil Aviation Organization (ICAO), International Labor Organization (ILO), and World Health Organization (WHO). Table 3 lists the Secretariat and the agencies, along with the number and status of Americans on board as of December 2000. (These figures represent only the professional posts funded from the agencies' assessed budgets.)

At first glance the hiring pattern seems clearly discriminatory

Table 3 Number and Status of US Nationals in the UN Secretariat and
Selected Agencies, as of December 2000

UN Agency	Filled	US Desirable Range or Quota	Number of Americans on Board	Percent of Americans on Board	Current Status
UN	2,400	314–424	315	13.1	In range
FAO	992	186–248	126	12.7	Underrepresented
ICAO	221	28	16	7.2	Underrepresented
ILO	659	101–135	87	13.2	Underrepresented
WHO	1,138	174–237	152	13.4	Underrepresented

Source: State Department, US Participation in the UN, 2000, p. 125.

against the US. However, the report explains that the failure of the US
to pay its dues on time, and in some cases to pay its contributions to
specific agencies either on time or at all, caused a realignment of
hiring patterns in favor of other donor nations. The case for "discrimination" is therefore unclear.

Additional Funding

Not all UN funding comes directly from member states. UNICEF
holiday cards, for example, have long provided additional income for
efforts to aid children. In addition, UN agencies and organizations
sometimes receive grants from foundations, such as the Turner Foundation or the Bill & Melinda Gates Foundation. Recently, however, a
new line of fiscal opportunity has opened up with the creation of
partnerships between the UN and large businesses.

The appeal is obvious. By tapping corporate support the UN can
possibly avoid having to raise the amounts that member states pay,
thus sidestepping the contentious issues associated with who pays
how much, and how funds should be spent. A danger is also evident:
the appearance of undue business influence in the affairs of an organization that is supposed to act disinterestedly.

The overture to the corporate world has alarmed some observers as a potential sellout to business interests. An early outcry came when it was learned that one UN agency had asked sixteen large transnational corporations for donations of $50,000 each to pay for a Global Sustainable Development Facility. The UNDP was criticized by international watchdog groups for selling out to corporate interests, a charge the agency strongly denied. Rather, the agency claimed it was seeking to demonstrate that corporations can be both profitable and good citizens.

Shepard Forman has offered his own, tongue-in-cheek solution for the UN's funding problems. "I once suggested rather facetiously that there should be a reverse scale of assessments in which countries that act badly and therefore cost the UN more to patch things up than to fix things up should have to pay more dues. There should be a system where if you misbehave very badly your membership should be suspended or something else occurs. Otherwise anybody can do what they want, they can get away with anything they want, and the membership doesn't live up to the organization's own set of standards."

CHAPTER 13

A Tour of UN Headquarters

In many ways [the UN is] a direct throwback to the '50s. The building itself is a throwback to the '50s with [period] chairs and everything, and there are still a lot of people that are stuck with the . . . mentality of North vs South, blaming the US for all their evils.
—Nancy Soderberg, former US Ambassador to the United Nations

Nancy Soderberg's quip has a kernel of truth, in that walking through the UN headquarters complex in New York City can feel like being in a museum. Never having enjoyed or endured a major renovation, the building and its furnishings are pretty much as they were when opened to the public during the early 1950s. As for her complaint about old ways of thinking, we can't blame that on the architecture, which has retained its freshness and still delights any eye that can overlook the worn fittings, cracked plaster, and peeling paint. The UN's leadership must find a way of maintaining the buildings while also making them better work spaces, and they must do that soon if the structures are to remain safe for both tenants and the thousands of visitors and tourists. The UN has cut its operating budget so much that it can't do proper maintenance, let alone renovate. There's too little heat in winter and not enough air conditioning in summer.

The United Nations headquarters in Manhattan.
UN photo 165054 by Lois Conner.

Despite its signs of wear and tear, the UN complex remains a popular tourist attraction. Opposite the complex, stretching from 48th
Street and First Avenue to 42nd Street, is a long line of flagpoles—191
of them—each bearing the flag of a UN member state. The flags are
arranged alphabetically, with Afghanistan starting at 48th Street and
Zimbabwe finishing at 42nd Street. The line nicely frames the UN
complex, like a grand boulevard.

Immediately beyond the flags, the blue-green glass slab of the Secretariat building, which houses UN staff, is so instantly recognizable
and well placed in the complex that it seems to grow organically from
the soil. It was designed by an international team of architects who
adapted a concept of the French architect Le Corbusier. John D. Rocke-

Flags of UN member states fly at the UN headquarters. UN photo 185522 by A. Brizzi.

feller Jr. donated the eighteen-acre UN Headquarters site, which was
cleared of its structures in 1947. The thirty-nine-storey Secretariat
building was finished in 1950, and on the thirty-eighth floor are the
UN Secretary General's offices.

Before entering through the glass doors to the visitors reception hall
in the General Assembly building with its central information booth,
visitors pass through UN security, located in a large tent erected after
September 11 to provide an expanded checkpoint at the UN's visitor's
entrance. The complex draws tourists and schoolchildren, as well as
members of the media and consultants who have business related to
the UN. Since 9/11, the UN security force is more visible and active
than ever before. So, although the security tent has ruined the view of

A stained glass memorial designed by Russian-born French artist Marc Chagall in memory of Dag Hammarskjöld. UN photo by Lois Connor.

the building façade, this seems a small price to pay for prudence. In addition to the security force, the UN operates its own postal administration (UN postage stamps are available only in the complex) and fire department.

Exhibition spaces are located in the eastern portion of the complex. Exhibits include artworks from a permanent collection and traveling shows such as children's art from around the world. One of the most eye-catching artistic features in the complex is a stained glass window by Marc Chagall, a gift from the artist and United Nations staff members. It was presented in memory of Secretary General Dag Hammarskjöld and fifteen others who died in a plane crash in 1961. Among the many paintings that hang on the walls are objects displayed in cases. Ironically, though, no maps are displayed. You would think a global organization would obsess on maps, but it turns out they're too politically sensitive. In the General Assembly Hall, discussed below, is a map of the world—without national boundaries drawn. Here it's the art that has been subjected to political correctness: none has been donated by any member nation; instead the walls feature two abstract murals by Fernand Leger, donated anonymously through the United Nations Association of the USA.

The complex consists of four large, interconnected buildings: the General Assembly Building, the Conference Building, the Secretariat building, and the Dag Hammarskjöld Library. In the basement of the General Assembly Building, visitors will find restrooms, a book and gift shop, and a post office.

Guided tours of the complex start in the General Assembly Building, which is the site of the General Assembly Hall. The hall is open to the public when the assembly is not in session. It's the largest room in the complex, seating more than 1,800. The delegates sit in alphabetical order, according to lots drawn before each annual session. Certainly this is a space made for speaking, although a former US Ambassador here, Richard Holbrooke, always complained about its having bad acoustics. Delegates have earphones that provide them with simultaneous translations into Arabic, Chinese, French, Russian, Spanish, or English.

Next on the tour is the Conference Building, which includes the chambers of the Security Council, the Trusteeship Council, and the Economic and Social Council, all lined up in a row. The Security Council Chamber is a clean and workable space, a gift from Norway designed by architect Arnstein Arneberg. The main room features the famous horseshoe table where the delegates confer during the "formals," the public sessions. A small side room is for the "informals." The decoration here is inspirational—a big canvas depicting a phoenix rising from the ashes, and a blue and gold silk tapestry. The images on the drapes of the windows overlooking the East River symbolize faith, charity, and hope.

The Economic and Social Council Chamber, a gift from Sweden, was designed by Sven Markelius, one of the original architects of the complex. The ductwork in the ceiling was left exposed as a reminder that the UN's economic and social work is never finished.

One of the least known and most interesting rooms in the complex

The UN is one of New York City's most popular sites to visit, drawing about 400,000 visitors every year. Since 1952, some 37 million visitors have taken a tour.

If You Go

You might consider first orienting yourself by taking the UN's online tour, *http://www.un.org/Overview/Tours/UNHQ/*

Guided tours of the UN operate daily from the General Assembly Public Lobby and take visitors to some of the main council chambers and the General Assembly Hall. In the public concourse, downstairs, the Public Inquiries Unit offers additional information materials relating to the UN and its agencies. Also in the concourse is the United Nations postal counter (which sells UN stamps), along with a UN bookstore, gift shops, coffee shop, and restrooms.

HOURS

January and February: Monday–Friday, 9:30 am–4:45 pm
The rest of the year: 7 days a week, 9:30 am–4:45 pm
May is usually the busiest month. English tours leave every half hour and last for about one hour.

The UN is closed on Thanksgiving Day, Christmas Day, and New Year's Day. A limited schedule may be in effect during the general debate of the GA (mid-September to mid-October), between Christmas and New Year, and during special conferences and events.

DIRECTIONS

The UN Headquarters is on First Avenue between 42nd Street and 48th Streets. The visitor's entrance is located on First Avenue at 46th Street. The UN does not offer public parking.
Subway: 4, 5, 6, or 7 line to Grand Central Terminal, then walk 42nd St. to First Ave.
Buses: M15, M27, M42, or M104

TOUR PRICES

Adults: $10.00
Senior citizens: $8.50
Students: $6.50
Children* (ages 5–14): $5.50
*Note that children under 5 are not admitted.

RESERVATIONS AND GROUPS

Reservations are required for 12 or more people and should be made by calling 212–963–4440, faxing 212–963–0071, or emailing *unitg@UN.org*
    A complimentary ticket is issued for the first 15 tickets purchased and one free one for every 20 tickets thereafter.

CONTACT INFO

General info: 212–963-TOUR
Languages other than English: 212–963–7539
Group reservations: 212–963–4440

LANGUAGES

Tours are conducted in the following languages: English, Arabic, Croatian, Danish, French, German, Greek, Hebrew, Italian, Japanese, Korean, Mandarin, Polish, Portuguese, Russian, Spanish, Swedish. Call to be sure a tour in your language is available the day you plan to visit.

HANDICAP ACCESS

The UN is accessible to people with disabilities and provides wheelchairs for those visitors who require them. People with hearing disabilities may obtain written information on the tour.

is the Trusteeship Council Chamber. A gift from Denmark, it was designed by the Danish architect Finn Juhl. The acoustics are reportedly excellent, but this hardly matters because the Trusteeship Council no longer meets. This room, designed for what was once a major part of the UN, has fallen silent because its main tenant is no longer relevant to the functioning of the UN. Delegates no longer sit around the table here, gazing at the large wooden statue of a woman with her arms outstretched and releasing a bird. The sculpture, donated in 1953, when the UN still had trust territories (islands and lands lacking self-government), is carved from teak, a wood associated with some of those territories.

The final building in the complex is the Dag Hammarskjöld Library. The building was a gift from the Ford Foundation (whose headquarters is down the street, on 42nd Street). Although its collections are available to the public, the library is used mostly by UN staff and diplomats. As you might guess, the library includes vast stores of information about the UN.

The staff cafeteria is one part of the UN that has definitely improved over the years; the food is better and in greater variety. Best of all is the view, overlooking the East River through huge windows. The cafeteria isn't open to the general public, but, oddly enough, the Delegates' Dining Room is. Rated a "NY secret treasure" by the *Zagat Survey of New York City Restaurants,* the dining room is on the fourth floor and is open to the public for lunch, featuring a "diverse selection of international cuisine." It too offers a view of the East River. According to Richard Holbrooke, food is what holds the UN together.

Delegates have two lounges in which to relax. Both are located in the Conference Building and are very popular sites for delegates to sit with one another after a meeting adjourns to talk over negotiations or details of a meeting, or just socialize. These lounges could be considered the "informal" chambers of the different councils, where horse-trading takes place. Of course, no lounge would be complete without a huge rug depicting the Great Wall of China, a gift from the Republic of China. On upper floors are the tiny offices of the journalists and other media people who report on the UN. And of course, the UN personnel are there too.

Several schemes have been floated to pay for renovating the complex, but none of them has gone anywhere yet. Recently, Kofi Annan asked the US State Department to consider making a $1 billion interest-free loan to the UN, to pay for renovation of the complex and construction of an additional building to house UN agencies. By stretching out repayment to twenty-five or thirty years, it would be possible for the UN to repay the loan without straining its budget. There is another way to go, but no one seems willing to consider it. The UN doesn't have to be located in New York City. It could move, if another nation offered it a more economical deal. Just as sports franchises move from city to city in search of the best domed stadium, the UN could shop around for the best offer. A few years ago a media report claimed the German government was interested in providing the UN with space in Bonn vacated by government offices moving to Berlin. Was this a serious offer? Would the members of the UN ever consider leaving New York and all it has to offer? The future will tell.

CHAPTER 14

The Coup Against Boutros-Ghali

Every country probably trashed us. I guess they didn't like the way we did it, but there was no other way. We tried to do it more subtly, we tried to ask Boutros to step down. He had promised he was a one-term, and he reneged on that promise. It got uglier and uglier, so we finally decided to stick to our guns.
                                                                    —Michael Sheehan

If you think the US government is at the mercy of the UN, or that the UN can dictate policy to the United States, consider the case of Boutros Boutros-Ghali, who was Kofi Annan's predecessor as Secretary General. Boutros-Ghali served one term as SG and declared his intention to run for another. But he never made it, because, to put it bluntly, he fell afoul of key US diplomats and political leaders, who blocked him through a carefully staged coup. The coup is no secret. Boutros-Ghali has described his experiences in writing, and many participants and observers have offered their own contributions. The story merits a brief retelling as an example of the fine line that the SG has to walk in threading a path to successful leadership.

Boutros-Ghali's downfall had two main roots. One of them was the disaffection of his middle managers, who did not lift a finger to defend him when the Americans and their accomplices made their move. Mark Malloch Brown blames Boutros-Ghali's background as a senior official in the Egyptian government for giving him an exalted view of his office, which was exactly the wrong thing to emulate as Secretary General. Instead of making himself indispensable by helping nations solve problems, too many saw him as doing "the diplomatic equivalent of stamping his foot while simultaneously staring down his nose. It didn't make most heads of state and foreign ministers particularly want to work with him."

A highly placed UN insider confirms this picture of an arrogant, isolated Secretary General. "The thing about Boutros that we were most unhappy about as staff was he didn't really like the institution that he headed. He was completely aloof and detached from all of us." His bullying caused the staff to either remain silent or tell him what he wanted to hear, which meant "he was no longer getting the best opinions from people." His manner of working, says the insider, "was hopeless." He would leave managers out of the loop, presenting them with constant administrative and policy surprises. They would often find an ambassador or minister coming to them and saying, "As your boss said the other day" or "As we said to your boss the other day," and they hadn't even been given a copy of the notes on the meeting. "That was really bad for efficiency and for morale."

The Secretariat's staff had to endure these indignities, but not the United States. Once Boutros-Ghali got on the bad side of US Permanent Representative Madeleine Albright, it was all downhill. "Personal dislike was a real issue on policy," says the insider. "In the case of Boutros and Madeleine, he didn't like her style, she didn't like his nature, and their dislike coincided with the fact that professionally they didn't see eye to eye."

Early in 1996 Albright became leader of an American effort to prevent Boutros-Ghali from seeking a second term. It was a period of strained relations between the UN and the US, owing to a string of failed operations (fighting in Somalia and genocidal massacres in Rwanda and Srebrenica). Michael Sheehan, who was on the National Security Council staff at the time, recalls that he found him-

Secretary General Boutros Boutros-Ghali greets President Clinton prior to the president's address before the General Assembly on Sept. 24, 1996. UN/DPI photo by Evan Schneider.

self one of the initial conspirators. "We got together and said Boutros needs to go, he is not good for the UN, and he's not good for the US, and not good for the US and the UN."

The conspirators quickly discovered that while Boutros-Ghali had little solid support in the UN, they had greatly underestimated his determination to run for a second term and his skill in marshalling support. He used "every trick he knew, with very subtle and not so subtle promises and threats to countries. No one wanted to oppose him." "We ended up standing alone in broad daylight," reflects Sheehan, "instead of slipping it to him." The deed would have to be done very publicly, in the modern-day equivalent of the Roman forum.

The conspirators acted with growing support from President Clinton and Secretary of State Warren Christopher, who were put off by Boutros-Ghali's lobbying of member states. "They recognized that he forgot what his job was," Sheehan says. "He was a servant of the member states, a servant for the organization not an entity unto himself." Realizing that they needed to have an appealing alternative candidate, the coup team wrote a memo to Clinton in spring 1996 that offered three candidates—Lakhdar Brahimi, Olara Otunnu, and Kofi Annan—each of whom was from Africa. Sheehan favored Annan or Brahimi. "I had been working for both of them and I loved both of them. At the time I didn't know Otunnu, who was being pushed by another member of the NSC staff. The President approved this strategy and said that, yes, he needs to go, that sounds good. We also discussed the Asian option and others, but we thought the post was going to stay in Africa."

When the Americans began looking for votes in the General Assembly, they discovered that Annan seemed to have the strongest support, so he became the lead candidate. "The French extracted a promise from us to support them to get the Under Secretary for Peacekeeping, which we granted, and they have now. And that was the deal. Kofi Annan became SG to the delight of everyone." Actually, much of the "delight" was after the fact. Sheehan recalls that after the vote, mass amnesia struck and "it was like rats off a sinking ship." "Now everyone supported Annan from day one, so he was the choice. I remember differently. We were under enormous pressure to cut a deal, particularly from [French president] Chirac and [South Africa's] Nelson Mandela, who called the president on many occasions to lobby for Boutros-Ghali. I never felt more pressure from anything I ever did during five years in the White House. It was hard." Sheehan praises Albright for not bending to pressures on Boutros-Ghali's behalf. "It wouldn't have happened without her. She hung in there. It was the right thing to do."

Even Sheehan is astonished by just how good a Secretary General Kofi Annan has been. "I don't think anyone foresaw that level of greatness. We knew he was solid, we knew he was good, we liked him, we trusted him, we respected him. I don't think anyone would dream that he would rise to this stature, but we'll take credit anyway for foreseeing it."

But was it right? Should a dominant nation be able to decide that it doesn't like the Secretary General and methodically force him out? Our UN insider has no problem with that, though faulting the reasons offered by the US government. "The Americans were right to get rid of Boutros but not on the ground that he wasn't reforming the UN. The official reason they gave was that he was resistant to reform, which was nonsense. In fact he did want reform more than anyone else. He may have done it in a way that we, the staff, didn't like, but he decisively slashed posts, slashed high-level functions, really did reform."

The real reason for Boutros-Ghali's ouster, the insider claims, was that he became a political liability in the US presidential election of 1996. "He let the Republicans have a useful piece of ammunition: they said if there's a Republican president, we would not allow our foreign policy to be made by an un-elected Egyptian bureaucrat sitting in New York. Of course he wasn't making policy. Of course the Americans could do what they want with Boutros. But perception was bad enough politically for Clinton because what mattered was what people thought the truth was. Clinton was, I think, increasingly convinced that he had to get rid of this liability. Why did he need to give the Republicans a stick to beat him on the head with?"

CHAPTER 15

UN Advocates, Donors, and Friends

The United Nations once dealt only with Governments. By now we know that peace and prosperity cannot be achieved without partnerships involving Governments, international organizations, the business community and civil society. In today's world, we depend on each other.
—Kofi Annan, Secretary General of the United Nations

Aside from Kofi Annan, now an international luminary in his role as UN Secretary General, some of the heads of UN agencies and commissions have shone brightly in their public careers, like Carol Bellamy of UNICEF and Mary Robinson of the Office of the High Commissioner for Human Rights. But there are also other kinds of stars—some more comfortable before a camera or a theater audience, some at home in the corporate boardroom—who have aligned themselves with the UN.

Ted Turner and Bill Gates, for example, don't just applaud the UN but throw money too. Turner singlehandedly endowed the United Nations Foundation (discussed below), while the Bill & Melinda Gates Foundation has pledged tens of millions of dollars for various programs, either as sole donor or as part of a consortium of donors. Gates

Secretary General Kofi Annan with wife, Nane Annan, and UN Goodwill Ambassador actor Michael Douglas on July 4, 2000, in Philadelphia. UN/ DPI photo by Eskinder Debebe.

has earmarked $50 million for UNICEF and partners to prevent deficiency in dietary micronutrients. The Gates Foundation is a major player in the effort to develop an AIDS vaccine. In addition, the foundation established the Global Fund for Children's Vaccines, which pledged $750 million over five years to improve the health of children in developing nations by funding immunization efforts.

Peace Messengers and Goodwill Ambassadors

The UN's most visible supporters are probably the forty-odd actors, athletes, and other celebrities who have become official Goodwill Ambassadors, Peace Ambassadors, and Peace Messengers. On their own time they volunteer to travel the world, representing the UN before every imaginable kind of audience and spreading word of its programs and concerns. Some of these celebrity volunteers serve at-large and represent the UN as a whole, while others sign on with a part of the system like the UN Development Program (UNDP), the UN Population Fund (UNFPA), or the UN Children's Fund (UNICEF). Actor Danny Kaye became the first Goodwill Ambassador in 1953, with UNICEF, and Audrey Hepburn joined shortly afterward. Soon there were many more: actor Peter Ustinov, singers Harry Belafonte and Judy Collins, and actresses Vanessa Redgrave and Linda Gray. Today, Angelina Jolie is working to help refugees. High-profile helpers come from everywhere: from China, singer Leon Lai; from Italy, actors Lino Banfi and Simona Marchini; from Greece, singer Nana Mouskouri; from Portugal, actress Catarina Furtado.

Peace Ambassador Luciano Pavarotti has raised money for the UN's refugee agency, including some $2 million at one event for Angolan refugees. Actor Danny Glover has toured widely in Africa promoting development, and Mia Farrow has campaigned for polio immunization.

The United Nations Foundation

On Sept. 18, 1997, businessman and philanthropist Ted Turner made an unprecedented gesture when he announced a $1 billion gift in support of UN causes. His historic donation was made in the form of Time-Warner stock, given in ten annual installments. In response to Turner's gift, the UN Foundation (UNF) was created for "promoting a more peaceful, prosperous, and just world," which it seeks by publicizing and funding various UN activities. Its four main functions are to (1) provide additional funding for programs and people served by UN agencies; (2) help forge new partnerships between UN agencies, the private sector, and nongovernmental organizations in order to improve support for the UN while also enhancing the effectiveness of service delivery; (3) in cooperation with a sister organization, the Better World Fund, sponsor or conduct efforts aimed at educating the public about the UN's unique role in addressing global issues; and (4) encourage public and private donors to help demonstrate what the UN and the world can do when the public and private sectors cooperate and co-invest.

An example of how these goals play out in the real world can be seen in the Adopt-A-Minefield campaign. In many parts of the world the land is sewn with small land mines, relics of civil wars and other violent outbreaks that remain lethal to humans long after the fighting has ended. The mines are invisible and their location is seldom known with accuracy. The UN agency most involved in clearing mines is the UNDP, which has collaborated with the Better World Fund and the UNA-USA (see below) to sponsor "Adopt-A-Minefield," enabling companies or individuals to pay for mine removal in more than 100 locations. Costs vary considerably, from $27,000 to clear a village of land mines in Croatia to $34,000 for a field in Cambodia.

The UNF also funds "UNWire," which compiles press stories and original reporting about the UN and makes them available online (*www.unwire.org*). In addition, as noted earlier, Turner also personally provided $34 million to cover the shortfall caused by the reduction in the US scale of assessments to the 2001 regular UN budget. The UNF is active and visible, ready to ride the next economic boom into humanitarian good deeds.

United Nations Association of the United States of America

For those of us who haven't yet made our first billion, an excellent way to participate (at least indirectly) is to join the United Nations Association of the United States of America (UNA-USA), a nonpartisan, nonprofit group. About 23,000 Americans belong to UNA-USA, the country's largest grassroots foreign policy organization, which seeks to educate Americans about the issues facing the UN and to encourage support for strong US leadership in the UN. It is a leading center of policy research on the UN and generally promotes participation in global issues. It offers forums and seminars about major international issues, and helps coordinate the Model United Nations (see Appendix D), an innovative simulation in which students act the roles of diplomats. It also reaches out to the business community through its Business Council for the United Nations. The headquarters of UNA-USA is in New York City, with chapters in more than a hundred other cities. They can be reached at their website (*www.unausa.org*) or by phone (212.907.1300).

Probably the best known program of UNA-USA is the Model United Nations, which the UNA-USA website describes (using a fine oxymoron) as "an authentic simulation" of the General Assembly and other bodies. This program catapults students into the world of diplomacy and negotiation, encouraging them to "step into the shoes of ambassadors from U.N. members states to debate current issues on the organization's vast agenda." Playing the role of delegates, students draft resolutions, "negotiate with supporters and adversaries, resolve conflicts, and navigate the U.N.'s rules of procedures," with the goal of focusing "international cooperation" to solve problems that affect almost every country on earth. A twist on the Model UN is the Global Classrooms program, which brings the simulation into the classroom through curriculum units designed for grades seven through twelve. The curriculum materials include a teacher's guide and an accompanying student workbook.

The Business Council for the United Nations (BCUN) reaches out to the private sector through meetings and partnerships. Through the BCUN, business owners and managers learn about the UN and world issues, and gain access to the largest diplomatic community in the world. The council cites its value in promoting investment flow to the developing world and helping to bridge the "digital divide."

The Academic Council on the United Nations System (ACUNS) is another UN-friendly organization, created to encourage education, writing, and research that contribute to the understanding of international issues and promotion of global cooperation. A primary goal is to strengthen the study of international organizations and to foster ties among academics, the UN system, and international organizations. The ACUNS was created in 1987 at Dartmouth College as an international association of scholars, teachers, practitioners, and others who study or are active in the United Nations system and international organizations. Ongoing projects include research and policy workshops, an annual meeting about UN and international issues, a summer workshop for younger scholars and practitioners hosted in cooperation with the American Society for International Law (ASIL), and a dissertation awards program. The organization also co-sponsors an email discussion listserv with the International Organization section of the International Studies Association (ISA). The ACUNS website is: *www.acuns.wlu.ca/*.

CHAPTER 16

Keeping Tabs on How Nations Vote

A country's voting record in the United Nations is only one dimension of its relations with the United States. . . . Nevertheless, a country's behavior at the United Nations is always relevant in its bilateral relationship with the United States, a point the Secretary of State regularly makes in letters of instruction to new U.S. ambassadors. —US Department of State

We are hardly surprised to learn that because the US is the biggest player at the UN, its words, actions, and nonactions are parsed a hundred different ways by the world's media, governments, and analysts. But the public is not generally aware that the US government does its own parsing of member states' behavior, especially their voting record in the General Assembly and the Security Council. Section 406 of Public Law 101–246 requires that the State Department inform Congress annually about how UN member states have voted in comparison with how the US has voted on the same issues.

Each year, the State Department's UN analysts tote up all the issues, all the votes, and then examine them according to several criteria, such as the geographical distribution of the member states (Europe, Asia, etc.) or their tendency to vote with or contrary to the US voting position.

Table 4 General Assembly Voting Coincidence with the US, 1995–2000, for Issues Resolved not by Consensus but by a Vote

Year	Arms Control	Middle East	Human Rights	Overall Votes
2000	66.1%	11.9%	55.7%	43.0%
1999	57.9	22.7	52.5	41.8
1998	64.0	22.5	62.8	44.2
1997	65.8	26.2	61.9	46.7
1996	62.3	28.3	68.3	49.4
1995	60.9	35.2	81.0	50.6

Source: US Department of State, 18th Annual Report on Voting Practices in the UN, 2000, p. 2.

The most recent such State Department report covers the UN for calendar year 2000. The 55th General Assembly adopted 275 resolutions, 209 (76 percent) by consensus. The really interesting numbers concern the nonconsensus issues, where a vote was taken, because these reflect how nations may differ from the US position. As Table 4 shows, the overall rate of voting coincidence declined over the six-year period, particularly regarding the Middle East and human rights, two areas where the US has historically taken strong positions that do not always find broad international support.

Information on how individual nations voted is available elsewhere in the State Department report (available at *www.state.gov/plio/conrpt/ vtgprac*). The report finds, among other things, that Israel almost always voted with the US, and the UK was not far behind. But among the sixteen countries that voted with the US less than 25 percent of the time were several obvious suspects like Libya, Cuba, and North Korea, and a few surprises like Egypt and Pakistan.

When we move to the Security Council, there is no suspense about the numbers. The tight club almost always acts through consensus. Of some fifty resolutions adopted in 2000, forty-three (86 percent) were adopted unanimously. John Negroponte sees the numbers as clear proof that "for all the talk about how people worry about the US

The voting board in the General Assembly in 1974. UN photo by T. Chen.

and our being unilateral, the number of resolutions and issues that we succeed in dealing with on a totally consensus basis is really quite striking."

But what do these numbers mean in terms of US foreign policy? As the report observes, although a nation's UN voting record "is only one dimension of its relations with the US," it is nevertheless a significant factor and "always relevant to its bilateral relationship with the US." The report goes on to say, "The SC and the GA are arguably the most important international bodies in the world, dealing as they do with such vital issues as threats to peace and security, disarmament, development, humanitarian relief, human rights, the environment, and narcotics—all of which can and do directly affect major US interests." The State Department gives copies of the report to the foreign ministries and UN missions of UN member states, as a friendly reminder that Uncle Sam is watching.

CHAPTER 17

Making a Career at the UN

We were dealing with actual human beings, and I could put my head to the pillow at night knowing that what I did made a real difference in people's lives—people I could see and feel and meet and touch and actually talk to. That kind of direct connection, that's something that UNHCR affords that's truly extraordinary.
—Shashi Tharoor, UN Undersecretary General for Communications and Public Information

To put a face on the career UN staffer, it's helpful to listen as one of them talks about his early years in the UN as an idealistic young administrator out to learn about the world. Shashi Tharoor was born in India, educated there and in the US, and in 1978 became a staff member of the UN High Commissioner for Refugees (UNHCR), which assists refugees in resettling. He was sent to Singapore (1981–84) to help organize efforts to aid the thousands of Vietnamese fleeing their homeland in the aftermath of the collapse of the Saigon government and the takeover of the country by the Communists in 1975. From 1989 to 1996, Tharoor was part of the peacekeeping office of the

Secretariat as a special assistant to the Under-Secretary General for Peacekeeping Operations. In 2002 he became Undersecretary General for Communications and Public Information. In an interview at his UN office Tharoor recalled his challenging work as a new staff member of the UNHCR:

The High Commissioner for Refugees was a great place to begin my career because it really attracts a lot of idealists, in those days in particular. What really brought me to a conviction of the indispensability of the UN was working for UNHCR in the field. I arrived in Singapore at the peak of the Vietnamese boat-people crisis. There were 4,000 refugees living at the camp, sleeping 25, 30 to a room this size. The situation had become totally unmanageable. When refugees left Vietnam by boat, they were picked up by boats sailing into Singapore. The Singapore government was very unhappy about having refugees come in, and they manifested this by making difficult the disembarkation of some of these refugees and having nothing to do with the camps themselves. Other countries who were receiving Vietnamese refugees ran their own camps, usually with their military, whereas in Singapore the UN was asked to run their camps.

UNHCR in those days believed it was not an operational agency, so we weren't supposed to be running camps. It was an extraordinary challenge for someone who was in their twenties as I was. I essentially invented operational partners by going to churches and church groups and saying, "Put your label on us and say you're the operational partner, and I will raise money to get the staff and we will run the camp." I got volunteers from the city, including wives of diplomats, to come in and teach refugees and run camps. I took donations from the community for the benefit of the refugees. I got refugees to run their own democracy, elect their own camp leader.

On the diplomatic side, there was dealing with a tough government, trying to use the power of my office to get them to cooperate. Church groups can go and help refugees, volunteers can go and help refugees, but only the UN can go to a government. I would tell officials, "You

Vietnamese refugees, often called "boat people," are rescued in the South China Sea in 1975. UNHCR/1505 photo by P. Deloche.

have an obligation to honor your international commitment to this organization." Even if they're not signatories to the UN convention, as a member of the General Assembly they're bound by the statute of the organization, which is a General Assembly resolution. We expect them to honor their role as a government and a member of the UN.

We had to invent whole new procedures. For example when ships came in, [the authorities] insisted that every ship that had refugees had to provide a guarantee that the refugees would be resettled. Then they realized that some of the guarantees were worthless because some of the ships were from Bangladesh and India and flag-of-convenience ships flying the Liberian flag or the Panamanian flag. What use was a letter of guarantee from Liberia that they will resettle their refugees?

The Singaporeans then wanted a letter from a country of resettlement. We had to invent a scheme, where we had looked into the ownership of a ship, and got a country of registration to actually provide the guarantees, and then there were the weekly meetings in my office with the immigration chiefs of embassies. It's a sobering thought that there are kids growing up French, or Canadian, or American today because of my skill or lack thereof in persuading an immigration officer to bend the rules.

Every month more were arriving, I would imagine somewhere between 12,000 and 20,000 refugees passed through my hands in Singapore. In one case, for example, a family left for Singapore on a tiny boat with a cannibalized tractor engine. It wasn't a proper motor and sure enough it conked out and they were drifting on the high seas. They ran out of food, out of water, and they were subsisting on rainwater and hope. What do the parents do? They slit their fingers to get their babies to suck their own blood in order to survive. They were finally rescued by an American ship and they were so weak they couldn't stand up, they had to be lifted out of the boat. We rushed them into intensive care in the hospital as soon as we could disembark them. Now, to see that same family three or four months later, healthy, well fed, well rested, well dressed, heading off to new lives in the US, there is simply no job that could compare with that sort of thing—pure human satisfaction.

When Poland declared martial law in December of 1981, do you remember the Solidarity movement [labor union] and all of that? A Polish ship docked in Singapore on a Saturday and four or five Polish seamen jumped ship and looked up the UN in the phone book and came to my office and wanted asylum. I had no authority to grant asylum. I woke up the director of international protections of the UNHCR and said, "What do I do?" The guy said, "Follow the convention, interview these people, and determine if in your view they should have refugee status. If you do, they are refugees."

It was quite a drama. I interviewed them. I felt that they had a credible case. They said they were supporters of Solidarity and if they went back they would be locked up, so they jumped ship. I said, "I recognize you as refugees," and basically said to the Singaporeans, "You've got to let these people stay." The Singaporeans were furious, but I contacted some embassies and said, "Could you try and take these people?" We worked out a scheme. The Singaporeans retaliated by banning shore leave for all Polish seamen. They kept saying, "You are only here to look after the Vietnamese." And I said, "No, I'm with the UN High Commissioner for Refugees. Vietnamese happen to be my caseload, but anybody else who comes in, I'm legally mandated under the statute of the office to help them."

A couple of months after this first episode, I got a frantic call from the Singaporeans and the Americans, one after the other. A Polish sailor had jumped ship, swum to an American destroyer in the port. Singapore naval police and immigration police said he had to be handed over because he was illegal. The American captain said that the sailor was fleeing communism and he would not surrender him. There was a diplomatic standoff. Neither side wanted this to hit the press, but the Singaporeans wouldn't let the American ship sail with the Polish seaman on board, and the Polish seaman couldn't go back to his ship. The Americans allowed the Singaporeans to take him off the ship under the condition that he be brought to me. He was brought to the US consul's office in the embassy, where it was determined he had refugee status, at which point we took charge and put him in a little hotel in Singapore (where it's not an inexpensive proposition for the UN, I can tell you).

Then I started putting heat on the Americans, saying, "Take him because we solved the problem for you and you have to resettle him." It dragged on for a couple of months before the US agreed to take him. A new consul arrived and was very helpful and said that he would take charge.

I got a lovely postcard from San Diego from this Polish seaman, saying, "I never will forget you, Mr. Shashi." One of the precious souvenirs of my career!

Singapore was such an extraordinary period, and among other things it convinced me about the indispensability of the UN cause. Most things I've done under the UN, only the UN could have done. The UN has a hell of a lot of advantages in dealing with authorities. There are so many stories in which the governmental influence that the UN can bring to bear changes the lives and fortunes of people who are in danger or distress.

CHAPTER 18

ECOSOC

*The worst two years of my life were spent as Canada's representative on
ECOSOC. A complete waste of time.*
—David Malone, former Canadian diplomat and
Director of the International Peace Academy

A quick look at the UN organizational chart reveals that one of the
Principal Organs—in fact, the only one we haven't discussed yet—is
something called Economic and Social Council (ECOSOC). ECOSOC
is a key coordinator and mediator among the constituent bodies of the
UN system. But it has struggled to find a clear identity among its
many functions and as a result has been accused of being unfocused.
David Malone's comment above is not unique; others have also remarked on ECOSOC's talent for fostering endless debate that leads to
no apparent action. Admittedly, ECOSOC was created to be mainly a
deliberative rather than operational body, to help other parts of the UN
system examine and shape their programs. In addition to being a
forum for discussing international social, economic, and humanitarian issues, it coordinates the work of nearly all UN agencies and
bodies concerned with those issues. As part of its coordinating role,

From the UN Charter, Chapter X:
The Economic and Social Council

ARTICLE 62

1. The Economic and Social Council may make or initiate studies and reports with respect to international economic, social, cultural, educational, health, and related matters and may make recommendations with respect to any such matters to the General Assembly, to the Members of the United Nations, and to the specialized agencies concerned.
2. It may make recommendations for the purpose of promoting respect for, and observance of, human rights and fundamental freedoms for all.
3. It may prepare draft conventions for submission to the General Assembly, with respect to matters falling within its competence.
4. It may call, in accordance with the rules prescribed by the United Nations, international conferences on matters falling within its competence.

ARTICLE 63

1. The Economic and Social Council may enter into agreements with any of the agencies referred to in Article 57, defining the terms on which the agency concerned shall be brought into relationship with the United Nations. Such agreements shall be subject to approval by the General Assembly.
2. It may coordinate the activities of the specialized agencies through consultation with and recommendations to such agencies and through recommendations to the General Assembly and to the Members of the United Nations.

ARTICLE 71

The Economic and Social Council may make suitable arrangements for consultation with non-governmental organizations which are concerned with matters within its competence. Such arrangements may be made with international organizations and, where appropriate, with national organizations after consultation with the Member of the United Nations concerned.

ECOSOC commissions studies, writes reports, and makes policy recommendations to the General Assembly and other parts of the UN.
Membership in ECOSOC—which holds a major session every July—
is coveted, owing to the body's central role in the UN universe. Its
fifty-four members, elected by the General Assembly, serve three-year
terms.

Flirting with Irrelevance?

Perhaps because its mission is so extensive, and it does a lot of coordinating among groups and organizations, ECOSOC lacks a clear public
profile and has suffered from a lack of conceptual and administrative
focus. It is almost everything but not exactly anything. Many diplomats, like David Malone, have found the organization's fuzziness and
endless discussions hard to endure. This has produced a plethora
of recommendations for reworking the body. Malone's advice is for
ECOSOC to make itself more relevant to the UN by working closely
with the Security Council on a vital issue, such as peace-building.
Peace-building involves addressing the causes of violence rather than
the deadly effects. It has particular relevance to today's world, where
so much violence occurs within nations rather than between them.
Peace-building involves strengthening basic civil institutions and the
rule of law, promoting respect for human rights, and rebuilding administrative and economic infrastructure. Many of the activities of
peace-building are actually done by UN agencies, nongovernmental
organizations and other organizations, frequently under the umbrella
of a Security Council peacekeeping mission. Malone thinks the Security Council would be open to having ECOSOC take the leading role
in peace-building but that ECOSOC "has yet to pick up the challenge."

Nongovernmental Organizations

One of ESOSOC's most important and delicate functions is to act as
intermediary between the General Assembly and nongovernmental
organizations (NGOs), which are independent, nonprofit, voluntary

The ECOSOC chamber. UN/DPI photo by Andrea Brizzi.

associations that focus on one or more areas of interest to the UN, such as human rights or environmental protection. In the United States, we usually refer to them as "nonprofit organizations" because we make a sharp distinction between private enterprise (which is profit-making) and civil society (which is not), but in most of the world, where the crucial distinction is between governmental and nongovernmental, NGO makes more sense as a category. (Outside the US, business is often included in civil society, again because the crucial distinction is between governmental versus nongovernmental.)

The UN has taken a growing interest in NGOs because they represent the interests of civil society, which is gaining visibility as a foundation of democracy. Kofi Annan recently acknowledged the importance of creating partnerships between the UN and civil society to achieve "a new synthesis between private initiative and the public good, which encourages entrepreneurship and market approaches together with social and environmental responsibility."

ECOSOC negotiates the agreements that define relations between the UN and the nearly 2,200 NGOs that have "consultative status," which gives them the right to participate in certain types of UN meetings, studies, and projects, and to submit reports to ECOSOC. When the UN was founded there were only a few NGOs, but in recent decades the number has risen dramatically, and they have become crucial in helping implement many important programs such as those related to human rights, literacy, health care, and economic development. More than 20,000 transnational NGOs existed in 1996, and the average nation now has almost 500 of them, compared with fewer than 20 per nation back in 1960.

A Public-Private Partnership

"NGOs play a more and more important role not only in the policy debates but equally important, maybe even more important, are critical in implementing many of these policies. A lot of the aid and emergency humanitarian assistance, like food distribution by the World Food Program, is done through the NGOs. There really is a public-private partnership, or a public-NGO partnership, that is very important. NGOs are effective, and part of the reason is they are private and they are accountable, they watch their pennies. People have a choice as to whom to give their money."
—John Negroponte, US Ambassador to the UN

Human rights NGOs such as Amnesty International and Human Rights Watch attend the meetings of the UN's Human Rights Commission, participate in the discussions, and submit reports on matters that concern them. NGOs have their own liaison body, the Conference on Non-Governmental Organizations in Consultative Status (CONGO), to represent their interests before ECOSOC and hold meetings about issues of common interest. Those NGOs holding consultative status remain independent bodies and do not become actual parts of the UN. To the contrary, their influence often depends on their reputation for independence from outside authority.

CHAPTER 19

Agencies, Programs, and Commissions

Article 55

With a view to the creation of conditions of stability and well-being which are necessary for peaceful and friendly relations among nations based on respect for the principle of equal rights and self-determination of peoples, the United Nations shall promote:

a. higher standards of living, full employment, and conditions of economic and social progress and development;

b. solutions of international economic, social, health, and related problems; and international cultural and educational cooperation; and

c. universal respect for, and observance of, human rights and fundamental freedoms for all without distinction as to race, sex, language, or religion.

—UN Charter

The Secretariat, Security Council, General Assembly, and other Principal Organs are the UN bodies that most command the public's attention. Yet, they have only general oversight of the UN's huge array of global efforts to advance human rights, help refugees or earthquake victims, combat infectious diseases, or coordinate international trade, finance, development, and communications. The direct control of these vital activities is usually in the hands of entities known as agencies, programs, and commissions, which make up the UN's less publicly exposed side. And, although these groups remain mostly in the background, they play key roles in the UN system. Some of the agencies, for example, actually pre-date the UN, and many act quite independently.

These supporting entities consist of nearly sixty organizations, divided into six categories. Moving from left to right on the UN organizational chart (see Chapter 1), we see first the Programs and Funds. Each of these was created to address a particular issue the General Assembly has deemed important. That is true also for the next category, Other UN Entities, such as the Office of the High Commissioner for Human Rights, and for the Research and Training Institutes, such as the International Research and Training Institute for the Advancement of Women (INSTRAW). Moving to the upper right we have the Commissions, of two types, Functional and Regional. The remaining two boxes contain the Related Organizations and the Specialized Agencies, which are autonomous organizations that have formal working relations with the UN. You can see from their names that the related organizations and specialized agencies cover virtually all areas of economic and social endeavor.

Coordination of these organizations is one of the greatest challenges facing the UN, for they have offices all over the map, with thousands of staff of all nationalities, and they address every imaginable issue. As a further complication, the categories of organizations each relate to the UN in a different way. The Administrative Committee on Coordination is charged with choreographing this ungainly ensemble.

To an outsider, these supporting organizations all look pretty much the same. Only the insider can perceive and fully appreciate their differences in terms of administrative position and prerogatives. The public, however, is more interested in the basics: what they do and how they do it. To find out what and how, a functional approach is best, because the organizations share many interests and methods of operation.

In a nutshell, the UN helps keep peace, promotes human rights, protects the environment, fights poverty, discourages nuclear proliferation, strengthens international law, provides humanitarian aid, promotes democracy, advances women's rights and human rights, provides safe drinking water, eradicates disease, promotes education, reduces child mortality, and improves global communications.

There are many ways of defining the major issues addressed by the agencies, programs, and commissions. The UN has its own ideas about how to describe the issues that shape their agendas. For example, at the Millennium Summit, Kofi Annan divided the UN's work into four broad areas: freedom from want, freedom from fear, a sustainable future, and renewal of the UN.

Rather than use the UN's categories, I prefer to identify a set of issues relevant to the average reader: first are human rights, followed by the related areas of economic and social development, then the natural environment. Next comes disaster relief, then the control of dangerous agents like toxins and nuclear materials, and finally the UN's role in globalization—first, in shaping world trade; second, in dealing with the expansion of international crime.

I don't claim these categories are definitive, but they do enable us to look at the supporting organizations in a systematic and functional manner. Keep in mind that these entities could easily fill a whole book by themselves. The Further Reading list at the back of this book provides a list of source material for those curious to learn more.

CHAPTER 20

Rule of Law and Human Rights

Strikingly, the centrality of human rights to peoples' expectation about the future role of the United Nations was stressed both at the [Millennium Summit regional] hearings and in the [public opinion] survey. The current level of performance, especially of government, was judged to be unsatisfactory. —Kofi Annan, Secretary General of the UN

Rights come first everywhere you look at the UN. The purpose of the organization, according to Article 1 of the Charter, is to promote and encourage "respect for human rights and for fundamental freedoms for all without distinction as to race, sex, language, or religion." The Universal Declaration of Human Rights, as we saw earlier, is literally all about rights (see Appendix B). Nearly all states that join the UN have agreed to accept its principles through the signing and ratifying of two international covenants, one addressing civil and political rights and the other economic, social, and cultural rights. The International Covenant on Civil and Political Rights and the International Covenant on Economic, Social, and Cultural Rights, which entered force in 1976, are legally binding documents. When combined with the Universal Declaration, they constitute the International Bill of Human Rights.

In addition, most member states have signed and ratified some eighty treaties that cover particular aspects of human rights. To give an idea of what they cover, here are only a few, with their initiation dates:

1948 Convention on the Prevention and Punishment of the Crime of Genocide

1961 Convention Relating to the Status of Refugees

1965 International Convention on the Elimination of All Forms of Racial Discrimination

1984 Convention Against Torture and Other Cruel, Inhuman or Degrading Treatment or Punishment

1990 International Convention on the Protection of the Rights of All Migrant Workers and Members of Their Families

The UN is justifiably proud of having enabled the creation of such wide-ranging safeguards of human rights. It has, additionally, been able to use its influence and authority to improve human rights in some nations, such as South Africa. There the UN led an anti-Apartheid campaign, including an arms embargo, that helped end official racial segregation. It then sent an observer mission in 1994 that monitored free elections and facilitated the transition away from official segregation.

A Commission and a High Commissioner

All offices and staff of the UN and its peacekeeping operations are responsible for adhering to international human rights law and reporting possible breaches of it to the proper authorities, but several have a special responsibility for rights. We have already seen how creation of the International Criminal Court (ICC), for example, will make permanent the capacity for investigating and prosecuting large-scale crimes against humanity.

The Commission on Human Rights, created in 1946, is the main body for making policy and providing a forum for discussion. It meets for six weeks each year in Geneva, Switzerland, and holds public meetings on violations of human rights. In 1993, the General Assembly

From the UN Charter, Chapter III: Organs

ARTICLE 8

The United Nations shall place no restrictions on the eligibility of men and women to participate in any capacity and under conditions of equality in its principal and subsidiary organs.

established the post of UN High Commissioner for Human Rights (HCHR), to provide a secretariat for the commission and to oversee the UN's human rights activities, help develop rights standards, and promote international cooperation to expand and protect rights. The current High Commissioner is Sergio Vieira de Mello.

The reports of the Human Rights Commission probe the status of rights in specific countries and hold them accountable for how they treat their citizens. The commission has the option of censuring nations with poor human rights records, but that happens on a selective basis that is heavily influenced by politics on the commission. For example, many experts on human rights rate China's record in this area as very poor, and the US representatives on the commission have long urged an investigation of China's human rights record, yet the commission has not acted. In 2001, for example, the commission adopted resolutions condemning rights violations in Afghanistan, Burma, Burundi, Chechnya, Congo, Cuba, Iran, Rwanda, and Sierra Leone—but not China.

When necessary, the Human Rights Commission appoints experts, called special rapporteurs, to examine rights abuses or conditions in specific countries. In some cases, when an international rights convention enters force, the UN may create a watchdog committee charged with ensuring that the treaty provisions are honored by member states. For example, when the Convention on the Rights of the Child entered force in 1989, it was accompanied by the creation of the Committee on the Rights of the Child, which meets regularly and has become an

Rights Hotline

The UN Office of Commission on Human Rights, in Geneva, Switzerland, maintains a 24-hour fax hotline to report violations of human rights. The number is 41 22 917 0092.

international voice for children. Other committees created to monitor specific conventions are the

Committee on the Elimination of Racial Discrimination
Committee on Economic, Social, and Cultural Rights
Committee Against Torture
Committee on the Elimination of Discrimination Against Women

Periodically the UN identifies groups that merit attention because their rights have been abridged. For example, the Secretary General has appointed Olara Otunnu as a Special Representative for Children in Armed Conflict—in other words, an advocate for child soldiers. Again, in 1993, the UN launched the International Year of the World's Indigenous People as a way of calling attention to the rights (and other needs) of groups like India's Tribals and Peru's Indians, who have suffered various forms of social, economic, and legal discrimination. Often these "Year of . . ." events lead to follow-up activities that may produce international treaties, as happened with children in 1989, as noted above. The UN regards rights as so important that it has given them not their own year but their own decade, the UN Decade for Human Rights Education (1995–2004).

Mainstreaming Human Rights

Earlier we touched on Secretary General Kofi Annan's "rights-based" approach to development, which highlights the importance of human rights as a positive and necessary component to social and economic progress. If the UN can "mainstream" human rights issues as part of the broader development agenda, it may achieve a breakthrough, because then rights would be seen not simply as a noble addition to society but as integral to it.

The rise of an international women's rights agenda offers a possible mainstreaming model. Experts in development are now arguing that society benefits greatly when women can take control of their work, property, and bodies. The UN has been advancing this line of thought through a variety of mechanisms, and although progress has been slow and uneven among nations, much has changed during the past few decades. The UN's constant publicizing of women's issues has contributed to a growing consensus among experts that rights are good for everyone.

For women, as with anyone else, the exercise of rights begins with an understanding of what "rights" are. The Preamble to the Universal Declaration specifies gender equality as a basic right. Even before the Declaration was finished, the UN had established the Commission on the Status of Women, which meets regularly and makes recommendations and suggests international legislation about women's rights. The UN's impact also comes through its public awareness campaigns and its major conferences. Soon after the surfacing of the women's movement during the late 1960s and early '70s, the UN declared 1975 to be International Women's Year and 1976–1985 the UN Decade for Women. The momentum generated by these efforts led to adoption in 1979 of the Convention on the Elimination of All Forms of Discrimination Against Women (CEDAW). This has been described as both "an international bill of rights for women" and "a blueprint for action by countries to guarantee those rights."

Complementing these public relations measures, the UN convened the first global conference ever held on women (in Mexico City), followed by world conferences in Copenhagen (1980), Nairobi (1985), and Beijing (1995). UN Conferences often attract high-profile delegations from most of the world's nations. A major purpose of the conference is to agree on a set of shared principles or an agenda for action (often referred to as a "platform for action") for the years until the next major conference. At Beijing, for example, the US delegation was led by then First Lady Hillary Rodham Clinton, who gave one of the major addresses. The conference produced the Beijing Declaration and Platform for Action.

Five years later, the General Assembly conducted Beijing +5, a review of the platform. In preparation for the review, the Commission on the Status of Women met in New York City in February and March 2000. With due ceremony, the General Assembly special session met from June 5 through 9, 2000, with Secretary of State Madeleine Albright chairing the US delegation and Secretary of Health and Human Services Donna Shalala and US Permanent Rep Richard Holbrooke co-chairing. Among outcomes of the session was a review of gains and hindrances in advancing the status of women worldwide.

Leading UN Actors

Most organizations within the UN system deal with human rights in one way or another, but several have special competence in this area. Note that some of those listed below are not focused fully on human rights but are included here because their goals are closely connected with rights issues.

- The Commission on Human Rights was established in 1946 and is based in Geneva, Switzerland.

    The commission makes policy, commissions studies, and monitors human rights worldwide. URL: *www.ohchr.org*
- The Office of the High Commissioner for Human Rights (OHCHR), created in 1993, is based in Geneva, Switzerland. URL: *www.unhcr.ch*

    The OHCHR has principal responsibility for UN human rights activities. The first High Commissioner was Jose Ayala-Lasso of Ecuador, who was succeeded in 1997 by Mary Robinson, former President of Ireland. The OHCHR has staff in about 30 countries, who provide technical services, monitor rights, and investigate alleged rights abuses (more than 100,000 annually).

- The Commission on the Status of Women, established in 1946, is based in New York. URL: *www.un.org/womenwatch/daw/csw/*
  The commission promotes implementation of equal rights for women and men.
- The International Research and Training Institute for the Advancement of Women (INSTRAW), established in 1976, is headquartered in Santo Domingo, Dominican Republic. URL: *www. un-instraw.org*
  INSTRAW is an autonomous body of the UN governed by an ECOSOC-appointed 11-member board of trustees. INSTRAW supports women's full participation in the economic, social, and political spheres through training, research, and information.
- UN Development Fund for Women (UNIFEM), created in 1976, is based in New York City and works closely with the UN Development Program (UNDP). URL: *www.unifem.undp.org*
  UNIFEM funds innovative development activities to benefit women, especially in rural areas of the developing world.

CHAPTER 21

Social and Economic Development

We know the answers to development problems, it's often just a matter of applying them and implementing them. We've had huge successes. Life expectancy has gone up, fewer kids are dying, more kids are in school. But poverty is still a huge problem out there. Money matters, but so do ideas and partnerships and consensus-building politics and all the things the UN's good at. —Mark Malloch Brown, Administrator of the UNDP

The word "development" has undergone an amazing rise in popularity in recent years, owing largely to its association with an even more popular word, "globalization." Globalization has raised our awareness that the level of the wealth among nations differs greatly, for reasons that are often hard to identify. This variation has renewed an old debate about why some nations develop rapidly while others seem hardly to change at all. The UN is a big player in development through its programs and agencies, including the World Bank. These bodies have mandates to pay special attention to the poorest nations.

The international debate about the pace of development has often pitted the poor nations against the rich, with the poor ones claiming

A homeless couple huddles by railroad track in Jakarta, Indonesia, in 1986. UN photo 155256 by John Isaac.

they are the victims of an oppressive global system that prevents them from escaping debt and poverty. Experts are increasingly agreeing with this analysis, at least in one sense. There is growing consensus that the old approach to economic development no longer works well. It is not enough just to raise the level of economic growth and assume that all boats will be lifted by the rising tide. "Old-school prescriptions of supplementing rapid growth with social spending and safety nets have proved inadequate," one recent UN report noted. In addition, many experts are advising that governments need to be more accountable to their citizens, who should have a significant role in running anti-poverty programs.

Mark Malloch Brown is head of the UN Development Program (UNDP), one of the leading bodies in the development effort. He emphasizes the need to strengthen the internal capacity of nations rather than trying to insert infrastructure or industry into a nation without taking into account its social and economic context. Malloch Brown defines development as, "How the hell do you make sense of countries where they are not training people, where there are not strong institutions? Managing one's response to that with some prudent capacity-building, institution-building, and training of people before throwing money . . . is incredibly important." He cautions that development "is not a linear thing where you see human suffering and you throw money at it and suffering is solved." Rather, both developing nations and those who assist them, like the UNDP, should invest in people through education, health, and making space for a strong private sector, with suitable rewards along the way in the shape of aid from the World Bank and other donors. This process, he believes, can help move a nation from dependency on World Bank loans to establishment of private investment flows. "It's a ladder you go up, from the early UNDP help."

Kofi Annan has pushed the UN to examine and embrace the new thinking. He wants an emphasis on sustainable development rather than the single-minded emphasis on a few aspects such as heavy industry or hydroelectric projects. He wants real poverty reduction and greater input from ordinary people. The UN responded with the Millennium Summit, discussed in Chapter 7, which met in 2000 to debate Annan's proposals as set forth in a special report written by his office. The report suggests initiatives to advance four fundamental goals: freedom from want, freedom from fear, a sustainable future, and renewal of the UN.

Malloch Brown finds an interesting parallel between the goals of the Millennium Summit and the evolution of European and American thinking about social reform and the so-called social safety net. "We are in the early stages of an interesting transformation of what politicians consider their responsibility. Many of the people who were around to form the UN . . . were domestically part of FDR's reforms and Britain's welfare state reforms. But they were too early for the export of their social policies abroad—for a global safety net—and now suddenly the world's ready for their vision of fifty years ago."

Some insiders are less sure that a major change has occurred. They have seen so much "new thinking" fizzle during the past few decades that they remain skeptical or downright hostile to the UN's development effort. This critique argues that many UN bodies, such as the UNDP, are liable to overestimate the ability to influence the pace and scope of development. That is always a danger with large organizations that have a strong top-down bureaucratic perspective, no matter how well-intentioned the executives and staff may be. In addition, competition among organizations for support from donors can lead to inflated claims of effectiveness, according to the critique. Malloch Brown does see cause for optimism because of a waning of the turf battles that have often kept UN bodies from collaborating and maximizing their impact. "The UN has come to a fundamental transition," he says, "from a rather intellectually sterile, politically fierce inside competition to the much more constructive mode where we've made our institutional peace." Now the UNDP accepts the World Bank's long-held emphasis on the need for macroeconomic stability, and the bank accepts the UNDP's focus on social spending and social policy.

But Malloch Brown wants to go further. "You need much more innovative social policy. You don't need just macro economic stability and a social safety net, you need targeted social spending programs which reach vulnerable groups." The key, he argues (echoing Kofi Annan), is to add strategies that "are not economic and social in character, but human rights in character to bring marginal core groups around the world into the mainstream political economy." This is another way of stating the rights-based approach to development, which places the emphasis on individual initiative rather than bureaucratic control. "We've done social spending in a big macro sense and still people are poor. But the center of the political debate, the intellectual debate about development policy, is going to shift back towards the UN with its more holistic view of poverty strategies, which embraces the cultural, the social, and the political, not just the economic."

Leading UN Actors

Among the many UN organizations that participate in the global development effort, several are prominent:

- The UN Development Program (UNDP) is based in New York City and was founded in 1945. URL: *www.undp.org*

  The UNDP concentrates on four aspects of development: poverty, the environment, jobs, and women. Among its many projects, it promotes small businesses in Bulgaria, helps devise development plans in Nepal that include local participation, and helps institutions in Botswana improve their ability to deal with the HIV/AIDS epidemic.

  A recent US government report observed that the UNDP gives the US an "important channel of communication, particularly in countries where the US has no permanent presence." Not surprisingly, the US has been the organization's biggest donor; its allocation for 2002 was $87.1 million. The US has praised Mark Malloch Brown, UNDP Administrator, for making important administrative reforms.

- The Food and Agriculture Organization (FAO) has been operating as a specialized UN agency since 1945, first from Washington, DC, and since 1951 from its headquarters in Rome, Italy. URL: *www.fao.org*

  Most of the FAO's work relates to agriculture in a direct way, such as providing technical assistance about farming or nutrition, but it also tries to address factors like AIDS that significantly affect farming communities. Because most hunger today is the result of political or economic factors rather than poor crops, the FAO has begun concentrating on the effective delivery of food to those who need it. In 2000, for example, it collaborated with the World Bank to provide cattle and farm machinery to jump-start farming in Kosovo. The FAO's statistics on agriculture, forestry, food supplies, nutrition, and fisheries are authoritative and highly regarded. Many countries, including the US, have applauded the FAO's efforts to protect commercial fisheries from overexploitation by developing an international plan of action. In 1996 it hosted the World Food Summit, where 185 nations issued the Rome Declaration on World Food Security and pledged to cut the number of hungry people in half by 2015.

The largest autonomous UN agency, with some 4,300 staff, the FAO has an annual budget of approximately $325 million, of which the US paid about one quarter for 2000.

- The International Fund for Agricultural Development (IFAD), founded in 1977, is a specialized agency of the UN based in Rome, Italy. URL: *www.ifad.org*

  IFAD is mandated to combat hunger and rural poverty in developing countries by providing long-term, low-cost loans for projects that improve the nutrition and food supply of small farmers, nomadic herders, landless rural people, poor women, and others. IFAD also encourages other agencies and governments to contribute their own funds to these projects. The agency's largest contributor is the US, which has provided about $575 million since 1977.

- The International Labor Organization (ILO), created in 1919, is based in Geneva, Switzerland. URL: *www.ilo.org*

  The ILO formulates international labor standards through conventions and recommendations that establish minimum standards of labor rights, such as the right to organize, collective bargaining, and equality of opportunity and treatment. It also offers technical assistance in vocational training and rehabilitation, employment policy, labor relations, working conditions, and occupational safety and health. One of the ILO's most important functions is to investigate and report on whether member states are adhering to the labor conventions and treaties they have signed. The US, which has a permanent seat on the ILO's governing body, considers the organization vital for addressing exploitative child labor. The ILO's Program for the Elimination of Child Labor was allotted $45 million from the US Congress for 2001, with another $37 million targeted at improving educational access to working children. A recent US government report claims that the programs have "removed tens of thousands of children" in Central America, Bangladesh, Pakistan, and elsewhere "from exploitative work, placed them in schools, and provided their families with alternative income-producing opportunities."

- The UN Industrial Development Organization (UNIDO), which became a specialized agency in 1985, is based in Vienna, Austria. URL: *www.unido.org*

  UNIDO helps developing nations establish economies that are globally competitive while respecting the natural environment. It mediates communication between business and government and works to encourage entrepreneurship and bring all segments of the population, including women, into the labor force. Its staff of 650 includes engineers, economists, and technology and environment specialists. Its budget for 2000–2001 was $133 million.

- The UN Office for Project Services (UNOPS) is headquartered in New York City and was founded in 1973. URL: *www.unops.org*

  UNOPS provides technical services and management for developing nations that seek to boost their economic base. Its staff of approximately 1,100 is providing a way for all the world's nations to tap into the vast industrial, commercial, and business experience and expertise of the developed nations.

- UN Volunteers (UNV), established in 1970 as a subsidiary organ of the UN, is based in Bonn, Germany. URL: *www.unv.org*

  During the past 30 years, more than 20,000 professionals have volunteered through the UNV to work on community-based development projects, humanitarian aid, and the promotion of human rights. In any given year, the organization deploys about 4,000 specialists and field workers.

- The UN Center for Human Settlements (Habitat), created in 1978, is headquartered in Nairobi, Kenya. URL: *www.unchs.org*

  As the world becomes more urbanized, with nearly half of all people living in cities and towns, there is a growing need to find solutions to slums, infectious diseases, and other ills that accompany overcrowding. Habitat describes itself as promoting "sustainable human settlement development through advocacy, policy formulation, capacity-building, knowledge creation, and the strengthening of partnerships between government and civil society." Its technical programs and projects focus on a wide range of urban issues, including poverty reduction, post-disaster reconstruction, and water management. It has a staff of some 240 and an annual budget of about $160 million. At Habitat II, the Second UN Conference on Human Settlements (Istanbul, 1996), delegates approved the Habitat Agenda, in which governments committed themselves to the goals of adequate shelter for all and sustainable urban development.

- The World Bank was established in 1945 with the goal of reducing global poverty by improving the economies of poor nations. URL: *www.worldbank.org*

This bank makes loans to countries, not grants. The loans, amounting to $17 billion in 2001, go only to governments, but in recent years the bank has tried to ensure that local organizations and communities are included in projects in order to increase the chances for success.

The World Bank consists of five parts, all based in Washington, D.C.:

1. The International Bank for Reconstruction and Development began operations in 1946. It offers loans and financial assistance to member states, each of which subscribes an amount of capital based on its economic strength (a total of about $11 billion since 1946). Voting power in the governing body is linked to the subscriptions. Most of its funds come from bonds sold in international capital markets.

2. The International Development Association offers affordable financing, known as credits, to countries with annual per capita incomes of less than $895. Most of the funds come from the governments of richer nations. IDA lends approximately $6 billion annually.

3. The International Finance Corporation is the developing world's largest multilateral source of loan and equity financing for private-sector projects. The corporation encourages the growth of productive business and efficient capital markets, and invests only when it sees an opportunity to complement the role of private investors.

4. The Multilateral Investment Guarantee Agency provides

The UN Secretariat building is lit with the red AIDS ribbon on June 23, 2001, to signify the commitment to the battle against HIV/AIDS. UN/DPI photo by Eskinder Debebe.

guarantees (that is, insurance) to foreign investors in developing countries. The guarantees protect against losses from political and other factors such as expropriation and war.

5. The International Center for Settlement of Investment Disputes provides arbitration or conciliation services in disputes between governments and private foreign investors.

• The World Health Organization (WHO), founded in 1948, is based in Geneva, Switzerland. URL: *www.who.int*

One of the largest specialized agencies, with a staff of about 3,800 and an annual budget of approximately $240 million, WHO is charged with improving health and with the eradication or control of diseases. Probably the organization's best known success is the eradication of smallpox in 1980. Almost eradicated are leprosy and river blindness. WHO has been addressing other destructive infectious diseases such as tuberculosis, malaria, HIV/AIDS, and polio. With six other UN agencies, WHO belongs to the Joint United Nations Program on HIV/AIDS (UNAIDS), described as "the leading advocate for a worldwide response aimed at preventing transmission, providing care and support, reducing the vulnerability of individuals and communities, and alleviating the impact of the epidemic." WHO's global campaign to eradicate polio began in 1988 and has established partnerships with governments and NGOs. It has reduced the number of cases worldwide to only a few thousand (from 350,000 in 1988) and is expected to achieve eradication by 2005 if adequate funding can be found. Immunizing entire populations against especially deadly diseases is an important part of the WHO program. From 1980 through 1995 it collaborated with UNICEF in a campaign to immunize against polio, tetanus, measles, whooping cough, diphtheria, and tuberculosis. In 1999 it received startup funding from the Bill & Melinda Gates Foundation to establish the Global Alliance for Vaccines and Immunization, which is providing immunization against two major killers, hepatitis B and haemophilus influenza type B.

CHAPTER 22

Protecting the Biosphere and Its Inhabitants

We are failing to provide the freedom of future generations to sustain their lives on this planet. —Kofi Annan, Secretary General of the UN

Concern for the natural environment has moved up on everyone's agenda over the past three decades, as rapid population increases and economic development have strained the world's forests, farmlands, atmosphere, rivers, and oceans. The UN has taken the lead through its efforts to safeguard our natural heritage. This is an area where the UN's global reach and ability to act as an honest broker has produced impressive results.

The Biosphere

The Earth Summit and the Kyoto Protocol are two UN-sponsored events that have helped transform how we think about our responsibility to the natural environment. The 1992 Conference on Environment and Development, commonly known as the Earth Summit, met in Rio de Janeiro and adopted Agenda 21, a plan for global sustainable development that is being monitored by a UN body, the Commission on Sustainable Development. Five years after the summit, the General Assembly held a special session, Earth Summit +5, to assess progress (which was very uneven) and suggest further action.

The Kyoto Protocol addresses global warming caused by human action. By the 1990s, a scientific consensus was emerging that carbon dioxide and other "greenhouse gases" emitted largely by industrialized nations were causing the world's climate to warm, with potentially serious long-term consequences for vital human activities such as agriculture. One-fifth of the world's inhabitants were producing about 60 percent of annual carbon dioxide emissions, the largest offender being the United States. Delegates at the Earth Summit had been given the opportunity to sign the UN Framework Convention on Climate Change (1992), which urged industrialized nations to reduce their emission of greenhouse gases to 1990 levels by 2000. The need for action was then documented, in 1995, in a report by the Intergovernmental Panel on Climate Change (IPCC), whose work was coordinated by two UN bodies, the UN Environment Program (UNEP) and the World Meteorological Organization (WMO).

Despite mounting evidence of climate change, some highly developed nations such as the US refused to comply with the 1992 Framework, claiming potential loss of economic growth. To push matters along, the UN sponsored a meeting in Kyoto, Japan, in December 1997, where major industrialized nations signed a protocol setting hard-and-fast targets for decreasing the emission of six greenhouse gases by more than 5 percent by 2012. The main job now is to enforce the protocol and persuade skeptics like the US government to comply.

Meanwhile, the UN has had much more success with another global climate issue, the ozone hole at the poles. In response to clear scientific evidence that certain manufactured chemicals, especially chlorofluorocarbons (CFCs), can catalyze the breakdown of ozone in the upper atmosphere and thus increase the amount of harmful ultraviolet sunlight reaching earth, the world community took decisive action under leadership of UNEP. Under the terms of the 1987 Montreal Protocol, the industrialized countries banned production of CFCs beginning in 1996, while developing countries were granted a grace period for compliance. All signs indicate that the plans are helping avert an environmental and human catastrophe.

Plants and Animals

We share the biosphere with creatures that are helpless to control human activity and are victims of human folly. We destroy habitat by logging forests and burning prairies or filling in wetlands, and we damage habitat by polluting the air, water, and soil. Plants and animals suffer, including many that we value for their beauty, economic value, or importance in the food chain. The UN Convention on Biological Diversity, signed at the Earth Summit, requires that nations preserve habitats and take other measures to protect plant and animal species. Desertification and deforestation have been identified as major threats to both natural and human habitats. When human misuse turns prairies into desert and forests into acres of denuded soil, all living beings pay the price. Current estimates are that some 900 million people are at risk of losing their livelihood and food supply through desertification. The UN's response is the Convention to Combat Desertification, which entered force in 1996. In the battle to save forests, the Food and Agriculture Organization (FAO), a UN agency, "monitors forest loss and trade in timber and assists developing countries in managing forests."

Plants and animals suffer not only through loss of habitat but through direct human exploitation. Some thirty years ago concern over the growing trade in rare birds, reptiles, fish, and mammals led the UN to create the Convention on International Trade in Endangered Species, which is administered by UNEP. This convention has served as a weapon in the fight against poachers who kill elephants for their tusks, rhinoceroses for their horns, or small mammals for their furs. Fish and fisheries have attracted a great deal of attention in recent decades, owing to a huge increase in the size and effectiveness of commercial fishing fleets, which may be taking fish faster than they can be replaced. The FAO is the world's accepted authority on the

Secretary General Kofi Annan (right, in vehicle) tours Ngorongoro Crater National Park in Tanzania. UN/DPI photo by Milton Grant.

size and exploitation of fish stocks worldwide. In 1995, UN members adopted a legal agreement that would regulate fishing on the high seas, but it has not been ratified by enough nations to make it enforceable.

Now the UN is beginning to deal with yet another human intervention in nature, bioengineering. Advances in cloning promise to alter the living reproductive cycle, while new skills in implanting genes across species make possible the creation of completely new organisms. The potential is vast and unsettling.

Leading UN Actors

Many UN organizations participate in projects or programs that include an environmental aspect: one of them focuses solely on environmental issues.

- The United Nations Environment Program (UNEP), founded in 1972, is based in Nairobi, Kenya. URL: *www.unep.org*

A US government report in 2000 credits UNEP with setting the world's environmental agenda, promoting the environmental dimension of sustainable development, and being an authoritative advocate of the global environment. The US government values its function as a global catalyst of ideas and action and has been UNEP's biggest donor from the beginning. The US government was especially impressed by UNEP's success in concluding the Stockholm Convention on Persistent Organic Pollutants, which regulates potentially hazardous chemicals that are no longer commonly used in the US but remain in the environment and the food chain for a long time and can be transported long distances by water and wind.

- The United Nations Educational, Scientific, and Cultural Organization (UNESCO), founded in 1946, is based in Paris, France. URL: www.unesco.org

  UNESCO has a varied mission involving education, research, and public outreach in the sciences, culture, and communications. With 188 member states and a staff of 2,000, it includes 178 national commissions and some 5,000 UNESCO associations, centers, and clubs. The budget for 2000–2001 was $544 million. In 1984, the US withdrew from UNESCO owing to policy differences but retained official observer status and is likely to rejoin soon. In 2000, the US government gave $2.25 million in voluntary contribution to UNESCO programs for the free flow of ideas, open access to education, the transfer of scientific knowledge, and protection of cultural and natural heritages.

- The World Meteorological Organization (WMO), founded in 1951, is based in Geneva, Switzerland. URL: www.wmo.ch

  The WMO is a specialized agency that provides current scientific information about the atmosphere, freshwaters, and climate. Depletion of the ozone layer, global warming, floods and droughts, and El Niño are among the concerns it addresses. Its staff of 246 serves 179 member states and 6 territories. Its budget for 2000–2003 was $152 million.

CHAPTER 23

UN to the Rescue

The usual face of the UN in the most difficult spots today is not the face of peacekeepers. It's the face of the World Food Program person, it's the face of the refugee person, it's the face of the UNICEF person.
—Carol Bellamy, Director of UNICEF

The UN has always regarded disaster aid as one of its primary missions, defining "disaster" in broad terms that range from earthquakes and floods to disease and famine. Humanitarian aid organizations operate in collaboration with the UN Emergency Relief Coordinator and a committee of representatives from UN agencies and major nongovernmental organizations like the Red Cross.

Which body of the UN responds to a given emergency depends on the nature of the situation. If food and shelter are needed, the World Food Program might be the lead agency. Although the WFP engages in social and economic development, its main focus is on helping victims of disaster, long-term refugees, and displaced persons. In 2000, the program's full-time staff of 2,355 fed almost 90 million people in more than 80 nations. The WFP is the largest UN provider of grant assistance to Africa, and it provided vital food supplies in

A young Somali mother and her children
await medical treatment at a UNICEF/
Swedish relief clinic. UN photo 159385 by
Milton Grant.

2000 to the Horn of Africa, North Korea, the Balkans, Afghanistan,
the former Soviet Union and Eastern Europe, and Latin America and
the Caribbean, particularly Haiti, Nicaragua, Bolivia, and Honduras.

Often the WFP collaborates with other UN bodies, such as the High
Commissioner for Refugees (UNHCR) or the UN Children's Fund
(UNICEF), and with NGOs that help distribute aid and ensure that it
goes where most needed. The UNHCR is charged with helping and
protecting refugees, fulfilling this mission so successfully that it received Nobel Peace Prizes in 1954 and 1981. It has developed "quick
impact projects," or QIPs, to bridge the gap between emergency assistance for refugees and for refugees returning home and longer-term

development aid undertaken by other agencies. Typical QIPs rebuild schools, repair roads, or restore water supplies. Media coverage has made the UNHCR's blue plastic tents familiar to Americans as they view events in Kosovo, West Africa, and elsewhere.

UNICEF looks after children in need. Its main task is to help children in developing countries achieve their full potential as human beings, which it does by focusing on rights, needs, and opportunities. Its bedrock statement of belief is the Convention on the Rights of the Child (CRC), ratified by all the world's nations (except the United States and Somalia, which are expected to ratify it soon), which lays out a kind of Bill of Rights for children. The convention expresses a rights-based approach that encourages governments to adopt internationally recognized ethical standards and to go beyond minimal assurances that citizens have the basics to survive. UNICEF addresses children's needs through research and information programs, partnerships with governments and NGOs for provision of vital services, and emergency operations. And it addresses opportunities for children by working with governments and other organizations to ensure good medical care and upbringing.

Leading UN Actors

Four organizations are preeminent in the UN's relief efforts:

- The World Food Program (WFP), created in 1963, is headquartered in Rome, Italy. URL: *www.wfp.org*

  The WFP underwent a major administrative reformation under Catherine Bertini, the organization's first American and first woman Executive Director. A recent US government report praised her internal reforms and noted that "significantly, the WFP has the largest budget, the smallest staff, and the lowest percentage of administrative costs within the UN system." In fiscal 2000, the US was the WFP's biggest benefactor, contributing $795.7 million of its $1.685 billion budget.
- The Office of the United Nations High Commissioner for Refugees

New residents arrive at the Rogani refugee camp in Chaman, a Pakistani
border town where children and young people make up a large portion of
the population. UN/DPI photo by Luke Powell.

(UNHCR), established in 1950, is based in Geneva, Switzerland.
URL: *www.unhcr.ch*

The UNHCR publishes a biennial report on the status of the
world's refugees. A staff of about 5,000 works in 281 offices in 121
countries and looks after 21.6 million people. In 2000, operations
were concentrated in western Asia (some 2.6 million Afghan refugees), the former Yugoslavia, and the Great Lakes region of Africa.
Almost all of the $965.2 million budget came from voluntary dona-
tions from governments.

- The United Nations Children's Fund (UNICEF), founded in 1946,
  is headquartered in New York City. URL: *www.unicef.org*

  UNICEF has become embedded in the American consciousness
  through its famous holiday cards. The organization has 8 regional
  offices and 126 country offices, a staff of 9,000, and an annual
  budget of $1.2 billion. Its director since 1995 is Carol Bellamy,
  formerly president of the New York City Council. The US government has invariably been UNICEF's largest single donor.

• The UN Relief and Works Agency for Palestine Refugees in the Near East (UNRWA), founded in 1949, is based in Gaza City, Palestine. URL: *www.unrwa.org*

Founded to provide emergency humanitarian aid to Palestinians displaced during the creation of the state of Israel, the UNRWA has become a permanent social services agency. It provides health, education, and social services to more than 3.6 million registered Palestinian refugees in the Middle East, under the eye of a UN Coordinator. The US government has usually been the largest donor, contributing $101 million in 2000.

CHAPTER 24

Nuclear, Biological, and Chemical Threats

We need a reaffirmation of political commitment to reduce the dangers from existing nuclear weapons and from further proliferation.
—Kofi Annan, Secretary General of the UN

Building homes on old chemical dumps like Love Canal or sending anthrax spores through the mail may seem like plots from bad movies. Unfortunately, the bad movies are getting a second showing in the theater of real life. Today, there are even scarier plots, involving deadly nerve gas and nuclear weapons smuggled into urban centers and airports. The UN's global presence makes it a natural leader in identifying and monitoring these dangers and confining them so they harm no one.

The UN has long been a forum for talks about arms control and disarmament, and some of these discussions have produced solid results. UN-sponsored or related negotiations have led to such major agreements as the Nuclear Non-Proliferation Treaty (1968), the Comprehensive Nuclear-Test-Ban Treaty (1996), and treaties outlawing chemical (1992) and bacteriological weapons (1972) and the placement of nuclear weapons on the seabed (1971) or in outer space (1967).

Equally important, the UN has helped establish methods to control weapons of mass destruction. The International Atomic Energy Agency (IAEA), for example, has set up a system of nuclear safeguards and verification, and the Organization for the Prohibition of Chemical Weapons (OPCW) monitors compliance with the Convention on Chemical Weapons.

One of the more insidious weapons of war is the land mine, a small explosive device that can be buried in the ground, where it explodes with deadly force when stepped on. Cheap and easy to deploy, land mines have proliferated in all kinds of conflicts, even civil wars, where they become silent killers. Even worse, when hostilities end, a mine typically remains buried in the ground, often forgotten until some innocent person steps on it and loses a leg or worse. It is estimated that each year some 2 million mines are laid worldwide, and during that year they kill and wound more than 20,000 people. The UN is credited with encouraging countries to support the 1997 Ottawa Convention, which bans the production, export, and use of land mines. The UN operates mine clearance projects in seven countries and also trains de-miners. It offers public education programs and improves medical and rehabilitation services for land mine victims.

Leading UN Actors

Of the three UN bodies responsible for overseeing nuclear, biological, or chemical threats, the IAEA is best known to the public, owing to its monitoring of the nuclear arms potential of Iran and North Korea.

- The International Atomic Energy Agency (IAEA), established in 1957, is based in Vienna, Austria. URL: *www.iaea.org*

  The IAEA is an independent intergovernmental agency that helps coordinate the fields of nuclear science and engineering and eases the transfer of technology among nations. Safety and the protection of people against excessive exposure to radiation have been important concerns as well. The organization is probably best known as the watchdog for international treaties aimed at containing the unauthorized spread or distribution of nuclear weapons or materials. Its inspectors watch more than a thousand nuclear installations worldwide that are covered under the IAEA Safeguards Program. The US government strongly endorses the work of the agency and provides more than one quarter of the $300 million annual cost. In the aftermath of the attack on the US on Sept. 11, 2001, the IAEA has become a leader in the debate about preventing terrorists from using nuclear weapons.

- The Organization for the Prohibition of Chemical Weapons (OPCW) is headquartered at The Hague, Netherlands. URL: *www.opcw.org*

  The primary task of the OPCW is to monitor the provisions of the 1972 Convention on the Prohibition of the Development, Production, and Stockpiling of Bacteriological (Biological) and Toxin Weapons and on Their Destruction and the Convention on the Prohibition of the Development, Production, Stockpiling, and Use of Chemical Weapons and on Their Destruction.

- The Preparatory Commission for the Comprehensive Nuclear-Test-Ban Treaty Organization (CTBTO), established in 1996, is based in Vienna, Austria. URL: *www.ctbto.org*

  The commission's main job is to devise a verification plan to ensure that the signers of the Nuclear-Test-Ban Treaty are adhering to its terms.

CHAPTER 25

Guiding Globalization: How the UN Helps Make Things Work

The surest route to growth is through successfully engaging in the global economy, combined with effective social policies.
　　　　　　—Kofi Annan, Secretary General of the United Nations

Free markets work best when they have strong government under-pinnings, but no one government is in charge of global markets. This is where the UN has become invaluable as the monitor, administrator, and facilitator of the many "soft infrastructures" that enable complex international financial and industrial markets to work reasonably well most of the time. The UN has also provided vital aid to governments trying to cope with the fast pace and intensity of modern economic relations, including the rapid swings in currency and capital that can send a seemingly sound national economy into sudden crisis.

Capital Opportunities

The smooth flow of capital is crucial for market systems, and here the UN has been a key player on both modest and global scales. A modest example is the recent collaborative efforts between the UN Confer-

ence on Trade and Development (UNCTAD) and the International
Chamber of Commerce, which are compiling investment guides to
the forty-eight least developed countries as a way of publicizing opportunities and encouraging capital inflows. Some thirty companies are
participating in a pilot venture in six countries. Another example is
UNCTAD's joint effort with information technology companies to
develop an automated customs system that has been implemented in
more than seventy developing countries.

Far bigger and better known is the work of the International Monetary Fund (IMF), a specialized agency that offers capital, fiscal and
monetary advice, and policy recommendations to national governments. Unlike the World Bank, the IMF's writ runs to all nations, not
just the developing ones. Most of its work proceeds quietly and consists of complex services aimed at easing international monetary cooperation, establishing a multilateral system of payments, eliminating
foreign exchange restrictions, and promoting stable and orderly exchange rates. In times of crisis, when a member nation is unable to
meet its foreign obligations or its financial system becomes unstable,
the IMF can offer essential aid in the form of large loans. However, the
loans often come bound with strings of fiscal reform that some nations find difficult to untie. The IMF's insistence, for example, that Indonesia and other developing countries cut their government spending as part of receiving bailout loans is cited by some as a contributing
factor to the Asian economic collapse of the late 1990s. The IMF has
conceded that it may have acted with undue severity and has reex-
amined its policies.

Soft Infrastructure

For every piece of machinery, every length of fiber-optic cable, every
chemical reagent, there has to be a technical standard that permits the
enforcement of consistency and standardization. UN bodies set technical standards for machines and the like, and also for laws, procedures, and other intangible elements of the infrastructure.

Another kind of soft infrastructure is the individual capacity to
acquire and process information. The UN Secretary General has spo-

ken often about the importance of information access as a basis for economic and social improvement. Alluding to the "digital divide" that helps separate the affluent from the poor nations, Kofi Annan has proposed that the UN should begin targeting specific information needs through its programs. In 2001 he announced the creation of the Health InterNetwork, which will have 10,000 on-site electronic information access locations in hospitals, clinics, and public health facilities throughout the developing world. The World Health Organization is the lead agency in this effort to bring the latest medical information to literally billions of people.

Soft infrastructure also includes the rules and standards for the creation, ownership, and development of intellectual property. Software, songs, and genes can all be regarded as forms of property that have value. And as with any form of property, disputes arise about ownership and use. The UN has a specialized agency that deals with exactly these kinds of concerns. The World Intellectual Property Organization (WIPO) provides services such as helping nations harmonize their laws and procedures about intellectual property, so that creators in each country can more easily be protected in other countries. WIPO also develops common international standards and procedures regarding issues like patents, copyrights, and trademarks. It administers eleven treaties that set out internationally agreed rights and common standards, which the signatory states agree to enforce within their own borders. The Internet, digitization, and e-commerce have made WIPO even more important by raising basic issues of the right to copy and use intellectual property, especially music and films. WIPO has developed global registration systems for trademarks, industrial designs, and other intellectual property. The Patent Cooperation Treaty (PCT), for example, establishes an international patent application that has legal force in signatory nations. WIPO provides another vital service, helping inventors determine whether their invention is truly new. Anyone who applies for a patent in their home country must show that their idea is new and that no one else owns it. The search for this kind of information can involve a vast amount of work, so WIPO has simplified matters by creating a classification system that organizes information pertaining to inventions, trade-

marks, and industrial designs into indexed structures for easy re-
trieval. The system defines about 70,000 technology categories,
grouped under major headings such as biotechnology and medicines.

Global Compact

One of the more ingenious ideas at the UN has been to engage the
business community in a common effort to act according to internationally accepted standards, such as treaties against child labor. Kofi
Annan proposed the Global Compact, as he dubbed it, at the 1999
World Economic Forum in Davos, Switzerland. He challenged the
business community to accept and enforce a set of core values in the
areas of human rights, labor standards, and environmental practices.
Annan asked them to:

Respect the protection of international human rights
Check to be sure they are not committing or abetting human rights
   abuses
Support freedom of association and the right to unionize
Eliminate forced and child labor
Eliminate occupational discrimination
Be more environmentally responsible and responsive

If businesses do this globally, the UN's agenda would advance substantially, without the need to create more bureaucracy or laws. It is
an elegant approach, certainly worth trying. In response, the International Chamber of Commerce formally accepted Annan's challenge
on behalf of its 7,000 business organizations in 137 nations. The
Global Compact is now operating as a grand experiment in advancing the UN's agenda through cooperation rather than the traditional
mechanisms of censure and sanctions.

Leading UN Actors

The following organizations are among those that facilitate globalization.

- The International Monetary Fund (IMF), established in 1944 at the Bretton Woods Conference, is based in Washington, D.C. URL: *www.imf.int*

  The IMF facilitates international monetary cooperation and provides loans to member states. The 182 member nations are each represented on the board of governors, which sets policy and has general oversight. Regular operations are managed by a twenty-four-member executive board. Member countries subscribe to the IMF through contributions to the budget, and can draw on IMF loans according to the level of their subscription. The IMF publishes two important reports: *World Economic Outlook* and *International Capital Markets.*

- The World Intellectual Property Organization (WIPO) was founded in 1970 and became a UN specialized agency in 1974. It is based in Geneva, Switzerland. URL: *www.wipo.int*

  WIPO's mission is to help protect intellectual property worldwide. Its annual budget is 410 million Swiss francs, 85 percent of which it raises through earnings from registration systems.

- The International Civil Aviation Organization (ICAO) was created in 1944, has been a UN specialized agency since 1947, and is based in Montreal, Canada. URL: *www.icao.int*

  ICAO sets the international standards and regulations necessary for the safety and efficiency of air transport. It does this by establishing international standards for aircraft, pilots and flight crews, air traffic controllers, ground and maintenance crews, and security in international airports. It is also concerned with flight rules and telecommunications systems. At a 2002 ICAO ministerial conference on anti-terrorism airline regulations, attendees agreed on a security plan that includes audits of airport security. The US, a strong supporter of the ICAO, provided one quarter of its $52.58 million budget for 2000.

- The International Maritime Organization (IMO), founded in 1959, is headquartered in London, England. URL: *www.imo.org*

  The IMO's mandate is to make the process of shipping goods for international trade safer and less likely to pollute the seas. Through its meetings, 40 conventions, and 800 codes and recommendations, the IMO has helped develop common standards of safety and efficiency in navigation, technical regulations and practices, and pollution control. The IMO founded the World Maritime University in 1983 in Sweden and has also established the IMO International Maritime Law Institute and the IMO International Maritime Academy.

- The International Telecommunication Union (ITU), founded in 1865 in Paris as the International Telegraph Union, became the ITU in 1934. It became a UN specialized agency in 1947 and is located in Geneva, Switzerland. URL: *www.itu.int*

  The ITU helps government and the private sector coordinate and improve global telecommunication networks and services. The staff of some 740 also offers technical assistance to developing countries.

- The Universal Postal Union (UPU), established in the Berne Treaty of 1874, became a UN specialized agency in 1948. It is headquartered in Berne, Switzerland. URL: *www.upu.int*

  The UPU regulates and facilitates cooperation among international postal services, as well as providing advice, mediation, and technical assistance. The Universal Postal Congress meets every five years.

CHAPTER 26

Drug Trafficking

Drug abuse is a global phenomenon. It affects almost every country although its extent and characteristics differ from region to region. Drug abuse trends around the world, especially among youth, have started to converge over the last few decades. —UN Office on Drugs and Crime

A downside of globalization has been the spread of international organized crime, often centered around the illegal trade of drugs, weapons, or humans. Crime is an abridgment of human rights. The mugger who steals a man's wallet has abridged his rights to security of person and property. The computer hacker who steals personal financial information abridges a woman's right to privacy. And perhaps most insidious and destructive of all is the combination of criminal activity and drug addiction. The drug lords who supply cocaine, heroine, Ecstasy, and other substances diminish the human capacity for independent living, often subverting local law enforcement through bribery. The drug trade has recently become even more ominous through its connections with international terrorism.

The UN Response

The rapid growth of the international narcotics trade has led the UN to streamline and better coordinate its anti-drug resources under the Office on Drugs and Crime (UNODC), established in 1997. The office consists of two parts: the Crime Program (discussed in Chapter 8) and the Drug Program, formally known as the UN Drug Control Program (UNDCP). Through the Drug Program, the UNODC offers an integrated approach that begins with the farmer and ends with the drug dealer and money launderer. The UNDCP also monitors implementation of drug-related decisions by ECOSOC and other UN bodies.

The governing body of the UNDCP is the Commission on Narcotic Drugs (CND), a functional commission of ECOSOC and the UN's main source of drug-related policy. Three international conventions form the basis for the CND's policies: the Single Convention on Narcotic Drugs (1961), which tries to confine drugs to medical use only; the Convention on Psychotropic Substances (1971), which seeks to control synthetic drugs; and the UN Convention against Illicit Traffic in Narcotic Drugs and Psychotropic Substances (1988), which deals mainly with drug trafficking and related issues like money laundering. However, the CND does not actually monitor implementation of these treaties. That task is the responsibility of the International Narcotics Control Board (INCB), an independent panel of 13 persons elected by ECOSOC and financed by the UN.

Among the UNODC's major efforts are the Global Assessment Program (GAP), which provides accurate information about the international drug problem; the legal Advisory Program, which assists governments in writing laws against the drug trade and helps train judicial officials; and the Illicit Crop Monitoring Program (ICMP), whose projects in six major drug-growing countries (Afghanistan, Bolivia, Colombia, Laos, Myanmar, and Peru) aim at discovering the extent and nature of drug crops such as coca bush and opium poppy. The Alternative Development Program tries to nip the drug problem at its source by offering farmers alternative crops that will enable them to earn a decent, and legal, living. This approach is being tested through projects in Latin America, Southwest Asia, and Southeast Asia.

The UNDCP encourages the cultivation of alternative crops to replace opium poppy, as on this farm in Thailand. UN/DPI photo by J. Sailas/UNDCP.

The UN's drug experts are becoming increasingly concerned about changing perceptions of drugs among youth. If our future lies with young people, we need to pay attention to the relation between youth and drugs. Things change, and old approaches may no longer work. That was the message the director of the UNDCP's youth programs delivered at a conference in 2002. He noted that young people are increasingly drawn toward synthetic drugs rather than those, like heroin, derived from poppies and other biological organisms. Such drugs are worse, in some ways, he claimed, because although they usually don't cause physical dependence and the painful withdrawal symptoms associated with heroin use, they do cause lasting and irreversible physical and neurological damage that may not become manifest until later in life. As the director observed, most young people who use Ecstasy think of it not as doing drugs, but merely as having a good time. Intervention or advice from adults usually doesn't work because of the generation gap, so the alternative is to encourage peer-to-peer education. Accordingly, UN narcotics experts are considering methods for reshaping their programs to include more youth as role models.

The Connection with Terrorism

Many reports in recent years have shown that some terrorist organizations rely on the drug trade to raise money for their operations. Obviously, any dent in the narcotics trade may therefore also help combat terrorism, but a more focused approach would have an even greater impact. One UN plan has been to identify the nations that are the largest producers of opium and strongly encourage them to take action. That has put the spotlight on Afghanistan, which has been the world's largest opium producer in most recent years.

The UN and the US leaned hard on the former Taliban regime to stop the growing of poppies, which had become virtually the basis of the national economy. They succeeded, and as Afghanistan's output rapidly declined, the distinction of being the global opium capital moved to Myanmar (formerly Burma). However, experts also began noticing that the Afghan drug networks were stockpiling much of the opium and processed heroin rather than destroying it, which meant that a large supply was available to anyone who could control it, including the Taliban regime. And because the Taliban and the Al Qaeda terrorist network had become virtually synonymous, it did not take much imagination to see how drug money could become terrorist funding.

When the US and its allies intervened in Afghanistan in late 2001, the Taliban ended its controls over poppy growing, and, predictably, the supply of opium in the region began rising. The collapse of the Taliban regime in winter 2001 enabled farmers to act with impunity and begin planting as much acreage in poppies as they could manage, an absolutely alarming thought to the European nations, who had been inundated with Afghan opium in previous years. At meetings sponsored by the Commission on Narcotic Drugs in Europe and Japan, experts warned that Afghanistan was poised to regain its premier status as an opium producer. The new Afghan government has committed itself to a strong anti-drug, anti-poppy-growing policy, although it is uncertain if it can carry this out. Afghan's farmers have few options in their choice of cash crops, and opium heads the list for profit per unit of investment and ease of transport along the country's bad roads. If the new government acts too harshly it will alienate some of its supporters, and if it moves too slowly it will anger the US and its allies. But finding an alternative crop will not be easy, and making the changeover on the farms will require investment capital that the government doesn't have.

A lot is riding on success. An agricultural system based on legal crops would enable the nation to prosper and participate fully in the international community. Yet the return of poppy cultivation would inevitably bring organized crime, official corruption, and possibly links with terrorist organizations. All the world's nations have an interest in the fate of Afghanistan's poppy fields, and the UN has begun aligning its bodies to act effectively. Among other things, the UN has reestablished its UNDCP Afghanistan office.

Leading UN Actors

Three bodies oversee most of the UN's fight against the trade in illegal drugs.

- The UN Office on Drugs and Crime (UNODC), established in 1997, is based in Vienna, Austria. URL: *www.unodc.org*

   The UNODC has two components, the Crime Program and the Drug Program. The Crime Program focuses on corruption, organized crime, trafficking in human beings, and terrorism. The Drug Program compiles and disseminates information about illicit drugs, monitors illegal drug-related agriculture, fights the laundering of drug-related money, seeks alternative crops for farmers in drug-growing regions, and helps governments write anti-drug legislation. The UNODC has some 350 staff and 22 field offices. Most of its funding comes from voluntary contributions by member states.
- The Commission on Narcotic Drugs (CND) was established in 1946 and has its headquarters in Vienna, Austria. URL: *www. uncnd.org*

   The CND makes UN policy about drugs and is the governing

body for the UN Drug Control Program (UNDCP). It is a functional commission of ECOSOC.

- The International Narcotics Control Board (INCB) was created in 1968 and is located in Vienna, Austria. *www.incb.org*

  The INCB is an independent body, funded by the UN, that monitors compliance with the three international conventions on narcotics and drug trafficking.

Conclusion

The campaign to end Afghanistan's opium industry offers powerful evidence that the UN is a deadly serious organization. For most Americans, who have little direct interaction with the world organization, it is easy to think that the UN's main value and mission lie far away. And often they do. Yet in our interconnected world, far away may also be right next door, as the terrorist attacks of September 11, 2001, demonstrated with brutal force. A prudent person must conclude that global safety and security come from many sources, in many ways, and that whatever the awesome power of the US, it should not, and need not, march alone.

By the same token, the UN cannot succeed without the US. We have seen that the UN has a tremendous mandate, greater than that of any other organization—even its predecessor, the ill-fated League of Nations (to which the US never belonged). The UN, by itself, lacks the resources to fulfill much of its mandate, and its partners—the nations of Europe, Asia, Africa, and the Americas—cannot act without unity of purpose and the material resources available to the US.

The attacks of 9/11 have jolted both the UN and the US into seriously redefining their historic relationship. The current Secretary General, as we have seen, understands the mutual interests and needs of the two and seems to realize that he has a rare opportunity to reinvent their relationship. The US government, for its part, now has a clear basis for its foreign and domestic policy in the form of international terrorism, which has replaced the Soviet Union, the "evil empire" of cold war days, as the major external threat to the nation. Perhaps as a result, Americans may replace the consumerism and market-economy rhetoric of the acquisitive 1990s with moral and psychological clarity. That focus could make the US a much more effective player at the UN, where, as our insiders have noted, the American government generally gets what it wants when it knows what it wants, but flounders when it is uncertain about its policies or goals.

Something to Think About

"I'm struck by the relevance of the UN to United States foreign policy and national security interests. If you look at the agenda that we've had since I've been here, it very much tracks with the agenda of our foreign policy and of our national security policy. To those who would question the relevance of the UN, my answer would be: absolutely the UN is relevant, no question about it, all you have to do is look at our agenda. The degree of UN involvement in any specific issue will vary from case to case, but there will always be a UN role. The debate is going to be over the precise definition of that role, and it seems to vary from situation to situation."   —John Negroponte, US Ambassador to the UN

Will the UN be capable of delivering on its end of the bargain? Partly that depends on how much it promises to offer, and how much the US expects. The UN, remember, is not a government but rather a creature of the world's governments, and is constrained by severe limits on its ability to raise money and impose its decisions. It is therefore vital that US legislators and policy makers, as well as the general public, understand how the UN is constituted and, even more important, how it functions—not just on a flowchart but in real life and real time. If it is true, as French statesman Georges Clemenceau once said, that war is too important to be left to the generals, the UN and its relationship with the US are too important to be left solely to the experts.

Membership of Principal United Nations Organs in 2002

GENERAL ASSEMBLY

The General Assembly is composed of all 191 United Nations Member States.

The States, and the dates on which they became members, are listed in Appendix C.

SECURITY COUNCIL

The Security Council has 15 members. The United Nations Charter designates five states as permanent members and the General Assembly elects 10 other members for two-year terms. The term of office for each nonpermanent member of the Council ends on 31 December of the year indicated in parentheses next to its name.

The five permanent members of the Security Council are China, France, Russian Federation, United Kingdom, and the United States.

The 10 nonpermanent members of the Council in 2002 are Bulgaria (2003), Cameroon (2003), Colombia (2002), Guinea (2003), Ireland (2002), Mauritius (2002), Mexico (2003), Norway (2002), Singapore (2002), and Syria (2003).

ECONOMIC AND SOCIAL COUNCIL

The Economic and Social Council has 54 members, elected for three-year terms by the General Assembly. The term of office for each member expires on 31 December of the year indicated in parentheses next to its name. In 2002, the Council is composed of the following 54 States:

Andorra (2003), Angola (2002), Argentina (2003), Australia (2004), Austria (2002), Bahrain (2002), Benin (2002), Bhutan (2004), Brazil (2003), Burkina Faso (2002), Burundi (2004), Cameroon (2002), Chile (2004), China (2004), Costa Rica (2002), Croatia (2002), Cuba (2002), Egypt (2003), El Salvador (2004), Ethiopia (2003), Fiji (2002), Finland (2004), France (2002), Georgia (2003), Germany (2002), Ghana (2004), Greece (2002), Guatemala (2004), Hungary (2004), India (2004), Iran (2003), Italy (2003), Japan (2002), Libya (2004), Mexico (2002), Nepal (2003), Netherlands (2003), Nigeria (2003), Pakistan (2003), Peru (2003), Portugal (2002), Qatar (2004), Republic of Korea (2003), Romania (2003), Russian Federation (2004), South Africa (2003), Sudan (2002), Suriname (2002), Sweden (2004), Uganda (2003), Ukraine (2004), United Kingdom (2004), United States (2003), and Zimbabwe (2004).

TRUSTEESHIP COUNCIL

The Trusteeship Council is made up of the five permanent members of the Security Council—China, France, Russian Federation, United Kingdom, and the United States. With the independence of Palau, the last remaining United Nations Trust Territory, the Council formally suspended operations on 1 November 1994. The Council amended its rules of procedure to drop the obligation to meet annually and agreed to meet as the occasion required; by its decision or the decision of its President or at the request of a majority of its members or the General Assembly or the Security Council.

INTERNATIONAL COURT OF JUSTICE

The International Court of Justice has 15 members, elected by both the General Assembly and the Security Council. Judges hold nine-year terms, which end 5 February of the year indicated in parentheses next to their name.

The current composition of the Court is as follows: Awn Shawkat Al-Khasawneh (Jordan) (2009); Nabil Elaraby (Egypt) (2006); Thomas Buergenthal (United States) (2006); Carl-August Fleischhauer (Germany) (2003); Gilbert Guillaume (France) (2009); Géza Herczegh (Hungary) (2003); Rosalyn Higgins (United Kingdom) (2009); Shi Jiuyong (China) (2003); Pieter H. Kooijmans (Netherlands) (2006); Abdul G. Koroma (Sierra Leone) (2003); Shigeru Oda (Japan) (2003); Gonzalo Parra-Aranguren (Venezuela) (2009); Raymond Ranjeva (Madagascar) (2009); José Francisco Rezek (Brazil) (2006); and Vladlen S. Vereshchetin (Russian Federation) (2006).

Universal Declaration of Human Rights

PREAMBLE

Whereas recognition of the inherent dignity and of the equal and inalienable rights of all members of the human family is the foundation of freedom, justice and peace in the world,

Whereas disregard and contempt for human rights have resulted in barbarous acts which have outraged the conscience of mankind, and the advent of a world in which human beings shall enjoy freedom of speech and belief and freedom from fear and want has been proclaimed as the highest aspiration of the common people,

Whereas it is essential, if man is not to be compelled to have recourse, as a last resort, to rebellion against tyranny and oppression, that human rights should be protected by the rule of law,

Whereas it is essential to promote the development of friendly relations between nations,

Whereas the peoples of the United Nations have in the Charter reaffirmed their faith in fundamental human rights, in the dignity and worth of the human person and in the equal rights of men and women and have determined to promote social progress and better standards of life in larger freedom,

Whereas Member States have pledged themselves to achieve, in co-operation with the United Nations, the promotion of universal respect for and observance of human rights and fundamental freedoms,

Whereas a common understanding of these rights and freedoms is of the greatest importance for the full realization of this pledge,

Now, Therefore THE GENERAL ASSEMBLY proclaims THIS UNIVERSAL DECLARATION OF HUMAN RIGHTS as a common standard of achievement for all peoples and all nations, to the end that every individual and every organ of society, keeping this Declaration constantly in mind, shall strive by teaching and education to promote respect for these rights and freedoms and by progressive measures, national and international, to secure their universal and effective recognition and observance, both among the peoples of Member States themselves and among the peoples of territories under their jurisdiction.

Article 1.
All human beings are born free and equal in dignity and rights. They are endowed with reason and conscience and should act towards one another in a spirit of brotherhood.

Article 2.
Everyone is entitled to all the rights and freedoms set forth in this Declaration, without distinction of any kind, such as race, colour, sex, language, religion, political or other opinion, national or social origin, property, birth or other status. Furthermore, no distinction shall be made on the basis of the political, jurisdictional or international status of the country or territory to which a person belongs, whether it be independent, trust, non-self-governing or under any other limitation of sovereignty.

Article 3.
Everyone has the right to life, liberty and security of person.

Article 4.
No one shall be held in slavery or servitude; slavery and the slave trade shall be prohibited in all their forms.

Article 5.
No one shall be subjected to torture or to cruel, inhuman or degrading treatment or punishment.

Article 6.
Everyone has the right to recognition everywhere as a person before the law.

Article 7.
All are equal before the law and are entitled without any discrimination to equal protection of the law. All are entitled to equal protection against any discrimination in violation of this Declaration and against any incitement to such discrimination.

Article 8.
Everyone has the right to an effective remedy by the competent national tribunals for acts violating the fundamental rights granted him by the constitution or by law.

Article 9.
No one shall be subjected to arbitrary arrest, detention or exile.

Article 10.
Everyone is entitled in full equality to a fair and public hearing by an independent and impartial tribunal, in the determination of his rights and obligations and of any criminal charge against him.

Article 11.
(1) Everyone charged with a penal offence has the right to be presumed innocent until proved guilty according to law in a public trial at which he has had all the guarantees necessary for his defence.
(2) No one shall be held guilty of any penal offence on account of any act or omission which did not constitute a penal offence, under

national or international law, at the time when it was committed. Nor shall a heavier penalty be imposed than the one that was applicable at the time the penal offence was committed.

Article 12.

No one shall be subjected to arbitrary interference with his privacy, family, home or correspondence, nor to attacks upon his honour and reputation. Everyone has the right to the protection of the law against such interference or attacks.

Article 13.

(1) Everyone has the right to freedom of movement and residence within the borders of each state.

(2) Everyone has the right to leave any country, including his own, and to return to his country.

Article 14.

(1) Everyone has the right to seek and to enjoy in other countries asylum from persecution.

(2) This right may not be invoked in the case of prosecutions genuinely arising from non-political crimes or from acts contrary to the purposes and principles of the United Nations.

Article 15.

(1) Everyone has the right to a nationality.

(2) No one shall be arbitrarily deprived of his nationality nor denied the right to change his nationality.

Article 16.

(1) Men and women of full age, without any limitation due to race, nationality or religion, have the right to marry and to found a family. They are entitled to equal rights as to marriage, during marriage and at its dissolution.

(2) Marriage shall be entered into only with the free and full consent of the intending spouses.

(3) The family is the natural and fundamental group unit of society and is entitled to protection by society and the State.

Article 17.

(1) Everyone has the right to own property alone as well as in association with others.

(2) No one shall be arbitrarily deprived of his property.

Article 18.

Everyone has the right to freedom of thought, conscience and religion; this right includes freedom to change his religion or belief, and freedom, either alone or in community with others and in public or private, to manifest his religion or belief in teaching, practice, worship and observance.

Article 19.

Everyone has the right to freedom of opinion and expression; this right includes freedom to hold opinions without interference and to seek, receive and impart information and ideas through any media and regardless of frontiers.

Article 20.

(1) Everyone has the right to freedom of peaceful assembly and association.

(2) No one may be compelled to belong to an association.

Article 21.

(1) Everyone has the right to take part in the government of his country, directly or through freely chosen representatives.

(2) Everyone has the right of equal access to public service in his country.

(3) The will of the people shall be the basis of the authority of government; this will shall be expressed in periodic and genuine elections which shall be by universal and equal suffrage and shall be held by secret vote or by equivalent free voting procedures.

Article 22.

Everyone, as a member of society, has the right to social security and is entitled to realization, through national effort and international co-operation and in accordance with the organization and resources of each State, of the economic, social and cultural rights indispensable for his dignity and the free development of his personality.

Article 23.

(1) Everyone has the right to work, to free choice of employment, to just and favourable conditions of work and to protection against unemployment.

(2) Everyone, without any discrimination, has the right to equal pay for equal work.

(3) Everyone who works has the right to just and favourable remuneration ensuring for himself and his family an existence worthy of human dignity, and supplemented, if necessary, by other means of social protection.

(4) Everyone has the right to form and to join trade unions for the protection of his interests.

Article 24.

Everyone has the right to rest and leisure, including reasonable limitation of working hours and periodic holidays with pay.

Article 25.

(1) Everyone has the right to a standard of living adequate for the health and well-being of himself and of his family, including food, clothing, housing and medical care and necessary social services, and the right to security in the event of unemployment, sickness, disability, widowhood, old age or other lack of livelihood in circumstances beyond his control.

(2) Motherhood and childhood are entitled to special care and assistance. All children, whether born in or out of wedlock, shall enjoy the same social protection.

Article 26.

(1) Everyone has the right to education. Education shall be free, at least in the elementary and fundamental stages. Elementary education shall be compulsory. Technical and professional education shall be made generally available and higher education shall be equally accessible to all on the basis of merit.

(2) Education shall be directed to the full development of the human personality and to the strengthening of respect for human rights and fundamental freedoms. It shall promote understanding, tolerance and friendship among all nations, racial or religious groups, and shall further the activities of the United Nations for the maintenance of peace.

(3) Parents have a prior right to choose the kind of education that shall be given to their children.

Article 27.

(1) Everyone has the right freely to participate in the cultural life of the community, to enjoy the arts and to share in scientific advancement and its benefits.

(2) Everyone has the right to the protection of the moral and material interests resulting from any scientific, literary or artistic production of which he is the author.

Article 28.

Everyone is entitled to a social and international order in which the rights and freedoms set forth in this Declaration can be fully realized.

Article 29.

(1) Everyone has duties to the community in which alone the free and full development of his personality is possible.

(2) In the exercise of his rights and freedoms, everyone shall be subject only to such limitations as are determined by law solely for the purpose of securing due recognition and respect for the rights and freedoms of others and of meeting the just requirements of morality, public order and the general welfare in a democratic society.

(3) These rights and freedoms may in no case be exercised contrary to the purposes and principles of the United Nations.

Article 30.

Nothing in this Declaration may be interpreted as implying for any State, group or person any right to engage in any activity or to perform any act aimed at the destruction of any of the rights and freedoms set forth herein.

UN Member States

The 191 member states, with the date on which each joined the United Nations:

Afghanistan   Nov. 19, 1946
Albania   Dec. 14, 1955
Algeria   Oct. 8, 1962
Andorra   July 28, 1993
Angola   Dec. 1, 1976
Antigua and Barbuda   Nov. 11, 1981
Argentina   Oct. 24, 1945
Armenia   Mar. 2, 1992
Australia   Nov. 1, 1945
Austria   Dec. 14, 1955
Azerbaijan   Mar. 2, 1992
Bahamas   Sept. 18, 1973
Bahrain   Sept. 21, 1971
Bangladesh   Sept. 17, 1974
Barbados   Dec. 9, 1966

Belarus   Oct. 24, 1945
Belgium   Dec. 27, 1945
Belize   Sept. 25, 1981
Benin   Sept. 20, 1960
Bhutan   Sept. 21, 1971
Bolivia   Nov. 14, 1945
Bosnia and Herzegovina   May 22, 1992
Botswana   Oct. 17, 1966
Brazil   Oct. 24, 1945
Brunei Darussalam   Sept. 21, 1984
Bulgaria   Dec. 14, 1955
Burkina Faso   Sept. 20, 1960
Burundi   Sept. 18, 1962
Cambodia   Dec. 14, 1955
Cameroon   Sept. 20, 1960
Canada   Nov. 9, 1945
Cape Verde   Sept. 16, 1975
Central African Republic   Sept. 20, 1960
Chad   Sept. 20, 1960
Chile   Oct. 24, 1945
China   Oct. 24, 1945
Colombia   Nov. 5, 1945
Comoros   Nov. 12, 1975
Congo (Republic of the)   Sept. 20, 1960
Costa Rica   Nov. 2, 1945
Côte d'Ivoire   Sept. 20, 1960
Croatia   May 22, 1992
Cuba   Oct. 24, 1945
Cyprus   Sept. 20, 1960
Czech Republic   Jan. 19, 1993
Democratic People's Republic of Korea   Sept. 17, 1991
Democratic Republic of the Congo   Sept. 20, 1960
Denmark   Oct. 24, 1945
Djibouti   Sept. 20, 1977
Dominica   Dec. 18, 1978

Dominican Republic   Oct. 24, 1945
Ecuador   Dec. 21, 1945
Egypt   Oct. 24, 1945
El Salvador   Oct. 24, 1945
Equatorial Guinea   Nov. 12, 1968
Eritrea   May 28, 1993
Estonia   Sept. 17, 1991
Ethiopia   Nov. 13, 1945
Fiji   Oct. 13, 1970
Finland   Dec. 14, 1955
France   Oct. 24, 1945
Gabon   Sept. 20, 1960
Gambia   Sept. 21, 1965
Georgia   July 31, 1992
Germany   Sept. 18, 1973
Ghana   Mar. 8, 1957
Greece   Oct. 25, 1945
Grenada   Sept. 17, 1974
Guatemala   Nov. 21, 1945
Guinea   Dec. 12, 1958
Guinea-Bissau   Sept. 17, 1974
Guyana   Sept. 20, 1966
Haiti   Oct. 24, 1945
Honduras   Dec. 17, 1945
Hungary   Dec. 14, 1955
Iceland   Nov. 19, 1946
India   Oct. 30, 1945
Indonesia   Sept. 28, 1950
Iran   Oct. 24, 1945
Iraq   Dec. 21, 1945
Ireland   Dec. 14, 1955
Israel   May 11, 1949
Italy   Dec. 14, 1955
Jamaica   Sept. 18, 1962
Japan   Dec. 18, 1956

Jordan   Dec. 14, 1955
Kazakhstan   Mar. 2, 1992
Kenya   Dec. 16, 1963
Kiribati   Sept. 14, 1999
Kuwait   May 14, 1963
Kyrgyzstan   Mar. 2, 1992
Lao People's Democratic Republic   Dec. 14, 1955
Latvia   Sept. 17, 1991
Lebanon   Oct. 24, 1945
Lesotho   Oct. 17, 1966
Liberia   Nov. 2, 1945
Libya   Dec. 24, 1955
Liechtenstein   Sept. 18, 1990
Lithuania   Sept. 17, 1991
Luxembourg   Oct. 24, 1945
Madagascar   Sept. 20, 1960
Malawi   Dec. 1, 1964
Malaysia   Sept. 17, 1957
Maldives   Sept. 21, 1965
Mali   Sept. 28, 1960
Malta   Dec. 1, 1964
Marshall Islands   Sept. 17, 1991
Mauritania   Oct. 27, 1961
Mauritius   Apr. 24, 1968
Mexico   Nov. 7, 1945
Micronesia (Federated States of)   Sept. 17, 1991
Monaco   May 28, 1993
Mongolia   Oct. 27, 1961
Morocco   Nov. 12, 1956
Mozambique   Sept. 16, 1975
Myanmar   Apr. 19, 1948
Namibia   Apr. 23, 1990
Nauru   Sept. 14, 1999
Nepal   Dec. 14, 1955
Netherlands   Dec. 10, 1945

New Zealand   Oct. 24, 1945
Nicaragua   Oct. 24, 1945
Niger   Sept. 20, 1960
Nigeria   Oct. 7, 1960
Norway   Nov. 27, 1945
Oman   Oct. 7, 1971
Pakistan   Sept. 30, 1947
Palau   Dec. 15, 1994
Panama   Nov. 13, 1945
Papua New Guinea   Oct. 10, 1975
Paraguay   Oct. 24, 1945
Peru   Oct. 31, 1945
Philippines   Oct. 24, 1945
Poland   Oct. 24, 1945
Portugal   Dec. 14, 1955
Qatar   Sept. 21, 1971
Republic of Korea   Sept. 17, 1991
Republic of Moldova   Mar. 2, 1992
Romania   Dec. 14, 1955
Russian Federation   Oct. 24, 1945
Rwanda   Sept. 18, 1962
Saint Kitts and Nevis   Sept. 23, 1983
Saint Lucia   Sept. 18, 1979
Saint Vincent and the Grenadines   Sept. 16, 1980
Samoa   Dec. 15, 1976
San Marino   Mar. 2, 1992
Sao Tome and Principe   Sept. 16, 1975
Saudi Arabia   Oct. 24, 1945
Senegal   Sept. 28, 1960
Seychelles   Sept. 21, 1976
Sierra Leone   Sept. 27, 1961
Singapore   Sept. 21, 1965
Slovakia   Jan. 19, 1993
Slovenia   May 22, 1992
Solomon Islands   Sept. 19, 1978

Somalia   Sept. 20, 1960
South Africa   Nov. 7, 1945
Spain   Dec. 14, 1955
Sri Lanka   Dec. 14, 1955
Sudan   Nov. 12, 1956
Suriname   Dec. 4, 1975
Swaziland   Sept. 24, 1968
Sweden   Nov. 19, 1946
Switzerland   Sept. 10, 2002
Syria   Oct. 24, 1945
Tajikistan   Mar. 2, 1992
Thailand   Dec. 16, 1946
The former Yugoslav Republic of Macedonia   Apr. 8, 1993
Timor-Leste   Sept. 27, 2002
Togo   Sept. 20, 1960
Tonga   Sept. 14, 1999
Trinidad and Tobago   Sept. 18, 1962
Tunisia   Nov. 12, 1956
Turkey   Oct. 24, 1945
Turkmenistan   Mar. 2, 1992
Tuvalu   Sept. 5, 2000
Uganda   Oct. 24, 1962
Ukraine   Oct. 24, 1945
United Arab Emirates   Dec. 9, 1971
United Kingdom   Oct. 24, 1945
United Republic of Tanzania   Dec. 14, 1961
United States   Oct. 24, 1945
Uruguay   Dec. 18, 1945
Uzbekistan   Mar. 2, 1992
Vanuatu   Sept. 15, 1981
Venezuela   Nov. 15, 1945
Vietnam   Sept. 20, 1977
Yemen   Sept. 30, 1947
Yugoslavia   Nov. 1, 2000
Zambia   Dec. 1, 1964
Zimbabwe   Aug. 25, 1980

How to Set Up a Model UN Meeting

The following is taken from *modelun@unausa.org*

The Model United Nations is a simulation of the United Nations System. In this simulation students assume the role of diplomats. They represent various countries and participate in debates about current issues in the UN agenda. Role-playing in a model UN meeting should enable you to learn:

- The concerns and hopes of people in different regions of the world;
- How people's lives worldwide can be improved through the UN;
- Skills and behavior which contribute to international cooperation.

Model UN meetings also help participants to understand the United Nations and appreciate the complexities and accomplishments of international cooperation. There are three basic components to the Model UN experience: first, an intensive preparation process researching the countries the participants represent; second, role-playing in a model UN debate where each participant assumes a role, usually that of an "ambassador" representing a country; and a final component evaluating the experience.

The first step in a Model UN experience is to prepare yourself to be a delegate.

You will need to learn about three things:

- The country you are to represent;
- The subject or issue on the agenda;
- The work of the United Nations related to the subject or issue.

You may begin the process by doing research about the country you will represent. This particular part of the preparation is very important. You will need to know some basic facts about "your" country, which might affect its policies. Such information can be found in an up-to-date encyclopedia or a similar source. You may also want to contact the nearest diplomatic mission/embassy of the country you will represent.

Here are a few features you may want to look at: economic and political systems; social structure and values; and cultural, national, and international priorities. For example, under political, topics could include: political system today; history (former colony or former colonial power); neighbors; allies; does it belong to any regional or other grouping of nations? In what ways does your country consider the UN important?

In addition to finding factual information, you will want to try to "get inside" to see with a delegate's eyes and feel as he or she does about the world today. The objective of your research is to ascertain the ways that your country perceives the United Nations and its application to your country's interests and policies.

The country research segment of your preparation is an ongoing activity, which will take considerable time. It will also be a group effort if the Model UN you are attending requires that a delegation of several people is needed to represent a member state.

The second stage of your preparation should focus on understanding the issues or subjects that are on the Model UN's agenda. In many instances, you and your colleagues will have to deduce what your country's views may be on these matters.

A Model UN may have a singular theme, such as human rights or economic development, or it may cover several different areas of the UN's work, such as regional conflicts, disarmament, refugees, children's issues, external debt of developing countries, or the environment. Your job is to find out what your country's position or views are on these issues and to develop a strategy for the country for the Model UN session.

The last stage of your research will focus on the UN system and its work. Understanding the role and functions of the various parts of the UN system on the issues and concerns is essential to your role as a delegate. This part of your research should help you better understand the role the UN plays in international affairs and how the UN operates as a diplomatic and policy-setting body for the international community.

Once you have researched the country you will represent, the issues on the Model UN's agenda, and the UN system, you will be ready to prepare a "position paper." This should be concise, consisting of the main points you think your country would consider important for the issues to be discussed. During the simulation, you can use these points as the basis for a speech or as items you might try to have included in resolutions. As you negotiate, you will undoubtedly modify them, or you may even abandon them altogether.

STEP #2: ROLE-PLAYING

The second step in the model UN experience is applying the information and knowledge you have acquired during your preparation. Once you and the other delegates arrive either in the meeting room or at the conference facilities, you are no longer a student. You are the "official" representative of the country you have been assigned. You are a diplomat. Your purpose and that of your colleagues representing the other

UN member states is to address the issues and the problems on the agenda and to develop a workable resolution which the largest number of nations can support.

The Model UN meetings are structured by rules of procedure which provide the ways and means for countries to express their views, to consider proposals and resolutions, and to come to decisions on resolving the issues and concerns on the agenda. You will have two principal concerns:

- To express the viewpoint of the country you represent for the purpose of sharing the ideas and experience of "your" government and procuring a resolution acceptable to "your" country;
- To contribute to developing an international response fair to all nations.

Most participants in the Model UN exercise will play the roles of delegates who represent a broad spectrum of political, economic, cultural, and geographic backgrounds. If you have sufficient participants, delegations can include specialists in different areas of industrial development and environment, such as toxic wastes and hazardous chemicals.

Additional participants could play members of the press, interviewing key delegates, filing dispatches to home newspapers, etc. Others might be representatives of nongovernmental organizations (NGOs) invited as observers.

You should also invite a knowledgeable person to observe and comment on the meeting. Best would be someone who has worked for the UN or on a national delegation to a meeting at the United Nations. To role-play well will require serious research—and imagination. You will need to be a skillful diplomat, aware of your nation's priorities, but flexible, sensitive to other's viewpoints, and willing to work for consensus and the common good.

Role-playing involves working in a group and making speeches. As soon as you begin the meetings, you will want to meet informally with delegates of countries with backgrounds and concerns similar to yours in order to coordinate ideas and actions. In the Model UN these groups are often called "caucus groups." These groups are all un-official and are not bodies that can bind "your" country to any position or viewpoint. The purpose of these groups is to facilitate the negotiating process. For example, the developing countries have formed the "Group of 77," which concentrates on forming a common agenda among over 130 countries in Africa, Asia, Latin America, and the Middle East. Similarly, most western European countries are now grouped under the European Union (EU).

Negotiations are very intense and can be very frustrating, especially in the larger groups. Most of the diplomatic work is accomplished during the informal caucuses producing draft resolutions, amendments, and the important compromises needed to reach consensus.

Speech-making during formal proceedings is another important part of role-playing. These public pronouncements permit delegates to "show their stuff" as orators and thinkers to the rest of the group. Yet not everyone is a polished speaker, and in the Model UN debate, substance is as important as the style at the podium. A careful balance of listening and speaking must be struck in order to generate support and to find consensus on the problem.

The end result of the process is the adoption of a resolution or resolutions by a vote, reflecting the aggregate of interests of the member states at the meeting. Therefore, your purpose at the Model UN is not to make the best presentation or to have "your" resolution win. Successful diplomacy is reaching a consensus on a resolution or proposal.

STEP #3: EVALUATION

Once the simulation is over, you should evaluate what you have learned from the experience. Here are some ways you might want to do this.

- What did the meeting accomplish from the point view of the country you represented?
- How closely did the Model UN simulate the real UN?

As your country's representative you would report to your Ministry of Foreign Affairs. Write such a report, include your evaluation of whether the resolution passed included points considered important by "your" country, whether they did not include such points but were nonetheless acceptable, or whether they were unacceptable. You may also add your suggestions on what actions your country might take to carry out the resolutions.

You and [your] colleagues should also discuss whether the simulation accurately reflected the situation in the world and in the UN today. An attempt should be made to explain what the main obstacles to agreements were and how such obstacles could have been overcome. Finally you might want to analyze how the real delegates at the UN addressed the same issue by looking at UN documents and resolutions on these issues.

From start to finish, the Model UN experience is an excellent way to learn about the United Nations and international relations. The world's issues and concerns actually come alive and you are at the center of it all. All it takes is dedication and enthusiasm to be a part of the ultimate diplomatic experience.

FOR FURTHER READING

- *Basic Facts about the United Nations.* This book provides a general introduction to the role and functions of the United Nations and its related agencies. Very helpful for students at secondary and higher levels. Copies should be ordered through UN Publications.
- *Everything You Always Wanted to Know about the United Nations.* A question and answer book, written for students at intermediate and secondary levels. For copies, write to the Public Inquiries Unit.
- Annotated preliminary list of items in the provisional agenda of the General Assembly. Issued every year prior to the beginning of the UN General Assembly. A must for all Model UN participants. For copies, write to UN Publications.
- *The Model UN Survival Kit.* Contains four publications, which provide comprehensive information for students and faculty participating in a Model UN. Issued annually by UNA-USA.
- *Model UN Security Council Kit.* A simulation package designed for use in the classroom and as a community program activity. A UNA-USA publication.

If you want to place an order for a UN publication listed above, please write to UN Publications, 2 UN Plaza, Room DC2–853, New York, NY 10017. Tel (212) 963–8302; Fax (212) 963–3489; e-mail: *publications@un.org*

For further inquiries, contact: Public Inquiries, GA-57, United Nations, NY 10017. Fax (212) 963–0071; e-mail: *inquiries@un.org*

For more information regarding Model UN conferences, please contact Lucia Rodriguez, Executive Director, Education and Model U.N., UNA-USA, 801 Second Avenue, 2nd Floor, New York, NY 10017, *modelun@unausa.org*

The sources for this book are available in libraries and on the Internet, except for the interviews that I conducted with diplomats, UN officials, scholars, and the like. Unless otherwise noted in the text, all quotations in the book come from these interviews.

For basic information about the UN system I relied heavily on the websites of the UN and its various organs, agencies, commissions, and programs. I also consulted the standard reference work by the UN, *Basic Facts about the United Nations* (New York: United Nations, 2000). Three US State Department reports, available on the State Department's website (*www.state.gov*), provided detailed information about important aspects of the UN. The first is the *US Report to the UN Counterterrorism Committee,* December 19, 2001, which describes the US government's actions taken in compliance with Security Council resolution 1373, against terrorism. The second is the *18th Annual Report on Voting Practices in the UN,* 2000, which analyzes how UN member states voted in comparison with US voting patterns. The third, *US Participation in the United Nations,* 2000, minutely describes the relationship of the US with all parts of the UN system, including financial assessments and contributions.

I used the United Nations Foundation's website to access UNWire, an electronic database that contains English-language news stories about the UN for about the past three years. The entries provide summaries and in

many cases full text of the articles. I have not referenced UNWire at each
point where I used it, but I acknowledge here that it was an invaluable tool.
In those instances where I quoted from or relied heavily on news stories,
these are noted below, by chapter, in the order in which they appear.

Chapter 3.   Newton Bowles, *Diplomacy of Hope*, provided information on
UNAMIR and General Romeo Dallaire in Rwanda. David Malone, in a letter
to the *Toronto Star*, Jan. 5, 2000, praised Annan for commissioning the
report on the Rwanda genocide.

Chapter 11.   US pleasure at the creation of the Office of Internal Oversight Services is expressed in the State Department report *US Participation
in the UN*, 2000, p. 119; it describes the results-based budgeting initiative on
p. 55. The GAO report, *United Nations Reform Initiatives Have Strengthened
Operations, But Overall Objectives Have Not Yet Been Achieved*, was published
in May 2000. Barbara Crossette's *New York Times* story on it (May 29) is presented in UNWire, May 31, 2000. The UNICEF quotation is from Reshma
Prakash's story in the *Earth Times*, Oct. 4, 1999. The mess at UNESCO is
presented in articles by Jon Henley of the *London Guardian*, Oct. 18 and 20,
1999; *Agence France-Presse*, Oct. 18, 1999; and Michael Binyon, *Times* (London), Aug. 8, 2000.

Chapter 12.   The "unprecedented act" by the US is described in the State
Department's report *US Participation in the UN*, 2000, pp. 112–13. The
debate about the outreach to the corporate world is in UNWire, summa-
rizing stories by Patricia Lumiell in the *Washington Times*, Mar. 13, 1999,
Joan Oleck in *Business Week*, Mar. 22, 1999; and in UNWire, Sept. 6, 2000.
The Adopt-A-Minefield program is described by Kevin Newman of ABC in
UNWire, Dec. 10, 1999.

Chapter 18.   The data on the proliferation of NGOs comes from Curtis
Runyan, *World Watch*, November/December 1999.

Chapter 21.   The report criticizing traditional development was issued by
the UNDP and is summarized in UNWire, Apr. 5, 2000.

Chapter 23.   See the story about Carol Bellamy by Barbara Crossette,
"From City Hall to the World's Stage," *New York Times*, Apr. 22, 2002.

Chapter 26.   Prime Minister Fini was quoted in *Corriere della Serra*, Mar.
15, 2002, translated by UNWire. The UNDCP's director of youth programs,
Stefano Berterami, was quoted in *Corriere della Serra*, Mar. 13, 2002, translated by UNWire.

The appendixes are drawn from the UN's Office of Public Inquiries.

UN and Other Websites

UN Homepage: *www.un.org*
UN Main Bodies: *www.un.org/aboutun/mainbodies.htm*
UN News: *www.un.org/news*
UN NGOs: *www.un.org/esa/coordination/ngo/*
UN Organization Website Locator: *www.unsystem.org*
UN Permanent Missions: *www.un.it*

Better World Campaign: *www.betterworldfund.org*
Center on International Cooperation: *www.cic.nyu.edu*
Council on Foreign Relations: *www.cfr.org*
Foreign Policy Association: *www.fpa.org*
International Crisis Group: *www.intl-crisis-group.org*
International Peace Academy: *www.ipacademy.org*
Model UN: *modelun@unausa.org*
UN Association of the United States: *www.unausa.org*
UN Foundation: *www.unfoundation.org*
UN Wire: *www.unwire.org*
US State Department: *www.state.gov*
World Affairs Councils of America: *www.worldaffairscouncils.org*

General

Annan, Kofi A. *We the Peoples: The Role of the United Nations in the 21st Century.* New York: United Nations, 2000.

Boutros-Ghali, B. *Unvanquished: A US-UN Saga.* New York: Random House, 1999.

Bowles, N. R. *The Diplomacy of Hope: The United Nations Since the Cold War.* Ottawa, Canada: United Nations Association in Canada, 2001.

Emmerij, L., and R. Jolly. *Ahead of the Curve?: UN Ideas and Global Challenges.* Bloomington: Indiana University Press, 2001.

Gorman, R. F. *Great Debates at the United Nations: An Encyclopedia of Fifty Key Issues, 1945–2000.* Westport, Conn.: Greenwood Publishing, 2001.

Hoopes, T. *FDR and the Creation of the United Nations.* New Haven: Yale University Press, 2000.

Luard, E. *The United Nations: How It Works and What It Does.* New York: St. Martin's Press, 1994.

Malone, David M., and Y. F. Khong, eds. *Unilateralism and U.S. Foreign Policy: International Perspectives.* Boulder, Colo.: Lynne Rienner Publishers, 2003.

Mingst, K. A., and M. P. Karns. *The United Nations in The Post–Cold War Era,* 2nd edition. Boulder, Colo.: Westview Press, 2000.

New Zealand Ministry of Foreign Affairs. *United Nations Handbook: 2001.* Wellington, New Zealand: New Zealand Ministry of Foreign Affairs and Trade, 2001.

Patrick, S., and S. Forman. *Multilateralism and US Foreign Policy: Ambivalent Engagement.* Boulder, Colo.: Lynne Rienner Publishers, 2002.

Ruggie, John Gerard, ed. *Constructing World Polity: Essays on International Institutionalization.* London: Routledge, 1998.

——. *Multilateralism Matters: The Theory and Praxis of an Institutional Form.* New York: Columbia University Press, 1993.

Russett, Bruce, ed. *The Once and Future Security Council.* New York: St. Martin's Press, 1997.

Sutterlin, James S. *The United Nations and the Maintenance of International Security: A Challenge to Be Met.* Westport, Conn.: Praeger, 1995.

Taylor, P., and A. J. R. Groom. *The United Nations at the Millennium: The Principal Organs.* New York: Continuum, 2000.

Tesner, S. *The United Nations and Business: A Partnership Recovered*. New York: Palgrave Macmillan, 2000. *http://unbisnet.un.org/newacq/toc/627403.pdf*

United Nations. *Basic Facts About the United Nations*. New York: United Nations, 2000.

US Department of State, *www.state.gov. US Participation in the UN, Yearly Reports*. 1990–2000.

———. *18th Annual Report on Voting Practices in the UN*, 2000.

———. *US Report to the UN Counterterrorism Committee*, December 19, 2001.

Weiss, T. G., and D. P. Forsythe. *The United Nations and Changing World Politics*. Boulder, Colo.: Westview Press, 2001.

Humanitarian Aid

Forman, S., and S. Patrick, eds. *Good Intentions: Pledges of Aid for Post-Conflict Recovery*. Boulder, Colo.: Lynne Rienner Publishers, 2000.

Helton, A. C. *The Price of Indifference: Refugees and Humanitarian Action in the New Century*. Oxford: Oxford University Press, 2002.

Shaw, D. J. *The UN World Food Programme and the Development of Food Aid*. New York: Palgrave Macmillan, 2001. *http://unbisnet.un.org/newacq/toc/666373.pdf*

Human Rights

Glendon, M. A. A. *World Made New: Eleanor Roosevelt and the Universal Declaration of Human Rights*. New York: Random House, 2001.

Human Rights Watch. *World Report: Human Rights Watch*. New York: Human Rights Watch, annual.

Power, S., and G. Allison. *Realizing Human Rights: Moving from Inspiration to Impact*. New York: St. Martin's Press, 2000.

Schoenberg, H. O. *The World Conference Against Racism: The Adoption and Repeal of the Z=R Resolution and the Implications for UN Reform*. Wayne, N.J.: Centre for United Nations Reform Education, 2001.

United Nations. *Human Rights Today: A United Nations Priority*. New York: United Nations, 1998.

Peace and Peacekeeping

Annan, Kofi A. *Prevention of Armed Conflict: Report of the Secretary-General.* New York: United Nations, 2002.

Barnett, M. *Eyewitness to a Genocide: The United Nations and Rwanda.* Ithaca, N.Y.: Cornell University Press, 2002.

Berdal, M., and D. Malone, eds. *Greed and Grievance: Economic Agendas in Civil Wars.* Boulder, Colo.: Lynne Rienner Publishers, 2000.

Boulden, J. *Peace Enforcement: The United Nations Experience in Congo, Somalia, and Bosnia.* New York: Praeger Publishing, 2001.

Chesterman, S. *East Timor in Transition: From Conflict Prevention to State-Building.* New York: International Peace Academy, 2001.

Cortright, D., and G. Lopez. *Sanctions and the Search for Security: Challenges to UN Action.* Boulder, Colo.: Lynne Rienner Publishers, 2002.

Cousens, E. M., and C. K. Cater. *Toward Peace in Bosnia: Implementing the Dayton Accords.* Boulder, Colo.: Lynne Rienner Publishers, 2001.

Cousens, E. M., and C. Kumar. *Peacebuilding as Politics: Cultivating Peace in Fragile Societies.* Boulder, Colo.: Lynne Rienner Publishers, 2001.

Durch, William J., ed. *The Evolution of UN Peacekeeping: Case Studies and Comparative Analysis.* New York: St. Martin's Press, 1993.

Haass, Richard N., ed. *Economic Sanctions and American Diplomacy.* New York: Council on Foreign Relations, 1998.

Hampson, F. O., and D. Malone. *From Reaction to Conflict Prevention: Opportunities for the UN System.* Boulder, Colo.: Lynne Rienner Publishers, 2002.

Hirsch, J., and R. Oakley. *Somalia & Operation Restore Hope: Reflections on Peacemaking & Peacekeeping.* Washington, D.C.: U.S. Institute of Peace Press, 1995.

International Development Research Centre. *The Responsibility to Protect: Report of the International Commission on Intervention and State Sovereignty.* Ottawa, Canada: International Development Research Centre, December 2001.

Jones, B. D. *Peacemaking in Rwanda: The Dynamics of Failure.* Boulder, Colo.: Lynne Rienner Publishers, 2001.

Khan, S. M. *The Shallow Graves of Rwanda.* London: I B Tauris & Co Ltd, 2001.

Luck, E. C. *Mixed Messages: American Politics and International Organization, 1919–1999.* Washington, D.C.: Brookings Institution Press, 1999.

Machel, G. *The Impact of the War on Children: A Review of Progress Since the 1996 United Nations Report on the Impact of Armed Conflict on Children.* New York: Palgrave Macmillan, 2001.

MacKinnon, M. G. *The Evolution of US Peacekeeping Policy Under Clinton: A Fairweather Friend?* London: Frank Cass & Co., 2000.

Martin, I. *Self-determination in East Timor: The United Nations, the Ballot, and the International Intervention.* Boulder, Colo.: Lynne Rienner Publishers, 2001.

Martin, L. *Democratic Commitments: Legislatures and International Co-operation.* Princeton, N.J.: Princeton University Press, 2000.

Ould-Ablallah, A. *Burundi on the Brink, 1993–95: A UN Special Envoy Reflects on Preventive Diplomacy.* Washington, D.C.: United States Institute of Peace, 2000.

Rikhye, I. *The Politics and Practice of United Nations Peacekeeping: Past, Present and Future.* Cornwallis, N.S.: Canadian Peacekeeping Press, 2000.

Shawcross, William. *Deliver Us from Evil: Peacekeepers, Warlords and World of Endless Conflict.* New York: Simon & Schuster, 2000.

United Nations. *An Agenda for Peace: Preventive Diplomacy, Peacemaking and Peacekeeping.* A/47/277-S/24111, 17 June 1992. Full text available at *http://www.un.org/Docs/SG/agpeace.html*

——. "Report of the Panel on United Nations Peace Operations," A/55/305, S/2000/809, 2000. Full text available at *http://www.un.org/peace/reports/peace_operations/*

——. *UN Peacekeeping: 50 Years (1948–1998).* New York: United Nations, 1998.

United Nations Association of the United States. *The Preparedness Gap: Making Peace Operations Work in the 21st Century: A Policy Report of the United Nations Association of the United States of America.* New York: United Nations Association of the United States, 2000.

CARDS MUST REMAIN IN THIS
POCKET AT ALL TIMES
a charge will be made for
lost or damaged cards

BERKELEY COLLEGE
WESTCHESTER CAMPUS LIBRARY
99 Church Street
White Plains, NY 10601

ALSO BY ANNE FRASIER

Hush

SLEEP TIGHT

Anne Frasier

AN ONYX BOOK

ONYX
Published by New American Library, a division of
Penguin Putnam Inc., 375 Hudson Street,
New York, New York 10014, U.S.A.
Penguin Books Ltd, 80 Strand,
London WC2R 0RL, England
Penguin Books Australia Ltd, 250 Camberwell Road,
Camberwell, Victoria 3124, Australia
Penguin Books Canada Ltd, 10 Alcorn Avenue,
Toronto, Ontario, Canada M4V 3B2
Penguin Books (N.Z.) Ltd, Cnr Rosedale and Airborne Roads,
Albany, Auckland 1310, New Zealand

Penguin Books Ltd, Registered Offices:
Harmondsworth, Middlesex, England

First published by Onyx, an imprint of New American Library,
a division of Penguin Putnam Inc.

First Printing, April 2003
10 9 8 7 6 5 4 3 2

 REGISTERED TRADEMARK—MARCA REGISTRADA

Printed in the United States of America

PUBLISHER'S NOTE
This is a work of fiction. Names, characters, places, and incidents either
are the product of the author's imagination or are used fictitiously, and
any resemblance to actual persons, living or dead, business establishments,
events, or locales is entirely coincidental.

for my father

Prologue

He hovered over the unmoving girl, deftly drawing a thick black line on her eyelid, curving it upward at the corner. That was followed by a smidgen of rouge to her colorless cheeks. Next came the lipstick, blood red in a gold metal tube.

He could hear his own rasping breath as he carefully applied the color to lips that had been soft and full but were now chapped and cracked. As carefully as a mortician he worked, and as he did he could feel his heart beating in his head.

He had the desire to kiss her and leaned closer.

Wake up, my princess. My little princess . . .

Her cracked lips opened under his. He felt her deep inhalation sucking the air from his lungs—a cat, trying to steal his breath. He pulled back to see her staring silently at him, her pupils dilated and glassy from drugs and the dark, windowless basement where she'd spent the last two weeks. Had she learned her lesson? Would she finally act like a lady? Would she ask him how his day had been? Would she ask him what he wanted for supper? Later, would she sit on the living room floor near his feet while he listened to music? Would she bring him something to drink, with perhaps a slice of cake, and rub his temples until his headache stopped, saying in the most soothing of voices, "There, there"?

"You're mine now," he told her. "You may as well get used to it."

She continued to stare, and he briefly wondered if there was something wrong with her, if she wasn't quite right in the head.

Unlike the first girl, he felt that this one could be changed. At seventeen, her knowledge of the world was skewed by mall society and MTV. But she was coming around.

Control was the key.

He'd tried taking away her Britney Spears, which he'd put on REPEAT and played to keep her occupied while he was at work, but she'd been *glad* when it was finally gone. Evidently even she had a saturation point.

TV would have helped in the training department, but unfortunately he didn't have cable. He could have cut off her music videos if she refused to do what she was told. Depriving someone of what she loved was an effective way to bring about desired behavior. Reward and deprivation. A very good method, to his mind.

Instead, he'd had to resort to drugging her and locking her away. Not a bad method. Seclusion. Isolation. It was how brainwashing worked. He'd read all about Patty Hearst, about how they kept her locked in a closet and in no time she was a new person named Tania.

It was called personality transformation.

Pretty soon she's waiting to hear your footsteps, your voice. Pretty soon she's looking *forward* to your return, your visit. Pretty soon you're the most important person in her life. Because you are her entire world. You are the one who feeds her and gives her what everyone needs and craves: human companionship. People were funny that way.

"Nobody is looking for you," he told her. Leaving her wrists bound, he coaxed her from the stale, damp room with its dusty rodent skeletons and spiderwebs that caught in her hair.

"Nobody misses you," he told her. "I'm all you have."

He shoved her down until she was sitting on the wooden steps, collapsing like a doll in a strapless red satin dress. Her skin was transparent. He could see the meandering blue veins running beneath it. Her knees were bony and sharp. Had she lost weight? It looked like she had. Quite a bit of weight now that he thought about it. She would have to start eating more. He didn't like skinny girls.

He fussed with her blond hair. Gone was its original vitality. It hung lank and lifeless on either side of her face. It didn't appear to be nearly so light as it had been when he'd picked her up. In fact, the roots were suspiciously dark.

"Do you bleach your hair?" he asked with sudden, deep dread.

"N-no."

"You're not lying, are you?"

"N-no. Of course not. L-lemon juice."

He had to lean close to hear.

"S-sometimes, in the summer, I put l-lemon juice on it."

"Why are the roots so dark?"

"They always get th-that way when my hair needs to be washed."

Satisfied with her answers, he adjusted the f-stop and lifted the camera that hung around his neck until he found her in the viewfinder. He focused, then pushed the button. The shutter clicked, the flash

briefly illuminating the gloom of the stairs. Not
enough for her eyes to respond. Her pupils, once the
film was developed, would be huge and flat. Like a
doll's.

Black and white.

He never shot anything but black and white.

He paused, but continued to watch her through the
camera. "Tell me that you love me."

She blinked and abruptly seemed to come to life.

Now, he thought with trembling anticipation. Now
she would say what he needed to hear.

"I hate you." Her words rang out against the cata-
comb walls.

He gasped and dropped the camera; it banged
against his stomach, caught and suspended by the
strap around his neck.

He bent closer and placed a hand on her bare knee,
feeling a tremor running through her body. He looked
deep into her eyes—and saw fear. "Repeat that," he
dared.

She made a sound deep in her throat. *Splat*—something wet hit his cheek.

Spit.

She'd spit in his face.

The thankless bitch! The thankless little bitch!

Rage roared through his veins until he thought his
skin would crack, until he thought his eyeballs might
pop from his head. He grabbed her by both arms and
jerked her to her feet. "I've been working my ass off
every day, out punching the clock, and this is the
thanks I get?"

He'd wanted her to be his ingenue. They could have
been so right together. They could have been so
happy.

He wrapped his hands around her neck. "I slave

over you, trying to teach you how to be a woman! You bitch!" He shook her. "You spoiled, spoiled bitch!"

He squeezed and he squeezed, and when she went limp he kept on squeezing until he was certain she would never insult him again.

She was still watching him with accusation in her eyes even after he placed her carefully in the trunk.

Chapter 1

There had been a time when the FBI thought it needed to update its image. During that lapse of sanity, younger people like Agent Mary Cantrell were recruited. She began her career at the Academy in the Behavioral Science Unit, but was later transferred to the National Center for Analysis of Violent Crime.

FBI director Nelson Roberts had worried that her age would be a handicap. What he hadn't known was that Mary Cantrell was an old soul, wise beyond her years. While most violent crime agents eventually reached their psychological limit, Cantrell was able to take whatever was thrown at her without flinching. The most horrendous murderers left her unscathed.

Even Cantrell's partner, Anthony Spence, sometimes exhibited signs of a meltdown. There had been rumors of heavy drinking, and then, six months ago, his wife left him. Not an uncommon story among agents, especially if both parties weren't in the Bureau. It was hard to mix two worlds. A guy couldn't be expected to deal with the deaths of innocents by day and take his wife to the latest romantic comedy at night. You couldn't just shut it off. The human mind didn't work that way.

Unless you were Mary Cantrell.

Roberts had taken time to familiarize himself with
her confidential bio, a bio that was a part of the agent
application process and psychiatric evaluation. He
knew she'd survived a childhood tragedy that had left
her scarred in ways she probably wasn't even aware
of. Ironic, but that very tragedy was probably what
made her the agent she was today.

She stood in front of him, waiting to receive new
orders. She was dressed in a caramel-colored suit, her
straight mahogany hair cut short. Pale skin, dark cir-
cles under her eyes, shadows beneath her cheekbones
belied the tough, no-nonsense image she normally
projected. It had been a month since she'd sustained
a gunshot wound to the shoulder, and he could still
detect lines in her face. Pain did that. Left its mark.

After receiving an injury like Cantrell's, most people would have jumped at the offer of a desk job.
They would have at least taken a couple of months
off. The day after the shooting, Cantrell had been on
the phone, asking that someone bring her case files to
the hospital, acting as if her injury were nothing more
than a minor inconvenience.

That wasn't normal. He and Agent Spence were
worried about her.

"I have an assignment for you," Roberts announced.

It was in Cantrell's hometown, and since she refused
to take the temporary leave the Bureau recommended
after suffering a gunshot wound in the field, he and
Spence thought a trip home would be the next best
thing.

"In Minneapolis," he said, watching for her reaction, not getting one. "Two young women have been
murdered in a period of eight weeks. One was the
daughter of a good friend of the governor of Minnesota. So far an unequivocal connection between the

murders hasn't been established, and they don't know if they're looking for one killer or two."

"I'm not sure I could do any better than the local FBI. Minneapolis has an excellent field office."

"I agree, but their profiler retired four months ago, and they haven't replaced him. Budget cuts. Cheaper for them to call us."

"What about the child poisonings in Denver and the murders in Texas?"

"Agent Spence can handle those."

"With all due respect, sir, working in my hometown might be a bit distracting to me. Wouldn't it be better to send someone else?"

Her reluctance was obvious, and Roberts wondered if returning her to the site of her childhood tragedy was a good idea. "I've never known you to allow yourself to be distracted. And it's common sense to send an agent to a city he or she is familiar with. Everything's already arranged. You're to meet with Agent Elliot Senatra in Minneapolis day after tomorrow. Pack with the intention of staying awhile. They're requesting that you remain until the case is close to being solved or until there are no more leads."

As he leaned back in his chair, she continued to stand straight before him. "Don't you have family there?" he finally asked, although he knew the answer.

"My mother and sister."

"Minneapolis . . . ," he said reflectively. "My brother was in the Olympic speed-skating trials there years ago. Coldest damn place I'd ever been. I seem to recall something about a famous sculpture. . . ."

"The *Spoonbridge and Cherry*?"

"That's it. Isn't there a strange story about it?"

"Not that I know of, sir."

He sensed she was hedging. "Hmmm. I could have sworn . . . Oh, well."

His phone rang. Reaching for the receiver, he dismissed her.

Mary Cantrell exited the building and slipped into her tan Camry. The interior smelled like french fries. On the passenger side floor was a rumpled fast-food bag: evidence of a meal she'd eaten . . . when? Two days ago. The molded plastic holder was overloaded with stacked, insulated cups, each containing an inch of forgotten sludge. She didn't usually leave as much as a receipt in her car, but ever since the shooting she seemed to have become a slob.

She pulled out of the parking lot, rolling down her window a couple of inches as she headed in the direction of the National Center for Analysis of Violent Crime, located a few miles from Headquarters and the Academy.

At the NCAVC building, she found her partner in his office, lolling in front of a computer.

She and Anthony Spence had begun their acquaintance while training together at the Academy. One day he'd made some chauvinistic remark about women and their physical limitations, and she'd never forgotten it. Months later she was able to admit to herself that if he hadn't been so good-looking, she probably would have given him another chance. Beauty could sometimes be a handicap.

By some odd string of events, they were thrown together on a child abduction case. Soon afterwards, their "temporary" partnership became permanent because, as Director Roberts had put it, they were "a perfect team."

"I'm being sent to Minneapolis," she announced.

Anthony shut off the monitor and turned around, hands on the arms of his swivel chair. He wore a white dress shirt and loosened tie. His hair was straight and dark brown, his eyes a gray that sometimes looked black. He was handsome, and women of all ages noticed him.

"But I have the feeling you already knew about that," she added, wondering why she needed to hear him admit to his involvement in the decision to send her home. "I have the feeling you're behind this whole thing. Am I right?"

"Minneapolis . . . Don't they have some famous sculpture there?" he asked, ignoring her question.

"Among other things." A flash of anger began to smolder. Anthony had a way of doing that to her. "I didn't come here to discuss art."

But Anthony appeared to be in one of his obnoxious, teasing moods. "The spoon and cherry. I think I heard that people have sex in it. Is that right?"

"It's just a rumor."

He dropped the attitude. "Come on, Mary. Can't you let me return the favor?" He picked up a pen and began tapping it against the desktop. *Tap, tap, tap. Tap, tap, tap.* "For chrissake." He paused. Then, without making eye contact he continued in a quiet voice. "You put your life in jeopardy. You shouldn't have done that."

He was talking about a botched raid on a child pornography ring. She and Anthony had been sent to Boston at the last minute—a move that caused deep resentment within the local departments.

It wasn't the FBI's job to go into the warehouse with guns blazing, but when they radioed for the SWAT team to take over, nobody came. Later the head of the squad reported that he never received the call, but both Anthony and Mary knew better. They were being put in their place.

By the time she and Anthony made the decision to abort, it was too late. Bullets were flying. When Mary saw her partner in danger, she stepped from the safety of a brick wall and shouted a warning, her weapon drawn.

The shooter got her instead of Anthony.

As she lay bleeding on the cement floor, the rhythmic clatter of the SWAT team rang out as they finally arrived, boots charging past her. And then Anthony was there, his shaking hands covered in her blood, frantically shouting for a trauma team, all of his cool gone.

They weren't going to allow him in the ambulance, but Anthony shoved a medic aside and jumped in at the last second as tires spun over rain-washed cobblestones. Mary wished he hadn't made it because all the way to the hospital he kept asking, "What the hell were you thinking?" He repeated those words now.

"Is that what this is about?" she demanded. "Are you ashamed that a woman saved your life?"

"If that's what you want to believe of me, go ahead."

This was familiar ground. One thing they did well together was argue. But for once words deserted her and she felt herself dissolving. Ever since the shooting, she'd been having these strange moments of emotional weakness. She hated the thought of coming undone in front of him.

This is not a good time to go home. I'm not strong enough.

An image flashed in her mind. Her best friend, murdered, lying in a pile of leaves, her face white, eyes empty. She hadn't thought about Fiona in years. The memory had been assigned to a cold case file in her mind. It was over.

"Are you okay?"

I'm afraid to go home.

She and Anthony had spent the last three years tracking down serial killers, pedophiles, and child abductors, and she was afraid to go home. It was weird how certain things, certain personal horrors, never faded.

"I'm fine."

If he noticed she was lying, he didn't show it. "When you're finished with the case, take some time off. Relax. Forget about this place. If you need me, call."

"We've been good together," she said, acknowledging something she'd never admitted before. "You know that, don't you?"

He nodded.

She'd been arguing with him for years, and now, at this moment, she had no idea why. It seemed unimportant—childish, really. She was suddenly extremely glad she'd saved his life, even if it meant getting shot.

"What's with the smile?"

She almost told him, but she knew her present state of mind was fragile, and she didn't want to give him ammunition to use against her later. "I'm wondering how you'll survive without me," she said.

An odd, unreadable expression came over his face. "The same way I survive with you."

He reached into the trunk and dragged out a heavy bundle of black plastic. Heaving it over his shoulder, his knees sagging under the weight, he carried it to the dilapidated shed.

His interest in horticulture had started when he was a kid. He liked to make things do what they hadn't been designed by nature to do. He'd made tulips bloom in the middle of January. He'd forced crocus to blossom in the fall. From there, he'd moved on to bonsai—the art of restraint. Then he'd discovered grafting. With grafting, he did more than toy with nature. He could make a weak tree strong. He could even create a completely new breed of tree, vine, or shrub. For an artist—and he was an artist—it was the ultimate satisfaction. That's why his foray into finding the right woman had been such a disappointment. He demanded perfection from himself and others, and he hated to admit to failure.

He thought of the girls who hadn't worked out as returned merchandise. If he'd been required to fill out a return form, he would have marked the box that said, "Wasn't what I expected." Everything else would have fit: size, style, quality, price. All of those would have been okay. Because from the outside, they'd appeared to be exactly what he had in mind.

Funny thing was, once they were gone, he'd missed them for a while. When he went in the house, he could still feel their presence, still smell them. They'd been like one of his migraines. He hated the headaches when he was in the middle of one, but rather enjoyed the heaviness that came afterward, rather enjoyed pampering himself.

He wasn't an idiot. He hadn't gone into this blindly. He'd known they'd require modification, but he hadn't realized it would be so hard. When he'd come across the first one at the nature preserve, he thought she was the one, but she hadn't worked out. Number two had come from the mall. In retrospect, he could see that getting a girl from a mall was a bad idea.

He'd never have been able to turn either of them into the woman he'd wanted them to be. No amount of grafting or forcing could have changed them enough.

So he'd returned them. That's all.

Taken them back to where he'd found them.

I'd like a refund, please.

He'd kept them both for almost three weeks. An adequate length of time. To have returned them sooner would have meant playing a much too active role in today's disposable society. So he'd had to start the quest for the perfect mate all over again, because once he got something in his head, he couldn't let it go. And now he was working on breaking in a new one. Third time's the charm, people always said. But was he fooling himself? Looking for something that didn't exist? Everyone had a perfect mate somewhere, didn't they? And you couldn't find her by sitting at home doing nothing. A guy had to make his life happen.

But a disturbing pattern was emerging. Number three—What was her name? Justine? Yeah, that was it. Justine was beginning to get on his nerves. He wasn't sure why. She wasn't anything like number one or two, he'd made certain of that. In fact, the new one had come with him willingly. (Could she be a slut?)

At a bar he'd asked, "Wanna come to my place?"

"Sure." Grabbed her purse.

Too easy. Way too easy. Of course, she didn't much like it when he told her she wasn't *leaving* his house.

He spent the afternoon grafting rosebushes. A dull blade guaranteed failure, so he liked a sharpened grafting knife. He made the cut to the green stem in one slice, starting at the base and moving to the tip in one single motion. So it wouldn't dry out, he stored the sliced scion in his mouth as he went to work on the rootstock. Then he quickly and dexterously attached the cuts of scion and rootstock, wrapping them with budding tape, stretching the tape almost to the breaking point.

Number three didn't much like it when he took her into the basement and stuffed her in the refrigerator, where she was at the moment.

He was quite proud of his new restraining device. It was an old refrigerator that hadn't worked in years. He'd cut a notch for her neck, tucked her in there when she was bad, and left the freezer door hanging open so he could see her face, talk to her if he felt like it.

Put her in a pumpkin shell and there he kept her very well.

He could tell her heart wasn't in it. She was just going through the motions, like an actress. (Or a slut?) The little actress was actually what he'd started calling her. And now he spent a large part of his day thinking about killing her, chopping her up, using her for compost. He actually began to dream about cutting off her fingers and grafting grapevines to her stubs. As the vines grew, he tied her to an arbor where her feet shot out roots that dug deeply into the ground. Fruit came on thick and lush, growing between her thighs.

He picked the fruit and ate it, blood dripping down his chin while she smiled lovingly at him from the wooden trellis.

Chapter 2

The 757 came in low over the scattered suburbs and blue, reflecting lakes that stretched to the horizon. In the far distance stood the IDS Center. In front of it, the Foshay Tower. As she stared out the window at the beauty of Minneapolis, Mary's stomach clenched. Instead of feeling a glow of sentimental attachment upon seeing the skyline, she experienced something that felt uncomfortably like fear.

She loved her hometown. Whenever someone asked where she was from, she would tell them Minneapolis even though she'd been born in Pennsylvania.

When Mary was seven and Gillian four, they moved to the cozy Minneapolis neighborhood of Lynwood Park, where they quickly fell under the spell of a charming, two-story Tudor. The girls had their own space, upstairs, in tree-shadowed rooms with green-trimmed windows. On hot summer days, they read books their mother recommended, such as *Silent Spring* and *Anne Frank: The Diary of a Young Girl*. In the house, in the yard, the sisters played together for hours.

Then Fiona Portman moved in, across the street and up three houses.

Fiona was someone everybody noticed, especially

boys and grown men. Even at ten years old, the beauty she would become stared out from a child's face. She had shiny black hair that fell from a white center part, a perfect contrast to her pale skin and thick-lashed blue eyes. The moving van had hardly pulled away when Mary and Fiona began their friendship, whispering, clinging to each other, and laughing so hard they fell into a tangled heap. From that day on, they were inseparable. People would see them walking down the sidewalk, and even though the girls looked nothing alike, neighbors were apt to say with a chuckle, "Here come the twins. Joined at the hip."

Looking back, Mary was always amazed and mystified by the strength of their union, by the power of a youthful friendship that was frightening and inexplicable in its steadfast unity.

Mary would often find her volatile younger sister staring at them from a distance, arms crossed at her chest, acting jealous and abandoned and left out. At the beginning, Mary would ask Gillian to join them, but she always refused, and eventually Mary quit asking.

Fiona vanished on October 29, the day of her sixteenth birthday. Even now, if Mary saw someone cutting cake with fluffy white frosting, she got a freeze-frame image in her head of Fiona's body, half-covered by dead leaves.

The birthday party was under way at Fiona's house. Mrs. Portman, arriving with the tidy presence of Betty Crocker, presented a white birthday cake to the gathering of classmates. When Fiona didn't show up to blow out the candles, Mrs. Portman shrugged and fed the cake to the hungry kids. An hour later, when Fiona still hadn't shown up, her mother began to worry.

The Portmans' backyard rolled down a gentle slope

to a dark, secret world guarded by ancient oak and hickory trees. When younger, Mary and Gillian, and later Fiona, had played in those damp, mossy, mysterious woods, often remaining until the mosquitoes and lightning bugs came out and their mothers called them home.

The house was searched from top to bottom, bottom to top. Then the teenagers, boys and girls, went running into the woods, calling Fiona's name. Mary laughed and spun around addressing the trees, telling her friend to come out, quit hiding—the joke was over and everybody was going home.

"We're going to open your presents if you don't show up!" Mary threatened. "We're going to take them back home with us!"

The oak leaves were deep enough to disguise the terrain. Mary would think she was on flat ground, but then she would step into a hole and sink to her knees. Sometimes tangled tree roots tripped her and sent her sprawling.

She thought about the place where she and Fiona used to play, a tree house her father had made. Briefly disoriented, she finally found the tree. It looked different, not so welcoming.

"Fiona!"

Mary circled the tree, looking upward into the spiraling branches. A heavy, black, snaking root snagged her foot, pulling her down into another pile of leaves. Mary put out her hands to catch herself, one palm connecting with something strange, something solid yet soft.

There, almost under her, was the body of her best friend.

Mary stared, still hoping it was a joke, a trick.

Fake blood. Almost Halloween.

Fake blood, fake blood, fake blood.

Fiona was lying on her stomach, her face in profile, her blue lips parted, one eye open, unfocused, staring at nothing, at no one. Dried blood clung to her nostrils, to the side of her face, fanning out like thick black cat whiskers.

And Mary knew, with a certainty that would become the driving force in her life, with the certainty that evil was the polar opposite of goodness and that it could lurk in the most innocent of places, that Fiona was dead.

The airplane wheels hit the ground, bringing Mary back to the present. The jet engines reversed, and hydraulic brakes engaged. The craft bobbed in a heavy, ungainly way, awkward now that it was no longer airborne.

The FASTEN SEAT BELTS sign went off. Metal seat belts clicked, and passengers began moving about, gathering up their belongings, preparing to disembark.

People often accused Blythe Cantrell of having found the secret of eternal youth. Maybe it was Mary's mother's penchant for constant change that kept her young, and the fact that she was a lifelong learner, always immersing herself in something new. There is so much to experience, she said.

Her hair was a different color and style from the last time Mary had seen her, gone from a red bob to something shorter and multicolored in shades from white to brown. She wore a gauzy skirt that fell to her knees in bright colors, her toenails painted red in brown leather sandals. She was adorable, and she looked about twenty-eight.

If her life had gone differently, Mary might have flown to Minneapolis unannounced so she could surprise her mother. But the practical Mary had called first. She'd told Blythe she'd rent a car, but Blythe had insisted upon picking up her daughter at the airport.

It was a strange thing, hugging a mother who was much smaller than her child. Mary let herself be pulled into her arms, careful of her injured shoulder, which was aching.

Together they took the escalator to the baggage area. In the congestion of people, they made small talk.

"They've added a new terminal, more parking, more places to eat," her mother said.

"I've always liked this airport." But then, Mary liked all airports. Airports brought you back, but better than that, they took you away. She'd spent a large part of her life in airports and on planes. Always moving on to the next case.

They gathered her luggage, one large bag and one small, and headed for parking. A few minutes later they were exiting the ramp and getting on 494.

A major problem with the Twin Cities, Mary remembered, was getting from point A to point B, and then finding a place to park once you finally arrived. Everybody traveled by car because they were either too cool for buses or knew the buses became mired in traffic like everything else.

"They're finally putting in the light rail," Blythe said, jockeying for position so she could hit the next exit ramp.

"They've been talking about it since the sixties."

"Eventually, the tracks will extend from Northfield to Saint Cloud."

Mary figured they'd all be dead by the time that happened, but she didn't want to dampen her mother's enthusiasm.

It was said that Minnesota had two seasons: winter

and construction. Even though it was early October, roadwork was still in full swing, and they had to take detour after detour. At a stoplight, a bumper sticker on a nearby car brought back a memory. "Remember the summer we went to Disney World?" Mary asked.

"I didn't want to go," Blythe said with a smile.

She hadn't approved of the place, calling it a "giant, sterile, artificial wasteland of the mind and soul," but Gillian had begged and begged, and one summer Blythe had finally broken down and taken them to Florida. Until then their vacations had been planned to invoke thought and provide mind expansion. To Blythe's chagrin, the trip to Disney World had been wonderful, and she'd later admitted that sometimes it was good simply to enjoy the moment.

Their street ended in a cul-de-sac—there was no way to avoid going past Fiona's house.

"Do the Portmans still live there?" Mary asked.

"They divorced, but Abigail won't sell the place." Blythe pulled the car into the driveway, cutting the engine. The river birch that Mary and Gillian had planted when they were in Girl Scouts had grown as tall as the house.

Except for a neglect that betrayed the absence of a man and the lack of things men did—like keeping the window trim painted and maple seeds from sprouting in the soffits—the house looked much like everyone else's on the block, all stucco-sided Tudors. But when you stepped inside, you entered the world of Blythe Cantrell. A flower child who'd refused to become a yuppie, Blythe spent her time creating her own unique brand of pottery, which she fired in a studio that used to be the garage. During the snow-bright, bitterly cold Minnesota winters, Mary and Gillian had spent time in the studio with their mother, slicing air bubbles out of clay while Blythe spun her foot-driven potter's wheel.

Inside the house were plants that reached the ceiling, oriental rugs spread over hardwood floors, antique furniture, and weird lamps that cast muted orange light. On the walls hung various pieces of art that Blythe had purchased over the years from struggling artist friends. The eclectic disarray flowed into the kitchen, where Blythe poured some iced tea and produced a plate of scones. She put everything on a tray and carried it to the little bistro table in front of the sliding doors that overlooked the lush, overgrown backyard and deck.

Her daughter, her tall, beautiful, stoic daughter, stood looking out at the bird feeders. Her face was pale, and it seemed as if she might be in pain, but Blythe knew if she asked, Mary would never admit to such a weakness.

Blythe's husband, a war correspondent, had been killed while covering an uprising in South Africa. Mary was eleven at the time, and had adored her father. It had been hard on them all, but they'd come out of it eventually. Then Fiona was killed. Her death marked the beginning of an awful change in Mary. A change that intensified six months later, when Gillian began writing and visiting Gavin Hitchcock—the imprisoned man who'd killed Mary's friend.

Why had Gillian done it? Blythe still wondered. Out of spite? To get Mary's attention? Or did Gillian, who had known Hitchcock since grade school and had befriended him since junior high, really believe her childhood friend was innocent?

It was hard to remember what Mary had been like before Fiona's death. Blythe often had to think hard, to pull the old Mary to the front of her mind so she could see her the way she used to be.

When Mary had announced her plans to become an FBI agent, Blythe had rejoiced because at least she'd finally wanted *something.* It meant she was looking toward her future once more. But as years passed, Blythe wondered if it had really been the best thing for Mary. Sometimes feeding an obsession only led to self-destruction.

Mary eased out of her dark, knee-length coat and hung it over the back of the chair. Under it she wore a short-sleeved white blouse and a black leather shoulder holster and gun.

"Is something wrong with your arm?" Blythe asked, noticing how carefully her daughter moved.

"I injured it during a raid," Mary said a little too casually as she sat down. "A stupid mistake."

"Why didn't you tell me?"

"It wasn't anything."

Blythe suspected her injury was more serious than she let on. That's the way Mary was—quiet and secretive.

Blythe had visited her daughter in Virginia several times, yet no matter how often Blythe saw her with a weapon strapped to her tall frame, she could never get used to it. She'd never allowed guns in her house, never allowed her girls to even *pretend* to have a gun.

Blythe had always thought of Mary as strong and capable, fearless. But at the moment she looked exhausted and vulnerable.

"Is it so awful being here?" Blythe blurted out. It hurt to know her daughter didn't want to come home. "Good things happened here. A lot more good than bad. Don't ruin those memories for yourself."

Mary looked up. "It's hard," she said quietly.

Blythe was surprised by her admission and felt her eyes begin to tear. She blinked rapidly. "I know. I just want you to be happy."

"I'm not sure I'm the kind of person who can be happy."

Blythe pulled her tea nearer and began drawing patterns in the condensation on the glass. "You used to be happy. When you were little you were happy. Always laughing. I think you have the capability to be happy again if you allow yourself the luxury."

"It's the curse of violent crime agents. We spend so much time around death and evil. Pretty soon everything is bad."

"Have you ever thought of doing something else?"

"Please. Don't start that again."

Blythe glanced at the clock. It was later than she'd thought. She reached across the table and squeezed her daughter's hand. "Mary, Gillian's coming over." She braced herself for an unpleasant reaction.

Mary stared at her in disbelief. "She isn't living here, is she?" she asked, demonstrating the first real emotion she'd shown since stepping off the plane.

"No, she has an apartment in Dinkytown."

Mary dropped back against her chair in relief. "What about Hitchcock?"

"When he got out of prison, Gillian helped him find a place in St. Paul. The Midway area, I believe."

Mary nodded and pursed her lips. "No surprise there." She leaned forward, her gaze suddenly intense. "You know he did it, don't you? You know he killed Fiona."

"Of course he did. I think deep down, Gillian must know it, too. She doesn't talk about him much. It upsets me. I don't like her hanging around somebody like that. I've always tried to be open-minded and embrace everyone, but . . . a killer? . . . I can't do it."

"When will she be here?"

Blythe looked up at the clock again. "Soon. You have to talk to her, sweetheart. She's your sister."

Mary reached for her coat, as if to get something out of the pocket, then stopped.

"Still smoking?" Blythe asked.

"No, but I'm seriously thinking of taking it up again."

Chapter 3

Gillian stood staring at the red front door of her mother's house, afraid to go in.

Mary was home.

Gillian turned and took two steps toward her car, then stopped, curbing the impulse to get the hell out of there. Detective Wakefield was always telling her to face her fears head-on. She was an adult now. A cop now. There were things she had to tell Mary—things her sister wasn't going to like.

Gillian took a deep breath and pushed open the door. "Hi, Mom! It's me!" Even though her heart was hammering, the greeting was her usual.

"In here!" Blythe shouted from the direction of the kitchen.

She found her mother loading the dishwasher. "She's outside."

Gillian followed Bythe's glance. Her older sister was standing in the backyard, hands in her coat pockets, studying the fall flowers and vines that lined a wooden fence.

"How does she seem?"

"Different. A little different, I think."

Gillian knew she was the reason Mary hadn't been home in five years. That knowledge sometimes made her feel physically ill. There hadn't been any huge fight. No confrontation. Just an initial aloofness that Gillian had figured Mary would eventually get over. Time passed. Holidays came and went. Mary didn't return.

Frightened as she was to finally be coming face-to-face with her sister, she also saw it as an opportunity to begin to patch things up. Gillian opened the sliding glass door and stepped outside. The day had been warm for October, but the sun was going down, and the air suddenly smelled like fall.

She and Mary had always loved fall, especially Halloween. They liked dressing up and making people try to figure out who they were, their costumes reflecting Blythe's influence.

"Let me guess," a neighbor would say, bending down to their eye level. "A couple of hobos?"

"No! Walt Whitman and Henry David Thoreau!"

The following year—"Guess who I am!" Mary had shrieked.

"A nurse? A mental patient?"

"No! Sylvia Plath!"

"Oh, what a cute bunny."

"I'm not a bunny, I'm Gloria Steinem!"

The trick or treating eventually evolved to staying home and passing out treats—homemade trail mix or granola squares.

Now fall always reminded Gillian of the day Fiona died.

Heart hammering, Gillian spoke. "Hi, Mary."

Her sister turned around. She'd always considered Mary beautiful, but now she was struck by an added maturity and serenity. Dark hair, dark eyes. Mary took after their Irish-Italian father, Gillian after the light, petite, Swedish Blythe. Mary would always be beautiful, bordering on exotic; Gillian was often described as "cute."

"Mom's flower garden is flourishing as usual," Mary said, as if Gillian had just returned after stepping out to get a paper. "These mums are spectacular."

Gillian came closer. "I think they're a new variety. Called Star something. You know how crazy Mom is about mums."

"Mum's mums."

An old joke. A childhood joke. Gillian smiled. "Yeah."

"Still have Birdie?" Mary asked, referring to the parrot Gillian had had since grade school.

"Yeah. He's as obnoxious as ever."

The trip down memory lane didn't last. "Mom said you wanted to talk." Mary had quickly reverted from sister to cool professional, as if instantly regretting the brief, shared moment. "That you had something to tell me."

Gillian was shaking inside, and she struggled to hide her nervousness. "You may have heard that I got a job with the Bureau of Criminal Apprehension." A state agency, the BCA had been established over seventy years ago to assist the police in complex investigations.

"You're kidding." Mary made no attempt to hide her surprise, looking as if she equated Gillian's position to that of a fox guarding the henhouse.

Why was her having a job at the BCA so hard to believe? Mary's reaction to her announcement gave Gillian's nervousness a jolt and rapidly replaced fear with irritation. Her next words, the words she'd been so afraid to utter, were delivered with a slight taunt. "I've been assigned to the case you're working on."

Mary frowned. "Analyzing evidence?" she asked, as

if struggling to imagine her sibling in such a setting. She still didn't have a clue how Gillian's news was going to impact her.

"No." Pause for effect. "I'm a field agent now."

Mary grew very still as she processed the information.

Here it comes, Gillian thought.

"You shouldn't be involved in this case," Mary told her with authority. "You're going to have to turn it down for personal reasons."

She was *so* controlling. Blythe kept saying how much Mary had changed, but this was the same bossy sister Gillian knew from childhood. "Because of *you*?" she asked.

"Because of Gavin Hitchcock," Mary said, her voice rising.

"Gavin? What does Gavin have to do with it?"

"Oh, come on. It must have crossed your mind. He gets out of prison and suddenly teenage girls are being killed."

"Is that why you took this assignment?" she said heatedly. "Because of Gavin Hitchcock?"

That hadn't taken long, Mary thought. So much for a meeting of mature adults. Gillian hadn't changed. She was equipped with sibling radar that directed her to the quickest way to get under Mary's skin.

"You've always been blind when it comes to Hitchcock," Mary said.

Gavin Hitchcock was sentenced to twenty years with the possibility of parole after nine. He should have gotten life. He should have been put to death, but unfortunately Minnesota didn't have the death penalty.

He'd been in prison six months when Gillian took it upon herself to write to him. That was bad enough, but then she began visiting Hitchcock. At a time when

Mary needed the love and support of her sister, Gillian had chosen to bestow her sympathy on the man who had killed Fiona. On the heels of her death, it was a double blow from which Mary had never recovered.

"He killed my best friend," she said.

"I don't think Gavin did it."

"I can't believe you still take his side!" How in the hell could she be a cop if she blindly sympathized with every killer out there? "What about his fingerprints? His semen? Wake up, Gillian. For chrissake, he was found staggering down the street with Fiona's blood on his hands! He all but confessed!"

"He was young. Seventeen. If he *did* do it, it was an accident."

"Ed Kemper was fifteen when he shot and killed both his grandparents. He got out of prison at age twenty-one. After that, he went on to kill eight women before he finally turned himself in—not out of remorse or regret, but because he wasn't getting the publicity he thought his horrific murders deserved."

"Gavin's *changed*. The prison psychiatrist said he isn't a threat to anyone."

Mary could have cited more case blunders where killers had been released with the support and backing of social workers and psychiatrists. Why? Because the idealists wanted to believe that basically people were good, and that bad "habits" could be changed.

"You're giving Hitchcock qualities he doesn't possess. You feel sorry for him, but he doesn't deserve your sympathy or your time."

"Do you feel any sympathy for anyone anymore? I don't think so. I don't think you're capable of sympathy."

"I feel sympathy, but I'm more selective with it than you are," Mary said, her voice biting. "I happen to save it for the victim, not the son of a bitch committing the crime." The tension in her body was making her shoulder ache. It was bad enough when strangers and madmen stabbed you in the heart, but your own family? Your own sister?

"You betrayed me." There. It was out. Words she'd never spoken to Gillian.

"I'm sorry you see it that way, but I did what I had to do. I did what was right for me."

"What made you want to become a cop?" Mary really wanted to know. From where she stood, it made no sense at all. She knew the idea was ludicrous, but it almost seemed like another way for Gillian to get to her.

"I have my reasons," she said evasively.

Mary had had more than enough of their reunion. She felt ill. She needed to get out, get away. "I'm going for a walk." Without looking in Gillian's direction, she cut across the yard, slipped out the gate, and began striding rapidly down the sidewalk, hands in her pockets, the hem of her dark coat slapping against her knees.

She ran across the street, ducking under the shadows of an elm tree. She wanted to keep running, but after a couple of minutes she forced herself to slow to a brisk walk. She hadn't yet recovered enough from her injury to take up jogging again, and the repetitious jarring motion was making her shoulder ache even more. The pain was actually a comfort, something to concentrate on, something to take her mind off a different kind of pain.

Why had she come here? she wondered with fresh dismay. Why hadn't she simply refused the case?

She heard the sound of shifting gears; then a small red car rounded the corner, came roaring down the street and pulled up beside her. Gillian leaned across the passenger seat and swung the door open. "They just found another body."

The interior of the car was an isolated pod of stony silence as they rushed to the crime scene. Gillian seemed to be entirely focused on driving like a New York City cabdriver, while Mary tried to avoid looking at her. Even though traffic was heavy, they made it to the Lake Harriet Rose Garden in fifteen minutes.

Mary had been there a few times. It was near the lake, with a bird sanctuary, boardwalks that spanned marshes, and secluded trails winding through thick stands of trees.

Police cars, silent with lights flashing, were parked at odd angles, as if the drivers had rushed in and jumped from the vehicles before they'd stopped. Yellow crime-scene tape had been strung around light poles and trees. Several officers were dealing with crowd control. Others were interviewing bystanders and possible witnesses, getting what information they could. A large, frazzled-looking man in a dark suit was barking out orders.

Gillian approached him. "Detective Wakefield?"

He swung around. "Gillian? Can't talk now. Remember, you aren't here in an official capacity tonight, just an observer. Don't forget slippers and an escort."

"Thanks."

The body had been found inside the bird sanctuary, near a blacktop jogging and walking path, about a quarter of a mile from the parking lot and lake. After sliding paper slippers over their shoes, the sisters were escorted to the crime scene by a young female officer with a high-powered regulation flashlight. They followed a paved path lined with yellow marking flags to an area that was ankle deep in leaves.

Night crime scenes were surreal. Generators hummed and high-powered lights illuminated the area until it was bleached and shadowless. In contrast, just past the circle of intensity, a person could drop off the face of the earth into a pit of blackness. Just as surreal for Mary was being at a Minneapolis crime scene with her sister beside her. Was this Gillian's first homicide? Mary wondered. How would someone who used to get light-headed at the sight of blood react to violent death?

The body belonged to a woman. She was lying face-down, partially covered in leaves. . . .

She'd found a body just like that before. The years evaporated, and Mary was once again staring at Fiona's lifeless body. *"She's dead, Mrs. Portman! She's dead!"*

Mary wasn't sure how long she stood there before realizing Gillian was talking and that she was being introduced to Agent Elliot Senatra, her local FBI contact. She hoped the confusion of the surroundings covered any strangeness in her reaction as she made the transition from past to present.

"I'd shake, but as you can see—" Agent Senatra held up a latexed hand. He was nice-looking, black, about thirty-five, with small wire glasses and a gold earring. He was dressed in an expensive suit, and Mary guessed he'd been pulled from a fancy dinner or an evening on the town.

"That's perfectly all right," Mary said. "Please—don't let us distract you."

Someone called to him. He gave them a half-wave and moved away.

Cameras were flashing; a video camera was running. Evidence was being collected. Finally the body was rolled onto a transparent plastic sheet—and a collective gasp was heard.

No eyes.

She had no eyes, just dry empty sockets looking blankly at them.

"Were the last victim's eyes removed?" Mary whispered to her sister.

Gillian leaned close, appearing unafraid and unfazed. She'd obviously been in this situation before. *"Yes."*

Here it was, their first nonhostile conversation in five years, and they were discussing missing eyeballs. But the role of FBI agent was second nature to Mary. She fell into it with ease and found comfort in its familiarity. And like the professional she was, she pushed all remnants of her fight with Gillian from her mind to focus on the scene before them. "And the other body?"

"We don't know. The coroner's report said she'd been in the woods approximately ten days before being found. What hadn't rotted was eaten by animals."

"Eyes are a delicacy in the scavenger world."

"What's the deal with her hands?" The question came from a young male police officer.

Mary pulled her gaze from the empty sockets to track down the partially nude body. The woman's right arm, stiff with rigor mortis, was bent at an odd angle, the hand—now a claw—gripping the air. Attached with green tape to the tip of each finger were what looked like small branches. Mary leaned closer until she recognized the spiny shape of a familiar leaf. She straightened. "Rose stems." She looked at her sister. Gillian was staring at the clawed hand, her mouth a small *O*. Somebody whistled. Somebody else let out a nervous laugh.

"We'll get out of here so you'll have more room to move around," Mary said, addressing Agent Senatra.

Senatra, along with almost everyone else, was still staring at the hand. He looked up slowly and spotted Mary. Recognition dawned. "Detective Wakefield's gonna try to rush this through and get an autopsy done tonight," he said. "Hopefully I'll have some information when we meet." He pointed at her with a gloved hand. "FBI building. Nine o'clock tomorrow. You need directions?"

"I know where it is."

An officer guided them back to the parking lot; then they were on their own.

"That was weird as hell," Gillian said, sounding slightly out of breath as they both removed and tossed their slippers into a nearby container before heading toward the car. "Have you ever seen anything like it?"

"Never. Nothing that even comes close." Mary couldn't remember when she'd last been surprised by a murder scene, but she'd been surprised tonight.

"What do you think it means?"

"I'm not certain, but it looks to me like he was grafting her."

"Grafting?"

"Trying to turn her into something else, something she could never be."

Their earlier conflict had been pushed to the background. They were two officers trying to make sense of possible clues.

"Graft her into what? A *plant*?" Gillian sounded unconvinced. "A *rosebush*?"

"Have you read *Symbolic Death* by Ivy Dunlap?" Mary had worked with Ivy on a Chicago serial killer case. Since then the two of them had become good friends. "In it, she theorizes that oftentimes killings are symbolic, that the manner and style in which the killing takes place has a deep, personal meaning for the killer."

"And what do roses symbolize?"

"Love. Beauty. Loyalty. Perfection. Femininity. Any number of things depending upon one's viewpoint. It's too early for speculation—I haven't seen any information on the other two victims—but in this instance the simplified message is telling us that the woman didn't live up to his expectations."

"It seems like a twisted fairy tale."

"Or twisted romance."

Chapter 4

It took twenty minutes to get from Lynwood Park to the FBI office in downtown Minneapolis. Mary circled the block in her rental car—a green Ford Taurus—and ended up in a lot between Marquette and Nicollet.

Years ago, the local division of the FBI had moved across the street and up the block to an ultramodern facility they shared with other businesses. Mary walked through the revolving doors of the skyscraper and took the escalator to the second floor. At the security desk, she flipped open her FBI photo ID. That garnered her access to a silent elevator that carried her to the eleventh floor, where she was directed down a carpeted hallway to Agent Senatra's office.

He shook her hand this time. The earring, which wasn't approved FBI dress, was gone. He'd traded his expensive suit for a more conservative gray.

The office was military tidy, with filing cabinets, a TV, and a VCR in the corner and maps of Minnesota and the Twin Cities on the wall. On a shelf was a framed photo of Agent Senatra and a laughing little girl.

"My daughter," he said, sitting down at his desk and motioning for Mary to take the seat across from him.

"She's beautiful." Fortunately, Mary could be honest in her response—something that wasn't always possible.

"She just turned eight and is a handful." He adjusted his burgundy tie. "Got any kids?"

"No," she said in a way that always sounded like an apology. It was good to make small talk before getting down to business, but the subject of parenting was something Mary knew very little about.

"We work closely with the Minneapolis Police Department's Homicide Unit. I hope you don't mind, but I've taken the liberty of arranging for you to meet privately with Detective Wakefield after your briefing here."

Wakefield. The detective Gillian had spoken to the night before. "That's fine."

They were lucky. In some cities, the police didn't work closely with the FBI. In some cities, if a crime occurred, the FBI might not know about it until after the media chewed it up and spit it out.

"Here's what we've got."

Senatra put an eight-by-ten color photo of a dead, eyeless girl on the desk. "Four weeks ago seventeen-year-old April Ellison was kidnapped from the Mall of America. No leads. Nobody saw anything. A lot of people speculated that she'd run away. One week ago, her body showed up. Where? In one of the mall elevators. At that point, we treated it as a single, isolated incident. Five days before that, a body was found in a Minneapolis nature park." He put down another photo, this of an unrecognizable decayed body. "Turned out to be an eighteen-year-old named Bambi Scott."

"Bambi?"

"I know. You can imagine how that played out with the investigative team. Finding a dead Bambi in the woods."

"No doubt," she said dryly.

"Because of the decomposition of the body, we have even fewer leads with this victim than with the previous one."

"Any similarities other than age?"

"Here are high school photos of both victims."

He pulled out eight-by-tens of two smiling girls, both blond. "If the perpetrator is the same in both cases, then I'm guessing he likes 'em young and he likes 'em blond."

"Had the Scott girl been reported missing?"

"No. Her parents were divorced, and her mother had custody. As soon as she turned eighteen she left home. The mother said she hadn't seen or heard from her in two months, but didn't think it was strange."

"Where was she living?"

"In a house where transients hang out. Nobody there seemed to know much about her. A couple of druggies remembered her, but said she basically stuck to herself and didn't stay there all the time. Said they never saw her with anybody strange, but everybody there seemed a little strange to me."

"We need to try to determine whether she was abducted from the park where her body was found."

"We've been trying to piece together a timeline, but keep running into dead ends."

"I see three possibilities: She visited the park and was killed on the spot—which would signify that her murder was unrelated to the other earlier case. She was abducted somewhere else, killed, and dumped at the park. Again, probably unrelated to the other. Or, she visited the park, was abducted by our Romeo, then killed and returned to the same place."

"I asked her mother if she liked the outdoors," Elliot said. "The woman didn't know." He pursed his

lips in disgust. "That's what I call parental involvement."

"What about the father?"

"Hadn't seen Bambi since she was seven."

He handed her two folders, one labeled APRIL EL-
LISON, the other BAMBI SCOTT. "When the governor got
after us about getting a profiler in here, I really didn't
think there was a connection between these two cases.
But now, with this new body showing up last night—"

"Was an autopsy performed?"

"Yeah, but we won't have any lab results back yet."

She shuffled through the Ellison paperwork, searching for the medical examiner's report. "Any drugs
show up in the lab tests?"

"She tested positive for morphine and pheno-
barbital."

"Pharmaceuticals."

"Here's the only videotape we have of the guy."
He popped a tape in the VCR and pushed the PLAY
button.

It took a moment for Mary to realize the camera
was located in an elevator. The door opened. A man
in a ski mask dragged a bundle inside, then punched
a number on the control panel before exiting the
elevator.

Senatra shut off the tape. "Some computer whiz at
the BCA has been working on enhancements, trying
to find something, but so far she hasn't had any luck."

The phone rang, and Senatra answered it. The con-
versation was brief. "She'll be there in ten minutes."
He hung up. "Detective Wakefield," he explained.
"He's ready to meet with you."

The Minneapolis Police Department was located in
the historic City Hall just up Third Avenue. Mary

walked the few blocks, taking the Fifth Street entrance
where the statue of Hubert H. Humphrey stood. Then
it was down a hall of fossil-embedded marble to Homicide Detective John Wakefield's office.

Wakefield was around fifty, stocky, with hair that
was as much gray as black. His suit was wrinkled, his
eyes puffy—evidence of a sleepless night.

"I understand you're Gillian Cantrell's sister. She
was assigned to Homicide a couple of months ago."
They both sat down, Wakefield behind his desk. "We do
that sometimes," he said, adjusting a jacket that looked
uncomfortably snug. "Borrow people from the BCA."
He had a rural Minnesota accent she hadn't picked up
on the previous evening. "Gillian's a bit impulsive, but
I think she might be detective material."

Apparently Wakefield didn't know what a task he'd
set for himself, Mary thought. Gillian's gullibility and
attraction to strays could prove an insurmountable
handicap.

He checked his watch and got down to business.
"Okay, here's the deal. You already have all the information on the first two homicides, so what I'm going
to tell you is exclusively about the body found last
night near the rose garden."

He handed her several photos of the murdered
woman, some taken at the scene, some at the morgue.
The morgue views were all close-ups of the woman's
face and the clawed, grafted hand.

"We've already got a problem. The eyes of the mall
victim were removed with almost surgical precision.
The latest victim's eyes were gouged or ripped out."

"Did the media know about the victim's eyes?"
Mary asked.

"Oh, hell yes," Wakefield said with disgust. "The
old couple that found her told everybody. But that's

not all that's different about the third body. This one was blond like the other two, but she was older. We don't have a positive ID yet, but the coroner puts her at about twenty-two. So we have three murders, all of blond women, but nothing else about them is the same. One left in the woods, one in the mall where she was kidnapped, one in a park. Two had their eyes removed, but removed differently—which immediately warns of a copycat. Two were left facedown, the third we don't know about. Animals can really make a mess out of a crime scene."

Mary lined up three eight-by-tens of each crime scene, all taken before the bodies had been touched. "The dress April Ellison was wearing. Did it belong to her?" The fabric looked old. Maybe vintage.

"I don't know. Here, let me have my assistant check on that." He picked up the phone and told his assistant to call April Ellison's parents.

When he hung up, Mary continued to follow her thought processes. "What about the body that was found last night? She's partially nude, but she's wearing something. Did you attend the autopsy?"

"Yeah." He rubbed his forehead. "They sent her clothes to the BCA for analysis. It was a dress."

"A sexy dress, like the one in this photo?" Mary pointed to the shot of the girl in the elevator.

"It appeared to be a plain, ordinary dress, but it was hard to tell because it was torn up. We'll have photos of everything by this evening. I'll get copies to you. Now," he said, inching forward, "what do you make of the hands?" He pulled out a photo of the clawed hand, minus the taped branches. "Both hands were mutilated, the nails removed and the branches slipped into the quick."

Mary elaborated on the theory she'd discussed with

Gillian. "The woman wasn't what he wanted, so he tried to mold her into something else. When that didn't work, he killed her."

Disgust, but not surprise, registered on his face. "It's one of the weirdest things I've ever seen."

"Any suspects?"

"I had the research department do some cross-referencing, and we came up with over a hundred possibilities." He handed her a stack of papers. Names, mug shots, and offenses that spanned years. Some of the rap sheets took up several pages. She riffled through names, aliases, faces, fingerprints, body art, and distinguishing physical characteristics until she came to Gavin Hitchcock. His life of crime had begun as petty thefts and minor offenses to finally culminate in murder.

"How long will it take you to come up with a profile?" he asked.

"About a week."

"A week?" He gave her a pained look. "I'm not sure we can wait a week."

"It can't be rushed. It takes a few days to study the information, then put a profile together. After that, I send it to Virginia, where it's gone over by a team of behaviorists."

"I was hoping you could come up with something quickly so we can narrow down the list of suspects."

He expected too much. The FBI had spent years building and training profilers, but the Behavioral Science Unit was no longer getting the funding and attention it had received in the past. Time had proved that while profiles could provide a useful adjunct to a case, they were by no means infallible. For a brief period, the FBI had even attempted to phase out the word *profiler* from the FBI vocabulary, but it was too late. It was already too deeply ingrained in the public mind.

"I'll do what I can, but in the meantime I would suggest you begin interviewing suspects," Mary said.

"Already got people on that. Sent half the list to the BCA, the other half to our department. Officers started the interviews this morning. We're also running everything through VICAP, CJIS, and are in contact with Wisconsin, South Dakota, North Dakota, and Iowa, trying to cross-reference information. Since every department is run independently, that can take a helluva long time."

"I know," she said with sympathy.

Wakefield dug into his pocket, pulled out a roll of antacid tablets, and began popping them into his mouth. He was sweating profusely, and it wasn't even hot in the room. It occurred to Mary that he looked more than just tired. He looked ill.

"Can I get you something?" Mary asked. "A drink of water, maybe?"

"Oh, Christ." He began opening desk drawers. "I've got some around here somewhere." He pulled out a bottle of water. "You know what's really bugging me? I have a daughter. A seventeen-year-old daughter. With blond hair." He suddenly stopped. "Oh, hell. I'm sorry."

"That's okay."

He put up his hands. "No, it's not. I want you to focus on this case. My personal situation has nothing to do with it."

"You'd be surprised how many times this kind of thing happens to me." She didn't have a degree in psychology, but because her job dealt with behavioral science, people often felt the need to confess their anxieties to her.

"Valerian root." He held up a brown bottle. "It's supposed to calm your nerves. I've been taking it for a month, and I don't think it does shit."

"Have you tried yoga?" she asked.

He let out a derisive snort. "You've gotta be kidding."

"I know agents who swear by it."

"FBI agents?" he asked in disbelief.

She nodded.

"You try it?"

"Me? No, but I've cut down on caffeine and quit smoking."

"If I cut down on caffeine, I wouldn't be able to function. Okay, I gotta go. Have another meeting to get to with Chief of Homicide. I'll get a copy of all pertinent information to Agent Senatra by this afternoon, and I'll be calling a meeting with all the departments when we get everything organized."

Mary gathered up the photos and papers and added them to the ones already in her briefcase. "I'll put together an unofficial profile in order to prioritize the suspects. That should give you enough to work with until I hear back from Headquarters." She stood and extended her hand.

He took it. "The governor personally asked for you," he said. "Not because you're a hometown girl, but because he knew you were one of the best. Here in Minnesota, we're proud of the work you've done."

"Thank you."

He was looking at her as if he had no doubt about her ability to solve the case given enough time. She had a decent track record—he was right about that. But then the FBI didn't advertise unsolved cases.

Chapter 5

Before concentrating on the profile, Mary had to talk to Gavin Hitchcock. She'd never been one to allow herself to jump to conclusions, always waiting for the evidence to point the way. Now she needed to know if there was any basis for suspecting him of these new murders—or were her emotions skewing her judgment?

The automobile repair shop where Hitchcock worked was on University Avenue in an area of St. Paul known as Midway.

She soon spotted a hand-painted sign that said ABE'S REPAIR. Parking spaces on University Avenue were at a premium, so Mary pulled her rental car into the alley behind the shop. To the left of an open door was a lot with weeds poking between broken-down cars that had been towed and abandoned years ago. Those carcasses were sprinkled with washing machines and mowers, stacks of tires, gas cans, broken beer bottles, and bed frames.

Mary inched the car to the side of the alley, trying to avoid the broken glass while leaving room for another vehicle to squeeze past if necessary. She got out, locking up with the remote. Up four bowed, rotten steps, she hesitated and checked to feel the reassurance of her gun beneath her jacket, irritated and slightly alarmed by the way her hand shook and her heart hammered.

This would be the first time she'd come face-to-face with Hitchcock since the murder trial during which she'd recounted finding her friend's dead body. All the while she was on the witness stand, Hitchcock, dressed in an orange jumpsuit, leg shackles, and handcuffs, had stared emotionlessly at her from his seat next to the state-appointed defense attorney.

Despite that, she was able to speak clearly and effectively, describing her years of close friendship with Fiona, describing exactly how the young girl had looked when she'd tripped over her body that day in the woods. The way the flies had gathered at the corners of her sightless eyes, the way bees buzzed around her mouth and crawled out her nose.

Mary hadn't called the repair shop first. She wanted her visit to take Hitchcock by surprise so he wouldn't have a mental script prepared.

Inside the door stood an L-shaped counter. Along one wall was a row of chairs where two people waited, flipping mindlessly through greasy magazines while a fluorescent light hummed and flickered above them.

"Can I help you?" the man behind the counter asked in a heavily accented voice. His crisply ironed blue shirt said JESUS MONTOYA, MANAGER under a motor oil logo. When she told him she needed to speak to Gavin Hitchcock, he opened the office door and stepped out on a wooden landing that overlooked the work bay, yelling to a man under a raised Cadillac. Then he hurried back into the office, where the phone was ringing.

Mary waited on the landing, one hand gripping the wooden rail. She watched as Hitchcock put down his tools and walked toward her, stopping at the bottom of the stairs.

"Yeah?"

He was seventeen when she'd last seen him, which now made him twenty-six or -seven. He'd been thin and wiry, a lanky teenager with stringy brown hair hanging in his empty eyes. Now he was an adult, a man. His hair was still stringy, but much shorter, and his eyes were no longer empty—they were cold and bitter.

As he stood staring up at her, ineffectually trying to wipe the grease from his hands with a red rag, she thought of how those same hands had bludgeoned a young girl to death.

Even though her position at the top of the landing put him at a physical disadvantage and should have lent a subconscious intimidation to the scene, he didn't seem to notice.

"I'm Mary Cantrell," she announced, feeling herself mentally retreating. Her name didn't elicit any response of recognition from him. "Gillian Cantrell's sister."

"So?" He glanced up and behind her, toward the office. Through the glass, the shop manager was still on the phone.

"I want to talk to you."

"I'm busy." His voice was deep and emotionless.

It had been up to the jury to decide whether or not he would be charged with premeditated murder. . . .

"Was it your intention to inflict bodily harm upon Fiona Portman?"

"No."

"Did you meet with Fiona Portman with the specific purpose of killing her?"

"No."

"*Can you describe for the jury what happened that afternoon of October twenty-ninth?*"

"*I'd been drinking.*"

"*That wasn't uncommon for you, was it? To spend the day drinking?*"

"*Not really.*"

"*Isn't it true that you'd been kicked out of school for fighting?*"

"*Yeah.*"

"*Isn't it true you'd been in the woods that day?*"

"I want to ask you a few questions," Mary now said.

"I can't talk."

"It won't take long."

"Gillian got me this job," he said. "I don't want to lose it."

He turned away, heading toward the car on the lift. His job wasn't the issue here—he was only using it to avoid her. And mentioning her sister was a handy dig, a way of getting to Mary at the same time.

She followed.

"Are you a cop?" he asked, picking up a heavy wrench. "I think I remember Gillian saying you were a cop."

"FBI."

Behind them someone banged on the office window. She turned to see the manager gesturing wildly, his face contorted.

"Get out of here," Hitchcock said. "No customers allowed in the bay area." He stared at her another moment. "The hydraulic could slip. The car could come down and crush you."

"And you don't want that to happen?"

"I don't care if you get killed, I just don't want to lose my job."

Right. She checked her watch. "When do you take a break?"

"I don't."

"What time do you get off work?"

"When I'm done."

Two hours later Mary was sitting in her car, which she'd maneuvered into a better position. From her new vantage point, she could see both the front and back areas of the auto repair shop.

It was getting dark by the time she spotted Hitchcock leaving the building. She pulled up beside him as he made his way along the sidewalk, hands in the pockets of his dirty jeans, walking in the direction of the bus stop.

She reached across the seat and opened the passenger door. "Get in."

He stopped and looked at her.

"Get in the car," she repeated. "I'll give you a ride to wherever you're going."

He opened the door wider and dropped into the passenger seat. She sped away from the curb before he could change his mind.

"Aren't you afraid to have me sitting beside you? When I could just reach over like this—?"

He put his hand to her throat, pressing his fingers against her trachea—just hard enough to make her gasp and pull back, a survival instinct.

She knocked his hand away. Intense, blinding pain knifed through her injured shoulder. She swerved to the right and slammed on the brakes, stopping in a parking space.

He laughed at the loss of control he'd caused. "A lot of women don't want anything to do with a guy who's been in prison. Except for your sister."

The pain in her shoulder didn't subside, and she visualized ripped muscles and nerves. She tried to push her physical discomfort aside to focus on the man

next to her. The son of a bitch was baiting her, toying
with her. He smelled like grease, and oil, and hot
metal. She imagined him behind heavy iron bars
painted with layer upon layer of institutional green.

"You've probably heard about the three murders
that have recently taken place in the area." A good
agent never jumped in with the prime question. A
good agent went for the slow build, getting the suspect
to relax, gaining confidence—then hit him. She didn't
have the luxury of that kind of strategy. Hitchcock
could bolt at any second.

He laughed and shifted in his seat, getting more
comfortable. "I've wanted to tell you something for a
long time. Your friend, Fiona. She liked to portray
herself as a goody-goody, somebody as pure as a nun,
but let me tell you, she was no nun. But then maybe
you knew that. Maybe you were whoring it up, too."

He was trying to throw her off, distract her from
the real reason she'd come.

"Are you like your sister?" He reached over and
put a hand on her bare knee. His fingers were rough
and hot. "Do you get off on guys that've been in
prison?"

A drop of sweat trickled down her forehead, catching on an eyebrow. It took an amazing amount of
willpower to keep from pulling out her gun.

"Get your hand off me."

He removed it, but not before giving her knee a
little caress. "Behavioral Science, right?"

How much had Gillian told him about her?

"That means you hunt down serial killers, right?"
When she didn't answer, he repeated his question.
"Right?"

"Yes."

"Child molesters? How about child molesters?"

"Those too."

"I have a theory about why people like you go into such disturbing fields," he said. "Want to hear it?"

She shrugged. "Sure."

"Because you're obsessed with death."

She wasn't going to let some killer psychoanalyze her. "If I'm obsessed, it's with finding the people who are causing death."

"No, you're obsessed with death itself. You have to see it, have to be around it."

"Is that the way *you* feel? Is that how you've come to this theory? Because you've killed?"

"I'm not talking about me. I'm talking about you. How old were you when you found your friend's dead body?"

He was talking about it so calmly, as if it were something he'd read about, not participated in.

She wanted to look away, but she forced herself to keep her eyes on him. "Seventeen."

"An impressionable age, wouldn't you say? A time when everything can turn upside down, when good can suddenly be bad, and bad good."

Not wanting to miss the opportunity to keep him going, she allowed herself to be pulled into the conversation. "Seventeen is the age you were when you killed Fiona Portman," she said.

"I think that once somebody sees death, feels death, sees death's emptiness, they want more. Suddenly life's biggest mystery is an even bigger mystery. And that mystery is something *you* were a part of and want to be a part of again."

Was this his twisted way of telling her he'd killed the three girls? Was it a sick plea for help? "Are you seeing a psychiatrist?" she asked, hoping she wouldn't lose him by introducing a new topic.

"Not since I got out of prison. I don't need one. Haven't you heard? I'm a new man."

"You should be under psychiatric care."

"I've had enough of shrinks."

"Do you have urges to see dead bodies?" she asked carefully.

"Right now I'm imagining what you'd look like dead."

"Is that a threat?"

"How many dead people have you seen in your life? Other than Fiona Portman? I'll bet you've seen a lot."

"Too many."

"How many?"

"Over a hundred."

"I'll bet you like that, don't you?"

"Of course not."

"Oh, come on. Why don't you admit that when you aren't around death, you aren't whole? You aren't complete?"

His intelligence and the skill with which he manipulated the conversation surprised her.

"Did you have anything to do with the recent murders?" Her stomach knotted at the question.

His attitude suddenly changed. "Fuck you." He was through with the game.

She'd been in a lot of dangerous situations in the course of her career, and had prided herself on remaining unflappable. This was different. After joining the FBI, she'd become tough and hard and fearless. But returning to your past had a way of screwing things up. Had a way of poking holes in that new person until pretty soon you were leaking like a sieve.

The old Mary was sitting on the seat next to Gavin Hitchcock. The old frightened, weak, young, vulnerable Mary.

"I've heard enough of your bullshit." Without another word, he got out and walked away, his shoulders hunched in his saggy, brown corduroy jacket.

Gavin Hitchcock sat down on the bus stop bench. He'd missed the 6:50, thanks to the woman pulling away from the curb and disappearing down University. He usually drove to work, but he'd run out of gas money and had been forced to take public transportation. Everything was fucked.

Mary Cantrell. He remembered her from the trial. Remembered her white face, her big eyes. Sitting there stone-faced, describing everything so graphically that a juror puked and another one fainted. He'd always figured it was the passionless eloquence of her testimony that won the jury over and lost him all sympathy.

He'd been intrigued with her just now because she was Gillian's sister. Otherwise he wouldn't have bothered talking to her, and he certainly wouldn't have gotten in her car.

His bus finally showed up. It pulled to the curb, and he got on.

It wasn't crowded. It was just him, a few homeless people, and the crazy lady who worked the night shift at a nursing home preparing food for the next day. She never quit talking. Now she was engaged in a one-sided conversation with the bus driver, who'd driven the route long enough to know not to give her any encouragement by answering.

She finally gave up and moved to another seat, close to a homeless guy who was on his way to nowhere.

She was going on about the road construction, and how the buses were always behind, and how she had to leave home an hour early because yesterday she was late for work. Blah, blah, blah.

"Hey, lady," Gavin said, raising his voice to be heard above the shifting gears.

She looked at him, eyes alert and eager now that she had a participating audience.

"Why don't you shut the fuck up?"

She was instantly defensive. "Why don't *you* shut the fuck up?"

"Nobody wants to hear the shit that's pourin' from your mouth."

"I ain't got no shit in my mouth," she said, hands at her waist, head bobbing.

"Somebody should put you out of your misery."

She let out a short, one-syllable scream. Kind of like a single beep from a car alarm.

"What the hell's going on?" the driver asked, looking at Gavin in the rearview mirror.

"Oh, come on. Haven't you had the same thought? Listening to her blabbin' on and on and on. Haven't you at least wished she'd trip and hit her fucking head on the curb when she's getting off the bus? How 'bout you?" he asked, motioning to a man sitting huddled in the corner with a stack of old newspapers. "Haven't you wished somebody'd just make the bitch shut up?"

The little man shook his head.

The driver pulled to the side of the street. Gavin noted it wasn't a scheduled stop.

The doors opened. "Get out," the driver said.

"There you go, lady," Gavin said with satisfaction.

"I'm talking to you. Get out before I call the police."

The woman let out a high-pitched laugh and clapped her hands in a frenzy of excitement.

Gavin pushed himself up and lunged out the door.

He shouldn't have opened his mouth.

Another thought hit him: It would never have happened if the Cantrell woman hadn't antagonized him.

Behind him, the bus's hydraulics hissed as it pulled away.

His head was beginning to throb. He put a hand to his temple. He could feel the artery pulsing. With each pulse, his headache got worse.

Had to get home.

He staggered down the sidewalk, feeling the change coming, the darkness that would drag him down and smother him.

Keep going. Only a few more blocks. A few more steps.

He watched his boots slide across the cement, toes scraping, catching on cracks.

He could feel his muscles hardening. His penis became engorged, growing as huge as an arm, throwing him off balance.

Walk. Walk.

When he was little, his grandmother used to talk him out of his fits. She would distract him.

"Look at the pretty flowers. Look at the tree. See how the leaves are whispering? Telling you to breathe gently, telling you to breathe softly. Grandma's here. Grandma's here to catch you. Grandma's here."

His grandmother died when he was ten. Murdered in her own kitchen while two apple pies cooled in the window. Gavin had found her there, on the kitchen floor, her throat slit with a butcher knife. He'd tried to run, tried to turn and scream, but the blackness had come over him with the thickness and weight of a heavy blanket.

See the flowers. See the pretty flowers.

He was found unconscious, with blood on his hands, lying next to his dead grandmother.

Walk, walk.

It was coming. Coming fast.

His muscles began to contract, his penis shrank. He

tried to run, but couldn't. There was his house. He
could see it, just past the two-story brick apartment
building.

Run, run, run.

I can't.

You can. You can do anything.

He moved faster. Crossing the last street, he fumbled in his pocket, pulling out a set of keys.

Keys to the Kingdom. Keys to the Kingdom.

Around back. Past the shed and the flower garden.
To the kitchen.

He unlocked the door and fell inside.

Gavin came awake with a jolt. Disoriented, he finally realized he was lying in the dark on the kitchen
floor. He dragged himself to a sitting position. His hair
was soaked and plastered to his head, his clothes were
drenched. He put a tentative finger to the corner of
his mouth. Dried blood. He could feel his tongue,
thick and swollen and sore.

In his confusion, his first thought was to call Gillian.
But she'd told him not to call her again. When he was
in prison, she wrote to him. She even came to see him.
And when he got out, she was there waiting for him.

He thought she loved him. He thought she'd been
waiting for him all that time. He thought he would go
to her place, and they would live together, maybe even
get married. But when he told her how much he loved
her, she got weird, pushing him away.

"Gavin, *no,*" she'd said as he clung to her, struggling to pull her close, struggling to kiss her. He could
see unease in her eyes, and he suddenly felt like
crying.

"I thought you loved me," he said.

"I do love you. But not that way. I love you as
a friend."

Friend? Oh, shit. Oh, fuck. No, no, NO!

His future, the future he'd dreamed about all the years he'd been in prison, dissolved before his eyes.

A friend.

It was so hard. Hard to keep going. He just wanted it to end. He didn't want to get cancer or anything; he just wanted it to be like a pulled plug. Over. He just wanted it over.

He shoved himself to his feet and turned on the light. Opening the nearest cupboard, he pulled out a bottle of whiskey, unscrewed the cap, and took a long swallow. He spent the next several minutes drinking and leaning against the counter, waiting to stabilize. He wished to hell he had something better than alcohol, but he hadn't been out of jail long enough to make any drug connections.

He hadn't had any attacks in a long time. It had been so long that he'd quit taking medicine, but now he'd had two attacks in one week.

The visit from Gillian's sister had brought on this second one. That was obvious.

Finally steady enough to walk, he made his way down the hall to the bathroom, where he took a piss.

The house had belonged to an old lady who'd spent the last ten years bedridden. The place had been so run-down and had smelled so bad that nobody wanted to rent it. An ex-con and convicted murderer didn't have much chance of finding a place to live or getting a job, but Gillian knew some people, and she'd helped him.

The place still looked like an old-lady house—with floral wallpaper and shit. Some of her clothes were still hanging in the closet. Jars of canned food lined the basement shelves. He'd originally planned to give the place a coat of paint, but he didn't give a shit anymore. He'd managed to hang some of his black-

and-white photos before deep depression had washed over him. He had more photos. Lots more . . .

He didn't have much furniture—he kept his clothes in cardboard boxes under a bed that was shoved into the corner of the room. Bad feng shui, he sometimes mockingly told himself, but what the hell? The house and everything about it was a reflection of his soul.

In the living room, he pushed around some open boxes until he came to the one with pictures of apples on it. He dug down past phone books and porn magazines until he found the bundle of envelopes—letters from Gillian.

He took them into the kitchen. He pulled out a plastic lighter.

One by one, he held up the envelopes and let the fire lick one corner until the paper burst into flame. He dropped them in the sink where they curled and burned, continuing until there was nothing left but a pile of ashes.

Love, Gillian.

Gillian. She was the perfect woman. He was afraid he'd never find anyone as perfect as her again.

Chapter 6

Gillian stood in the observation room of the Minneapolis Police Station. Beside her was a student intern named Ben Collins. From the second Ben had stepped into the BCA building for his first day on the job, the poor kid had been labeled a lost cause.

His hair was dyed jet black and combed down over his forehead. His fingernails were usually painted purple. If he'd gone to see a band the night before, he could almost always be counted on to have remnants of eyeliner lingering between his lashes. But it wasn't his unconventional looks that made people reluctant to work with him. He talked. All the time. And not about anything remotely related to what was going on. Three people had taken him for a test drive, and none of them had been able to stand him for more than a day. They were getting ready to kick him out of the intern program when Gillian stepped in and offered to be his mentor. She thought he was a nice kid. He just needed to learn to curb his impulsiveness and stay focused.

Less than twenty-four hours after the third victim had been found near Lake Harriet, Gillian and Ben were sent out to interview suspects. The most recent victim had been identified, and when they flashed her photo, a housemate of one of the suspects recalled seeing her at their place a couple of times.

The suspect's name was Sebastian Tate, and his rap sheet was two pages long. At twenty-eight, he had a record of assault and battery, plus two rape charges. Somehow he'd never served time.

So now she and Ben stood in front of one-way glass as Tate was led into the interview room by Detective Wakefield. The door clicked closed, and Tate glanced around, then immediately walked to the window. He rapped his knuckles against it. "Anybody in there?" He put his face two inches from the surface.

"This is so cool," Ben whispered. "Just like *The Long Goodbye* with Elliot Gould playing Philip Marlowe. Ever see that movie?"

Actually she had, but didn't want to encourage Ben's chatty conversation. Once he got going on a movie, he didn't stop. "I'm not sure."

Tate began making faces.

Ben let out a loud snort. "If you saw it, you'd remember. Elliot Gould is the coolest. He gets called in, and he's fingerprinted; then he starts wiping the ink on his face while he's lookin' through the one-way glass. It's so cool. You should rent it. They have it at Intercontinental Video. They have everything at Intercontinental."

"I'll have to look for it sometime," Gillian said dryly. There were only two years between them, but sometimes she felt like his mother.

Detective Wakefield finally got Tate corralled so they were sitting across from each other at the long, narrow table.

"What is your full name?"

Tate turned to the glass and smiled. "Sebastian Griffin Tate."

"How old are you?" Wakefield continued.

"Why don't you just invite them in?" Tate asked, obviously enjoying his stardom. "Whoever's behind the glass."

Wakefield lifted his eyebrows and looked in the direction of Gillian and Ben. *What do you think?*

"Who's there? A couple of detectives? Or how about the agent who came to my place? Gillian Cantrell. Yeah, that was her name. She seemed pretty cool."

"This is going nowhere," Gillian said, moving toward the door. "I may as well make an appearance." Ben started to follow, but she stopped him with a hand on his arm. He might just get the notion to strike up some inane conversation with their suspect. "Stay here. Maybe you'll catch something we miss."

"Ah-hah!" Tate said as soon as Gillian stepped into the interview room. "I knew it was you!" The guy was beaming at her.

Until questioning Tate yesterday, she hadn't thought about the similarity between herself and the victims, and now it was creepy standing there knowing she came close to fitting the physical description of all three of the dead girls.

She sat down at the end of the table, and Wakefield resumed the interview. "How old are you?"

Tate glanced at Gillian, then back to Wakefield.

She could tell he was one of those arrogant guys who thought every girl in the room was attracted to him. Trouble was, a lot of girls probably *were* attracted to him. She supposed he was nice-looking in a high cheekboned, big-lipped, spooky model sort of way.

"Twenty-eight."

That was followed by his address and phone number.

"What do you do for a living?"

"I'm a full-time student." With every answer, he looked in Gillian's direction and smiled.

"Where do you attend school?"

"The U."

"Would that be the University of Minnesota?"

"Uh-huh."

"What's your major?"

"Theater."

"Have a minor?"

"Photography."

Fraternities were big at the U, and Tate had the closely cropped hair and pumped-up body of a frat weight-room addict. If Tate were the murderer, Gillian found something especially unnerving about a psycho hiding in plain sight while posing as an average student.

"Have you ever seen any of these girls?" Wakefield spread three eight-by-tens on the table. The third victim's name was Justine Ramsey, a twenty-two-year-old former university student who had a reputation for going home with a new guy every night.

Tate leaned forward and looked at the photos one at a time, then fell back in his chair. "No."

"Are you sure? Care to take another look?"

"I don't need to take another look. I've never seen any of 'em."

Wakefield separated the photo of the Ramsey girl from the others. "We checked school records and discovered you had some classes with this individual." He pushed the photo across the table in case Tate wanted to examine it again.

"So? Some of my classes have four hundred kids. How would I recognize everybody?"

"Someone said you and Ramsey went out a few times."

"Who told you that?" he asked, his face turning red.

"Someone reliable—that's all you need to know. Did you maybe forget about going out with Justine Ramsey?" Wakefield paused, giving Tate time to think about the corner he'd painted himself into. "You're a good-looking guy. Probably gone out with a lot of girls. I know how girls can be. Maybe you stop and say hi to one of them, and pretty soon she's telling everybody you're dating."

Gillian had watched several of Wakefield's interviews. He had a nice technique, relaxed, friendly, not too aggressive. And he never directly accused the interviewee of anything if he could give him a way out.

Tate shot Gillian a nervous smile, some of his cool beginning to melt. "What'd you say her name was?" he asked, backpedaling.

"Ramsey. Justine Ramsey."

"You know . . . maybe that does sound kinda familiar. Yeah, now that I think about it—it does. I totally forgot about her, man. And this picture—" He tapped the photo. "It doesn't really look like her."

"But you remember her now?"

"Yeah. Yeah, I do."

"Do you happen to remember a 911 call she made from her residence about eight months ago? You beat her up and she required ten stitches. Do you remember that?"

Tate completely lost his too-cool-for-this-place attitude. "Those charges were dropped. It was an accident."

"What color was Justine Ramsey's hair?"

Tate looked down at the photo, then back up. "Blond. So what?"

"Maybe you can tell me."

"I don't know what you're talkin' about."

Wakefield shifted gears. "How you could forget the name and face of a woman you beat up, someone who called the cops on you? That doesn't make any sense to me," he said with false puzzlement.

"Am I under arrest?"

"Should you be? Is there something you want to tell me?"

"I've had enough of this bullshit." Tate grabbed his jacket and started to get to his feet.

"All I need to do is get a court order and you'll be right back down here. It always looks better if you come in of your own free will." Wakefield put a sincere expression on his face. "A guy just seems less guilty that way."

Tate considered that, then settled back in his chair.

"Why did you lie about knowing Justine Ramsey?"

Tate rubbed his head. "I wanted the interview to be over. I didn't want to get messed up in anything—especially murder. You can understand that, can't you?" He looked at Gillian for reassurance. "You can, can't you?"

She didn't reply or respond in any way.

"It makes it harder for everybody when you don't tell the truth," Wakefield said. "Because chances are, we already know the answer to the question we're asking. And if we don't, we'll find out."

"I'm not falling for that."

"Did I tell you I know your dad?"

That got his attention.

"We went to the same high school," Wakefield said. "He was two years ahead of me, but we were in band and Academic Bowl together. I wasn't surprised when he went into politics. He knew the ins and outs of everything. How's your dad doing nowadays? I heard he was going to run for state senator."

"Maybe. I don't know. I don't talk to him much."

"Only when you're in trouble, right?"

"I see him other times. Christmas, usually."

"Where were you Friday—the night Justine Ramsey's body was dumped near Lake Harriet?"

"Listen, if you're trying to say I killed Justine Ramsey just because I may have hit her once, you're crazy."

"We're not accusing you of anything. We're interviewing everybody who knew Justine. It's standard procedure."

Tate relaxed a little, but kept his arms crossed at his chest, his attitude belligerent. "I was at a party."

"Were you there all night?"

"I stayed a few hours, then went barhopping. Everybody goes barhopping on Fridays."

"Were you with anybody? Someone who can corroborate your story?"

"I left the party by myself."

"What about the bars? Can you give me a list of the bars you went to and the people you saw?"

"Some of them. Listen, I was drunk. I can't remember exactly where I went and who I saw."

Wakefield pulled out a tablet and a piece of paper. "Why don't you try?"

Half an hour later, Wakefield had several bars and names written down, and Tate was out the door.

"What do you think?" Wakefield asked.

"Other than the fact that he's an arrogant ass?" Gillian asked.

"Yeah, other than that."

Ben joined them. "That guy's got the hots for you." He seemed to think that was extremely funny. "He's so not your type."

"I found Tate's reaction to you as telling as anything we got out of him," Wakefield said, flashing Ben a look of resigned irritation.

"He didn't seem at all interested in hiding his attraction," Gillian said. "Which makes me wonder if what we just witnessed was some kind of strategy—or was he just trying to look cool?"

"I wouldn't be surprised if he's been in more trouble than we know and Daddy's gotten him out of it. He's avoided getting his name on the public-access sex offender blacklist. He avoided a prison sentence by agreeing to become a full-time student. That kind of thing is bullshit."

"I've seen him on campus," Ben said. "Girls seem to dig him."

"Not this girl," Gillian said.

"We'll try to get interviews with school acquaintances," Wakefield said. "See if we can come up with anything."

Outside the police station, Gillian and Ben split up. He headed for a class on West Bank. She needed to report back to the BCA in St. Paul.

She was walking toward her car on the third floor of the Federal Courthouse parking garage when someone jumped out from behind a cement pillar and landed flat-footed in front of her.

She let out a frightened yelp, at the same time recognizing Sebastian Tate.

"Hi." He flashed her a smile, proud of himself.

Her heart was pounding madly in her chest. "What *the hell* are you doing?" she shouted at him in disbelief.

"It's almost noon. I thought you might want to grab a bite to eat."

"Are you kidding?" If he hadn't just scared the hell out of her, she may have been a little more discreet in her response. As it was, she did nothing to hide her disgust.

He gestured with hands in the pockets of his unzipped, black leather bomber jacket, walking backwards while she strode toward her car. "Why not?"

he asked innocently, as if expecting her to say she was too busy.

"Why not? Because you're a fucking asshole, that's why not!"

He stopped walking, and his jaw went slack. She shoved past him, unlocked her car with the remote, and slid behind the wheel. With a trembling hand, she jabbed the key in the ignition. *Oh, that was good,* she thought sarcastically. She locked the door and pulled the seat belt across her shoulder. Real professional. Cussing out a suspect. She was sure Mary did that all the time.

Chapter 7

"Would you like to try out my new potter's wheel while you're here?" Blythe asked. She and Mary were sitting at the bistro table in the kitchen sharing a light lunch. "You were getting pretty good at one time."

"I think that may have been Gillian." Mary was trying to ignore the throbbing in her shoulder, which had been getting increasingly worse since her encounter with Hitchcock. It hadn't helped that she'd been working on the profile for almost forty-eight hours straight. "I was never very good at throwing pots."

"Oh, you were too! Let's make an evening of it. Gillian can come. We'll get a bottle of wine. Be creative. What do you think?"

"Let's not rush into things."

Mary had come to terms with the fact that she and Gillian would be working together. She didn't like it, but she was a professional, and professionals had to adapt to unpleasant situations. That didn't mean she was ready to hop in the sandbox with her sister.

"Later, maybe," her mother said, momentarily deflated. Blythe gathered up a large canvas bag, water bottle, and car keys. "I've gotta run. Try to get some rest." She gave Mary a kiss on the cheek, then left to teach her afternoon and evening pottery classes at the Pot House.

Mary went upstairs and took a hot shower. She'd hoped the heat might help the pain, but by the time she'd dried off, her shoulder was aching even more. She made an ice pack out of a plastic bag and kitchen towel, then settled in bed with the pack on her shoulder and laptop on her lap.

Her phone rang.

Gillian was calling to tell her about a suspect they'd brought in for questioning. "Sebastian Tate," she said. "He's a student at the university and dated the third victim a few times."

"What did you find out?"

Gillian filled her in on Tate's rap sheet and how he'd reacted to her.

"I'm not sure you should be involved in the questioning of suspects," Mary said, surprised that they'd sent Gillian out on the initial canvas.

"It's my job." Gillian didn't bother trying to disguise her resentment.

"Didn't anyone stop to think that you fit the victimology?" Mary had to work to keep her voice smooth, even though she was irritated by Wakefield's lack of judgment. She'd expected more from him.

"I know I fit the victimology. I thought my going on the canvas was a good strategy."

Had she really thought it out that thoroughly? Mary wondered. More than likely, it had come to her later, when Gillian was face-to-face with the suspect.

"The last victim was also identified," Gillian said. "Justine Ramsey."

"Had she been reported missing?"

"No. Lived alone, no close friends."

"Like the first girl."

"Exactly." The conversation shifted. "How are you coming on the profiles?"

"I'll have the preliminary paperwork ready to present to Detective Wakefield by early tomorrow. Hopefully I can get the Behavioral Science team to sign off on it in two or three days so the profile can be made official and the information gotten to the public."

There was a pause, as if Gillian were weighing her next words. "You sound tired."

Her concern took Mary by surprise. "I am," she admitted.

"Try to get some sleep."

"As soon as I wrap this up." Her voice was once again distantly polite.

"I'll let you get back to work," Gillian said, sounding rebuffed.

"Gillian?" Mary paused. "If Tate comes around, call the cops."

"I *am* a cop."

"You know what I mean. Don't try to deal with him by yourself. He could be dangerous." Mary disconnected.

The ice in the plastic bag had turned to tepid water; Mary dropped it and the towel on the floor. Would Gillian follow her advice about Tate? Probably not. Mary shouldn't have said anything about her being careful around the guy. Gillian had a history of doing the opposite of whatever her sister suggested.

For the next two hours Mary fine-tuned the killer and victim profile, adding the finishing touches before shutting off the computer and lying back in bed.

She was almost asleep when the doorbell rang.

She kept her eyes closed, trying to pretend she hadn't heard anything. The doorbell rang again. It was probably some sweet-faced kid selling something she didn't want to buy but would anyway. Dressed in navy blue cotton pajamas, she made her way downstairs, leaning forward to peer through the peephole.

Anthony Spence stood on her mother's front porch. She blinked. He was still there.

She opened the door, the chain lock catching. She slammed the door, undid the chain, and opened it again.

Instead of a greeting, he got directly to the point: "You look like hell."

On the other hand, he looked great. But when didn't Anthony look great? He was dressed in the FBI black he was so fond of, complete with trench coat.

"Nice to see you too."

The pain was making her dizzy. She turned around and plopped down on the steps, wincing as she jarred her arm. "What are you doing here?"

"Are you sick?" He stepped inside and closed the door behind him.

"A headache." It was the first thing that popped into her mind. It seemed childish and immature—always evading everyone—but she hated to be fussed over.

Anthony put a hand to her forehead. She closed her eyes for a moment, enjoying the coolness.

"You feel warm."

"Think so?"

"How's the shoulder?"

"A little sore," she admitted reluctantly.

"A little?" From his expression of disbelief, it was apparent she hadn't fooled him for a second. "I know your definition of 'a little.' Like the time you had a little pain in your side and ended up having an emergency appendectomy."

She gave him a weak smile, then tried to steer the attention away from her. "What are you doing here?"

"I thought you might need some help."

"You should have told me you were coming. I'd have met you at the airport."

"Let me see your shoulder."

"No."

"Come on."

"For some reason, you seem to think you own me now. That you *own* my shoulder." She was uncomfortably aware that she was in pajamas while he was fully dressed.

"Is that so unreasonable? I'm partially responsible for that shoulder."

Without asking permission, he unbuttoned the top button of her shirt. He slipped his hand inside, under the fabric. His touch felt wonderfully cool.

He frowned. "Hot."

Her heart sank, and then began to beat rapidly. What did *that* mean?

"Do you have your doctor's phone number?"

"Upstairs. In my data book." She started to get up.

"Stay there." His voice held urgency. "I'll get it."

"Take a right at the top of the stairs."

He disappeared, then quickly returned with a small leather booklet. Anthony flipped through the pages and located the number. He sat down near her on the stairs, pulled out his mobile phone, and dialed.

Dr. Farina was in surgery, but the problem was relayed to him and he insisted that Mary get to a Minneapolis physician immediately. "It could be one of three things," his nurse explained. "Inflammation due to overexertion, infection that has been incubating since the surgery, or staph." The nurse gave them the name of a reputable physician and added that Dr. Farina would call Mary that night.

Staph. Mary and Anthony looked at each other, and she saw her own fear reflected back at her. The best possible staph scenario might mean weeks in an isolation room while they pumped antibiotics into her veins in an attempt to kill the resistant bacteria. A bad scenario could mean a lost limb. It could mean death.

It took thirty minutes to get to the Edina office where Mary's doctor suggested they go.

Once there, she was put through a series of tests. She had blood drawn, cultures taken, and was sent to an adjoining hospital for an MRI. When that was completed, she met with Dr. Tabora. Anthony insisted on being in the room when the verdict was announced.

"You have quite a bit of inflammation," he said, "but the preliminary quick test didn't show any evidence of staph."

No staph. Mary wilted in relief and looked at Anthony. He was leaning against the wall, head tipped back, eyes closed, sending up his own thank-you.

"I'm going to put you on an anti-inflammatory drug. That should take care of the problem. Come back and see me in two weeks unless you're in Virginia. In that case, see Dr. Farina. I'll be sending him a copy of my report."

He handed Mary the prescription order. "Rest and take it easy. Try not to use your arm for the next few days; then begin exercises gradually, much the way you did after surgery. There are some excellent physical therapists in the building. I'll have the receptionist set up an initial visit."

At the front desk, Mary was handed a card that gave the date and time of her therapist appointment. She would cancel it later.

At the pharmacy Mary turned in the script, then moved away from the counter to wait. She was sensing a strong, negative energy coming from Anthony, and it put her on the defensive.

"I can tell you're thinking about having me pulled from the case," she said as soon as they were in his rental car. "Well, I'm not leaving." Which seemed weird when she thought about it, since she hadn't wanted to come in the first place. But it was like that first plunge into cold water. Once you were wet, you might as well stay in and swim.

"The doctor told you to take it easy."

"Anthony, I want to remain on the case. If you have me pulled off, I'll continue to investigate on my own."

"Why are you being so hardheaded about this?"

Anthony didn't know about Fiona. Once, he'd asked her why she'd wanted to become an FBI agent, and she'd mumbled something vague about the challenge and the desire to help people.

Pain stabbed through her shoulder, redirecting her thoughts. "You need to get in the right lane so you can get on 494 East. Oh, and Anthony? My mother doesn't know about my being shot, so don't mention it to her."

He pulled away from a green light and then cut to the right lane. "You're a little old to be hiding things from your mother, aren't you?" He sounded puzzled and slightly annoyed.

"She worries about me enough as it is," Mary explained. "So please don't say anything."

He shrugged, but didn't press the issue.

It was late afternoon, and traffic was heavy, adding fifteen minutes to their return trip. Once home, Mary took her pills, retrieved her laptop from her room, and handed it to Anthony, determined to get back to business as usual. "The profiles are finished. Would you mind going over my notes before I present them to Detective Wakefield and Quantico?" Every breath made her shoulder hurt. "I'm going upstairs to lie down for a while. The kitchen is that way, the bathroom over there." She pointed. "My mom should be home in a couple of hours."

After she left, Anthony wandered around the living

room. Over the years he'd conjured up a mental image of Mary at her childhood home in Minneapolis. The place he'd put her was nothing like this living room with its red walls, framed artwork, exotic rugs, wild plants, and strange sculptures. This wasn't at all the landscape he'd expected the rigid, unbending Mary Cantrell to come from.

Her shooting had scared the hell out of him.

She almost died.

Up until then he'd thought of them both as invincible, with Mary seeming even more of a superhero for some reason. Although she didn't know it, the trauma he'd experienced over her being shot had been crippling. So much so that he was seeing an FBI therapist, who'd suggested he and Mary quit working together for a while. The only problem was, he worried about her twice as much when she was out of his sight.

He settled into a soft ottoman, opened Mary's laptop, and turned it on. While waiting for it to boot up, his mind drifted to thoughts of his ex-wife. *Ex.* Such a negative word. As if she'd been crossed out of his life. Divorce papers didn't suddenly mean they no longer cared about each other, because they did. Things were just different now.

With hindsight, he could see that their marriage had been a recipe for disaster. She was so sensitive that TV ads for horror movies gave her nightmares. There was no way he could talk to her about his work, no way he could tell her what was bothering him. She'd begged him to quit, but he couldn't. She said he didn't love her enough, and he thought she might be right.

In the end, she was even jealous of Mary. "You spend more time with her than you do with me," she'd shouted at him one particularly ugly night. It was true, he'd realized. Then he'd had an ever more alarming thought: *This is never going to work.*

On Mary's laptop, the FBI screen saver was humming at him. He opened the writing program and quickly found the most recent file.

He read her notes, then looked at the background information on the murders and personal observations. That was followed by the profile.

The crime scenes reflect characteristics of the organized offender. Most likely a chameleon personality. Cunning. Cruises for victims.

Crime Scene: Kills at undetermined location, then disposes of body at abduction site. Very likely tortures victims, either psychologically or physically or both. Leaves little or no physical evidence.

Development: Has been hurt in some way, and is angry, yet feeling fear or loss. Thinks himself superior to others. Selects victims he can manipulate, dominate, and control.

He constantly feels the need for approval and feminine admiration. He is self-confident and arrogant, but may have doubts about his own sexuality. Could be attracted to men, and his denial of that attraction is taken out on innocent women.

Method: He usually preselects his victims, but if a victim doesn't work out, he may take one by opportunity. He uses the surprise approach, attacking between midnight and 5:00 A.M. The victim will always be alone.

Sex of Offender: Male

Race: White

Age: 24 to 35

Physical Description: 5'11" or above, muscular

Scholastic Achievement: High school, possibly some college.

Lifestyle: Single, but may have friends or relatives who only see one side of him.

Social Adjustment: Did well in grade school, but

when he reached adolescence, began to cause trouble. Has leadership qualities.

Demeanor: Confident, possibly quite charming.

Mental Problems: Phobias. Some type of stressor most likely occurred to bring about the first kidnapping and murder.

Grafted Rose Branches: Symbolic of his need to seek perfection in a mate along with his need to manipulate his victims in impossible ways.

The next file contained the victimology, which was every bit as important as the offender profile.

Sex: Female
Race: White
Age: 15 to 25
Height: 5'4" to 5'8"
Weight: 110 to 135
Hair color: Blond
Victim will most likely be someone who is young and healthy, dresses stylishly, yet can be manipulated. Offender is an opportunist, and if the right victim can't be found, he makes do.

A note at the bottom proposed sending the profiles to the media as soon as the FBI signed off on them.

As Anthony shut down the computer and put it aside, he heard a key turn in the front lock. He was getting to his feet when the door swung open and an attractive woman walked in. Mary's sister? Mother?

He didn't want to frighten her, so he quickly pulled out his ID, flipped open the leather case, and introduced himself. Did she know who he was? he wondered. Had Mary ever mentioned him? "I'm Mary's partner," he explained in case she hadn't.

"Anthony! How wonderful!" the woman said, extending a hand. "I'm Blythe. I'm so glad to finally meet you." She was looking at him with curiosity.

"Excuse my hands," she said, smiling warmly. "I've been mixing clay all afternoon, and you know how hard clay is on your skin."

He hadn't known, but now he did.

She glanced around. "Where's Mary?"

It was tempting as hell to blow Mary's cover for her own good, but if he did, he doubted she'd ever speak to him again. "She didn't feel well, so she's upstairs sleeping."

"I knew something was wrong with her earlier today." Blythe frowned. "Is it flu, do you think?"

This was Mary's mother. How could he lie to Mary's mother? "Hard to say," he replied uncomfortably.

"I'll just go up and check on her."

Blythe disappeared, then returned a few minutes later. "She's sound asleep, poor dear." She clasped him on the upper arm. "What about you? Did you just fly in? Have you had anything to eat? Come in the kitchen, and we'll have a chat while we wait for Mary to wake up."

She led him through the house to a kitchen that was as cluttered and as warm as the living room, with copper pans hanging above the stove. He noticed in particular a wire mesh bust in the corner. She talked while she pulled out condiments and heated water for tea. "Would you prefer beer? Wine? Soda? Oh, please sit down."

He could see that she was the kind of person who loved taking care of people, who would love to be taking care of Mary. Mary had recently told him she hadn't been home in five years. Not for the first time, he wondered why.

There was a little table in front of sliding glass doors

that looked out onto a deck and backyard. He chose one of the stools at the kitchen counter.

"You and Mary don't look much alike," he observed.

"Mary's dark, like her father," Blythe said. "And Gillian's light like me. As far as personality, Mary and I are nothing alike either," she added, slicing a tomato. "But believe it or not, she used to be a lot more like me."

"Really?" He was having a hard time picturing Mary fluttering around a kitchen, wearing bright colors and talking nonstop.

"You should have known her before."

"Before? Before what?"

"Why, before Fiona died."

Mary awakened abruptly.

She could hear the soft, indistinct murmur of voices coming from downstairs. Disoriented, she turned on the lamp next to the bed and checked her watch. A little after seven.

She changed clothes, slipping into a pair of jeans and digging out a long-sleeved top. Downstairs, she found her mother and Anthony huddled together in the kitchen.

Blythe got to her feet. "I was just getting ready to come up and check on you." She gave Mary a quick hug. "How are you feeling?"

"Much better."

She leaned back to examine her. "Do you think it's the flu?"

Mary glanced at Anthony, thankful he hadn't told her mother everything. "It's not the flu; it's my arm."

"I was afraid," Blythe said with drama, "that there was more to your injury than you were letting on."

"I'm going to have to take it easy for a few days."

"Can I get you anything?"

"No." She put her uninjured arm around her mother and gave her a hug. "Everything's going to be fine."

Blythe was an optimist, so it was easy to convince her that there was no reason to worry. Satisfied with Mary's response, she excused herself, leaving the two of them alone to "talk business."

"Did you look at the profile?" Mary asked once her mother was gone.

Anthony nodded and lifted a glass to his mouth. The liquid was light green—Blythe was already plying him with herbal tea. "The profile looks pretty good as far as I can tell."

"Do you have anything to add, or anything you feel different about?" When it came to crime scene psychology they were a perfectly synchronized pair, and Mary had total faith in his judgment.

"He has some strangely conflicting qualities."

"I know. I keep going over everything and coming up with descriptions that seem more suited to two people than one. That's why I wanted to get your reaction."

"I really can't say until I have time to go over the victims' case files."

She waved her hand in impatience. "I promised Detective Wakefield a rough draft by tomorrow morning."

"I'll try to get everything read before that. What about the decomposed victim? Were you able to link her to the other two murders?"

"It's going to take a crime lab to do that."

He gave her a disapproving look. "This wasn't quite the break I envisioned for you."

"I didn't need a vacation."

"Come on, Mary." It had to be one of his favorite lines.

"You're not going to win this argument. Believe me, I'll be fine. I'm feeling much better already."

He seemed to be considering something and then finally said, "I'm sticking around."

"To keep an eye on me?"

"You weren't sent here to do the work of two people. Take tomorrow off. I've got a reservation at a hotel a few blocks from police headquarters, so I'll deliver the profile to Detective Wakefield in the morning. If he has any questions, he can call you. How does that sound?"

His idea seemed a fair compromise. "You're welcome to stay here," she offered. "There's a private area at the back of the house that used to be my father's work space. It has a bed and shower."

He stared at her for what seemed like a full minute.

Why was he looking at her like that? Had he misconstrued her invitation? she wondered. She was just trying to be friendly. But of course he wouldn't want to stay at their house. Not when the government was putting him up in a nice hotel.

His eyes cleared as if he'd finally made sense of her offer. "You're not trying to keep me under your thumb, are you, Mary?"

"Idiot." They were back on familiar ground. That evasive cat-and-mouse teasing that was so much a part of their relationship.

"You really are feeling better."

"I was just trying to be nice."

"Well, cut it out. You're scaring me."

She laughed.

"Thanks for the offer, regardless of how it came about," he said. "But I have to turn it down. I wouldn't want to be any trouble."

"It's too late for that."

"I'm afraid you're right." He glanced at her shoulder.

"That's not what I meant."

A look of resignation crossed his features, and she suddenly became aware of how tired he was.

She cupped his face with her hands, feeling abrasive stubble against her palms. She'd never touched him in such a way. "Quit beating yourself up about my injury," she whispered. "It happened. It's over. Forget about it."

"I can't."

It was unsettling to catch herself looking so deeply into Anthony Spence's eyes. She broke contact and moved away, suddenly embarrassed by her impulsiveness.

"Yeah, well . . . I'd better get going." He bustled around to cover the awkward moment, gathering up his jacket, quickly shrugging into it. "I've got a lot of homework." Two minutes later, he was gone.

Chapter 8

The following morning, when she should have been resting, Mary decided to make a long overdue visit. She rang the doorbell and stepped back, her heart beating rapidly as footsteps inside the house came closer. The door opened, and there stood Abigail Portman, Fiona's mother.

Abigail had always seemed a throwback to a delusional fifties mom, the mother who had turned her back on a career to stay home and raise her only daughter. She wore aprons and baked cookies, and all the kids in the neighborhood seemed to end up at her house. And no matter how busy she was with all that cooking, and running Fiona from piano to cheerleading practice, no matter how busy she was with PTA and the latest school fund-raiser, she always looked immaculate.

Back then Mary had often regarded Fiona's life with longing and wished her own could be more like it.

Poor Mrs. Portman's once beautiful Betty Crocker hair was gray and frizzy, and her eyes looked out from deep, lined sockets. Her white sweatshirt was stained and ragged. On her feet were slippers Mary suspected rarely left her feet.

"Hello, Mrs. Portman. It's me. Mary."

The woman's blank expression disappeared. "Mary! Oh, Mary!" She opened the door wide and pulled Mary inside.

It was like stepping into a tomb.

The hallway was dark and stuffy, smelling as if fresh air and sunlight hadn't touched the house since Fiona's death.

Abigail Portman wrapped her arms around Mary, hugging her tightly. "You're so grown up!" she said, stepping back to look at her. "I can't believe it! I always think of you just like Fiona—a perpetual teenager. Are you still with the FBI?"

"Yes. Actually, I'm in town on a case."

The light left Abigail's face. "Those girls."

"Yes."

"I've read about them. I keep thinking of their poor mothers. I wondered about dropping them a note, but what words of comfort could I give when there aren't any? I would just remind them that they aren't in the middle of a horrible dream and that ten years from now they'll still be in pain."

"Is that how it is for you?" Mary asked, sad to see that things were so bad.

"Frank and I got divorced. He couldn't take it anymore. Said I was always moping around. He wanted to sell the house and move out West somewhere. He begged me to go. I thought about it, but I couldn't leave. It's different for men. He didn't understand that this house is my connection to my daughter. I can't imagine anybody else sleeping in her room. I can't imagine children running down the hall, laughing and screaming. I don't want happy children here. It wouldn't seem right. Like laughing at a funeral."

"I understand."

"I think you do." She waved her hand. "Come in and have a snack with me. Remember how you and

Fiona used to charge in after school for milk and cookies?"

Mary smiled. "I remember. You made the best chocolate chip cookies in the world."

"I don't bake anymore." It was a statement of the way things were. "I don't cook at all."

Mary followed her through a living room that was frozen in time. Being in Fiona's house gave her a weird feeling of dislocation. Nothing had changed. The furniture. The curtains. Where the furniture was placed. All the same. She almost expected to pick up a newspaper to see that it was dated the day Fiona had died.

The kitchen hadn't changed either. Same wallpaper. Same laminated table and matching chairs with plastic-covered cushions that left strange designs on a child's bare legs. Same bland motel oil painting on the wall. Abigail may have been Betty Crocker, but she'd never had an esthetic eye.

"Take off your coat."

Mary removed her trench coat and draped it over a kitchen chair.

"You became an FBI agent because of Fiona, didn't you?" Abigail asked, tearing open a bag of gingersnaps and getting two cans of diet soda from the refrigerator.

"I think you're right." Why not be honest? "I'm sure you're right."

They drank the soda and munched the gingersnaps, which turned out to be atrocious. Abigail talked about Fiona as if she'd been waiting for this day, for someone who would listen, for someone who would understand without telling her she needed to forget about what happened and move on—which was the last thing people like Abigail wanted to hear.

The conversation turned away from the tragedy to the sharing of fond memories of a girl who would always be sixteen. Abigail dragged out scrapbooks. Together she and Mary reminisced. They went through page after page of newspaper clippings about the spelling bees Fiona had won, and about recognition by the mayor for the money she'd raised for the homeless. There was a photo of her accepting a plaque for a state speech competition, another for Academic Bowl.

"She was such a special person," Abigail said, stroking the photo. "I never pushed her. I was never one of those mothers who pushed her kids to do things they had no interest in. She pushed herself."

"She had so much energy," Mary said. "She wanted everything."

"She wanted to be the first female president. Did she ever tell you that?"

"Yes. And I think she could have done it." Mary recognized an echo of the old enthusiasm she used to have for Fiona's ideas.

The last photos in the album were obituaries, cut from several papers. There was even a photo taken at the cemetery of the grieving mourners. With a weird jolt of recognition, Mary spotted her much younger self standing with Blythe. Gillian stood a little to one side.

Mary turned the page. Abigail had also cut out every single article about the murder and trial—and finally the conviction of Gavin Hitchcock. There was a four-by-five photo of him staring at the camera, looking both scared and pissed off.

"He's out of prison," Abigail said. "I can't believe he had the nerve to come back here and flaunt himself. You'd think he'd want to move to a town where nobody knew him, where nobody knew what he did."

"I was a little surprised myself when he didn't go somewhere else," Mary said. She didn't add that there was someone who'd encouraged him to return to his hometown, someone who'd helped him find a place to live and a place to work.

"He shouldn't have been released. He should have died. It's not fair that he's alive and running around free when my sweet little girl is dead. I have half a mind to drive over and see him someday."

"I don't think that would be a good idea," Mary cautioned.

"Tell him what a useless piece of work he is. He never even said he was sorry for what he did."

Mary waited until Mrs. Portman was looking at her. "Would you want that? Would it really make any difference?"

She thought a moment. "No, I don't suppose it would. But I'd still like to talk to him. I'd like to see his face when he opens the door and realizes it's me." She let out a burst of laughter, then pressed a hand to her mouth. "Can you imagine his expression? Oh, it would be priceless."

Maybe, Mary thought, she shouldn't have come. Her visit seemed to have set the poor woman off. She closed the book and stacked it with the others. "Thanks for letting me see these. I should get going. My mother's expecting me." No matter how old you got, mothers were still a good excuse when you needed to end a visit.

"Would you like to go upstairs?" Abigail asked. "To Fiona's room? It comforts me. Maybe it will comfort you."

Mary would never have thought, Gee, I'd sure like to see Fiona's old room. But now that the invitation was out there, something inside her was compelled to say yes.

The steps that led upstairs were covered with the same green carpet, and they creaked in just the same way.

Nothing had changed. Except for an underlying mustiness, Fiona's room even smelled the same.

On the walls were the posters of unicorns. There was her music box collection. Her stuffed animals, many of them huge, won at the fair by a legion of admirers. Her scrapbooks, her yearbooks. Tucked into the edges of the vanity mirror above a pink, skirted dresser were photos, many of Mary and Fiona. Hanging on a closet door hook was her cheerleader uniform, behind it her letter jacket.

The canopy bed, with its cream eyelet cover, was strewn with gaily colored wrapped packages, some with birthday paper, some Christmas. There were even Easter baskets overflowing with candy.

"I get her a present every year on her birthday and Christmas," Abigail said, sitting down on the bed and picking up one of the wrapped gifts.

Along one wall more gifts were arrayed.

"Sometimes I come up here and just sit. For hours. It's so peaceful, don't you think?"

A life derailed. "Yes." Sad was what it was. Mary wished she hadn't come. The room was stuffy, and she broke into a cold sweat. She suddenly felt as if she might pass out.

"Would you like me to leave you alone here for a while?" Abigail asked. "It might be good for you."

Mary nodded, stifling the urge to run. What with the buzzing in her head, she wasn't all that sure she could make it out of the house under her own steam. "That would be nice," she managed.

"You can light a candle and say a prayer," Abigail said, motioning toward a cluster of red votives on the dresser. Mary had forgotten the Portmans were Catholic, and now she remembered Fiona saying her nighttime prayers, "so I won't get a venial sin on my soul."

Abigail left, gently closing the door behind her.

Mary sank down on the bed and put her head between her knees, fighting light-headedness. She'd lost consciousness twice in her life. The first time had been when Blythe told Mary her father was dead; the second was when she got shot. Finding Fiona's body that day in the woods had had the opposite effect, sending her scrambling and screaming for help.

It was too much for her, being in Fiona's room. Too immediate. Too real. For years she'd mastered the fine art of retreat, but she couldn't hide here.

She kept her head down until the blackness behind her eyes disappeared and her heart quit thundering. Gradually her breathing returned to normal. She leaned back, lowering herself against the pillow, her feet on the floor, and looked up at the canopy above her head.

There were the stars that glowed in the dark. She and Fiona had put them there one summer. A crescent moon dangled from a thread, and there was the tiny stuffed lamb with angel wings Mary had given Fiona for Christmas.

Life had been so perfect then. So innocent.

But not real, of course.

Lying there, Mary realized her own life had stagnated. Differently from Abigail's, but stagnated all the same. Something had shut off inside her the day she'd found Fiona's body. For years she'd understood that she was no longer the person she used to be, and that as time passed Mary Cantrell was fading, but she couldn't seem to summon the strength or will to do anything about it.

She and Fiona used to discuss the future. They talked about what they wanted to be when they grew up, what it would be like, and where they would live, where they would travel, what they would see and do and learn.

"I don't want kids," Fiona had told Mary one day. "Kids just get in the way."

Mary had been surprised, because she'd always seen herself getting married and having children. Now she had no plans.

Lying there took her back to the days when she'd thought about that kind of thing. Now she tried to picture herself with a child and found it difficult. Any existence beyond her current one seemed hard to imagine.

Dizziness gone, she got up and moved around the room, leaning close to the vanity mirror to look at the photos. One in particular caught her eye. It was of Fiona, Mary, and Gillian. Fiona and Mary were smiling happily. Gillian had her arms crossed at her waist, a scowl on her face.

Poor Gillian. She'd been so jealous of Fiona. It was a shame, because they could have had so much fun together, the three of them. But Gillian refused to share Mary with anyone, and Mary had refused to be manipulated by her sister.

Gillian thought Mary hadn't noticed, but her jealousy was impossible to miss. Gillian sticking out her tongue, and later, throwing the finger. Gillian never giving Fiona a chance. Once, when Fiona stayed the night at Mary's, Gillian put a laxative in her Kool-Aid and bugs in her pink sleeping bag. The next time she came, she left dog crap in Fiona's purse. It would have been funny if Gillian's pranks hadn't been so cruel and calculated.

For a long while, Fiona refused to stay the night at the Cantrell house, and Mary was relieved because she never knew what Gillian might try next—her jealousy was so out of control.

When Gillian got to high school she found her own

circle of friends, and she and Mary didn't hang around together much unless it was a family function.

Mary lit one of the candles. She didn't pray, but she meditated, willing her mind to empty, allowing herself to drift. . . . She began to sense the comfort Abigail had talked about, and it was with a touch of regret that she finally blew out the candle and left the room.

"You'll come back, won't you?" Abigail asked, downstairs.

"I'll try." Mary retrieved her coat from the back of the kitchen chair. The visit had been cathartic, but she wasn't sure she could do it again. "Would you mind if I walked in the woods behind the house?"

"Oh, my." Abigail put a hand to her throat, horrified. "Why would you want to do that?"

"I think about the woods sometimes. And dream about the tree house. I thought it might be good for me to actually see it again."

"I can't go into those woods. That's one place I haven't been able to go. I hate those woods." Abigail put a hand to her hair, as if to smooth a style that no longer existed. "Developers are always hounding me, wanting me to sell the land. You'd think I'd want to, the way I hate it. It's worth quite a lot, you know. But even though I can't go in there, I can't sell it either. And what do I need money for?"

What, indeed? To buy more gifts for a dead girl who could never open them? "Do you mind?" Mary repeated gently.

Abigail waved her hand, shooing her away, looking irritated now. "Go ahead, then. I just don't know why you'd want to."

"Dark light," her grandmother used to call the weird cast the sun took in the fall. Mary always felt a tug of sorrow whenever she noticed the change. She never knew if it was simply because it signaled the passage of time and the end of summer, or because the sun had been low on the horizon the day she'd come upon Fiona's body, the trees casting long black shadows.

Today was cool, the temperature in the high fifties. Where the sunlight cut through bare trees, it offered no warmth. It had rained the night before, and the fallen leaves had been packed into a soft, damp cushion beneath Mary's feet. The magnificent scent of earth drifted up to her, and for a moment she was a child again, experiencing the woods with the innocence that came before the bad times.

When she was young, the woods had seemed huge and endless—as big as a small country from one end to the other. With the jaded eyes of an adult, Mary could see that the property was not more than four acres.

She deliberately avoided heading toward where she'd found Fiona's body. Instead, she circled around the edge of the woods, following a faint path made by deer and other wild animals, until she finally reached the tree where they'd spent so much time.

It wasn't as big as she remembered either.

The tree house her father had built with the permission of the previous owners was still there, at least the floor and most of the walls. The windows were just a memory, the glass gone, probably shattered and buried by years of fallen leaves. Sometime during their middle school years, she and Gillian had attempted to spend the night in the tree house, announcing themselves brave and independent enough to survive the wilderness alone. Less than two hours into the evening, Gillian had had enough. When Blythe came to check on them, she ended up carrying her frightened, clinging daughter home with Mary trudging behind, disappointed but resigned.

When Fiona arrived in the neighborhood, Mary took her to the tree house, and soon they were spending hours there talking about boys and music. There they fearlessly remained all night long, tucked into sleeping bags. If Blythe came to check on them, they never heard her.

Now that Mary had decided to immerse herself in the past, she wanted to do it totally.

For years she'd avoided even the faintest memory of this place, and here she was, wallowing in it. She was like the people who couldn't stop cutting themselves. The only difference was that they cut themselves as a distraction from reality. *She* was finally facing what she'd spent years avoiding. It hurt, but it also felt good in a weird way. Because even though she was where bad things had happened, she felt a strange sense of distance. Maybe time did heal. And unlike Fiona's mother, Mary had moved on. She was a functioning adult. Maybe not fully functioning, but functioning all the same.

The ground around the base of the tree was bare— a sign of activity. A new generation of kids probably came there to play. Maybe they could feel the energy of the young girl who had died nearby but interpreted it as something else, as the magic of the woods.

Mary was a practical person, but she'd been in enough places where evil lurked and powerful tragedies had occurred to know that such violent events could leave their imprint on a place—on the ground, in a building, or even in the air.

She wanted to climb into the tree, to look into the house her father had built, but there was no way she could do it without using her injured arm.

It's probably for the best.

But if she wasn't able to get up into the tree house, she was ready to find the spot where Fiona had died.

The leaves were thick under her feet, and the woods had changed since she'd played there. The deeper she walked, the denser the undergrowth. Multiflora rose, the bane of uncontrolled timberland, had taken over, spreading like cancer across the ground, choking out grasses and even small trees, suffocating the wildflowers and jack-in-the-pulpits. Sharp thorns caught on Mary's trench coat and snagged her corduroy pants. They caught in her hair and scratched the back of her hands.

Everything was so overgrown that at first she didn't think she'd be able to find the spot. And then she saw it—a white wooden cross stuck into the ground. She approached until she was able to read the lettering.

WE WILL ALWAYS MISS YOU
WE WILL ALWAYS LOVE YOU

Mary didn't remember the cross. But then, she didn't remember much of anything that had happened in those weeks after finding Fiona's body. For a time, her brain had simply shut down, her body moving on autopilot.

What struck her as odd now was the condition of the cross. It looked as if it was either fairly new or had recently been repainted.

She stepped closer, standing in the approximate area where Fiona's body had lain. There, at the base of the cross, was a bouquet of dead red roses. Beside it was a small stuffed teddy bear with a delicate gold chain around its neck. Mary crouched down. On the necklace was a charm shaped like a cheerleader.

She straightened and grabbed the top of the cross. She tried to wiggle it. A cross placed there ten years ago would have been rotten at the base. This had been driven firmly and securely into the ground. The bouquet couldn't have been over a week or two old; the stuffed bear looked to have been outside about the same length of time.

Who would be coming here, fighting the tangle of thorn bushes, to decorate the place where Fiona had died? Mrs. Portman would be the logical person, but Abigail said she never came into the woods.

Mary examined the ground, only to find that rain and falling leaves had obliterated any footprints. The sound of a breaking twig made her look up. She squinted through the undergrowth and strained her ears, listening for the sound to repeat.

Nothing.

She felt under her coat for the reassurance of her gun and remembered it was one of the rare occasions when she'd left it at home, not wanting to wear it when visiting Abigail.

She was being ridiculous. A grown woman, an FBI agent, jumping at every sound in the woods. It could very well have been a twig she'd heard, broken by a wild animal.

Nonetheless, she walked back as quickly as she could, while bushes grabbed her with their thorns. When she reached the street, she was a little out of breath.

At the Portman house, the shades were drawn.

Mary pulled out her cell phone and dialed a number she remembered from childhood.

Mrs. Portman answered.

It was probably a little silly, standing in front of the Portman house, talking to Abigail on the phone, but Mary didn't feel up to another face-to-face meeting at the moment.

"Do you know who put a cross in the woods?" Mary asked.

"A cross? For Fiona?"

"Yes. And also a stuffed animal—a bear, along with a bouquet of roses."

There was a pause as Mrs. Portman digested the information. "How odd," she finally said.

"Can you think of anyone who may have done it?"

"I haven't the vaguest idea. I mean, most people leave things at the cemetery."

"Thanks, Mrs. Portman. Sorry to bother you."

Mary hung up and crossed the street to her house.

Gillian went for a five-mile jog. By the time she was on the return path, it was almost dark. Approaching her apartment, she noticed an unfamiliar car parked in the driveway, a man standing beside it. She slowed to a walk and kept her eye on him.

"Oh, shit," she said once she was close enough to recognize Sebastian Tate. She was thinking about swinging around to the back door when he spotted her.

"Gillian!" He gave her a big wave and headed in her direction, meeting her halfway.

"What are you doing here?" she said.

"I have tickets to the Dylan concert tonight." He pulled them out of his coat pocket and held them in the air. "Wanna go?"

She'd tried to get tickets months ago, but the concert was sold out. She continued walking. "No, thanks."

"Oh, come on." He fell into step beside her. "I'll bet you like Dylan. Everybody likes Dylan. Plus, the show's at Northrop Auditorium. We could walk from here. No need to fight traffic. What do you say?"

"Did you get the tickets from a scalper?"

"I made a trade. I had something somebody wanted."

"What?" Detective Wakefield was always telling her to ask questions.

"Some photographs." He shrugged. "I'm a photographer."

So *he* said. "I don't want to go to the Dylan concert, and I don't want you coming around here again."

He followed her up the front steps. Mary had told her to call the police if he bothered her, but Gillian felt sure she could handle him. "Leave," she told him, with no intention of unlocking the door while he stood so near, afraid he might force himself inside. "Now."

He struggled to control his mounting anger. "I don't even like Dylan," he finally said, raising a hand as if to strike her. "I got the fucking tickets for you!" He threw them in her face, strode to his car, and left.

"Asshole." She bent and scooped up the tickets. Inside her apartment, the door locked, she grabbed the phone and called Ben Collins, the talkative intern from work. When he answered she asked, "How would you like to see Bob Dylan? I managed to get my hands on a couple of tickets."

Chapter 9

The phone was ringing.

Mary struggled through the disorientation of awakening in the middle of a sleep cycle. Where was she? Her apartment in Virginia? A hotel?

With each possibility, her mind conjured up the locale, complete with furnishings, until she settled on the correct location—her mother's home in Minneapolis and her old room with the India print spread.

With ease of practice, she felt around on the floor for her cell phone and caught it on the fourth ring.

It was Anthony. "A teenage girl's been kidnapped south of here," he said. "At a place called Canary Falls. A little town off Highway 52, between Minneapolis and Rochester."

Mary scooted higher in the bed. "I know where it is." She was wide awake now.

"I'm heading south on 35 West and can be at your place in ten minutes."

"I'll be waiting outside." She disconnected and jumped from bed. She brushed her hair and teeth, splashed water on her face, and then quickly slipped into a pair of jeans, a black shirt, her gun, and her trench coat. When she was ready, she gently woke Blythe to tell her she was leaving.

"Take an umbrella," her mother mumbled. "It's supposed to rain."

Downstairs Mary collected her laptop, notebook, and camera, grabbing an umbrella from the antique stand as she stepped out the door. Outside, birds were already up, singing like crazy. In the east the sky was beginning to lighten.

Anthony wasn't there, so she pulled out her phone and punched the single speed-dial number she'd recently entered for Gillian.

"Just getting ready to call you," Gillian said when Mary told her about the kidnapping. "My associate and I are already on our way."

Mary was impressed to find her sister sounding so professional and on top of things. "See you there." She disconnected and was slipping the phone into her pocket as Anthony pulled to the curb.

"You're going to have to give me directions," he said as she slammed the door and they sped away.

"Take 494 east. Crosstown will be a snarl right now."

"I picked up a coffee for you." He motioned to an unopened insulated cup resting in the drink holder.

"You're a lifesaver." She pulled back the plastic tab, and the smell of coffee filled the small compartment. Anthony knew her addictions.

As they drove, the sky darkened. The rain began with a few warning drops that quickly turned into a deluge that swamped the highway. The windshield wipers beat madly, but couldn't keep up with the downpour.

Anthony slowed the car to forty and turned the defroster on HIGH, trying to fight the condensation building on the glass. "There won't be any evidence left by the time this stops," he said, tension and frustration in his voice.

"They would have sent for a crime-scene team from the Twin Cities," Mary said. "I doubt they'll get there much ahead of us."

Thirty miles north of Rochester, they turned west. By the time they reached Canary Falls, the rain had stopped and the sun was out.

The town was split by a small river. Main Street was three blocks long and contained what looked to be the only stoplight. Along the edges of town were run-down fairgrounds, abandoned grain elevators, and the requisite forlorn Dairy Queen amidst a stand of weeds. The population was one thousand, and for those one thousand people there were several churches and even more bars. A farming community, it was the kind of place kids spent their childhoods dreaming of leaving.

"Seems to have drawn a crowd and then some," Anthony commented as he pulled up in front of a two-story, navy-blue-trimmed house. They had to park several blocks away from the area of concentrated activity and walk past clusters of loitering people. Upon reaching the crime scene, they flashed their IDs and ducked under the yellow tape.

"The missing person is a seventeen-year-old girl named Charlotte Henning," the officer in charge said, handing both of them a flyer with photo and description. She had a sweet face, Mary noted. Like the other girls, she was blond.

"National Guard is combing the area by foot, and they've got two helicopters in the air," the man continued. He had a Minnesota accent stronger than Wakefield's. "We'd hoped that the lab technicians would be able to lift some impressions, but it started rainin' before they could get here." He shook his head. "Tire tracks are soup now."

"Any other clues?" Mary asked.

"Charlotte closed up Gibby's—the pizza shop where she worked. We found a pizza that she must have dropped on the ground next to where her car would have been parked. He must have attacked her, driven her here in her car, then switched vehicles."

Mary nodded. It made sense.

"Do ya think this is connected to the kidnappings and murders in Minneapolis?" the officer asked.

"Until we have all the facts, there's no reason to even speculate," Anthony told him in the curt way he sometimes had when dealing with people he didn't know. He could certainly come across as a stereotypical FBI asshole, Mary thought.

"No," the officer said, all but squirming, "I guess not."

"We'd like to talk to the parents and anybody who was in the pizza shop last night," Mary said more kindly.

"Interviews are bein' conducted at the grade school." He pointed. "Go two blocks thatta way; then make a left."

"Thanks." Mary gave him a smile, trying to make up for Anthony's brusqueness. Apparently Anthony hadn't heard of "Minnesota nice."

The officer smiled back. "You betcha."

Before heading to the school, Mary wanted to check out the kidnapped victim's car. It was a small, green, rusty model she couldn't identify. Something cheap, something a high school student might drive if her parents weren't as affluent as April Ellison's.

Technicians in yellow ponchos were doing a ground sweep. She spotted a light-haired woman in BCA raingear: Gillian. With her was a young man of about twenty, jet-black hair plastered to his head. Introductions were made. The young man turned out to be a BCA intern named Ben.

Ben was thin and pretty, with remnants of eyeliner around his eyes. His fingernails were purple. He also seemed to be enjoying himself more than the situation warranted. Was he an ambulance chaser? Or one of Gillian's projects?

"Have they found anything of significance?" Mary asked.

Gillian shook her head. "The rain's completely compromised the scene."

Mary pulled out her camera and began taking pictures, just enough so she would have a record of the layout. Anthony wandered off to talk to one of the technicians.

"They've sealed the vehicle," Gillian reported as Mary tucked her camera away. "As soon as they're done combing the ground, they're bringing in a tow truck to take the car to the lab in St. Paul."

It was starting to rain again. Gillian and Ben pulled up their hoods, and Mary popped open her mother's umbrella. Yellow ducks. Not standard-issue FBI.

Gillian laughed. "I know where that came from."

Mary allowed herself a reluctant smile as Anthony appeared beside her, giving the umbrella an odd glance. "We may have a witness," he said. "A girl who was at the pizza shop last night. She's waiting at the grade school."

The umbrella was large enough for two. Mary held it high, offering cover to Anthony. They walked side by side toward the grade school under a canopy of yellow ducks while Gillian and Ben strolled behind them.

"How's your shoulder?"

Anthony's gaze was on her, and she knew better than to lie. "It still hurts off and on, but nothing like two days ago." A moment passed until she saw that he believed her.

He smiled. "Good."

Inside the grade school, Mary closed the umbrella and shook out the excess water. The four of them were led to a classroom where a young girl was waiting. Her name was Susan. She was thin with dark, straight hair and shabby clothes. She seemed to be enjoying the attention and related her story with relish.

"I go there all the time. It's kind of a hangout, you know. There's no other place for kids except for the DQ, and all the old people go there, you know. At Gibby's, you usually see the same kids, so I noticed when this guy came in and ordered a pizza." Susan gave Ben a shy glance, and Mary couldn't tell if the girl was afraid of him or attracted to him. Sometimes the two went together.

"Can you describe him?" Mary and Gillian each had pen and tablet in hand.

"He was kinda tall. Maybe six foot. About normal size, I'd say."

"How old?"

She thought a moment. "Maybe twenty-six, twenty-seven. But I'm not real good at ages."

"Was he white? Black?"

"White. Well, maybe a little something else too, you know. I'm not sure. Something about his eyes made me think that."

"Hair color?"

"Brown."

"Length?"

"Short."

"How short?"

"I don't know. Just not long."

"Anything unusual about his features?" Anthony asked.

"Only his eyes, but I already told you about that."

The girl shook her head. "What I don't get is why would a guy that cute have to kidnap somebody."

Anthony's eyebrows lifted. "People don't always do things that make sense."

"A sketch artist will be getting in touch with you," Gillian put in when they were done. "Hopefully today." She shot Mary a look that let her know she resented being cut out of the questioning. Mary merely shrugged. Too many interviewers could get confusing.

In the hallway, they searched for someone who could direct them to the room where the parents of the missing girl were waiting.

All schools had the same smell of floor wax and paper, books and sweaty bodies. And smells had a way of triggering dormant memories in a way nothing else could. Mary found her thoughts tumbling backward. . . .

Was it déjà vu, she wondered, if the scene that was being played out and the scene you seemed to recall weren't exactly the same?

Suddenly she was standing in the high school she and Gillian had attended—Lynwood High. Rather than Anthony next to her, it was Gavin. Gavin, who was about six feet tall, with brown hair and eyes that had a compelling tilt to them.

Fiona was laughing up at him, and he was laughing back. She handed him something. When Mary looked down, she saw a folded piece of paper in Gavin's hand. On the paper was his name written in bold black letters.

She felt dizzy and confused. Sweat rushed from every pore. She became aware of a feeling of suffocation that reminded her of when she was shot. There had been the white-hot pain of the bullet ripping through her flesh, followed by a rush of perspiration.

The ground had shifted. The next thing she knew, Anthony was bending over her, fear and anguish in his face.

Voices cut through the haze. Her mind sorted them out, pulling her back to the present, to Canary Falls High School, her sister, and Anthony.

"Are you okay?"

The voice was Gillian's, but when everything came back into focus, it was Anthony she saw regarding her with concern. She was standing frozen in the center of the hallway. But at least she was standing. In her mind's eye, she could still see the note. The handwriting on it had seemed familiar, yet she couldn't place it. . . .

"Mary?" Anthony asked.

She pressed her fingers to her forehead. "Oh, wow," she said breathlessly, attempting a light laugh. "I just had the strongest sense of déjà vu I've ever had."

"For a minute," Gillian said with a worried frown, "you looked like you'd stepped into another world."

"Did it have to do with the case?" Ben suddenly seemed to find her extremely interesting.

"You mean, like something psychic?" Mary asked suspiciously.

"Well . . . yeah." He shrugged.

"Why would you think that?"

"I've heard things. About some of the cases you've been on."

So . . . He *was* one of Gillian's projects. That knowledge added a sharper edge to her next words. "Are you trying to discredit my skills as a profiler?"

"Come on, Mary." Anthony was still watching her. "You're overreacting." His eyes seemed to be saying, *He's just a kid.*

"No." Ben held up both hands, palms out, and took a step back. "No way. I'm just really interested in psychic stuff, that's all. I know a guy who has a roommate that can bend spoons—"

"Whatever you've heard, I'm not psychic. What I do has nothing to do with anything psychic. Psychology, yes. But my little trip to another planet probably had more to do with an empty stomach than any kind of ESP."

Gillian laughed, sounding relieved now that Mary appeared to be back to normal. "You've insulted her, Ben," she said lightly. "Mary doesn't believe in that kind of thing."

"Sorry, man. I didn't mean anything by it. I just think psychic stuff is cool, that's all."

"I'm starved." Gillian gave Ben's arm a friendly, reassuring squeeze and a smile that verged on being conspiratorial. *Don't let my crazy sister get to you,* it seemed to say. "Why don't we see if there's any place in this town to grab some food?"

"Not until we interview the parents," Mary said.

Ben shrugged off his backpack and unzipped the front pocket. "My blood sugar gets weird sometimes, so I always carry a couple of these." He held a wrapped rectangle out to Mary, his arm straight. "It's a granola bar. I make them myself. Go ahead." He shook it at her. "Take it. It'll help until we get a chance to eat."

A peace offering.

It seemed they were all holding their breath, waiting to see how Mary would react. She smiled tightly. "Thanks." She unwrapped it and took a bite, hoping it didn't contain pot, quickly discovering that it was full of healthy things like raisins and nuts and sunflower seeds. It was delicious, and she told him so.

Ben beamed, happy to be of assistance.

The bar reminded her of some of Blythe's healthy

concoctions. "I can see that you're going to have to meet our mother," Mary said.

The parents had been put upstairs in a small office. In an attempt to make the interview as easy as possible on the distraught couple, it was decided that Mary and Gillian would speak to them while the men waited outside.

Mary stopped her sister near the door. "It will be less confusing if only one of us does the questioning," she whispered. She waited for Gillian's response, hoping she wouldn't have to pull rank.

At first Gillian seemed prepared to argue—a conditioned reaction. Mary watched as her sister's irritation gave way to understanding and finally relief. Wisdom and experience were on Mary's side.

"Good idea," Gillian said.

The mother, dressed in a red sweatshirt, jeans, and tennis shoes, was hysterical; the father, a burly man in a heavy plaid shirt, was emotionless and brittle with shock. Two others—a man and woman—hovered nearby. They all looked as if they were farmers—hard-working and earnest.

Mary began with the standard questions: Did their daughter know anyone she may have left with? Had she been acting differently lately? Hanging around with new acquaintances? Did she know anyone who may have talked her into leaving with him or her? Know anyone who may have taken her against her will? Had she mentioned meeting anyone new, anyone strange? What was her schedule? What was she wearing?

During questioning, the parents' minds would wander, and their attention would have to be gently coaxed back. Several times the mother broke down, and the husband held her in his arms.

Then came *their* questions, the ones Mary always dreaded.

"You'll find her, won't you?"

"She'll be okay, won't she?"

This was always the worst part, talking to the parents. Worse than watching the autopsy of a child. Worse than staring into the cold eyes of a mass murderer.

"There's no connection between her kidnapping and the deaths of those other girls, is there? Please tell us there isn't."

Mary glanced at Gillian. Her sister's eyes were glassy with tears; she didn't look in any shape to answer. "We don't know," Mary said.

"You must have some idea. Are you hiding something? Not telling us something?"

"We aren't hiding anything. As soon as we have any information, you'll be the first to know."

The man pressed his lips together and nodded. "My daughter's a good girl, a strong girl. She grew up on a farm and knows how to take care of herself. She'll be okay. I know she'll be okay."

Both parents looked from Mary to Gillian, desperately begging for reassurance that couldn't be given.

Chapter 10

After spending all day and into the evening investigating the Canary Falls kidnapping, Gillian returned to her apartment in Dinkytown, but she couldn't sleep. As she lay in bed, the events of the day kept replaying in her mind, especially the interview with the missing girl's parents. How did Mary do it? she wondered. Deal directly with the victim's families like that? Did she have trouble sleeping? Was she awake right now?

Gillian's reflections were disturbed by the sound of someone knocking on her door. She pressed the button on her digital alarm clock, and the numbers glowed green: 12:25 A.M.

The knocking continued.

A soft, rhythmic sound.

Wearing a gray BCA T-shirt and flannel pajama bottoms, she went downstairs and peeked through the living room blinds to see Gavin Hitchcock's car parked next to the curb in front of the duplex.

The knocking continued. The sound was so repetitive and monotonous that it could have been a loop. The style of delivery had Gavin Hitchcock's signature all over it. It was just like him to focus his entire concentration on one thing while blocking out everything else.

She turned the dead bolt and opened the door so the chain caught.

Gavin was a shadowy form standing on her porch.

"What are you doing here?" she whispered.

"Let me in." He sounded desperate. "I have to talk to you."

"It's late."

"Please. Let me in."

She'd always had a soft spot for Gavin, mainly because she knew how tough his life had been and what a struggle it continued to be.

"What's wrong?" she asked over the security chain. Most people were afraid of him, but she wasn't.

"I—I've been having . . . bad dreams."

The words came reluctantly, like the confession of a frightened child who knew he wasn't supposed to wake his parents.

Her resolve weakened. She closed the door, unlatched the chain, and opened the door. Gavin burst in.

"Don't turn on the light!" he said as she reached for the wall switch.

Instead, she crossed the room and opened the window blinds. "How's that?" Light from the street pooled inside.

He pulled a book of matches from the deep pocket of his army jacket and lit the candles on the coffee table, then tossed the matchbook down and collapsed into the sofa.

"I'm sorry," he said, shaking his head.

Gillian had grown up knowing who Gavin Hitchcock was. Everybody knew who he was. Every school had a Gavin Hitchcock. He was the kid nobody wanted to sit near. The kid who always had a runny nose. Every time there was a lice outbreak, all eyes turned to Gavin. Gillian had felt sorry for him from a distance, and secretly she'd thought he was kind of cute, that he would actually be good-looking if somebody took the time to clean him up. They didn't have any classes together—he'd been lumped in with the slow students at the beginning of his educational journey. Gavin would have remained someone she passed in the hallway, someone she saw on the playground, if she hadn't come to his rescue one day when they were both in junior high.

She'd been walking home the long way, the scenic way, taking a path over the stone bridge in Tandem Park when she heard a commotion underneath. She leaned over the side to see a group of older kids picking on Gavin, shoving him around, trying to steal the ragged coat he was wearing. On the ground was a tattered blanket, junk food wrappers, and remnants of a campfire, and she wondered if Gavin had been sleeping there.

Her moral senses were outraged, and without any thought she jumped into the battle, screaming and fighting like a wild animal. She was no match for five bullies, but the idiocy of her attack took them by surprise. They knew that what they were doing was wrong, and to be confronted by a scrawny girl made them feel ashamed. They stomped on the jacket, kicked up some dirt, and then ran away, shoving at one another as they did, laughing and acting tough so nobody would think a girl had scared them off.

Ever since then Gavin had looked upon her with awe and hero worship. She used to subject him to her reading obsession of the moment, from Blake to Burroughs to Rimbaud—which he'd suffered with stoicism and good nature.

She dived into her role as protector, caring for Gavin with the fervor of a big sister. Maybe he filled a need in Gillian, replacing the space vacated by Mary.

Unfortunately, Gavin hadn't seen her as strictly sister material.

Soon after Gavin's release from prison, Gillian discovered he'd spent his days there looking forward to getting out and marrying her. When she tried to explain, he refused to understand. She'd had no recourse but to cut herself off from him completely.

Yet she still worried about him. Her rejection of him went so much against her nature that she had trouble accepting her decision. But what else could she do if any time she spent with him gave him false hope? And now, here he was again, a wounded creature she couldn't turn away.

She sat down in the ottoman across from him, tucking her feet under her. "What kind of dreams have you been having?"

He chewed on his thumb while staring at a candle flame. "I keep dreamin' about girls."

Her heart beat a little quicker. "Girls? What do you mean?"

He continued to chew on himself. "About doin' things to them."

"What kind of things?" Gillian asked with sinking despair.

"I can't tell you, but it's bad. It's really bad."

Gillian pressed a hand to her mouth.

"It seems so real," he whispered. He looked up at her. The flame was reflected in his tear-filled eyes. "It seems *so real.*"

Had his release and return to society brought back what had happened years ago? Were the recent homicides preying on his mind? "Are you still seeing a psychiatrist?"

"You can help me more than any stupid shrink." He rubbed his face. "I'm so fucking tired, Gillian," he said quietly. "So fucking tired."

What should she do? Tell somebody? But they were *dreams*. Just dreams. Gavin was already under suspicion. She'd seen his name on the suspect list. If she said anything, it might be enough to have him thrown in jail. She couldn't do that. Gavin hadn't killed those girls.

The words had become her mantra. Did she believe them, or only want to believe them?

"A doctor could give you pills to help you sleep," she told him.

"I have to be able to wake up! I have to be able to wake up when the dreams come!"

"Shhh. Okay, okay."

"I wish things could be like they used to be." He fell back into the couch, his clenched fists on his legs. "When we were kids."

"Things can't ever be that way again. Not for us. Not for anybody."

"But wouldn't it be nice?" He gave her a pleading look. "If we could go back? Don't you ever wish you could turn back the clock?"

She thought of the horrible childhood he'd had, the poverty, the neglect. My God—he'd developed epilepsy due to head trauma caused by beatings from his alcoholic father. He'd finally found a bit of happiness when the court handed him over to his grandmother, but he'd come home one day to find her dead. After that, he was shoved from one foster home to another. What did it say about his current life if he wanted to return to *that*?

"You have to stop looking back," she told him. "You have to look forward now."

"I've tried, but there's nothing there." He shook his head in discouragement. "Just this dark hole, this pit waiting to swallow me. I want to go back to the time when you were my friend. I know you don't want to marry me. I've come to terms with that. I don't know why I ever thought you would. Sometimes I get these ideas. Games I play in my head. After a while, I begin to believe them. I know we won't get married. But I want you to be my friend again. My sister."

She wished she could tell him she would always be there for him, but she didn't want to hurt him any more than he'd been hurt already. Regardless of what he said, she was afraid that any kind of encouragement might get him going again, might lead to more delusional ideas.

His head fell forward. He caught himself, then straightened. Poor thing. He was exhausted.

She got up. "Gavin, come on." He couldn't stay there. "You have to go home." She pulled him to his feet and pushed him toward the door. Once there, he paused and turned. He reached for her, grasping her gently by one wrist.

"I love you."

The words hung between them.

She felt a little twist inside. She'd only wanted to help him. Instead, she'd ended up hurting him. "Don't say that."

"Why? I'm just telling you the truth. There's nothing wrong with the truth. My grandmother always said the truth will give you wings."

He let her go.

She watched him as he trudged toward his car, a solitary figure. When he was gone, she closed the door and blew out the candles. Then she went upstairs and sat on the edge of the bed, staring into the darkness.

It wasn't love—it was devotion, she argued with herself. Gavin Hitchcock was devoted to her. He'd been devoted to her ever since that day she'd rescued him from the bullies. She thought about how different things would be right now if they'd never met. If she hadn't taken the long way home on that particular day. Gavin had unwittingly played a pivotal role in their lives. It was strange, how one seemingly innocent connection could do so much damage. How one person, by his very existence, had forged the destinies of so many people.

Gillian had adored her sister. They'd been inseparable until Fiona Portman had come along. Then it was good-bye, Gillian. As the months stretched into a year, then two, Gillian's resentment toward Fiona grew. She hated her. She hated the way she laughed and tossed her hair around. She hated the way Fiona would give Gillian those sly, secretive looks that said she knew she'd come between sisters and was proud of it.

Sometimes Fiona would stay over. Whenever that happened, Gillian knew she was in for a night of torture and misery. Fiona would tell her scary stories, then slip into her room after the lights were out and make scratching noises under the bed, saying she was the hatchet man. As Gillian grew older, she distanced herself more and more from Fiona and Mary. She made her own friends. She had her navel pierced and got a couple of tattoos. She wore a lot of makeup and dressed in black.

During that time, she concentrated on giving Gavin a makeover. She helped him with his clothes and hair. She coached him. Pretty soon he was standing tall, looking people in the eye. At the mall, girls ogled him, giggling and flirting outrageously. For probably the first time in his miserable life, Gavin seemed happy.

Together he and Gillian would crash parties where nobody knew them. Girls tripped over one another trying to get to him first. He was "*so* cute" and "*so* cool."

One night they went to a party where kids were drinking and smoking pot. Fiona was there, stoned out of her mind. She spotted Gavin. When she hit on him, Gillian announced it was time to leave.

But Gavin didn't want to go. For the first time since they'd known each other, he refused to do what Gillian said. He stayed with Fiona, and probably made out with her in the upstairs bedroom. Gillian couldn't take it. She caught a bus and went home.

At school two days later, Gavin saw Fiona in the hallway and went up to her, his head high, his stride confident. She was standing with her clique, Mary included in the small, exalted group. Fiona brushed him off. He stood there smiling and talking to her, and the bitch just brushed him off. Acting as if he were invisible, she walked away.

Gavin's shoulders slumped. His head dropped.

Gillian wanted to attack Fiona the way she'd attacked the boys under the bridge, but this was Gavin's battle. She'd warned him about her, and he hadn't listened.

To her credit, Mary didn't follow Fiona. She stayed and apologized to Gavin. She made excuses for her friend. "I don't think she heard you," Mary told Gavin.

"Come on," Gillian said, knowing an argument was pointless. She took Gavin's arm. "Let's go."

Gavin looked at her from under his bowed brow and hanging hair, and his eyes were full of such bleak pain that for the first time in her life Gillian wanted to kill somebody. Fiona Portman.

She shared her desire with Gavin. The bleakness left his eyes, and that afternoon they discussed how it could be done. Together, they fantasized about kidnapping her. They would torture her. They would kill her.

Gillian forgot all about the incident until two

months later when Fiona was dead and Gavin was arrested for the crime.

Gillian never knew if Gavin killed her or not, but if he had, Gillian knew she was to blame for planting the idea in his head.

It had been bullshit, kid stuff, not anything she ever thought would be carried out. But she was young. She hadn't understood about Gavin, about how he sometimes had a problem separating fantasy from reality. As a child, he'd developed the skill to protect himself. That armor lent him the power to be able to move through the world without being crushed by it.

She pressed a fist against her mouth to muffle the sob that threatened to escape. She'd fucked up his life—that's what she'd done. All along, she'd convinced herself that once he got out of prison, everything would be fine. Well, now he was out and he wasn't fine. He was a million miles from fine.

She hadn't only fucked up Gavin's life; she'd also fucked up Mary's. If Fiona had lived, Mary would eventually have seen her for what she was: a spoiled little bitch. Now she'd been relegated to sainthood, and Mary—Mary, who used to be *funny,* who used to laugh and dance and act as crazy as a person could act—was now on some holy mission to right the wrongs of the world. She'd so immersed herself in darkness that she could no longer see a pinpoint of light. She was no longer Mary Cantrell. She hadn't been Mary Cantrell since the day she'd stumbled over Fiona's dead body.

Chapter 11

"I'm home!"

He hurried down the basement stairs. In one hand was a cup of hot chocolate and a carryout bag of food he'd picked up at an all-night gas station. He'd agonized over what to get her as a reward, and then he'd spotted the hot chocolate. Bingo. She would be hungry. She would be glad to see him.

His heart beat in anticipation. This was the one. He was sure of it.

He unlocked the door to the narrow room and leaned his shoulder into it, shoving it open.

The acrid smell of vomit hit him in the face. He recoiled and then forced himself to step inside. She was lying on the mattress, her hands cuffed behind her. He rolled her toward him; her body was heavy and cold.

"I brought you hot chocolate," he said with hesitation.

Skin the color of paste.

Eyes partially open and dried out.

He ripped the duct tape from her mouth to reveal blue lips and not a stirring of breath.

NO!

Dead! She was dead!

He roared like a bull elephant and threw down the cup. Hot chocolate exploded against his pants.

She'd suffocated.

NO!

Not Charlotte! Not *his* Charlotte!

He'd covered her mouth so she wouldn't scream while he was gone. How was he to know she would get sick? He didn't have all the answers. He wasn't the Answer Man.

He slammed the door and went upstairs. *This can't be happening.*

He sat down at the kitchen table and unwrapped the prepackaged sandwich he'd gotten for her. He wouldn't have picked it out for himself. It was something a girl might like, with thin slices of turkey, slimy cheese, and wilted lettuce. Light mayonnaise. He would have preferred regular. He was halfway through the meal when he started sobbing. He almost choked because his mouth was full of food that just wouldn't go down. He gagged and spit it out.

He quit coughing. He quit crying. He sat there trying to figure out what he was going to do.

Daylight will be here in a couple of hours.

"I know. I know," he said to the empty room. "Don't you think I know that? I'm thinking. Just let me think."

Twenty minutes later, he went back downstairs.

She was still there, just the way he'd left her, lying on the mattress he'd put there just for her. He would like to have kept her awhile, but he knew from experience that it didn't take long for a dead body to start smelling, start drawing flies.

It was hard getting her upstairs. He was out of breath, and his back hurt by the time he got her to the bathroom.

Once there, he removed her clothes, then put her

in the tub. He arranged her legs so she would be comfortable. He filled the tub with cool water and, with a washcloth, removed all traces of vomit. When he was finished, he crossed her arms over her chest. He caressed her hair, smoothing it on either side of her face.

"Not your fault, little girl." Not his, either. Like the bumper sticker said, *Shit Happens*. It was an oldie but a goodie.

Oh, she was beautiful and sweet and innocent. He was terribly afraid she'd been the one.

Don't think about that. You can't think about that.

He let the water out of the tub, then photographed her, snapping frame after frame. He shot close-ups of her face and shots that took in her entire body. He was caught up in the wonder of her. He wanted to have sex with her. Should he? Did he dare? He finally decided it wouldn't be right; she deserved to be treated like a lady. He wrapped her in the shower curtain and carried her back through the house, into the garage. He put her in the trunk of his car.

He could see her face through the plastic.

Under cover of darkness, he drove.

He wanted to take her back where he'd found her, but cops were crawling all over. They had dogs and helicopters. The National Guard. He'd seen it on the news. So he'd have to take her someplace else. She was special; she deserved a place that was special.

He didn't want to leave her where nobody would find her. He didn't want to leave her where animals might eat her. He wanted to baptize her. He wanted to give her extreme unction.

He took her to a spot where the river flowed swiftly, where the current would carry her away with cherished abandon. She was heavy, and he staggered under the weight as he walked along the old railroad tracks that led to the bridge.

The night was dark, and the water was black.

"I commit you to the night, to the water," he whispered, unwrapping her from the plastic shower curtain. Standing on the bridge, he let her go. A moment later, he heard a faint splash.

It was one of those autumn days that brought people out to enjoy the fall colors and possibly the last warm day of the season. Children perched on their fathers' shoulders, chubby hands splayed across foreheads. Bicyclists cruised the Mississippi Mile, and groups of people paused in their stroll across the Stone Arch Bridge to admire the river gushing through the dam.

"Ball," a baby said, pointing with a wet finger.

The object tumbled into view and then vanished into the churning, roaring water.

"Ball," the baby repeated, giggling.

"Where'd it go?" asked the mother, enunciating clearly.

They waited but didn't see it again.

"All gone," the father said with mock sadness. "All gone."

Just then, to the right of the tumbling falls, something bobbed to the surface where the water became silent and smooth as black glass.

"Ball," the baby said, happy again.

Everyone at the bridge smiled and looked. The object drifted closer, and the voices fell silent.

"What the—?" a man finally said.

It was near enough for the crowd of people to be able to make out two undulating arms, a back with the indentation of the spine. Deeper beneath the surface, legs and feet. A body, drifting facedown in the water.

*   *   *

The Behavioral Science team at Quantico had signed off on Mary's profile. She and Anthony put together a press release and were presenting it to Elliot Senatra when the call came.

Elliot's body language changed in a fraction of a second. He was tense, hypervigilant. "Where?" Elliot said into the receiver. Then, "We're on our way." He hung up and looked from Mary to Anthony. "A woman's body's been found in the river near the Stone Arch Bridge at Saint Anthony Falls."

All three charged out of the room, pulling on coats as they hurried down the hallway.

The falls, located just a few blocks from the FBI building, was a popular spot with its view of the locks and jogging paths that took in the Stone Arch Bridge, Mill Ruins Park, Nicollet Island, plus both sides of the Mississippi.

Mary, Anthony, and Elliot arrived on the scene as the victim was pronounced dead. There wasn't a lot that could be processed when a body was found floating in the water, but detectives, lab techs, and the medical examiner were doing what they could. Detective Wakefield was there, along with another officer who was snapping photos. Wakefield acknowledged them with a nod; then he bent his head to converse with a nearby policeman. Reporters with TV cameras swarmed, the media outnumbering crime investigators twenty to one.

"Could be a suicide," Mary commented, crossing her arms and scanning the crowd, not wanting anybody to get ahead of themselves. Both nearby bridges were packed with people hoping to see something. "Or an accident."

"Mind if we take a look?" Anthony asked, flashing his ID.

The man with the camera stepped back. "Go ahead."

The three FBI agents approached.

The body had been pulled from the water and put in a lined body bag. From there it was taken to shore, the bag unzipped for evidence collection and photos.

"Dead less than twenty-four hours, wouldn't you say?" Mary asked, glancing up at Anthony. He was bent, hands on his knees, dark hair falling forward.

"Yeah."

Mary crouched down. If the body hadn't been found in the water, they would have documented everything on the spot, rolling her over to get both sides. Now the main objective was to keep any possible evidence inside the bag with the body. But everyone knew water usually erased all traces of evidence.

"Any visible signs of trauma?" she asked the medical examiner, a heavy middle-aged woman with graying temples.

"Not readily apparent." The ME focused back on her tablet.

The body belonged to a female, about seventeen. Her hair was blond, her skin the color of marble, her lips blue. One eye was half open, the pupil a creamy white, like a cataract.

She still had her eyes.

Mary visually studied her fingernails. Except for abrasions most likely caused by banging around in the river, they seemed unharmed. She looked up at Anthony and could see that he'd made the same observations.

He moved closer, crouching down opposite Mary. "Looks like our girl," he whispered.

"We'll have to wait for the fingerprints or her family's ID, but I think you're right."

They moved back so the crime scene investigators

and medical examiner could finish up. The body was tagged, the bag zipped and secured with a seal to maintain the chain of evidence. It was then loaded into the van to be taken to the morgue.

Gillian and Ben arrived as the vehicle was pulling away. "Got caught in traffic," Gillian explained. "Looks like we missed the whole thing."

"Water cases don't take as long to process on-scene," Elliot commented.

Wakefield came up behind them. "A meeting in my office—right away." He began walking in the direction of the police station. As soon as he stepped under the crime scene tape, microphones were jammed in his face. "Come on, people. You know better than that. I can't talk to you until we have the facts."

One reporter wouldn't relent. He needed a sound bite for five o'clock. "Someone said it was a young girl. Can you confirm that?"

Wakefield stopped. "Yes. It appears to be the body of a woman. That's all I can say." He pushed them aside and continued on.

Elliot had his own technique for dealing with the mob. It could have been called pretend-they-don't-exist. It appeared to work extremely well, and Mary made a note to try it the next time she was bombarded with unwanted questions.

They must have made a strange group to anyone who met them on the city sidewalk outside the police station. Six stone-faced people, most dressed in black, moving silently and with purpose, their strides long and deliberate, looking like the opening scene of a police drama.

When they reached the seclusion of Wakefield's office, everybody began talking at once.

". . . still had her eyes."

". . . fingernails intact."

"Doesn't fit the MO."

"If it is Charlotte Henning, she wasn't killed right away." That comment came from Gillian.

Wakefield nodded in approval. "Anybody care to guess how long after she was kidnapped?" he asked.

"Twenty-four hours," Elliot said.

"Maybe longer," was Anthony's observation.

"So is it the same guy?" Ben asked, his face reflecting the confusion they all felt.

Everybody looked at Mary and Anthony. They were the experts. They were supposed to have the answers.

"Well?" said Wakefield.

Mary shook her head. "I don't know."

"We need more facts," added Anthony.

"You must have some initial feeling about it," Wakefield argued.

"There are similarities," Mary said. "But they could simply be coincidence. It could even be a sort of copycat. Not a deliberate copycat, but someone who was given the idea to kidnap and kill a blond teenage girl. I'm hoping the autopsy reveals something. I'd like in on it, if that can be arranged."

"Shouldn't be a problem," Wakefield said. "Anybody else want their name on the list?"

"I may not be able to make it, but put me down," Anthony said.

"Me too." That from Gillian.

"What about you?" Wakefield was looking at Ben, who'd suddenly turned a pasty white.

He glanced at Gillian, as if expecting her to come to his rescue. "Uh, I'm not sure I'm ready for an autopsy."

"This would be a good one to start on. She's pretty fresh."

Ben gestured with his hands buried deep in the pockets of his black hooded sweatshirt. "Sure. Okay."

Chapter 12

Ben didn't show up.

At least he called, telling Gillian he didn't think he was going to make it. She wouldn't hold his squeamishness against him. She remembered her first autopsy. The anticipation had been hell, but once she was in the suite with the body, nothing was what she'd expected. The experience was probably different for everybody. Maybe that's why nobody told her it would border on being spiritual. The cadaver's hands had especially intrigued her, and she'd finally gotten up enough nerve to ask the medical examiner if she could touch them, hold them, feel the muscles and tendons and bones.

She wasn't especially religious, and yet she couldn't help but think of one of the most beautifully written lines from the Bible: "Behold, I am fearfully and wonderfully made." The human body was truly amazing.

Mary and Anthony arrived together, looking cool and professional as always. What was their deal? Gillian wondered. There was a weird electricity between them. It was unnerving the way they were always finishing each other's sentences and exchanging those silent communications. Yesterday when they were walking to the police station, Gillian had noticed women furtively glancing in Anthony's direction. He was striking, that was for sure, but a little intimidating for her taste.

Mary looked around the preparation room. "Where's Ben?"

"I don't think he's coming."

"Oh." Mary nodded, immediately understanding.

They began putting on protective gear.

"I'd better warn you," Gillian said as she slid a pair of Tyvek pants over her jeans. "The pathologist—Dr. Phillips—he has the reputation for being an ass."

Bending at the waist, Mary pulled paper slippers over her shoes. "I've met some of those in my life. I think I've even been one upon occasion."

Gillian laughed, surprised that Mary had made a joke.

"Does he know we're coming?" Anthony asked.

"Sure, but he didn't *invite* us. Cough drop?" She extended an open tin.

Mary took a lozenge and popped it in her mouth.

Anthony shook his head. "I can't handle any of that eucalyptus stuff anymore. I associate it with dead bodies."

"Luckily I haven't reached that point," Gillian said.

After donning the bio safety hoods, they moved from the preparation room to the autopsy suite, their paper suits rustling.

The Hennepin County Morgue had four exam tables, each separated by a curtain. A special room to one side was reserved for the badly decomposed. Gillian had been in there only once—and had no desire to go again. When she was done she had to throw out her clothes, and a full bottle of lemon shampoo hadn't been enough to get the stink from her hair.

Several people were already present—two detectives Gillian recognized from Homicide, along with one of the crime scene investigators, and the two policemen who'd answered the initial call. Mary and Anthony slipped into a space near the foot of the body. Gillian took a position directly opposite the infamous Dr. Phillips, the stainless steel exam table between them.

"I don't know why you can't just read my autopsy report," Phillips grumbled. "Those Tyveks aren't cheap."

Gillian looked at Mary. *What'd I tell you?*

The table was equipped with one of the newer down vents rather than an exhaust fan above the work area. Next to the doctor were trays containing some of the tools of his trade: scalpels, saws, needles, tweezers, mallets, and shears. The exam hadn't started, yet the overpowering smell of formalin filled the room. The cough drop didn't help. Instead, the synergy of the two odors created something entirely new and repulsive, and Gillian decided Anthony might have a point about eucalyptus.

"It used to be nobody wanted to see an autopsy," Dr. Phillips remarked. "Now so many people want in on it that we've had cases where we had to hold a lottery."

The nude body was removed from the sealed body bag and placed on the funneled exam table, a case number attached to her shoulder: ME-02-652. Her skin had a waxy, transparent quality, her hair matted, her lips almost black. In death, there was something regal and beautiful about her. And, as with all the dead, something secretive and mysterious.

The exam began with the doctor recording vital statistics—name, race, social security number, date of birth, medical history, and case number—into the tiny microphone clipped to his scrub suit. "This is the body of a well-developed, well-nourished white female," Dr.

Phillips stated. "She is five feet seven inches tall, weighing approximately one hundred and thirty pounds."

The body had already been identified by the family as Charlotte Henning. Now it was gone over from head to toe. Case numbers were also affixed to various areas of the body as they were examined. Photos were taken with a digital and a 35-millimeter camera.

"I like to have negatives for the file," Dr. Phillips said.

The epidermis was examined.

"Some slight tissue damage on both sides of the mouth," he said. He pulled the swing-arm light closer. With a scalpel, he lightly scraped the abrasion. "I'm removing some foreign material from the right side of the face, below the cheekbone. Slide." His assistant stepped forward, and Dr. Phillips transferred the possible evidence from the scalpel to the slide.

He continued with the preliminary pass, examining the body from front to back, the diener helping at the appropriate times. More photos were taken. He made note of any birthmarks; those were also photographed.

"Abrasions on both wrists." Photos of the wrists were taken.

Scrapings were lifted from beneath the fingernails. Then, using the scalpel, he cut around the wrist and slipped the withered, unprintable skin of the entire hand away until it lay like a crumpled latex glove in his palm. As in most cases where the body had been submerged in water, the skin slipped free easily.

"Who has small hands?" he asked, eyeing the audience.

One detective and a cop took a step back. Gillian offered her gloved hand, which he accepted. He slipped the peeled skin over hers, smoothing the fingertips so a decent print could now be retrieved. His assistant produced the metal container of ink. Wearing the skin, Gillian inked all of the fingers and thumbs and then pressed the prints onto cards. Even when family or friends had visually identified a body, prints were always taken.

"You earned the right to be here," the pathologist said, helping her slip the skin from her hand.

Gillian had felt Mary's eyes on her the entire time. Now she looked up to see that her sister appeared impressed by her coolness.

The ME's examination continued. "Broken forearm, two broken ankles."

"Postmortem?" Mary asked.

"Most likely. The injuries are consistent with a body that's been found in water. The strong current would have banged it against rocks and outcroppings. I'd expect broken bones and lacerations such as these."

"Anything that looks like an inflicted wound?" The question came from Anthony.

"No."

With a syringe, Dr. Phillips drew blood by puncturing the heart; then he filled several tubes.

Now it was time for the internal exam.

Gillian braced herself for the initial cut.

He made a long, deep, Y-shaped incision, beginning at the shoulders and ending at the pubic bone. With shears, he snipped through the rib cartilage and removed the rib cage. More blood was collected for a microorganism culture.

The dissecting continued inside the neck. He removed the trachea and esophagus. "There's your probable cause of death," Dr. Phillips said, placing them in a stainless steel tray. Asphyxiation." With a scalpel, he poked around at the trachea, separating some small pieces of foreign matter. "Regurgitated food particles." He moved to the head, examining the eyelids. "Petechial hemorrhaging. A classic sign of asphyxiation."

"She choked on her own vomit?" Mary asked.

Using his foot, the doctor clicked off the tape recorder. "It would appear so."

He moved back to the face, touching the skin damage he'd pointed out earlier. "I would guess that she was bound and gagged, her mouth sealed with tape. During that time, she got sick and threw up. No place for the vomit to go except, of course, out the nose. The nostrils immediately became plugged, and that was that. Asphyxiation. Since the exam isn't finished, this information is off the record, and nothing is a hundred percent until I've sewn up the body, gone over the slides, and gotten the reports back from the labs."

He turned the recorder back on, then continued with the dissection, proceeding to the carotid artery and jugular veins. Half an hour later, he'd moved down to the abdomen.

"Sulfhemoglobin," Phillips noted, pointing to the green discoloration in the abdominal cavity.

A heavy, cloying, familiar odor filled the room, a smell that was as unforgettable as it was indescribable. Maybe if you put a combination of rancid gym shorts, dirty diapers, and rotten food outside in a hot, sealed car for a couple of days, then you might come close to recreating the stench. One thing for sure, it was a smell nobody ever forgot.

"What's this?"

From the vaginal cavity, Phillips pulled out a small sandwich bag with a plastic zipper. He unzipped the bag. Using a pair of tweezers, he extracted an object and deposited it on a tray. Everybody leaned closer. On the small stainless steel tray was a single red rose petal.

"That's a first for me," Phillips said.

"Weird as hell," said one of the police officers.

The other one started humming the song "Red Roses for a Blue Lady" under his breath.

Everybody cracked up.

"News of this finding can't be released to the public." Mary glanced around the table. "Having exclusive knowledge of this kind of evidence can be used in our favor."

There was a unanimous nodding of heads and verbal agreement.

"I've seen what I need to see," Anthony said. He turned and left the room. Gillian thanked Dr. Phillips; then the sisters followed Anthony out the door. In the changing area, they removed their masks, and stripped out of their scrubs, dropping them into the biohazard container.

Anthony wiped his arm across his face. "That smell will be in my sinuses for a week."

"Should have used Vicks," Mary said.

"You know how I hate that stuff."

They left the building, all three of them taking deep, cleansing breaths.

Anthony pulled out his mobile phone. "We are all pretty much in agreement that this is the same guy, right?"

"If it is, then he probably didn't intend to kill her—at least not yet," Mary said. "She was abducted. Her mouth was taped, her wrists tied. And like Phillips said, she got sick and choked to death."

"Pretty clear cut," Anthony added.

"I don't get the rose petal," Gillian said. "Is it a signature?"

"Could be a clue he left for us," Mary said. "Subconsciously he may even want to get caught before he kills someone else. And it definitely ties in with the grafting performed on the previous victim."

"He could be toying with us." Anthony checked his phone for messages. "I'm calling Wakefield. He needs to schedule a meeting—within a few hours, if possible." He talked while entering the number. "Charlotte Henning died by accident, so everybody needs to be on high alert. I'm afraid this guy could be extremely agitated and already trolling for a replacement."

Chapter 13

In the City Hall building Mary, Anthony, and Gillian made a beeline for the café on the first floor, a place called Larry's Canteen. There they were able to grab snack food and beverages from the vending machines—enough to get them through the next couple of hours.

The meeting room was on the same floor. When they arrived, Mary was relieved to see that Wakefield had been able to round up several detectives from the Minneapolis Police Department, officers from the Hennepin County Sheriff's office, plus agents from the BCA. Also present was the press liaison—quite likely the most important person in the room at the moment. Ben Collins was also there, lounging in a chair, feet crossed at the ankle, looking sheepish. Elliot hurried in at the last minute, out of breath and carrying a sack lunch.

It was good to see such diversification. In the old days, lack of organization, competition, and jealousy, made for little exchange of information among bureaus. Over the last several years there had been a deliberate movement toward sharing on all levels, with the various departments agreeing that they were after the same thing: capturing the criminal.

Chairs were lined up in rows schoolroom fashion.

People grabbed and rearranged them until they were U-shaped.

"I want to thank all of you for getting here on such short notice," Wakefield said, perching on the corner of a full-size desk at the front of the room. "We don't have an official autopsy report on the latest victim— who's turned out to be the missing Canary Falls girl— but we do have information that could be crucial to the safety of our citizens. I also have lab results to pass along, but we'll get to those later. Right now I'll let Agents Spence and Cantrell explain their immediate concerns."

Remaining seated, Anthony detailed what had occurred during the autopsy. His voice was low but clear.

"Is it your belief that the same person committed all of the homicides?" one of the female detectives asked.

"We can't say about the badly decomposed body," Anthony related, "but the last three were killed by the same person."

"I don't get it. What about the eyes? If it's the same person, why didn't he remove the eyes? Why didn't he stick branches in her fingers?"

"Because the girl died too soon," Mary explained. "She never had a chance to fail or disappoint him. There was no reason for him to remove her eyes or try to graft her, because she was still an enigma to him."

"I've been thinking about that eye deal." Without removing his hands from his sweatshirt pockets, Ben wiggled higher in his seat. He seemed to have shaken off his earlier no-show shame. "It's like Santa Lucia."

"Lucia?" Wakefield asked, looking both annoyed and baffled.

"Yeah, you know. The saint who gouged out her own eyes."

"Not familiar with that story." Wakefield glanced at Gillian, the big reader.

"This guy liked her—a lot, especially her eyes," Ben went on. "But she didn't want anything to do with him, so she gouged them out and sent them to him. Haven't you seen that picture of her with her eyes on a plate? At first you think it's just a couple of grapes she's offering somebody, but then, when you look closer, you see they're eyeballs."

People laughed, mostly at the inappropriateness of Ben's contribution.

"Isn't Lucia a Swedish celebration?" Mary asked, willing to follow Ben down his path. "I wonder if that in some way might tie in with the blond hair. Did all the victims have similar eye color?"

Several people flipped through paperwork and reports. "All blue."

"Ben may be on to something," Anthony said. "At this point I'm not sure what, but it's good to throw all ideas out there. You never know where it might lead or what kind of connection might later be drawn."

Wakefield checked his watch. "Okay, let's move on. What about the method in which the eyes were removed? We have one done with almost surgical precision, another torn out. How do you find a correlation there?"

"The removal itself is the correlation," Mary said. "How they were removed directly reflects the killer's emotional state at the time. With one he was cool and careful. With the other, angry and sloppy."

"What about the surgical precision?" Wakefield asked. "Your profile says nothing about the guy possibly being a surgeon."

"Nothing points in that direction. Although remember that a profile is only an educated guess. He's obviously proficient with a blade, has a fondness for roses, and could even be into propagation."

"We've got Records running the profile right now, matching it to people on our extended suspect list. We should have it narrowed down in a few days. As soon as that happens, I'll get copies to everybody."

"The city and surrounding areas need to be on high alert," Anthony said. "I don't want people to panic, but this is a grave situation. He could strike again at any moment."

"The department's scheduled a press conference in two hours," Wakefield said. He got to his feet and passed out lab results. "Here's what we've got so far. They found the same navy fiber on both April Ellison and Bambi Scott.

"The dress worn by the Ellison girl is a vintage 1960s number," he added. "We figure it's something the guy had around the house—maybe belonged to his mother, aunt, grandmother—or he picked it up in one of those little shops around town. We have people looking into that prospect, but so far no results. They've hit the vintage shops; now they're working on charity places like Goodwill."

Wakefield continued. "This guy just isn't leaving much in the way of clues. And I'll tell you something—Walgreen's can't keep dark hair color on the shelves. Light-haired women all over the place are dyeing their hair." He looked around the room. "Anybody got anything else?"

Gillian opened her folder. "Unfortunately, the BCA hasn't made much progress. We've reviewed the surveillance tapes from the mall hundreds of times, but can't pull anything together. We've had our experts enhance the visuals, coming up with several faces we've finally matched to names. None of them have fit the profile, and all of them look clean. Right now, we're hoping for a tip from the public."

The group broke up, with Gillian and Ben heading

back to St. Paul to report the most recent findings to the BCA. Elliot remained at City Hall. The mayor wanted to speak with him and Wakefield before the press conference. Mary and Anthony exited the building through the Fifth Street doors, moving toward the Third Avenue ramp where Anthony had parked his car.

"I've got to get something substantial to eat, how about you?" Anthony asked.

"There used to be a little pub up two streets."

They headed in that direction.

It was still there. People were getting off work, and the pub was dark, crowded, and intimate. The hostess put them at a small, highly varnished table near the front window.

They ordered sandwich baskets and iced tea.

The waitress brought their drinks, placing both glasses on small square napkins. Mary smiled at her and nodded her thanks.

"How's the arm?" Anthony asked.

"Almost normal. The anti-inflammatories seem to be working."

Mary was dressed in a dark blue suit Anthony recognized, along with a white top. Her skin was almost flawless, her mouth, even without its present touch of color, was perfectly shaped. She was lean and tall. He liked that.

She squeezed lemon into her drink. Evening light filtered in, illuminating one side of her face. Green eyes. That always surprised him about her; under most conditions her eyes looked brown.

"As one trained in the art of acute observation, I can't help but notice a certain amount of tension whenever your sister's around," Anthony said.

She gave him a pained, I'd-rather-not-talk-about-it

look. "We have some unresolved issues I'm trying to put aside so I can remain focused on this case." Her voice was dismissive.

In the time they'd been partners, he couldn't recall her ever volunteering information about herself. Anything he'd picked up had been sifted through casual conversation. But then, he'd never told her much about himself either.

He sensed that Mary was struggling with something Gillian had done to her, and Anthony knew forgiving someone for past grievances wasn't easy.

"Did I ever tell you my father was a football coach?" he asked.

Mary looked up, and he could see she thought he was joking. His family's obsession with football had been the crux of his childhood. He'd been a stranger in a strange land.

"It's true," he said. "I come from a real rah-rah family. My father coached, my three brothers played football, and my mother drove them all over the country to their games."

She leaned closer, chin in her palm. "Where did you fit into this picture?"

"I didn't. One of my earliest memories is of my dad trying to teach me to throw a football. I had no interest in it. I kept tossing it down and walking away. That lack of interest only intensified with age."

"That must have been alienating."

"That's the word for it. For years my father and brothers tried to shame me into playing until I eventually refused to attend any games." He took a swallow of tea. "We lived in a small town. Only one high school. Their rejection of me was contagious. I couldn't go anywhere without some redneck saying, 'Hey, Spence. Why ain't ya' playin' football? Are you afraid of hurtin' your wrist?' That line almost always called for a dangle of the hand. Then the guy and his buddies would fall all over themselves laughing."

"Is your dad still coaching?"

"Semi-retired."

"And your brothers?"

"They went on to play college football until injuries sidelined them." He nodded at the familiarity of the story. When he was a kid, it had seemed unique. Now he knew it was a plot that had replayed itself in towns across the country. "Of course, they're all proud as hell of me now. Last time I was home for a visit, the guy who started the limp-wrist thing was practically kissing my feet."

She was watching him with sympathy and understanding. "And you resent that."

"Hell yes." He smiled even though the subject was one that still filled him with bitterness. He'd been robbed of his childhood, while the very people who should have supported him were the bullies leading the attack, condemning who he was. Had something similar happened to Mary? If so, he could understand her reluctance to work with her sister. Yet he also knew bitterness was crippling and served no purpose.

"This is all very enlightening, but I'm suspicious. Why are you telling me your life story right now?"

He shrugged. "The atmosphere seemed conducive. Two people sharing a meal in a dark pub."

She was watching him with a half-smile—she wasn't falling for it. She wasn't going to show him her scars just because he'd shown her his.

As if to signal a change of subject, Anthony banged a long metal spoon around in the tall glass. "What are you doing tonight?"

She gave him a strange look, and he could tell she was wondering if he'd just asked her out on a date.

He could see the idea develop, see the instant it was dismissed as preposterous, see her finally pick it up again only to end with lingering confusion.

He put her out of her misery. "I was wondering if you could look over the details of the Texas case I'm working on. I've run into a couple of rough spots."

She relaxed, back on secure ground. "I'm going to be busy earlier, but how does nine o'clock sound?"

"That'll work." He reached across the table and grabbed her hand, holding it lightly in his. "Cat?" He ran a finger across the angry red scratch that showed up starkly against her white skin.

"No, I was out in the woods."

He sensed her discomfort with physical contact and held her hand a little more tightly. "You've never struck me as the outdoor type. Does this sudden interest have anything to do with the current case?"

"No."

"What about Fiona Portman?"

She pulled her hand away and, to discourage any attempt to renew contact, moved it to her lap under the table. "What do you know about Fiona?"

"That she was a friend of yours who was murdered when you were seventeen. Want to talk about it?"

"No."

"Sometime?"

"It's over. It happened years ago."

The longer you were around somebody, the easier that person got to read. Mary was hiding something. "Are you sure it's over?"

"Of course I'm sure."

"Then why were you in the woods?"

She tossed down her napkin and got to her feet. "I have to go to the ladies' room."

Anthony watched her walk away. Blythe had given him a general explanation of Fiona Portman's death, but he had the feeling she'd left out some important details. He and Blythe should have another talk, he decided. After all, getting information was his specialty.

Chapter 14

"I'm going into the woods tonight," Mary announced.

She and Blythe were sitting in the warm kitchen with its terra-cotta color-washed walls, drinking a horrendous green tea her mother claimed would reduce inflammation and speed healing. A CD was playing, something ambient, mysterious, and exotic. In the corner, a small fountain flowed soothingly over layered rocks while a scented candle burned.

Mary knew what her mother was doing—trying to create a relaxing environment to boost her immune system. Earlier she'd tried to talk Mary into visiting one of her friends—a healer who worked with crystals and heated rocks. Mary declined. She wasn't going to discount the benefits of such a strategy, but she felt the subject of such healings had to have a measure of faith and mental participation—something Mary didn't have the patience for. She had too many other things on her mind.

"You're going into the woods when it's dark?" Blythe put down her mug—one she'd made years ago. It was thick and heavy, with a burnt-umber glaze. "Why not wait until daytime? Do you FBI agents always have to do everything in the dark?" She reached across the table and gave Mary's hand a gentle squeeze. "It doesn't make sense, sweetheart. And why do you want to go at all?"

"It's strange that you and Mrs. Portman have never seen anyone coming or going. That means whoever is visiting the site doesn't want to be seen, which makes me think they have to be visiting at night. And yes," she said with a smile. "FBI agents like the dark. We're a gloomy bunch."

"Don't go," Blythe pleaded. "Not where Fiona died."

"I have to."

"It can't be good for you. I don't like to think about you out there, especially by yourself." That thought seemed to make up her mind. "If you're going, I'm going with you."

"It'll be cold and possibly muddy in places," Mary warned, appreciating her mother's offer. Not that she was afraid to go by herself, but the company would be nice.

"Look at these." Blythe held out hands with square, damaged nails and skin that was dry and prematurely wrinkled from years of working with clay. "I play in the mud all day long."

"This will be your first FBI stakeout," Mary joked.

They cleared the table, blew out the candle, went to their rooms, and changed into outdoor clothes and sturdy boots. It was getting dark by the time they convened downstairs.

Mary handed her mother a miniature flashlight and another small device. "It's a thermal scanner. It can detect a temperature change from over a hundred yards away. Push this button—" She demonstrated. "The reading is seventy-one, which is the temperature of the walls. Now point it at me."

"Ninety-eight point six," Blythe said. "That's amazing. Aren't these the things used by parapsychologists?"

Leave it to her mother to ask a question like that. "Yes, but we're looking for living, breathing human beings."

Blythe looked around as if she were missing something. "What about night-vision goggles?"

"Unfortunately, I left those at home."

"I was kidding."

"I actually have a pair," Mary said, laughing. "With the scanner, we won't be able to see what it's picking up. We can only determine the location."

With their flashlights off and stashed in their pockets, they headed out the kitchen door, through the backyard and side gate. The street ended in a cul-de-sac. Where the yellow sign said DEAD END, they continued down a dirt path people used to cut through a ditch in order to get to the adjoining street. At the bottom of the ditch Mary swung to the left, toward the woods. She plunged ahead, into the darkness.

"No flashlights," Mary whispered as her mother collided with her from behind.

"I can't see a damn thing," Blythe whispered.

Mary pulled out a key chain with a tiny orange squeeze light. Holding it toward the ground, she pressed the soft button. It created a small glow of light around her feet. "Hang on to me."

"I feel like Nancy Drew." Blythe grabbed her arm, and they began moving slowly through the woods, Mary keeping her eyes and ears tuned for anything unusual. Darkness was almost complete when, minutes later, they reached the area where Fiona had died.

"There it is." Mary directed the small glow of light on the cross.

"I can't believe I never knew this was here," Blythe

said, peering at it. "Who's taking care of it? And why?"

"That's what I want to know. People leave crosses and flowers where people have died in car wrecks, but the secretive nature of this memorial makes me suspicious."

Mary found a spot beneath the curved branches of some bushes where they could wait and see if anyone made a nighttime appearance.

Blythe switched on the thermal scanner and began monitoring the readings, turning it in different directions. The temperature hovered around fifty-five unless she pointed it at the sky. In that case, it dived below zero.

They soon discovered that fifty-five wasn't too cold for Minnesota mosquitoes. Mary tried not to slap too loudly.

Fifteen minutes into their vigil, Mary heard something moving through the leaves. Blythe trained the heat detector in the direction of the sound, where it registered a temperature above one hundred. Mary's flashlight picked up the glowing eyes of a raccoon or possum.

"People say they've seen coyotes in these woods," Blythe whispered. "Sometimes in the winter I hear them at night. It's so eerie. They sound like people—like tortured souls."

"Mom, we're going to have to be quiet."

"Oh. Sorry."

Mary patted her back. *"That's okay,"* she whispered.

They stuck it out for two hours. By the time Mary checked her watch and announced that Anthony would soon be stopping by, their teeth were chattering and their legs were stiff.

Thinking about Anthony reminded Mary of that afternoon in the pub. Had she read him wrong? Had he been slightly flirtatious? No, she thought, quickly dismissing the idea.

Silently they got to their feet.

Blythe, who continued to keep an eye on the scanner, suddenly pulled in a tight breath and tugged Mary's sleeve. Mary looked down at the readout in her mother's hand. Pointing away from them, in the opposite direction of the cross, it read 98.6.

Human.

They dropped back to the ground and stared at the glowing green numbers. As the person came nearer, their ears began to pick up the sounds of movement—the *shush*ing of leaves, the snagging of thorns on cloth. A beam of light cut through the branches, bouncing off tree trunks and a mist that had moved in.

Mary was aware of her own breathing, of her mother's fingers digging into her arm.

The person stopped.

A beam of light moved in front of them, illuminating the cross.

Slowly, silently, Mary reached inside her jacket pocket, her fingers wrapping around the leather flip-open case that held her ID. Afraid the person was getting ready to bolt, she straightened.

"Stop!"

She held up her ID. The beam of light shot in her direction, blinding her.

"FBI!"

The light was extinguished. The person backtracked in the direction he'd come, crashing through the underbrush.

Mary followed, turning on her high-powered FBI-issue flashlight as she ran. Behind her, Blythe shouted.

Thorns ripped at Mary's jacket. Ghost halos from the doused light blinded her. Unfamiliar with the path, she soon realized the person she was chasing had her at a disadvantage. Two minutes later, she'd lost him and was forced to give up.

With cold air burning her lungs, she turned and headed back to where she could see the light cast by her mother's flashlight.

"Look," Blythe said.

On the ground lay a bouquet of red roses.

Also illuminated in the pool of light was part of a footprint that appeared to be from a fairly large boot. Mary crouched beside it. "It looks like a man's nine or ten. Here—" She passed the flashlight to her mother. "Hold this." While her mother held the light, Mary pulled a camera from her pocket and took a quick series of photographs. Finished, she stowed the camera and picked up the bouquet of roses by a single stem.

"What are you doing with those?" Blythe sounded concerned.

"I might be able to lift prints from the cellophane."

"They don't belong to us." She was using a tone Mary remembered from childhood when most of Blythe's moralizing came by way of heavy suggestion or opinion. "I think you should leave them by the cross."

"Really?" Mary asked, hoping this didn't turn into a battle. She had no intention of putting the roses back.

"I feel bad about this. Does it matter who's visiting the place where Fiona died? Whoever it was just wanted to put flowers there. What's wrong with that?"

"He ran away."

"I'd run too if I came upon someone hiding in the woods right where a sixteen-year-old girl had been murdered."

"Come on," Mary said, heading back toward the house.

"You aren't going to leave the flowers?"

"No."

"But, darling. Think about it. Taking them is like . . . like grave robbing."

Mary stopped and turned around. "Do you always have to be my conscience?"

"Isn't that what a mother does?"

Mary sighed. "Okay, I'll bring them back. After I check for prints. How's that?"

"Much better."

When they reached the house Mary asked Blythe if she had any superglue. "And the heated tank I used to keep my lizard in. Do we still have that?"

She already knew the answer. Her mother never got rid of anything.

Wearing latex gloves, Mary arranged the cellophane-wrapped roses carefully in the reptile tank she'd positioned in the center of the kitchen counter. She squeezed superglue onto a small dish fashioned from aluminum foil. That she placed in the bottom of the container, which was then sealed tightly with plastic wrap and packing tape.

"Now we wait." Mary plugged in the heater cord. "Years ago somebody discovered that the heated vapors from superglue make fingerprints appear on hard-to-dust objects. And since I don't have any fingerprint powder . . ."

As they watched, smoke gradually filled the sealed tank. After several minutes white fingerprints appeared on the green cellophane.

"Now I feel like MacGyver," Blythe said.

Mary carried the tank outside and unsealed it so the vapors would evaporate. Back in the kitchen, she lifted the cellophane-wrapped roses from the tank. She'd been able to capture several clear prints. "Who says I can't cook?"

The problem with the superglue method was that

the prints couldn't be lifted and transferred to a slide or card without the aid of fingerprint powder. Mary ended up cutting off squares of cellophane, which she carefully taped to index cards. She was just finishing up when the doorbell rang. She checked the wall clock. Almost nine. Anthony.

Mary answered the door.

"Superglue?" he asked, stepping inside. He removed his coat and tossed it over a chair, excited at the prospect of a clue. "Did you find some prints?"

"It's nothing to do with the case," Mary quickly explained, gesturing toward a sitting area in the living room as she attempted to divert him. She didn't want him to know what she'd been up to.

But the smell of glue was overpowering, and he followed his nose into the kitchen, where Blythe was putting a bouquet of flowers in water.

"Those are the foulest roses I've ever smelled. He leaned forward to examine the prints on the index cards. "What's going on?"

"I'll let Mary tell you," Blythe said. "I'm freezing." She hugged herself and rubbed her arms. "I'm going upstairs to take a hot bath."

When she was gone, Anthony grabbed Mary's hand. "You're cold, too. What have you been doing?"

Mary pulled away to turn on the teakettle. "Would you like some hot tea?" She was wearing a bulky wool sweater, and her cheeks were bright red from the outdoors. On her feet were thick socks. She looked vibrant.

"Sure," he said.

She retrieved two cups and placed a tin of tea bags on the counter between them. "Help yourself."

He poked through the supply, passing on the florals and herbals to settle on Earl Grey. "Go on. I'm still waiting for an answer."

She hesitated, prepared to say something elusive. But then she thought about the occasions in the past when she'd evaded his questions only to later regret her silence. She didn't want to push him away anymore.

She briefly told him about the person in the woods, and the site where a sixteen-year-old girl had lost her life years ago.

"Your friend."

"Yes."

Once she got started, she didn't stop. She told him about the birthday party. She told him about Fiona and about how she'd found her in the woods. It all came pouring out.

At the end, he said, "Jesus. You were only a kid yourself."

"It was a long time ago."

"Time doesn't always mean that much when you're dealing with something traumatic."

She began to bustle around, as if suddenly embarrassed by how much of herself she'd let him see. The teapot was ready. She focused her attention on pouring steaming water into his cup, then hers.

"I still don't understand why you're investigating a closed case," he said.

The subtle disapproval in his voice set her on guard. "I'm not investigating it. I'm just curious, that's all."

"What about the current homicides?"

"I've worked several cases at a time before. I'm not being negligent, if that's what you're implying."

"I simply think it's a waste of time, energy, and focus. And I'm not sure it's healthy."

She crossed her arms. "Earlier today you wanted to know why I'm tense when my sister's around. It's simple and easy to explain: A buddy of hers killed my friend." She looked over her shoulder, in the direction her mother had gone. Upstairs water was running. "All these years," she whispered, looking deadly serious and terribly sad. "All these years I've suspected that my sister may have put the idea in his head, however unintentionally."

Anthony wasn't impressed. "You were a child. You've dealt with enough juvenile cases to know children often create their own reality, often misread something that has happened, especially when a high degree of fear is involved."

"I know that. I realize that. But Gillian hated Fiona. She despised her. And Gavin would do anything for my sister, including killing someone he knew was making her miserable. Even if that isn't the case, her betrayal has been an ongoing saga. She visited the bastard in prison. She helped him get a job and a place to live when he got out."

"He's out?"

She lowered her mug. "Released a couple of months ago." She looked at him, waiting for a reaction.

"Shortly before the girls began disappearing," Anthony said thoughtfully.

"Handy, isn't it?"

"Do you think there's a connection?"

"I haven't found anything to substantiate that idea. But if you're asking about my gut feeling, I'd have to say I think he may have something to do with it."

The extra heat in her voice made him pause. "Emotions can skew a person's perspective."

"I know. I hate this guy, and I would like nothing more than to see him back in prison where there's no chance of his hurting anyone again. And," she admitted, "I'm afraid every piece of evidence I look at is colored by those feelings."

Anthony nodded, taking it all in. "The person in the woods. The person who put up the cross. You think it might be this—what did you say his name was?"

"Gavin Hitchcock."

"You think it might be Gavin Hitchcock?"

"Doesn't it make sense? He got out of prison two months ago. Killers often go back to the scene of the crime. He never got the chance because he was arrested right after her murder. So now he can finally return and relive that day, even put up a shrine. And what about the roses? Red roses. It makes sense to me. Does it make sense to you?"

She was looking at him with a desperation that he'd never seen in her before. She wanted to be reassured that she hadn't lost perspective the way agents sometimes did when they were too close to a case.

"The roses could very well be a coincidence," he said slowly, "but what you're saying makes sense. It's a solid theory."

She let out a relieved breath.

"But you can't allow yourself to be sidetracked by this old case. You have to follow the clues from the new homicides, then see if they intersect with this Gavin Hitchcock."

She fully agreed. She'd been trying to do that all along. "The killer's in control of the game. He hasn't left much of anything, at least nothing he doesn't want us to find. Wakefield might not understand how in control he is, but you do."

Anthony knew what she was thinking. The cases where there were no clues, and the killers had never been caught. Those were the ones that haunted them.

He had another concern. "Have you said anything to anyone about Hitchcock?"

"Only Gillian. But his name is on the suspect list, and he fits the profile."

Thank God she'd understood the dangers of mentioning his name to people like Wakefield and Elliot Senatra, Anthony thought.

"Because of the lack of clues," Mary went on, "tantalizing information about Hitchcock could turn this investigation into a witch hunt. As much as I hate Hitchcock, I don't want that to happen."

"No."

Mary's thoughts flashed to an image of Charlotte Henning tucked into a body bag.

"My worry," Anthony said, putting voice to the concern foremost in both their minds, "is that the killer is stalking a new victim at this very moment."

Chapter 15

Blondes.

He'd always had an obsession with blondes. When he was little, he used to sit behind a little blond girl who had the most amazing hair. It was so blond, it was almost white. One time he touched it. She didn't stop him, so he touched it again, continuing to get braver until she turned her head and caught him with her silken locks spilling through his fingers. She cried. That hurt. After that, he went out of his way to avoid her . . . but he never quit thinking about her hair. . . .

He bought a paper and read up on the visitation and funeral of Charlotte Henning. He wanted to go. He desperately needed to see her, needed to make sure she'd completed her journey safely.

But he couldn't. He knew how these things worked. The police would be there looking for him. So he sent her a rosebush instead, one her parents could plant at the cemetery or in their yard. Whenever they saw the abundant, beautiful red blooms, they'd think of their daughter, and they'd think of him.

The funeral was scheduled for two o'clock.

At 12:30, he showered and shaved, then put on his only suit. The jacket sleeves were a little short, but if he pulled down the cuffs of his white shirt, it didn't look too bad.

At 1:30, he stepped into the basement and turned on the overhead lights.

He'd taken fifteen photos of Charlotte in the bathtub. Those he'd developed and enlarged to a variety of forty eight-by-tens. One wall was covered with her pictures—a memorial to a beautiful girl, a beautiful woman. In many of them he'd varied his developing technique, using different paper, different exposure times, filters, even some burning and dodging, so that even though many of the poses were the same, each was different.

He had several favorites, but the one he liked best was an eight-by-ten of her face—her sweet, angelic face.

He'd used a filter and fiber paper, both lending a softness to the finished product. She looked about twelve years old. She looked like an angel, with her blond, matted hair, her dark lips that had really been blue but since he worked exclusively in black-and-white, they could very well have been a lush red.

He checked the industrial clock on the wall. Five minutes.

He pulled out a chair, turning it toward the photos, and sat down, his hands clasped together on his lap.

He closed his eyes.

He imagined driving to the funeral. He imagined parking. He imagined stepping inside the church. And suddenly . . . he was there. . . .

Candle flames danced behind red glass. The air smelled of flowers. He was pleased to see that the roses he'd sent were displayed prominently by the altar, next to her open coffin.

Without feeling his feet on the floor, he glided down the aisle toward her.

She was beautiful.

Her hair had been washed so it lay softly on either side of her face. Her lips were no longer blue, but a healthy pink that matched her cheeks. She wore a flowing white gown, the neckline trimmed with lace.

He looked down past her breasts and trim waist to where her hands were lying delicately, one on top of the other, her fingernails as pink as shells.

He reached inside the coffin and touched her blond hair. It was soft as silk. He touched her hands, which were warm beneath his fingers.

"You're going home," he whispered, bending closer.

Her eyes opened, and she smiled up at him.

"Forgive me." His throat was beginning to hurt, his voice getting tight.

"Come with me," she said, an imploring look on her face. She lifted a hand to him. "Come with me—"

Tears welled up in his eyes. "I can't," he choked.

"Of course you can."

"No. No, I can't. Don't ask me that."

"The world is a cruel place. You said so yourself."

"I'm afraid."

"There's nothing to be afraid of."

"Yes. Yes, there is!"

"Shhh."

The sound came from several people seated nearby. They were staring at him with cross faces and fingers pressed to their lips.

The scene changed, and suddenly he was sitting at the back of the church. The service had begun. Beautiful songs were sung, but when it came time for everyone to follow the closed coffin outside, he couldn't make himself get up.

"I'm afraid," he whispered shamefully to himself.

He couldn't make himself go to the cemetery. Couldn't make himself follow her on the last leg of her journey. He didn't like cemeteries. He tried to stay away from cemeteries.

Good-bye, Charlotte.

He opened his eyes and stood up, the chair legs scraping against the floor. Exhausted, he walked to the wall of photos and pulled down his favorite, the soft close-up of Charlotte's face.

Why had she asked him to come with her? He was ashamed because he was such a coward. There had been many times in his life when he'd thought of killing himself. He believed in God, and he knew the next world had to be better than this one. He wanted to die, wanted to join her, but he'd been told that killing himself would be a sin. A mortal sin that could send him plummeting to hell.

But maybe *this* was hell.

Words came to him and he spoke them aloud: "The errors that are whispered to me, enchantments, false perfumes, childish melodies."

Who had written that? Somebody's favorite author. Rimbaud. Yes. Arthur Rimbaud had written those words.

He bent his head and kissed Charlotte, sweet, sweet Charlotte, on the lips.

He put the photo aside and left the darkroom to change out of his suit so he could return to work.

He thought about the other girls. Their annoying imperfections.

Sluts.

Bitches.

Undeserving of life.

He reached into the deep front pocket of his pants, feeling for the six round objects he kept there. They were dry and much smaller now, but he loved the way they felt. He rolled them against his fingertips, around and around. Like worry stones, they brought him comfort, comfort he sorely needed in a time like this when his quest for a mate had to start all over again.

The bartender kicked them out at 1 A.M.

There was a lot of noise as the five friends shuffled out the door of the rural Minnesota tavern.

"Comin' over, Todd?" Jerry asked as he searched through his keys. "I rented a coupla movies. Adam Sandler. You still like Adam Sandler?"

"Who doesn't?" Todd asked, not wanting to make Jerry feel bad even though he'd outgrown Sandler a while back. "I don't know. I'm a little tired."

"Come on."

"Yeah, come on. We're all going," chimed in two of the other guys.

The routine was familiar. Usually Todd dragged his feet, saying he was tired, but eventually Jerry and company convinced him to come to Jerry's place, where they would sit around drinking beer and watching movies until early morning. It had been fun when they were in high school, but they'd been out for four years now, and Todd was finding it increasingly depressing.

"I think I'll just go on home," Todd said, even though he knew once he got there he would lie in bed and stare at the ceiling and stew about his life until the sun came up. He was going through what was now being termed "quarter-life crisis," and he wasn't enjoying it.

"Sure?" Jerry asked, standing with his car door open.

"Yeah. Yeah, I'm sure."

They broke up, and Todd fumbled for his keys. Now that he was standing upright, he realized he was drunker than he'd thought. He'd just drive slow and take a back road. His truck was a piece of shit with over a hundred thousand miles on it, but it always got him home.

"Shoulda stayed in college," he said to himself as he turned onto a narrow, unmarked road that wound between a mixture of towering pines and deciduous trees. He'd gotten into a fender bender last winter, and one headlight didn't point straight anymore. Instead, it veered to the right, illuminating the trees as he passed.

The night was cold with patches of fog. Condensation settled on the windshield. The wipers were going, but they didn't help much. Todd craned his neck trying to find a clear area, the fog just dense enough to be disorienting as he tried to spot something that looked familiar, that would take him in the direction of his trailer. Why had he gone this way? Why hadn't he taken a road he was more familiar with? Had he missed the turn?

He continued on for ten minutes.

Too far.

He braked, coming to a stop in the middle of the dark, deserted road. He was about to swing the truck around using the ol' three-point turn when he caught a flash of movement out of the corner of his eye.

His scalp prickled.

Ever since he could remember, he'd heard stories about this road, about a ghost that had been seen by a lot of people. He'd never seen a ghost. Once, when he was twelve and sitting alone in his room, he thought he felt the pressure of a hand on his shoulder. But it never happened again, so as the years passed he figured he'd just imagined it.

He clicked on his brights.

Oh, shit.

Standing on the side of the road was a blurry shape. His first instinct was to turn the truck around and haul ass out of there. He fumbled with the gearshift, intending to put it in drive. But he'd already been in drive, and he accidentally slammed it into park instead.

He looked up, the sound of his heart thundering in his head. His eyes watered in fear.

The apparition turned to face him.

A girl.

He'd expected to see a skull for a face, or at least something withered and ugly, but it was a girl. A girl with blond hair. Wearing nothing but a red T-shirt, panties, and jogging shoes. She stood at the edge of the road, staring into the bright lights.

His fear dissolved. This was somebody real. This was somebody in trouble.

He pulled out the parking brake and stepped from the truck. "Are you okay?" he shouted to her.

She stared as if afraid of him—or as if trying to gauge whether he was friend or foe.

He began to move slowly toward her, the soles of his boots echoing hollowly and sounding unnatural on the deserted road.

"Stop!" She held up a hand, palm out.

He stopped.

"Don't come any closer!"

"Okay, okay. I won't. Look, I stopped. I'm just standing here. But I think you should get in my truck so I can take you—"

"Truck? You're driving a truck?"

"Yeah." He stepped into the headlight beam, his body cutting off the light, throwing her into darkness. "Now can you see it?"

"M-maybe." She raised her arm higher, like a person blocking the sun. "I'm not sure."

He stepped to the side so the light once again illuminated her. She was younger than he'd thought. Fifteen, sixteen, maybe. Her face was dirty and scratched, and there were tear tracks down her cheeks.

Something bad had happened to her. Something really bad.

He began blabbering, trying to gain her trust. "My name's Todd. I live around here." He scratched his head—a nervous gesture of his. "I should be going to college, but . . . I don't know, I thought it was a drag and quit. Now I wish I hadn't. It's not like it's too late, I guess. But it doesn't seem the same going when you're twenty-two." He paused, trying to pull together more of his biography. That was about it. Sad, really. "Let me help you."

He began to move again, slowly because he was afraid she might bolt.

She didn't, and soon he was close enough to touch her arm. It was like cold marble.

She spoke, and when she did her words came out a harsh, broken whisper through a throat that sounded raw. "Some guy. Some creepy, awful, creepy guy. He k-kidnapped me and p-put me in the trunk of his car. It smelled awful in there! Awful!"

"Oh, man!"

"I started gagging and couldn't breathe." She pressed madly trembling fingers to her mouth. Her eyes began to tear. "B-but t-that gave me the idea to play dead . . . and I got away."

Fuuuckkk! The hairs on the back of his neck shifted. He'd read about some crazy asshole who was kidnapping and killing girls. The people on the news had started calling him the Lucia Killer because the guy kept their eyes. Their fucking eyes! What kind of person did that? Nervously Todd checked up and down the road. Empty except for the fog. At least it *looked* empty.

He'd seen *Texas Chainsaw Massacre* over twenty

times, and he half expected Leatherface to come crashing out of the trees, chainsaw in his hand.

"Come on! Let's get the hell out of here!" He grabbed the girl. Stumbling, they ran for the truck.

The police station where Todd took Holly Lindstrom was located on the main drag in the small town of Hiawatha Springs. As soon as the officers on duty heard what had happened to her, they put in a frantic call to the country sheriff, the BCA, and the FBI. Now, in the predawn hours, Holly sat in a cramped room with two high, tiny windows and a row of buzzing fluorescent lights overhead while waiting to be interviewed by an FBI agent being sent down from the Cities.

She just wanted to go home. Go home and take a shower to wash the stink from her body, then crawl into bed and never get up. Sleep. She wanted to sleep forever.

But when she got home, would she be able to sleep? And if she did, what if he came back? What if he was lurking outside her house, outside her bedroom window, waiting for the lights to go out?

The FBI agent introduced herself as Mary something. Holly was having a hard time concentrating, and she'd never been good with names. Mary something had short dark hair and was wearing black pants, a black jacket, and white blouse. The clothes were too grown-up and business for Holly's taste, but there was something cool about the woman. Holly suddenly felt safer just having her in the room.

"Do you mind if I record this?" the agent asked, sitting across from her at a narrow table and pulling a small tape recorder from a brown leather briefcase.

Holly shook her head. "Somebody already explained how interviews have to be recorded." She shrugged. "And I don't care anyway."

"I know you've already answered a lot of questions." The woman flipped open a notebook and retrieved a pen. "But I specialize in abduction cases. I might ask you things the police aren't trained to ask." She looked at her and smiled in a sad, understanding way that made Holly feel better. "How about if we start with your name, age, and address?" She clicked on the recorder, entering a date, time, and location.

"Holly Lindstrom. Age seventeen." That was followed by her south Minneapolis address.

"What were you doing just before you were kidnapped?"

"I heard about the Lucia Killer—that's what everybody's calling him now. That's all people are talking about. We even had an assembly at school. They passed out flyers. Told us to be careful. Always walk with other kids. Adults, if possible. All that stuff, but it didn't seem real. I mean, we've had assemblies about other things. Drinking and driving. Drugs. AIDS. I never felt like any of them had anything to do with me. I mean, I heard that one of the girls who was killed was a runaway, and another was kind of a whore."

Her mother had warned her. Her father had warned her. "When you get off work, have the manager walk you to your car," they'd instructed. She'd promised, but only to lessen her parents' worry. She'd never had any intention of asking her boss to go with her. How uncool.

"I was at work," she explained to the FBI agent. "I work at a convenience store. Come and Get It. Stupid name, I know. My friends always tease me about it. They're always asking if I work at a pet store. Sorry." She looked down at her hands. Her knuckles were white. "I have a bad habit of getting off the subject. What did you say your name was?"

"Cantrell. Agent Mary Cantrell."

"Oh. Yeah. Sorry."

"That's okay. Take your time. We aren't in any hurry."

Holly took a deep breath and continued. "When I get off work it's usually dark. For some reason, I felt kind of creeped out and I actually thought about asking my boss to walk me to my car, but he was busy. A customer had . . . like . . . run into one of the gas pumps, and it was all crazy. It was late and I wanted to get home. I have a test tomorrow—well, today—and needed to study. My car was just a block away, around the corner. It was no big deal. Or I didn't think so, anyway."

She tugged a chunk of straight blond hair across her cheek and pulled it into her mouth. She gnawed on ends that were already wet, then let go. She was addicted to hair chewing. Also to eyebrow plucking. Not with tweezers—with her fingers.

"When I unlocked the car," she continued, "somebody grabbed me from behind. I thought it was one of my friends playing a trick on me. I yelled, mad. And then . . . the guy—he stuck a gun in my side and told me he'd kill me if I didn't shut up. After that I didn't say anything else. He, like . . . got in the backseat and told me to, like . . . drive away."

"Did you see him? See his face?"

"No. I was afraid to turn around. One time . . .

when I was waiting for a light to change . . . I looked in the mirror, but it was dark in the backseat."

"Then what happened?"

"He made me drive to this deserted place where his car was parked."

"Did you know where you were? Did you recognize the area?"

She shook her head. "I was too scared. All I was thinking about was dying. I knew this was the guy, the Lucia guy, and I knew he was going to kill me. The only thing I remember is that we pulled up behind these huge cement things. You know, those things you see by railroad tracks."

"Grain elevators?"

"Maybe. I'm not sure. I'm a townie. I don't know anything about that stuff."

"Did you go over any railroad tracks to get there?"

"I don't remember. I think. Oh, I don't know. Sorry."

"That's okay. Then what happened?"

"He taped my mouth and hands and made me get in the trunk of his car."

"Did you see the vehicle?"

"It was dark, really dark. But the trunk was big. It wasn't any little compact thing, that's for sure."

"When he was taping your mouth, did you see him at all? Even a little bit?"

"I could kinda make out a dark shape, and maybe a lighter area that would have been his face, but that's all."

"Did you get a sense of how tall he was?"

She thought a moment. "For some reason, I thought he was taller than me. Maybe close to six feet."

"How about his voice? A lot of times we can get a sense of how large a person is by the voice. Was his voice deep? Or high-pitched?"

"I don't know. I was too scared to notice. Maybe average. I don't know."

"What about an accent? Or possibly poor grammar? Did he sound like someone who was well educated?"

She gave it some thought. "I didn't notice anything weird about the way he talked, but like I said, I was scared. And he didn't say much. A few commands like, Drive. Turn right. Pull up there. Get out of the car. I was so scared that a couple of times I didn't hear him, and he got mad and yelled it again." Holly suddenly felt like crying. "I'm sorry. I don't know why I can't remember anything when it just happened a few hours ago. I feel so stupid. I'm not helping at all, am I?"

"You're helping immensely. You've already told me that he's most likely white, fairly tall, no strong accent, and drives a large car—a car that may have left tracks near a grain elevator. Don't feel bad about not being able to answer my questions. Don't apologize for being human and responding like ninety-eight percent of the population. It's a documented fact that when a person's heart rate reaches a high level, it becomes almost impossible to hear and even more impossible to comprehend what we're hearing. I'm going to continue to ask questions, but please don't worry if you can't supply an answer. Just be proud of yourself for having the guts and initiative to get away from him. That's something no one else has been able to do, because unfortunately it's also human nature to become passive when presented with such a situation. We tend to freeze and wait when facing the unknown. You didn't allow yourself to freeze—which is why you're alive. You are an amazingly strong individual," the agent told her sincerely. "And just the fact that you got away is going to help us catch this guy."

Her words of encouragement assuaged some of Holly's tenseness and made her fear recede. She *had* gotten away. That was pretty damn impressive.

Agent Cantrell glanced through the notes the police had taken, then up at Holly. "I know it may be impossible to answer this, but did you get any sense of how far you may have ridden in the trunk before he stopped to check on you?"

The mental block Holly had subconsciously erected when she'd been speaking with the police evaporated. All at once she was able to put herself back there, in the trunk.

"It smelled so bad," she whispered. "Like something rotten. Like something dead." She picked at the green scrubs she was wearing. "I'd let you smell my shirt, but the crime scene people took it. They picked things out of my hair too. And cut my fingernails—in case there was any evidence under my nails."

"They're very efficient."

"It was the Lucia Killer, wasn't it?"

"We don't know. The only way to substantiate that theory would be to link him to the other crimes."

Holly knew they couldn't assume the guy was the Lucia Killer without facts. She'd already been told that. It seemed stupid, when everybody was thinking it was him. "They asked if they needed to get a rape kit, and I told them no. I don't think they believed me at first until I yelled and cried. Anyway, I started thinking that maybe there was a dead person in there with me. In the trunk. The more I thought about it, the sicker I felt. Pretty soon I started gagging and even threw up. It shot out my nose or I would have choked to death. A little later the car stopped and the trunk flew open. The guy made some weird sound, like maybe he was upset or scared or something; then he pulled the tape off my mouth and put a hand over my face. Right away I wanted to scream, but then I

realized he was checking to see if I was breathing."
She paused, thinking about how she'd tricked him. "I
love to swim. I swim all the time. I can hold my
breath, like, forever—so I held it. He slammed the
trunk and took off. We drove for a long time. Or it
seemed like a long time. Then he stopped and opened
the trunk again. This time he cut the tape from my
wrists and pulled me out."

"Then what happened?"

"He drags me through the woods, all the while I'm
playing dead. It's dark. Pitch black, otherwise he
would have known, but the darkness helped, I think.
But I know he's going to kill me. He cuts off my jeans.
Slash, slash, rip, rip, and they were off." She hesitated
a moment, wondering if she wanted to mention what
happened next. She hadn't told the police.

"He took pictures of me."

"Pictures?"

"Yeah. The flash went off in my face. Two, maybe
three times."

"Did the camera make a sound? Or was it silent?"

"I heard something. Kinda like my 35-millimeter
camera, but faster. One shot after the other."

"Then what?"

"He starts fiddling with his own clothes. I can hear
the sound of a belt buckle and a zipper, and I know
he's going to rape me. *He* thinks he's going to have
sex with a corpse. What do you call those people?
Who have sex with corpses?"

"Necrophiliacs."

"Yeah. I saw a movie once about a girl who worked
at a morgue and had sex with the dead bodies. Anyway, that's what he was thinking was going to happen.
And I knew I couldn't play dead any longer, so I
jumped up and ran. I just ran. . . ."

Holly could still hear him behind her, panting, rip-

ping through the underbrush. She remembered making so much noise. Too much noise! But she couldn't
slow down. No way could she slow down! The sound
of her own heart was drumming in her head. She
heard the air being sucked into her lungs. Even though
branches tore at the flesh of her bare legs, she felt no
pain. All she thought about was moving, getting away.
She was fast. She was young. She was scared shitless.
She could beat him. She could outrun him. She just
had to keep going. Keep moving.

She didn't know how far she ran, or for how long.
All she knew was that she couldn't stop. There was
no way she could stop. Even when she no longer heard
sounds of pursuit, she kept going. He could still be
back there, moving silently. Because he could move
silently. He'd already proved that when he'd surprised
her getting into her car. So maybe he was still behind
her. Moving silently over the forest floor, silently over
skeletal leaves and tiny ferns and dark earth.

Suddenly she saw lights in the distance. The night
was foggy, but she was able to pick up the sound of
a single car rolling down the highway.

Was it him? Had he gone back for his car, and now
here he was, ready to cut her off? She voted against
revealing herself, but her body moved of its own accord. Before she could stop it, she stood at the side
of the highway with a pair of headlights cutting
through the fog, blinding her.

This could be the end, she thought distantly. *The
end of my life.*

She thought about her parents, about all they'd
done for her. She wished she hadn't been so nasty to
them the last couple of years. What was the point?
What had she been trying to prove? It seemed so stupid now.

The car stopped but remained idling. Someone

stepped out and began to move toward her. She could
make out the shape of a man, his legs scissoring black
silhouettes against the light. How would she know if
it was him? His face would tell her nothing. Seeing
him would do no good. This could be him and she
wouldn't even know it. Pretending to be stopping to
help. Hadn't she seen that trick in a movie?

Turn around.

Turn around and run back into the woods.

But his voice was young and compelling. He said
he was driving a truck.

Let me see it. Step aside so I can see it!

It *was* a truck. A crappy, rusty, wonderful truck!
And he was practically a kid! Nice, horrified, just as
frightened as she was.

"Todd," Holly told Agent Cantrell. "He said his
name was Todd."

"Yes, I met him in the hallway. I'm going to be
talking with him shortly."

"He yelled at me to run, like he was suddenly
scared to death." Now that she thought about it, it
was funny. Really funny. She laughed, a hand to her
stomach. "Here *I* was the one who'd been kidnapped,
almost raped, almost killed—yet *he* was scared. I think
he said, 'Let's get the hell out of here!' in this high-
pitched voice. Yeah, that's what it was. Let's get the
hell out of here! Oh, my God," she gasped. "That is
so funny! Isn't that funny?" she asked, waiting for
a reply.

Agent Cantrell stared at her a moment as if
weighing her words. "I'm guessing you had to be
there."

Chapter 17

Detective Wakefield called a private emergency meeting five hours after Mary's interview with Holly Lindstrom. Present in the first-floor room of the Minneapolis Police Department were Wakefield, Mary, Anthony, and Gillian.

"What's your opinion?" Wakefield asked the two FBI agents. He was popping antacid tablets and clutching a stained coffee mug that said WISHIN' I WAS FISHIN'. "Do you think this wacko who kidnapped the Lindstrom girl is the same guy who's killing women and cutting out their eyeballs?"

"Without more evidence," Anthony said, "we have nothing to tie them together."

"You're profilers. You were called in because we don't *have* enough evidence. Can't you just come out and say what you think? That's why I wanted only the four of us here. This is completely off the record, but I have to know what you're really thinking, and I have to know it now. Not tomorrow. Not in a week or ten days, or whenever the hell you can get those guys at Quantico to sign off on another profile. Let's quit beating around the bush about this. Let's cut through that FBI red tape and tell me what you think."

Mary looked at Anthony. To anyone else his expression may not have seemed to change, but Mary understood he was agreeing to go against protocol. She turned back to Wakefield. "Off the record," she said, "we think it's the same guy."

Wakefield let out a deep breath. "Thank you. That's all I wanted to know. Now let's proceed. We've got people out combing the woods where the Lindstrom girl was picked up. They found some footprints they're making casts of as we speak. They've also found some strands of hair caught on branches. But so far no torn clothing and no tire tracks."

"Holly said he took photos of her." Mary sat down in an unforgiving plastic chair. Anthony stood nearby, a hip against the window ledge, feet crossed at the ankles. "I doubt he'd want to take his film in to get it developed, which means he's probably processing it himself."

"Sebastian Tate's taking darkroom classes," Gillian offered, contributing for the first time.

Wakefield took a sip of coffee, then grimaced as if he knew it was going to hurt when it hit his stomach. "Tate's still on the suspect list. With the earlier profile we've been able to narrow the names down to roughly twenty. Have detectives out interviewing all twenty right now."

"We can't concentrate exclusively on the list," Mary said. "The killer might not be on it. I think we need to broaden the net."

"I agree," Anthony said.

Wakefield let out a groan. "You know how many people are into photography in the Twin Cities area? How many people have their own darkroom? We'll have Research go through data from places that sell darkroom equipment, but there are probably thousands. Still," he added reluctantly, "at this point, the photography angle seems to be all we got."

"Anthony and I have discussed this, and our opinion is that he'll try to come after Holly," Mary said. "She represents the one who got away. Not only physically but romantically as well."

"That's my feeling too," Wakefield agreed. "He's going to be pissed off. This girl has to be watched. She has to be protected."

"Have you explained the danger she's in?" Anthony asked.

"I thought I'd give her until this afternoon to equalize, then hit her with the bad news. Unfair as hell, but there it is. She's a target."

"Right now it looks as if our best chance of catching the killer is Holly Lindstrom," Mary said. "But the problem I foresee is high visibility. He's not going to try anything if he knows he's being watched."

"What we need is somebody who isn't so visible," Gillian said with enthusiasm. Until that point she'd been basically ignored. "I want to propose an idea. What if I move in with the Lindstroms?" Anticipating protests, she held up her hands. "Hear me out. What if I move in with them and go to school with Holly? Spend every second with her? That way she'd be better protected," Gillian reasoned. The plan appeared to be taking shape as she spoke. "And by being with her at all times, I would see everybody she sees throughout the entire day. We could say I'm a cousin or something. Somebody who is maybe having trouble at home and could use a change of scene while also keeping Holly company."

"You mean work undercover?" Mary asked skeptically. She suspected Gillian's proposal was based on the desire to put an idea, any idea, on the table. "Pose as a high school student?"

"Why not? People always think I'm younger than I am. A little change in wardrobe, hair, and makeup, and I could pass for seventeen."

Mary's heart pounded in alarm at the thought of her sister exposing herself to the Lucia Killer. Gillian was a master at getting her way, and Mary hadn't missed the father-daughter relationship between her sister and Wakefield. In one more minute he would be agreeing to the scheme. "A visiting relative might raise the killer's suspicion," Mary said, hoping to effectively halt the direction of the conversation before it began.

"Possible benefits could certainly outweigh the risks of a blown cover," Anthony interjected. "The idea is sound."

Why was he siding with Gillian? Mary wondered. "Even if we consider it, I don't think the visiting teenybopper should be Gillian."

Had Anthony forgotten about Gavin? If the kidnapper was Gavin Hitchcock, what good would Gillian's presence do? And if he wasn't Gavin—well, she didn't think her sister had worked in the field long enough to carry out such a deceptive and dangerous operation.

She got to her feet and grabbed Gillian by the arm. "Can I speak with you in the hallway?"

Once out of earshot of Anthony and Wakefield, Mary said what she had to say. "It's a bad idea. Period."

"I knew you'd be against it," Gillian said, clearly annoyed. "You know what your problem is? You'll never think of me as an adult. No matter how old I get, I will always be your silly little sister. When I'm ninety and you're ninety-three, you'll think of me as the kid who used to follow you around, who used to do everything you said. Well, I no longer operate on blind faith."

"I'd say that's all you operate on. At the moment you're working under the assumption that the killer isn't Gavin Hitchcock."

Gillian gave her a surprised look. "You're working under the assumption that it is."

"You won't be exactly undercover if it is Gavin."

"It's not Gavin. Get him out of your head."

This was how all of their arguments used to start, with Gillian jumping on whatever Mary said as soon as she said it. Until today, Mary had been impressed with Gillian's work. Now she could see she was showing a grave lack of experience.

"How in the hell did you get a job with the BCA?" Mary asked, fighting a rising tide of panic. What her sister was proposing was dangerous. She wasn't going to stand by and let Gillian get herself killed.

"You're too jaded," Gillian retorted. "I have an idea. Why don't we go back in there and you pretend you don't even know me? Then maybe you might treat me with some respect."

"Gillian, it's dangerous," Mary said, her every nerve screaming.

"And your job isn't?"

"You fit the victimology."

"Are you pretending to be worried about me?" Gillian asked in sarcastic disbelief. "Give me a break! I'm not that naïve."

"This isn't a game!" Mary said. "Young women are being murdered."

"Stop treating me like a child! I *know* women are being murdered. Why do you think I want to be a part of this?"

"Maybe because you have some misplaced notion that it's romantic? So you can be a hero? Or does it have some deeper meaning? Is it possible you're subconsciously trying to right something that happened years ago? Subconsciously trying to save another girl, a different girl?"

"What are you getting at?"

"Fiona's dead. Nothing you do now can ever change that."

"I think you've got the Cantrell sisters mixed up. Mary's the one suffering from post-traumatic stress, not me."

Why had she ever thought Gillian would feel bad about Fiona's death? Mary wondered bleakly.

"I'm perfect for the job," Gillian said. "Why can't you admit it?"

"I want you to know that I completely disapprove of your idea."

"I'm not asking for your approval."

There had been a time when Mary's approval had meant everything to Gillian, but that had been years ago.

Gillian lifted her chin, her nose high.

"The princess is in a snit," their grandfather would have said.

Mary stared, suddenly having trouble separating the old Gillian from the new. But then, maybe the two weren't so different. "If Wakefield gives you the go-ahead," Mary said, knowing fighting was useless, "I don't think you'll have any trouble passing for seventeen."

"Does that nasty comment mean I have your reluctant vote?"

"You won't get even that much from me."

It was happening again.

The sensation came over Gavin like a tidal wave, knocking him to the floor, kneecaps meeting solid wood, jarring him all the way to his fillings.

Talk yourself out of it. You can talk yourself out of it.

Crippling poison rushed through his arteries, pushing out to his extremities, curling his fingers and toes, locking them.

Don't let it get you. Don't let it control you.

He was weak, so weak, and it was so strong. Getting stronger every day.

I'm scared.

Don't be scared, sweetie. It won't hurt you. If you can't beat it, then relax and let it take you. Let it take you away. Grandma will hold you. Grandma will be here for you.

Grandma, grandma. Grand mal, grand mal.

He couldn't win.

It overtook him, tightening his muscles until it seemed like his bones would snap.

Somehow he managed to twist his head enough to look at the clock above the sink. 6:45 P.M.

When he was little, the seizures never lasted over thirty seconds. Now they went on for much longer. Writhing, he managed to grab the dish towel from the refrigerator handle. He jammed it in his mouth before losing control. . . .

The return to consciousness was slow and seductive. Bones and muscles that had been stretched to the limit were now weak and limp as a newborn's. The feeling wasn't unpleasant—druggy, like a heroin high. He drifted, enjoying the sensation, the lack of pain. He finally managed to open his eyes long enough to read the clock. 7:05.

What time had it been before he blacked out? 6:45? Could that be right? That meant he'd lost . . . He tried to figure it out, but he'd always been bad at math. And his head was so fucked up and fuzzy.

Almost twenty minutes. He'd lost almost twenty minutes.

His attacks were getting more frequent, and he was

noticing that afterward it was getting harder and harder to remember what he'd been doing when they started.

He heard a sound and held his breath. Lying on his back on the floor, he listened.

Knocking.

Nobody ever knocked on his door, not even people trying to sell things.

He pulled the towel from his mouth and rolled to his knees. With trembling muscles, he shoved himself to his feet. He looked down to see if he was dressed. Jeans. No shirt. Barefoot. He ran a hand over his face. His fingers came away stained with blood.

Bloody nose.

Knock, knock, knock.

Whoever was out there was persistent. Why did people always knock three times? He never knocked three times.

At the sink, he washed his face, then dried it with the kitchen towel he'd dropped on the floor. On weak legs, he went to the door.

It was Gillian.

He was suddenly aware of how shitty he looked. He needed to shave, and he wished he'd put on a shirt before answering. But how could he have known Gillian would be there? She'd come to his house only once, right after he got out of prison. She'd brought him a basket of fruit and cheese—along with some white flowers, because she knew he liked flowers. He and his grandmother used to plant them together.

"Hi, Gavin." She was looking as sweet as ever. "Can I come in?"

"Oh. Yeah." He opened the door wide and stepped back. After she was inside and the door was closed, he started moving around the living room, picking up dirty clothes and empty food wrappers. "I wish I'd known you were coming," he said, unable to make eye contact, ashamed of the way his house looked, the way he looked.

"You don't have to straighten up for me," she said, taking a seat on the couch.

Right beside her lay a girlie magazine. He swooped down and grabbed it, turning it over on the table he'd made from a door. On the back of the magazine was a garish ad for a phone sex line. He grabbed the magazine again, dropped it to the floor, and shoved it under the couch with his bare foot. "Can I get you something to drink?" he asked, wondering if he had anything other than beer. But then, maybe she'd want a beer. That would be nice, if they drank a beer together.

"No, thanks." She smiled up at him.

Most people were either afraid of him or suspicious of him. Gillian was the only person he knew who looked at him in a completely open way that seemed to mean she was genuinely glad to see him.

"I came to tell you that I'm going to be out of town for a while."

"For your job?"

"I can't go into any detail about it. I just wanted you to know in case you stopped by my place."

"What about your bird?"

"My mother's going to take care of him—are you feeling okay?"

He scratched his head and pretended to yawn. "I was asleep when you knocked." He hadn't told her about the recent attacks. She knew about his epilepsy. She was one of the first people he ever told. But he didn't want her to know it had gotten worse since getting out of prison. He had enough things to be ashamed of.

"Since I'm going to be gone, I wanted to give you my mobile phone number in case you need to get in touch with me. I won't have my phone on much, but I'll check it once or twice a day so you can leave a message on my voice mail and I'll call you back when I can. I'll also leave my pager number."

She was going undercover. "This is about the Lucia Killer, isn't it?" he asked, his heart beginning to thunder. He could feel it in his chest and in his head.

"I can't tell you what I'm doing."

That's what it was.

"Don't go. Don't do it."

"I've already made plans. Don't worry. It won't be any big deal."

When he was little, his grandmother used to tell him that the seizures brought him closer to God. Sometimes when he came back she'd say, "How was your visit with God, sweet pea?"

Now that his seizures were more severe, he figured he spent a lot more time with God, a lot more time letting him whisper in his ear. But was it really God?

His seizure seemed to have opened a direct path to Gillian's brain, and he suddenly felt as if she were made of transparent glass. He could see through her skull to the gray matter beneath. On a threadlike rope were sentences that exposed her to him. It was her slanted handwriting, written in little snippets of information.

I'll be working on the murder case.

Something secret.

Something I can't tell.

I love you.

What?

He stared at her brain. *I love you.* That's what it said.

He continued to stare at the lettering, wishing he could save it somehow. As he stared, she continued

to talk as she dug into her purse and pulled out a
piece of paper and a pencil. She jotted something
down, then pushed the paper across the door table.
He saw her mouth move, saw her smile up at him.

She got to her feet.

I love you.

Why hadn't she ever told him how she felt about
him? Why had she been hiding it, playing this game?

I wanted you to discover it for yourself.

Had she spoken those words out loud? Yes. He was
sure she had. And now his heart was singing with
happiness.

At last certain of her feelings for him, he stepped
forward and boldly grabbed her by both arms. He
pulled her to him and pressed his mouth to hers. Her
lips blossomed under his, all soft and welcoming and
warm. He pushed her backward on the couch and fell
on top of her, his mouth never leaving hers. He released her arm to shove a hand up her shirt, immediately working his way under her bra, her breast filling
his hand.

He breathed in her intoxicating scent, his head full
of her, his blood pounding, roaring through his veins.

I love you, I love you!

He felt her hands on his back, pulling him close,
tugging at him, pushing slapping, shoving, shoving,
shoving—

He broke away in surprise.

"What the hell are you doing?" she screamed.

Stunned, he jumped to his feet, away from her.

She was lying on the couch, her shirt twisted under
her armpits, her bra above one breast, her eyes large
and angry and frightened.

"I thought, I didn't mean—"

She sat up, dropping her blouse to cover her
nakedness.

"Gillian, don't be afraid of me. Please don't be afraid of me. You're the only friend I have. Please—"

"This is how you treat your friends? You try to rape them?"

Rape? "No." He raised an imploring hand to her. "No—"

"If it is, then fuck you, Gavin Hitchcock. Fuck you."

He heard the front door slam shut and her stomping footsteps, followed by her car squealing away from the curb.

And he realized it hadn't been God whispering in his ear at all—it had been the devil.

Chapter 18

Three days after her abduction and subsequent escape, Holly Lindstrom checked the peephole and then answered her front door. Standing on the step was a seventeen- or eighteen-year-old girl. She had blond hair with lighter streaks, cut very cool, curving in under a small, pointed chin. She wore a white crop top and beige hip-huggers with jogging shoes. Her flat stomach was tan, and her belly button was pierced.

Holly had secretly gotten her belly button pierced once, but it ended up getting infected and she'd had to tell her parents. The stud was taken out, the site cleaned, and she'd been put on antibiotics. The whole episode had been gross, but whenever she saw someone with a cool navel ring, she still wanted one.

"Yeah?" Holly asked.

"Don't you recognize me?" the girl asked, smiling broadly. "I'm your cousin, Gillian."

Gillian? *Oh, shit!* Holly thought in disbelief. Gillian? *This* was the cop who was supposed to be living with them?

Holly was standing there with her mouth hanging open when Gillian let out an excited squeal, wrapped her arms around her, and gave her a huge hug, the screen door hitting her in the ass.

"I can't believe I'm going to be living here with you," Gillian said. "Come help me get my stuff."

Holly followed her outside. "This is your car?" Holly asked, staring at the Mustang convertible.

"Isn't it great? It's a '65. Dad restored it for me." Gillian put down a huge suitcase and then made a face. "That was last year. Before I started getting into trouble."

Holly felt a little dizzy, trying to sort out what was real and what was acting. She'd been told the cop, when she came, would remain in character most of the time. Holly was already believing the crap she was telling her, even though she knew it was made up.

She helped carry her things inside, locking the door behind them. "Mom! Dad!" she shouted. "Gillian's here!"

Her parents appeared from around the corner. Their mouths dropped open, and Holly giggled. She could tell they were still trying to figure it all out when Gillian reached into her backpack and pulled out her badge. Now that she was inside the house, she must have thought it would be okay to come clean.

"I'm Agent Cantrell," Gillian said, her voice lower and smoother than it had been before. "We spoke on the phone."

Holly's father shook her extended hand, a perplexed expression on his face. "How old are you?"

"Twenty-three." She flipped her hair with one hand. "The stylist did an excellent job. I cut a picture out of *Seventeen* magazine, took it in, and told her I wanted to look like that."

"You could *be* seventeen," Holly said.

"I've always looked young for my age. You should see my mom. She's fifty and looks thirty."

"The FBI agent who interviewed me—her name was Cantrell."

"She's my sister."

"Cool." But Holly was really thinking about school. She'd spent the last two days moving through classes in a cloud, like nothing was quite real. Her friends didn't know how to act, so they avoided her. She would have been hurt, but it was like there was a fuzzy glass between her and everybody else. Now, at the thought of Gillian coming along, she felt a surge of excitement. "You're going to have the guys at school going crazy!" she said, laughing.

Gillian sat down with the Lindstroms at the kitchen table.

They talked about the detectives that were watching the house. They talked about being hypervigilant. They rechecked phone numbers in order of importance. Gillian told them what to watch out for and what to do in any given situation. "It's extremely important that you treat me like a seventeen-year-old relative, and not a BCA agent," she told them once all the pertinent details had been discussed.

Holly's parents nodded in agreement. The unforgiving ceiling light cast shadows, accentuating the exhaustion in both of their faces. "We want this guy caught and our daughter safe again," Mrs. Lindstrom said.

"That's what we all want," Gillian agreed.

Holly's father stretched his arms above his head. "You know, I might actually be able to sleep a little tonight."

His vote of confidence should have made Gillian feel good. Instead, she found it unsettling. They were counting on her. They had faith in her. Suddenly she began to wonder if Mary had been right. Was she ready for a step of this magnitude? Or had she jumped into a situation above her skill level just to prove herself to Mary, with no thought of the possible consequences? Now, with the victim and her family looking at her as if she were their salvation, Gillian was confused and a little scared—a reaction she was careful to hide.

Holly jumped to her feet. "Come on." She waved her hand, motioning for Gillian to follow. "I'll show you where you're going to sleep and put your stuff."

Holly's room was small, with a single window facing the street. The walls were papered with pink flowers— a design probably left over from early childhood. The rest of the room had been updated with funky lights, fake-fur-covered pillows, band posters, and candles. And, of course, stuffed animals.

"We brought a bed in here for you," Holly said, pointing to a twin bed covered with a purple spread.

Holly slid open the closet door. "I moved my clothes over so you can have this side."

"Thanks."

Holly plopped down on her bed, sitting on her hands. "I was so pissed when my parents told me you were coming. It sounded like such a lame idea. I was expecting some goofy older person in a wig or something. But this is going to be so cool." She bounced up and down. "This is going to be so much fun."

Gillian had spent the last two days pulling together a wardrobe, getting her hair cut and lightened, and talking the department into letting her lease the Mustang rather than a Fiesta. At first they were going to allow her only a hundred dollars for clothes. She finally convinced them that she would need at least five hundred. She'd looked into the school Holly attended and knew that even though Holly's parents were both teachers and weren't in the upper income bracket, most of the kids at the school came from wealthy families. The idea was for Gillian to blend, not stick out.

"You can't tell anybody about me," Gillian warned. "Not your best friend, not anybody."

"I'm good at keeping secrets, and this is one I won't have to feel guilty about. That's why it's so cool."

"I'm your cousin who's been having trouble at home, so I've come to live with you and keep you company. Period."

Holly nodded. "Right."

They went over various scenarios that might pop up, such as where Gillian was from, how well she and Holly knew each other. They decided to say they had met only a couple of times. That way there would be less chance of messing up their stories.

"Do you have a gun?" Holly asked out of the blue.

Gillian sat down on her bed and pulled up the hem of her flared pants. Strapped to her ankle was a little five-shot Smith & Wesson backup. "You can't as much as touch it."

"Don't worry."

Gillian didn't like guns. She wasn't comfortable with them. As a BCA agent she didn't wear one all that often, and she hadn't thought a gun would be appropriate to bring into a high school, but Wakefield felt it was necessary and had cleared it with the few school authorities who knew her true identity.

"Part of the reason you're there is to protect Holly," he'd pointed out.

Now Holly shrugged. "I've seen guns before."

"Your dad's?"

"No, kids at school."

Holy shit. "Kids have guns at school?"

"Well, not in the building, but in their cars. One guy had me come out and look, and he had three guns in his trunk." Gillian must have appeared dismayed, because Holly made a shooing motion with her hand. "Don't worry. He got kicked out last semester."

"If you ever see anyone with a gun, you have to

report it right away," Gillian said. "You know that, don't you?"

"I don't like to squeal on people, but yeah, I know."

The room grew dim, and Holly lighted some candles and incense. They settled back on their beds and talked, Holly hugging a stuffed animal.

This was the part of childhood that Gillian had missed out on. She'd been fourteen when Fiona was murdered. At that point, her world had changed, had lost its brilliance. At that point, she'd finally understood that life was real, and the things you said, every word you spoke, mattered. She had screwed up, and in the process Mary, Gavin, Fiona, and herself had been robbed of their youth. So lying in the candlelit bedroom, talking and confiding in soft whispers was bittersweet for Gillian because she'd spent her own years in silence, in shame, guilt, and fear.

They chatted lightly for a while; then Gillian asked, "What about the guy who kidnapped you? Do you mind if we talk about him?"

Holly looked up sharply. "I'd like to. Nobody here has even mentioned what happened. Like it's going to set me off or something. Like it's not something I'm thinking about every second anyway. Do you think he'll try to kidnap me again?" she asked, poking the eye of the stuffed bear she was holding. "Detective Wakefield said that's why you're here."

"It's a possibility. Are you afraid?"

"No. Worried, but not afraid. I got away from him once. I can do it again." Holly was quiet for a minute, thinking through the question. Then she said softly, "Have you ever killed anybody?"

Nobody had ever asked Gillian that before. "No." She couldn't imagine any other answer.

"If you had to, would you?"

Point a gun at someone and pull the trigger? Could

she do it? "Yes. If I had to. If someone's life was in danger."

Had Mary ever shot anybody? Gillian wondered. Had she ever killed anybody?

"But isn't that why you're here? To kill him if you have to?"

"Catch him, not kill him."

A knock sounded on the closed door; then Mrs. Lindstrom said, "Better get to sleep, girls. School tomorrow."

Gillian raised her eyebrows in surprise, and Holly pressed her face against the bear to stifle a giggle.

Once they were in bed and the candles were blown out, Holly had another question to ask: "Why did you become a cop?"

Gillian wondered how much she should divulge and decided upon a watered-down version of the truth. "When I was a little younger than you, something happened to me that made me question who I was and what I really wanted out of life. I had a friend who was put in prison for something he may not have done, or something that may not have been his fault. That led to my interest in crime investigation."

"What did your friend do?"

Gillian hesitated, then decided to be forthright. "He was found guilty of murder."

Holly gasped. "But you don't think he did it?"

"I never used to feel that he was capable of murder. But now . . . lately, I'm not so sure. . . . I always thought I knew him so well, but I'm beginning to wonder if I was just fooling myself. My sister says I see things the way I want them to be, not the way they really are, and maybe that's true."

Holly was quiet for so long that Gillian thought she was asleep.

"I lied," Holly suddenly said, the confession coming

out of the darkness. "When I said I wasn't afraid, I lied. I'm always afraid now. I think about him all the time. I can't think about anything else." Her words came in a panicked rush. "You'll catch him, won't you? You'll kill him or put him in prison so I can quit thinking about him, won't you?"

Mary headed for the U of M campus and the fraternity where Sebastian Tate lived. They'd uncovered some new incriminating information about him, and she wanted to get her own interview.

Three days had passed since Gillian had gone undercover, and Mary wasn't feeling any better about it now than she had that afternoon in Wakefield's office. The thought of her sister exposing herself to a warped killer scared the hell out of her. But Gillian was a grown-up, and Mary couldn't do a thing if Gillian decided to act like an idiot. Not that she'd ever listened to Mary before—not even when they were kids. Gillian may have been the youngest, but she'd always had a mind of her own.

Mary spotted the address Wakefield had given her and parked her rental car. It wasn't fair that obnoxious, partying frat guys got the coolest houses, but there it was. Sebastian Tate lived in a massive three-story stone building with an equally impressive wraparound porch and defaced cement lions guarding the front steps.

Dave Matthews was blasting from a radio somewhere, and two guys on the roof of the porch were rolling out sod. The temperature was in the low fifties, but that didn't keep them from going shirtless while they worked.

She shaded her eyes and shouted up at them. "Does Sebastian Tate live here?"

One of them straightened. He wore khaki shorts and a curled cap with a band logo on the front. "Tate? Yeah, most of the time. Go on in."

"What's the grass for?" she asked, curious.

"Homecoming. We're having a kegger, and we're gonna put lawn furniture out here. You aren't a cop, are you?" he asked, laughing.

She pulled out the leather case that held her photo ID and flipped it open.

"Oh, shit."

The other guy stopped working. "Nice going, Carver."

"Hey," he called down to her, "nobody here will be under twenty-one."

"I'm sure they won't," Mary said dryly, slipping the badge back into her pocket. She had zero interest in their drinking habits. "Where'd you say Tate is?"

"His room's on the third floor. Go on in."

"Thanks."

The place reeked of stale beer. As she took the stairs, she met two students on their way down, laughing and struggling to transport a half-finished keg.

She found Tate in a room that may once have been a library. Sunlight managed to filter through windows that looked as if they hadn't been washed in years. Two unmade double beds were shoved against opposite walls. Clothes littered the hardwood floor, and the room smelled like sweat and dirty socks. The radio she'd heard outside was blaring, the DJ shouting nonsensical patter.

Tate sat at a table, deeply engrossed in something she couldn't see.

She knocked on the molding of the open door.

He didn't hear her.

She walked over to the radio and turned it off.

"Hey!" He looked up. "Who the hell are you?"

She introduced herself, flashed her ID, and said she wanted to talk to him.

In his hand was an X-Acto knife he was using to cut out mat board for photos.

"You're pretty good at that," she said, noting the precise lines. She remembered trying to cut mat board and knew it was excruciatingly hard to do. In the right hands, an X-Acto knife could do as much damage as a scalpel.

"I've already been downtown." He leaned back, one hand braced on the table in front of him. He was shirtless. Didn't anybody wear shirts around there?

"I'd really like to talk to you myself." She found a chair and pulled it close, sitting down. "You don't mind, do you?"

"Cantrell . . . You aren't related to Gillian, are you?"

"You mean Officer Cantrell? She's my sister."

He gave her a big, predatory smile. "I'd rather talk to her."

Of course he would. "What kind of photography are you interested in?"

"Black-and-white."

"Nature?"

"People." He tossed down the knife. "I like taking pictures of people."

She fished around in her coat pocket and pulled out a page torn from *City Pages*, the Twin Cities free weekly entertainment paper. "Is this your ad?"

He glanced at the clipping, but couldn't have looked closely enough to see anything. When he didn't answer, she read it aloud.

"Models. Female. Eighteen to twenty-five. Blond. Some nudity required." She read the ten-digit number. "According to the phone company, that number belongs to you."

"So?"

She sensed his restrained rage, and maybe an urge to hit her.

"That's not against the law, is it?" he asked, his face taking on an angry flush.

"No. Not as long as they're willing participants."

"Oh, they're willing. If they answer the ad and find out it's not up their alley, they don't do it. Simple as that."

She wasn't letting this creep off so easily. "Would you mind showing me some of your photos?"

"I've got buddies in law school. I know I don't have to show you anything without a search warrant. And there's no way a judge or DA's going to give you one."

He was absolutely right. They didn't have anything to justify a search warrant. "How about names?" she persisted. "Do you have names of the girls you've photographed? I'd like to talk to them. Just to put my mind at ease. Just to confirm what you're saying."

He shoved himself to his feet, rummaged through a pile of papers in the corner of the room, and finally came back with two phone numbers written on a scrap of paper. "There," he said, angrily thrusting it into her hand. "Call them. They'll tell you I was a perfect gentleman."

"Thanks," she said, pocketing the numbers.

Outside in her car, Mary was able to reach one of the women, a girl named Poppy Adams, and arranged to meet with her at a bar in Brooklyn Park. She left a message at the second number.

Poppy was bottle blonde, about twenty-one, wearing a black tank top, hip-hugger jeans, and hemp chokers. She had several tattoos and piercings.

"I'm trying to get into acting," she told Mary, "and needed some publicity photos. Those cost like hell, so I told him I'd pose if he'd print up some extra shots for me."

"How did he behave when you did the photo shoot? Was he professional?"

"Do you mean, did he try anything? No, he just took the pictures. Then he gave me a few of his cards and said if I knew anybody else who might want photos to let them know about him."

"Have you passed his cards on to anybody else?"

"Yeah. A couple of girls."

"You wouldn't happen to have their numbers, would you?"

She had to think about it for a second. "One of them doesn't have a phone, but I can tell you where she lives. Her name's Jennifer." She gave her directions to an apartment building in Uptown. "The other girl . . . I don't even know her name. She used to come in here quite a bit, but I haven't seen her recently."

Mary pulled out four-by-six head shots of all the murder victims. "Do any of these look familiar?"

Poppy examined them, shook her head, and gave them back.

"If you do see the girl you told me about, will you ask her to give me a call?" Mary handed Poppy her card. "And if you think of anything else, please get in touch with me."

From Brooklyn Park, Mary drove directly to Uptown. The loft apartment Poppy had described was above a coffee shop. Uptown wasn't the cheapest place to live, but it was considered the hippest. In order to achieve that hip status, about a dozen people were occupying an apartment that looked more suited to two or three. Jennifer didn't ask her in. Instead, she stepped out into the dark hallway and shut the door behind her.

"Yeah, I got photos taken," she said, arms crossed below her breasts, shoulder blades sharp. She looked and sounded as if she had a bad cold. "But I got the idea I wasn't what he had in mind."

Jennifer had light brown dreadlocks, tattoos, and more piercings than Poppy.

"What type of girl do you think he was looking for?"

She shrugged. "I don't know. He's a frat guy. Frat guys don't go for girls like me. He'd want somebody more conservative. Somebody more Minnesota."

"Minnesota?"

"Yeah, you know those blond blue-eyed girls with white teeth and perfect skin? One of those."

"Did he not take pictures of you?"

"Oh, he took pictures. Even though I wasn't perfect, he didn't seem to mind seeing me naked." She stiffened at the memory. "I thought I was going to get paid. That's the only reason I did it. I needed the money. But he takes the photos, and when I ask for cash he gets mad."

"How mad? Did he threaten you? Hurt you?"

"No, but he was really pissed. He said he was an artist. That I should be honored that he took my picture at all. I asked for the negatives, and he unrolls them, then tosses them at me. I just left them there. It ends up they weren't even the right ones, because . . . well . . . a couple weeks later I get this nude photo of me in the mail that says 'Ha, ha, ha' written across the bottom in black Magic Marker."

"Do you still have it?"

She shook her head. "I burned it."

"Did you contact the police?"

"What for? It was my fault, you know? My own stupid fault. But now I'm worried that when I get famous—" She sniffled and wiped her nose with the back of her hand. "—he'll, like, sell the pictures to *Playboy*."

Chapter 19

Gavin cashed his check and headed for the nearest bar.

He loved alcohol.

During his time in prison, he'd forgotten how much he loved it. Its warm embrace. Its many moods, every high as different as a fingerprint. There were so many variables, so many small chemical factors that could tip the high one way or another—like the contents of a person's stomach, or how much sleep he'd gotten. The *kind* of alcohol. Wine was different from beer. Tequila, different from vodka. But most of all, his state of mind on any given night determined the path the evening would take.

Sitting at a bar where thousands of elbows had worn the wood smooth, Gavin looked around. Most of the patrons were working on the same project—becoming anesthetized as quickly as possible. Why was it cool to get wasted when you were a kid, and so pathetic once a guy passed thirty? Gavin had the answer. When a kid got drunk, he did it for sheer fun. An adult, on the other hand, did it to escape, to find oblivion.

Trouble was, oblivion never lasted, and you had to do it over again, enduring hangovers, humiliation, and shame for those few blessed hours of numbness.

Sometimes the alcohol turned on you. Instead of being a friend, it became the enemy. Instead of having a good time, you spent the evening sinking deeper and deeper into despair. When that happened, a guy had to go searching for another kind of drug to shut it off, to bring on that feeling of being satisfied in your own skin. And block out the things he didn't want to remember.

Kissing Gillian.

Attacking Gillian.

Almost raping Gillian.

The replay was like watching a movie, watching actors. Certainly the main character didn't seem like him at all. The attack wasn't something he would do or could do.

But he *had* done it.

Oh, God.

He squeezed his eyes shut and pressed his fingers against the lids. He'd killed a girl once, but didn't remember it. Some people said he killed his grandmother too. His grandmother, the only person who'd loved him.

Why? Why did I do such a thing?

Then there was Gillian's sister, the FBI agent. She'd been to see him again, nagging at him like an annoying gnat. She thought he'd killed those girls, and sometimes he wondered if she was right. Maybe he *had* killed them. Even if he couldn't remember.

He heard a sound and lifted his head to see the bartender placing a shot of tequila in front of him. "From the lady at the end of the bar," the man said, pointing.

Gavin looked through the smoky haze to see a woman with blond hair seated at the other end of the L-shaped bar. She gave him a prissy wave. He nodded, lifted the shot glass—*cheers*—and downed the burning liquid.

His mother died of a heroin overdose when he was three. He couldn't remember much about his father except for the beatings. The one that gave him epilepsy had put him in the hospital. After that he was sent to Minneapolis to live with his grandmother—his mother's mother. He was young, maybe six, and he used to think that everybody lost time, had gaps they couldn't fill. Later it was explained to him that the gaps had something to do with his epilepsy, courtesy of dear old Dad.

"Hi," said a soft voice in his ear.

He looked up from the empty shot glass to see the woman who'd bought the drink standing next to him, an elbow on the bar. She was about thirty, too much makeup, too much sun. One of those women who fried herself on the beach all summer and cooked herself in a tanning bed all winter.

She wanted sex.

But what kind of sex? he wondered. That was sometimes hard to tell. Was she a whore? Or just horny?

"Hi," he said. "What're you drinkin'?"

She slid onto the bar stool. "Gin and tonic."

He bought her a drink, and another for himself.

She began talking about being in town for a convention, something about selling digital cameras or cleaning products or something. He didn't care. He didn't give a shit. He'd already shut her out. The company she was with had to be shaky, because she was hanging out in one of the seediest parts of town. Or it could be she was just feeding him a line of bullshit, wanting him to think she was alone and unfamiliar with the area. Whores, the kind that robbed you once you passed out, liked to do that. The world was a great place. Yessirree.

Whatever she was selling, he wasn't interested.

He worked his billfold from the back pocket of his

jeans, flipped it open, and pulled out a piece of folded newspaper.

"What's that?" the woman asked, hanging over his shoulder.

"Something I saved."

He'd been closely following the Lucia Killer—which was what one of the local papers was now calling the guy. The other major paper, in a lame attempt to be original, had decided to call him the Scarlet Pimpernel since it was rumored that his signature had something to do with red roses. Gavin had read the killer's profile in the paper, trying to find some kind of connection, trying to find something that might spark a memory. It seemed familiar. But maybe that was because he'd read it so many times. . . .

How was a guy to know?

He unfolded the paper; it was soft and creased. And even though he'd read it a million times, he read it again.

It could be him. Almost everything about the profile sounded like him.

"That an article about the Lucia Killer?" the woman asked. "I'm getting sick of hearing about him, aren't you? Every time I turn on the TV, they're talking about it."

For a moment he'd forgotten about her, forgotten he was in a public place. She didn't fit the victim profile. She was blond, but she was too old.

"Yeah." He refolded the clipping and put it back in his billfold.

Gavin was tired of the place. He shoved himself to his feet and pocketed the pile of wadded-up bills from the counter, tucking them deep into the front pocket of his jeans. Without another word, he left.

It was a Friday night. Campus bars would be packed with much more interesting possibilities.

He took University Avenue west, to the U of M campus, in search of music and alcohol and young blondes. He would find some and see what happened. See if he got the urge to do anything weird, then maybe he would have the answer everybody was seeking, then maybe he would know.

Gavin wasn't a great-looking guy, but he'd been told there was something dangerous about him that appealed to the opposite sex. It must have been true, because within ten minutes of stepping into the first club, girls began hitting on him. College girls who were drunk and horny—and not shy about letting a guy know it.

He bought drinks and had drinks bought for him. He even danced, mostly slow dances that involved rubbing and making out. At one point, a bouncer came out to the floor and told him and the chick he was dancing with to cool it or he'd throw them out.

That's when Gavin looked at the girl he was holding tightly to his crotch. She was young and tan and blond. Perfect. He asked her if she wanted to come home with him, and she said yes.

This is easy, he thought. *Like picking dandelions. Maybe I am the killer.*

On the way to his place he stopped at a coffee shop where, if the right question was asked, a guy could buy his drug of choice. Gavin's drugs were pot and heroin. After the purchase, he slipped them into his pocket and made his way back outside, where the girl was waiting in the passenger seat of his car.

"You didn't get me anything to drink?" she whined, pouting.

"You want something?"

She stuck out her chest and cocked her head to one side. "Yeah."

He went around the block and pulled into the parking lot of a liquor store, where he grabbed a fifth of cheap whiskey. "I'll take one of these too," he said, pulling a red rose from a container next to the cash register. He tossed a ten-dollar bill on the counter.

The rose sure made up for any slacking off on his part. She sniffed it, and stroked it against her cheek, then against his face. She began to get so hot for him that he could barely drive. She had her hands all over him. When she started fiddling with the zipper on his pants, he pushed her away.

"Ten more minutes," he said. "We'll be there in ten minutes."

They stumbled into his house. He poured whiskey into glasses and handed her one. She dropped the rose on the table next to the portable phone, took a long swallow, and then began pulling off her clothes. He did the same, and pretty soon they were lying naked on the couch where he'd attacked Gillian, except that this girl was digging the hell out of him, screaming and clawing and biting. When it was over, they were both sweating and panting like two wild animals.

"Wanna do some smack?" he asked.

She shook her head and reached for the whiskey. She drank straight from the bottle, her head tilted back. When she straightened, the brown-tinged liquid ran down her chin, onto her bare breasts. Her eyes were glazed, her lips swollen, her blond hair hanging wet in front of her face.

He grew hard and took the bottle from her. He helped her to her feet and led her into his bedroom, where they fucked again. This time she didn't seem to enjoy it. This time she was almost comatose.

And he thought in amazement and disgust—for him, for her, for both?—*This wasted chick whose name I don't even know is somebody's daughter. Somebody's little girl.*

He left her passed out on the bed, tugged on his jeans, and went to the living room to smoke some pot and drink the rest of the whiskey. Time became weird. He forgot the girl was in his house. Then, a little later, he remembered her.

I'll bet it's me. I'll bet I'm the one.

The idea of being a famous murderer suddenly appealed to him. It made sense.

He got to his feet and stood there swaying for a few moments before spotting the wilted rose on the floor. Smiling, he picked it up and staggered to the bedroom. The girl was where he'd left her—naked and passed out. She was disgusting. She made him sick. He couldn't believe he'd fucked her.

He rummaged around and found some rope. He tied her hands to the headboard, then took the rose and rubbed it between his palms, the petals breaking and falling across her body. He got out his camera and took some pictures.

She slept through it all.

Killing her.

That's what came next.

He found a knife in the kitchen. He turned it in his hand, admiring it. The size and shape were remarkably similar to the knife left on the floor next to his murdered grandmother.

Kill her, he told himself. *Kill her now.*

He stood at the foot of the bed for a long time, clutching the knife in his hand, staring at the blond chick, feeling nothing for her. In his mind, he pictured Fiona Portman lying on the ground, blood pouring from a gash in her head. He could see his own hands on a massive rock, holding it high. . . .

The heroin.

He hadn't done the heroin yet.

He returned to the living room to snort the heroin he'd bought. He hadn't done any in a long time, but the rush, when it came, was well remembered. Well appreciated.

Nice. So nice.

Why didn't I do this before?

Niiiicccceeee . . .

He toppled headfirst across the table he'd made out of a door and cement blocks. He and the door crashed to the floor. He lay there for a long, long moment, staring, his gaze finally moving along the floor, under the couch, falling upon the piece of paper Gillian had left the day he'd attacked her.

He stretched out his arm, trying to reach it, his fingers finally coming into contact with the scrap of paper.

In case you need to get in touch with me, she'd said.

The paper felt weird. Thin and dry as moth wings.

It seemed to take days, weeks, months, but he finally rolled onto his back and unfolded the paper.

Gillian's phone number.

Gillian's pager number.

He should give her a call. Gillian, sweet Gillian.

Sinking. He was sinking, melting into the floor.

Find the phone. Find the phone and call Gillian.

It was like fighting a fit, holding it back as long as he could before finally allowing it to overtake him. Lying on his back, he twisted his head, looking around. There was the portable phone beside him.

He tried to pick it up—it slipped from his fingers. It took three tries, but he finally got it in front of him. He lifted the paper to his face. The numbers weren't in a line. Instead, they looked like they'd been thrown down in no order at all. He blinked. He blinked again. The numbers straightened. Before they began marching around again, he punched in the phone number, then waited through four rings to end up getting Gillian's voice mail.

"Fu-uck." The word came out funny, with a kind of "whoa, dude" cadence that reminded him of his high school days. He would have laughed if he'd had the strength.

He lay there with the phone to his ear, breathing, listening to the silence. *"Fu-uck,"* he repeated, and then hung up. The hand with the phone dropped to his stomach. He was drifting away when he remembered that Gillian had left her pager number too.

Chapter 20

Gillian's beeper went off.

Automatically, she reached out and silenced it. Pressing the button, she checked the caller's illuminated number.

Gavin.

The digital display read 3:46.

Not wanting to wake up Holly, she fumbled in the dark for her mobile phone. On her back, head against the pillow, she flipped it open and pressed the button to check her voice mail. There was one message, sent at 3:41. She punched in her PIN code, then listened to a long silence followed by a mumbled *"Fu-uck."*

According to the caller ID, the message was also from Gavin. No surprise there. He was known for his eloquence.

But had that *fuck* sounded strange? Thick? Groggy?

She sat up cross-legged in bed and punched his number. He didn't have voice mail or an answering machine, so she listened to endless ringing. She hung up and tried again. "Come on, you idiot. You just paged me."

No answer.

She sat there, trying to figure out what to do.

She could call the police and request that someone

check up on him, but it could be nothing, just another one of the weird things Gavin did. Or he could be smoking pot. If that were the case, he'd be sent back to prison.

With a resigned sigh, she got out of bed and searched for the clothes she'd worn earlier.

After getting dressed and strapping her Smith & Wesson to her ankle, she gave Holly a gentle shake. That was followed by a much harder shake when the girl failed to respond.

"Huh?" Holly said groggily.

Gillian leaned close and whispered, "I have to go look in on a friend." She mentally calculated how long it would take to get to Gavin's. "I should be back within two hours. If not, I'll be here before school starts."

Holly didn't answer.

Gillian shook her again. "Holly? Did you hear me? Don't leave the house without me."

"Uh? Oh, yeah. Back before school starts. Gotcha. Ten-four, Eleanor."

Gillian grabbed her coat and hurried from the room. Outside, she spotted the detectives parked halfway down the block. The night was cold and silent, and she could see her breath as she hurried to her car.

On the way to Gavin's, she pulled out her phone and tried his number again. Two miles later, when she didn't get an answer, she disconnected.

At least the traffic wasn't bad. She made it to Gavin's in under fifteen minutes.

She pulled to an abrupt halt next to the curb. All of the houses in the block were dark except for Gavin's. She hurried to the door and knocked. She hadn't expected an answer and didn't get one. She tried the doorknob.

Unlocked.

"Gavin?" She opened the door—and let out a startled gasp.

Lying on his back in the middle of a broken table was Gavin. Dressed in nothing but a pair of tattered jeans, he was unconscious, his face white, his lips blue. Beside him was an empty whiskey bottle. In the air hung the earthy, cloying scent of pot.

She ran to his side and dropped down next to him, grabbing him by the arm. His skin was ice-cold. "You idiot!" she shouted. She examined his hands: his fingertips were blue. Trembling, she felt for a pulse and thought she detected a weak flutter. She lifted his lids and checked his pupils. Pinpoints.

She pulled out her phone and dialed 911.

"This is Agent Cantrell of the BCA," she said when the operator answered. "I have an overdose victim with me. Request immediate transport."

"Do you know what the victim has taken?" the operator asked.

"No." She looked around and spotted a square of tinfoil in the litter surrounding him. Inside was a white powder residue. "Cocaine, maybe. Or heroin."

The operator double-checked the name and address and dispatched an ambulance.

Gillian disconnected. It could be too late by the time they got there. It could be too late already.

She punched number three on her speed dial: Mary's mobile phone.

Fortunately Mary slept with her cell phone on; she answered before the second ring.

"I'm at Gavin's house," Gillian said, shaky and breathless. "He's overdosed."

"Have you called 911?" Mary's voice sounded sleep-tinged but alert.

"They're on their way."

"I'll be right there."

* * *

Mary disconnected and quickly slipped into some clothes. She was heading out the bedroom door when Blythe met her in the hallway. "What's wrong?" With a white-knuckled hand, she clutched her robe together at her throat. "Is it Gillian?"

"Gillian's fine," Mary reassured her. "But Gavin Hitchcock overdosed. Gillian's at his house waiting for the ambulance, and she needs somebody there with her."

"I'll come too. Let me throw on some clothes." Blythe had started to turn back to her bedroom when Mary stopped her.

"Mom, stay here. You don't want to see this." Mary experienced a sudden, sweet ache that was the love of a daughter for her mother. Such things came at the strangest of times. She smiled softly. "You don't always have to be the mom."

Blythe's arms dropped to her sides. "You're right," she said in relief. "I'll wait here. Call me when you know something."

Mary kept the speedometer between seventy and seventy-five the entire way. She took 35W to 94, then 94 to Snelling, quickly cutting over to Midway. She reached Gavin's house just as the paramedics were wheeling him out the door, Gillian following.

Mary ran across the lawn. "Is he still alive?"

One of the attendants held an IV drip while two others loaded him into the back of the ambulance.

"Barely," Gillian said. "They gave him an injection of naloxone. I told them about his epilepsy, but that's the least of their concerns at the moment." She pressed a hand to her mouth. "It's my fault. I know it's my fault."

Mary wasn't going to stand there and watch Gillian flog herself. "Do you have to take responsibility for every idiot who comes along? This is nobody's fault but Gavin's."

Gillian wouldn't listen. She shook her head, saying, "You don't understand."

The ambulance was ready to leave. "What hospital?" Mary shouted at the attendant.

"Holy Cross."

"We'll meet you there."

The ambulance took off.

"I have to get my coat and phone."

Mary was waiting in the yard when she heard a high-pitched scream come from deep within the house. She pulled her gun and ran into the building, almost colliding with Gillian, who stood in the living room, her fuzzy teenybopper coat held limply in one hand, her gaze directed down the dark hallway.

"Did you scream?" Mary asked.

"Please. I haven't screamed since I was twelve." Gillian pointed. "It came from back there." She dropped her coat and hurried down the hall. Mary followed. At the bathroom door, Gillian paused and looked inside. Empty. She continued to the bedroom, coming to a halt in the open doorway.

"Oh my God."

Mary looked over her sister's shoulder.

In the muted light cast by a gauze-covered lamp, she was able to make out the nude body of a young girl tied to the bed by her wrists. Scattered across her body and the stained, sheetless mattress were red rose petals.

As soon as the girl saw them standing in the doorway, she began screaming and flailing against her bonds.

"Get me out of here!" she shrieked. "That madman did this! He tied me up and raped me! He's crazy! Get me out of here!"

Gillian seemed frozen to the floor. Mary slid her gun back into the shoulder holster and pushed her sister forward. Gillian took a few halting steps, then stopped again.

"Find a knife," Mary told her. "Scissors, anything to cut her loose."

Gillian nodded and left the room.

Mary pulled out her mobile phone and punched number one on her speed dial. Anthony answered and she quickly explained the situation, asking him to call Wakefield and Elliot Senatra. Then she hung up to concentrate on the victim.

Gillian reappeared with a steak knife. "This is all I could find."

"I wish we had latex gloves," Mary said. "This is a crime scene, and the less we mess it up the better."

"Get me out of here!" The girl was hysterical.

"I'm an FBI agent," Mary explained calmly. "And this is Officer Cantrell, from the Bureau of Criminal Apprehension. We're going to free you, but we have to be careful not to destroy any evidence."

"Evidence? Why do you need evidence? I know who did this to me!"

"We'll still need evidence to back up your story. You want him to pay for this, don't you? You don't want him to get away with it, do you?"

"Fuck no!"

"Hold still, and when you're free, try not to touch anything."

"I want my clothes!"

"I'll get them," Gillian said, handing Mary the knife. She'd been bound with clothesline cord. Mary cut through the bindings and the girl came shooting off the bed, grabbing her clothes from Gillian. Now that she was on her feet, it quickly became evident that she was drunk.

"I wanna cab," she said, staggering around, trying to get into her clothes, giving up on the panties, which she tossed on the floor along with her top.

"We have to wait for the police to come and take your statement," Mary explained, picking up the top and turning the triangle of fabric this way and that, trying to figure out what was what. "Then you're going to have to go to the emergency room so you can be processed with a rape kit."

"No."

The girl had managed to get into her shorts—tiny little things that her butt hung out of. Mary helped her with the crop top, tying it in back with strings as big around as pieces of spaghetti.

"Don't you want to see this guy convicted?" Mary asked.

"They'll check my blood alcohol. I'm under twenty-one. My parents'll kill me."

"Let's get out of here. We should wait where there's no risk of evidence contamination. Is there a room you haven't been in?"

"The kitchen."

Mary wanted to question her, but knew it would be best to wait for the police so the information wouldn't become diluted by repetition.

Everybody showed up at the same time. The police. Anthony. Elliot.

"I met him at a bar," said the girl, whose name turned out to be Cammie Curtis. "He asked me if I wanted to ride around and I said, Yeah, sure. Why not? He brought me here instead. I'm not the kind of girl who has sex with a guy she's just met, so he got mad and raped me. He tied me up!" She began to cry, and one of the female officers put an arm around her.

"We're going to have to ask you to come to the hospital so we can run some tests," she said quietly.

Seemingly subdued by the appearance of officers in uniform, Cammie sniffled and nodded. "Okay."

"After that, we'll take you down to police headquarters to get a more in-depth statement."

Again, the girl nodded.

Cammie lived in Wisconsin and was attending school at the U of M. "You're going to have to stay in town," Mary said, willing to play unpopular again. "At least for a couple more days." She knew Cammie's instinct would be to run for home and security.

"Fax us a copy of everything, will you?" Elliot asked.

The female officer nodded, then led Cammie from the house to the patrol car. Two officers remained to secure the scene and wait for the crime lab. Another officer took Mary and Gillian's statements.

When the crime technicians arrived, it was almost five o'clock.

Cammie had said that the first assault took place in the living room. Then he moved her to the bedroom to rape her a second time. The technicians went over everything inch by inch, bagging up fibers, body secretions, hairs. They dusted for fingerprints, coming up with what looked to be three sets—a small number of prints to find in one person's house, but then Gavin didn't know many people.

A butcher knife was found on the floor near the couch.

At that point, Mary realized she hadn't seen Gillian in a while. She searched the house and finally found her sitting outside on the front steps. The sky was beginning to lighten.

"I can't believe it," Gillian said, elbow on her knee, forehead to her palm. "He must have really killed Fiona."

Mary sat down beside her. She could feel the cold

of the cement through her jeans. She put her arm around her sister and gave her a gentle shake. "Don't feel bad about trusting him." Mary had spent years trying to convince Gillian that Gavin was bad news, but now she experienced no satisfaction in knowing that her sister finally saw him for what he was. Instead, Mary felt incredibly sorry for Gillian. "There's nothing wrong with having faith in people."

Gillian lifted both hands as if cupping a huge bowl. "But he was right there in front of me the whole time. I'm supposed to be a cop. How could I have been so blind?" She grabbed a fistful of her hair and tugged at it—something she used to do years ago when she was frustrated.

"I came to visit him the other day," Gillian said. "I wanted him to know I wasn't going to be around for a while. . . ."

Mary waited, but Gillian stopped in midsentence, swallowing her next words.

"What happened when you came to see him?" Mary prodded.

Gillian seemed to change her mind, as if she immediately regretted mentioning her visit. "Nothing. Not really. You know Gavin." She let out a tense, false laugh and motioned toward the inside of the house and the evidence of what had recently taken place in there. "You know how weird he can be."

The door slammed behind them as Anthony stepped outside. "There's one more person we need to talk to," he said. "If he's still alive."

Nobody had to ask who he was talking about.

Gillian had been staring at her hands. Now she looked up. Mary couldn't recall ever seeing that expression on her sister's face—a mixture of fear and revulsion. What had happened between her and Gavin? What had he done to her?

"There's no reason for you to go," Mary said. "You don't have to see him."

Gillian got to her feet. "I'm going. I know him better than anybody else. He'll talk to me. I may be the only one who's able to get a confession out of him."

Chapter 21

"He's breathing on his own."

The emergency room doctor made the announcement to the group of police and agents in the waiting room. Then he succinctly filled them in on details. "The patient rated a fourteen on the Glasgow Coma Scale. He was lucky—at twelve we usually intubate. Unfortunately, we had to give him another injection of naloxone, which has been associated with seizures. With Mr. Hitchcock's history of epilepsy, we'll have to monitor him closely for the next twenty-four to forty-eight hours."

"Can we speak with him?" Anthony asked.

"Two people for not more than ten minutes. And I mean speak to him. No interrogation."

It was decided that Gillian and Detective Wakefield would conduct the brief interview, even though Mary offered to go in Gillian's place. They followed the doctor down a long hallway with mint green walls and a cracked linoleum floor that had turned yellow. The fluorescent lights were unnaturally bright, and no one cast a shadow.

Gavin had been put in a private room. Outside, two policemen, a man and woman, stood guard.

Gavin was lying on a gurney, an IV drip in his arm

and oxygen tubes in his nostrils. A heart monitor beeped near his head. His eyes were closed, and his lips were still blue.

Gillian slowly approached the bed. She felt a wave of heat wash over her. Her ears started to ring. She was angry. Angry with herself for not seeing Gavin for what he was, angry with Gavin for tricking her for so many years.

Be professional, she told herself. Be a cop.

Wakefield moved to the opposite side of the bed, facing the door. He nodded at her to proceed.

"Gavin?" Gillian said.

Gavin heard Gillian's voice and relief washed over him. After a bleary struggle, he opened his eyes.

"Gillian? . . ." He lifted a hand to reach for her. She remained beyond his grasp.

"C-mere," he said thickly.

She didn't move any closer. "Gavin, this is Detective Wakefield of the Minneapolis Police Department. We're here to ask you some questions."

The curt tone of her voice made him retreat. "Sleep," he mumbled. "Wanna sleep." His eyes drifted shut.

"You can sleep later. We want to talk to you now."

He opened his eyes again.

The detective turned on a microcassette recorder and spoke into it, listing stuff like the date and time, location. Then he started with the questions, asking Gavin where he'd been last night.

Gavin wouldn't have answered—he was so fucking tired and his head hurt like hell—but Gillian was there, watching him. He wanted to be good for her. He'd always wanted to be good for her. So he told the guy about his evening, about how he'd ended up running into the chick they were asking him about. Guess he finally knew her name. Cammie.

"Where did you meet Cammie Curtis?" Wakefield asked.

"A bar. A bar on the U campus."

"Did you approach her, or did she approach you?"

"D-don't remember."

"Did you ask her if she wanted to go for a ride?"

"I asked her . . . if she wanted to come home with me," Gavin said. "She said yes."

"And you took her to your house?" Wakefield asked.

"Yeah."

"Did you have sex with her?"

Gavin looked at Gillian. Shit. Why was he asking those kinds of questions in front of her? He should know better than that.

"Answer the question," she said sternly.

So he answered the question. What else could he do? "Yeah."

"Consensual?" the detective asked.

"Huh?"

"Did she also want to have sex with you?"

Oh, *consensual.* They thought he was dumb, but he just hadn't heard right. "I think so."

"She claims that you raped her. Did you rape Cammie Curtis?"

Rape? Had he raped her? "I'm not sure."

"Did you tie her to your bed?"

Again, he looked at Gillian. *Tell the truth*, her body language seemed to say.

"She sure as hell didn't do it herself."

"Is that a yes?" the guy asked. "Are you saying you tied her to the bed?"

"Yeah."

"Why?"

"The occasion just seemed to call for it."

"Did you rape her?"

He was confused.

His brain was mush.

Were they supposed to be asking him questions when his brain was mush? Should he wait for a lawyer? Did it matter?

"Gavin?" Gillian prodded.

If she thought he needed a lawyer, she would have said so.

"Answer the question. Did you rape Cammie Curtis?"

Had he raped her? She'd wanted it, hadn't she? At least he thought she'd wanted it, but then he'd thought Gillian had wanted it too. "I don't know about the rape stuff." He thought about the knife—a knife that looked like the knife that had killed his grandmother. He thought about the huge rock that had crushed Fiona Portman's skull. "Is she dead?"

"Who?" the detective asked.

"That Cammie chick. 'Cause all I remember is that I was gonna kill her."

That shut them both up. Gillian and the detective looked at each other; then they looked at Gavin.

"Gavin, listen to me," Gillian said with insistence.

He complied, the way he always complied.

"Did you abduct Charlotte Henning?"

There was something odd about Gillian. She seemed like somebody else. "You're different," he stated.

She put a hand to her hair.

"Not your hair," he said. "You. You're different."

"Answer the question, Gavin." That command came from Wakefield.

Gavin continued to stare at her. "What was the question?" His mind had floated away.

"Did you abduct Charlotte Henning?"

He could see that Gillian wanted him to say yes.

He could see that she believed he'd done it, and if she believed it, then it must be true. His head hurt, and he wanted to sleep. "Yes," he said.

"Did you smother her—on purpose or by accident?"

"Yes."

Wakefield moved his palm-size recorder nearer, while Gavin continued to stare at Gillian.

"Did you throw her body in the river?" Gillian asked.

"Yes."

"Did you abduct Holly Lindstrom?"

"Yes."

The door opened. "Time's up," a male voice said. "No more questions."

"We've got enough for now." The detective sounded pretty damn satisfied. "Gavin Hitchcock, you're under arrest for the rape of Cammie Curtis, the murder of Charlotte Henning, and the abduction of Holly Lindstrom." He read him his rights, then shut off the recorder.

The detective and Gillian were stepping out the door when Gavin called her name.

She stopped and turned.

"Why didn't you let me die?"

For a moment he caught a flash of the old Gillian, the Gillian who had liked him and believed in him.

"Couldn't you see I wanted to die?" His voice was a rough, aching whisper.

Her only response was to leave the room.

Gavin heard the click of the closing door, heard the detective telling the officers that the patient was under arrest and would be transported to jail as soon as medically possible.

He'd be going back to prison. That was okay. Things were better in prison.

He squeezed his eyes shut, trying to forget the way Gillian had looked at him. Everything was so hard, too hard.

She was all he'd ever had, all he'd ever wanted, and now she hated him. His fault. Completely his fault. He was bad. Very bad.

He wanted to tell her he was sorry, tell her how much she meant to him, tell her he was glad she'd been a part of his life.

He pulled out the oxygen tubes, ripped out his IV, shoved himself to his feet, and staggered to the door, pulling it open.

"GILLIAN!" he shouted before the guards grabbed him and dragged him back into the room. *"GILLIAN!"*

It didn't matter. She was gone.

His body stiffened. His head flew back.

"He's seizing!" somebody shouted before oblivion came.

Holly was putting on makeup when Gillian returned to the house.

Upon leaving the hospital, Gillian had had to fight the urge to drive straight home. She wanted to be alone, but Holly was waiting. In the hospital hallway Mary had tried to stop her, concern on her face, but Gillian had barged past, afraid that any weakening, any personal contact—especially from her sister— would cause her to fall apart.

Why didn't you let me die?

She had to be tough; she had to be strong. And the only way to do that was to shut herself off, at least temporarily. Not like Mary, not for a lifetime, but for a few hours, maybe even a few days.

"Let her go," Wakefield had told Mary, his voice seeming to come from another dimension.

"What's wrong? What happened?" Mary had asked, worried.

"We got a confession."

We got a confession.

"Did you find your friend?" Holly asked, leaning close to the vanity mirror, a mascara wand in her hand, her mouth open as she concentrated on her reflection.

"Yeah. Yeah, I did." Gillian paced. She picked up a stuffed animal. She put it down. "I need to talk to you."

Holly swung around, her expression going from bored distraction to frightened in less than a second. "What happened?"

"The guy who abducted you—he's been arrested."

"Oh my God! Is it the Lucia Killer?"

"So far he's confessed to one of the murders. I'm sure the others will follow."

There was a long pause as Holly absorbed the information. She plopped down on her bed, as if suddenly too weak to stand. "Does this mean you're going to leave?"

Instead of being relieved, as Gillian would have expected, Holly sounded upset. "We have him in custody," Gillian explained. "There's no reason for me to continue to work undercover."

Holly hung her head and stared intently at the floor. "W-what should I tell the kids at school?"

"Tell them I patched things up with my parents and went back home."

Gillian heard a sniffle, followed by another—and realized it was the news of her departure that Holly was finding difficult to deal with. Poor thing. She'd been through so much. Her emotions were brittle right now, the shift too abrupt. She'd just gotten used to the idea of Gillian spending almost every moment with her; now she was leaving.

The mental distance Gillian had been trying to maintain fell away. "Don't cry," she pleaded, sitting down and putting an arm around her. "We'll still see each other."

"It won't be the same. You won't be my cousin. I know you haven't even been here a whole week, but it was starting to be so much fun."

Gillian held her as her shoulders quaked. "We can still have fun together. I'm not really that much older than you. Look—" She jumped up, grabbed pen and paper, and wrote down her address and home number. Holly already had her pager number. "Call me anytime you feel like it. In the middle of the night—if you need to talk to somebody—call me." She tucked the paper in the frame of the vanity mirror. "Maybe you can stay over sometime. We can rent movies and make popcorn."

Finally Holly raised her head and looked at Gillian, her face wet with tears. "What will happen to him?"

"He'll go to prison."

"For how long?"

"He's already done time, so he'll get a severe sentence," Gillian said sadly. "Probably life." An hour ago, she'd hated Gavin. Now she felt like crying for him.

Couldn't you see I wanted to die?

"I'm still afraid," Holly confessed, sounding surprised. "I thought when he was caught, I wouldn't be afraid anymore. But I don't feel any different. I still have this knot right here." She pressed a hand to her stomach.

"I'm sorry." Gillian wished she could assure her that the fear would subside quickly, but she would be lying.

"What was he in for before?"

"I don't think you need to know. Not right now."

"It'll be in the papers and on TV. Tell me."

"Killing a sixteen-year-old girl." For the first time, Gillian spoke the words without a shadow of doubt.

Chapter 22

Three hours after Gavin's confession, the Minneapolis Police Department, along with the FBI, held a press conference in which information about Hitchcock's confession was released to the media.

"The main purpose of this meeting is to inform the public that the killer terrorizing our young women has been apprehended," Detective Wakefield announced.

A cheer went up, and the relief in the room was palpable.

When questioned about the physical evidence, Detective Wakefield admitted that they didn't yet have much to back up the case. "But I'm confident more will surface." He knew a lack of physical evidence could severely undermine the prosecution, and Hitchcock's confession, especially taken as it was in the emergency room, could be withdrawn or considered inadmissible in court.

Immediately following the conference, Mary and Anthony headed to Gavin Hitchcock's home, where a crime lab team was combing the house and yard.

The living room was littered with bent yellow numbers used to mark areas of evidence. Fiber and hair samples had been collected from the couch, rugs, blankets, and bedding. Beyond the perimeter of the labeled area, technicians had methodically removed and examined the framed images that hung on the wall. They took the drawers from dressers, looking for secret hiding places.

"Find anything interesting?" Anthony asked a young technician in a navy-blue sweatshirt with the letters CSI across the back.

"We came across a box of black-and-white photographs," the young man said, "but there wasn't anything that looked suspicious."

"I'd like to see them."

The technician pointed to a cardboard box on the kitchen counter. "Be my guest."

Anthony pulled two pairs of latex gloves from a container on the floor and handed a pair to Mary.

The cardboard box was about twelve inches deep and full of black-and-white photos. Mary pulled out a handful and began sifting through them. Most were eight-by-tens, taken of different locations in the Twin Cities. St. Paul Cathedral. The Warehouse District in Minneapolis. Stone Arch Bridge. The Witch's Hat. There were several close-ups of flowers, some in various stages of decay.

"I don't know anything about photography," she said, "but these look pretty good."

"Nice contrast." Anthony turned a photo over and examined the back. "He must have developed them himself."

"Here's one of an old woman." She handed it to Anthony.

"I'd guess this was done from a color negative. It has that look to it."

"It could be his grandmother," Mary said. "I don't remember exactly how the story goes, but when he was in grade school, he was living with her and came home one day to find her dead. Burglary was the motive, but the perpetrator was never found, and some people believe Hitchcock killed her himself."

"His first kill, maybe?"

"Possibly."

"That's how some of these people start. They get rid of an annoying family member—out of anger or simple curiosity—then they move on past their immediate comfort zone."

Mary turned to the crime scene technician. "Have you come across any darkroom or developing supplies?"

"Nope. Those photographs are the only thing we've found that has anything to do with photography. Except for a camera. We found that in the bedroom closet."

"Any film in it?" Anthony asked.

"A half-finished roll. It's already been sent to the lab." The man looked at his watch. "That was two hours ago. It should be developed by now."

Mary pulled out her cell phone, called the lab, introduced herself, and got the scoop on the developed photos. "All architecture," Mary said, hanging up and slipping the phone back into her jacket pocket. "Except for four of Cammie Curtis. Taken in bed when she was unconscious."

"The pieces are falling into place," Anthony said. "It fits his MO."

"The lab already sent copies to Homicide, the BCA, and the local FBI."

They left the house. The day had turned out sunny and relatively warm for the end of October. In the front yard, two men were methodically going over the ground with metal detectors and a device that could determine whether or not the soil had recently been disturbed. So far they'd found a couple of quarters, a gum wrapper, and a cat-food lid. Gavin's car, a 1984

Oldsmobile, had been taken to the BCA lab, where it had been vacuumed with high-powered equipment. Every piece of lint sucked from every crevice would be examined.

"I'm heading out tomorrow morning." Anthony shoved his hands deep in the pockets of his black, knee-length coat. "I've got a couple of cases I need to get back to, and things are getting close to being wrapped up here."

Mary experienced a pang, and realized she would miss him. "My mom's having a sort of celebratory dinner tonight because the case is solved, and she'd like you to come if you can make it," she told him as they walked to their individual cars.

"What about you?" Anthony stopped and squinted against the sunlight. "Are you part of this invitation?" he asked with a nonchalance that seemed forced.

"Of course I am. What's that supposed to mean?"

"Do you really want me to come, or are you just being polite?"

The bluntness of his question took her by surprise. "Insecurity doesn't become you," she told him. "Have you ever known me to be anything other than straightforward?"

He thought about that. "Never. And just for the record, it wasn't insecurity that made me question your involvement in the invitation. My therapist suggested I be more honest and open in my dealings with people."

"Therapist? I didn't know you were seeing a therapist. Because of your divorce?"

He looked at her with an unreadable expression, then said, "No. Not because of the divorce." He paused, as if reluctant to continue. "Because of the shooting."

His words left her momentarily breathless. "*My* shooting?" she finally asked, needing clarification even though she knew the answer.

"You almost died because of me." His voice tightened. "That's a hard thing for a guy to live with."

She hadn't known the shooting had bothered him so much. He'd seemed more annoyed than anything else, an annoyance she'd attributed to wounded male pride. "Why didn't you say anything before this?"

He glanced around, hands deep in the pockets of his trench coat. There were people everywhere. He finally looked at her in a way that was direct and almost intimate. "I thought you'd been through enough already."

Her throat burned; she suddenly felt close to tears. She wanted to touch him, to offer him some gesture of compassion, but such an action seemed so alien to her that she couldn't bring herself to make it.

"You should have told me," she said softly.

"I'm telling you now."

For years she'd felt so alone. Now, standing there with Anthony, she suddenly realized she hadn't been as alone as she'd thought.

"I have to go," he said, flashing her a smile that was lacking its usual touch of cynicism. "See you tonight."

"Yeah," she said, distracted by his behavior. "Tonight."

As he drove away, Mary stood on the sidewalk staring at nothing, lost in her own thoughts as she tried to decipher what had just occurred. In the years she'd known Anthony, he'd had a tendency to occasionally reveal the quirky side of his nature, but it had always been a subtle flash, so subtle that any small revelation left her wondering if she'd imagined it. Like a glimpse caught out of the corner of her eye. Turn—and it's gone. But this Anthony . . . this Anthony was front and center.

Her phone rang, redirecting her thoughts to another puzzle. The call was from the fingerprint expert at Quantico.

"You know those prints from the cellophane you sent?" he asked. "Couldn't find a match in the database."

So, the prints from the roses left in the woods weren't Gavin's. Gavin's would have been on file. They probably belonged to the florist. Or the delivery person. Mary thanked him and hung up. After slipping into her car, she made a quick U-turn in the middle of the road and headed for Gillian's apartment.

Gillian's place was in Dinkytown, an area of Minneapolis Mary remembered with fondness. Located just north of the university, Dinkytown was populated by students, and rife with pizza joints and cafés.

The house where Gillian lived turned out to be a two-story monstrosity built when wood was cheap and plentiful. White paint was chipping away, and the porch slanted toward a tiny lawn that was worn to dirt where college students had cut corners on the way to and from class. The building had been divided into two living spaces, with Gillian's on the right.

Mary wasn't sure her sister had moved back home after being at Holly's, but after the third round of knocking Gillian answered the door and let Mary in. "Hi," she said, obviously wondering what Mary was doing there.

"I just came from Gavin's house," Mary said, dropping her coat on a nearby futon.

Gillian had her mother's artistic eye. Her apartment was warm and inviting, with antique furniture, rugs, and shelves overflowing with books. Gillian had always been an obsessive reader, devouring all genres and periods. Mary recalled that in high school she'd developed a particular fondness for French authors.

"There's Birdie." Mary walked over to the massive cage in the corner to say hello. The parrot let out a soft protest, ruffled his white feathers, and then tucked his face under his wing.

"Poor guy's getting old," Gillian said. "He sleeps more than he used to."

Another wounded soul to take care of. Mary turned to her with a smile. "Remember that time he got away?"

Gillian smiled back. "You totally panicked."

"I found a white feather on the neighbor's porch and thought their awful Siamese cat had eaten him. Remember that cat? Dogs trembled in fear when he came around."

Gillian laughed. "Didn't we pry his mouth open looking for Birdie?"

"I think that was your idea. I was just trying to reassure you that he wasn't in there. Poor Birdie." Mary addressed the bird in a soft, teasing voice. "We didn't want you to end up being the cat's meow, did we?"

For the first time in weeks, Mary felt relaxed. Gillian was safe, and the source of their estrangement would soon be put behind bars, probably for good.

"Have they come up with anything else?" Gillian asked.

Mary turned from the bird. "Some fibers they're hoping to match to ones found on the earlier victims." She told her about the eight-by-tens and the photos that had been developed from Gavin's camera. "But no darkroom equipment was found at his house. Do you know where he might develop his film?"

Gillian had to think about that one. "There are

places around town where you can pay a fee—something like ten bucks for the day—to use their darkrooms. There are also places where you can get yearly memberships. Then there's the university. I'm not sure how that works. I don't know if a person could just drop in and develop photos without attracting attention and suspicion. Or it could be he knows somebody who has a darkroom."

Mary put in a call to Elliot. "Have you seen the photos the crime lab sent over?"

"Yeah. We're trying to figure out where Hitchcock's getting his developing done."

"Have some people check out all the local darkrooms where you pay by the day. Also ones where you can buy a membership. They might check with the university to see if someone could just walk into a darkroom there. Call me if you find anything."

She ended the conversation and tossed the phone down on top of her coat. "Mom's having a dinner party tonight," she announced. "I know you probably don't feel like celebrating, but you know Mom. She's big on recognizing accomplishments."

"Will there be a lot of people there?" Gillian made a face. "You know how crazy her parties can be. I always end up getting dragged around, being introduced to so-and-so who used to live next door to so-and-so, who knew Uncle Jack when he lived in Phoenix but before he moved to Philly."

Mary jumped in, "It always starts like, 'You remember John Doe, don't you? His father went to church with Jane Doe, who used to be married to Fill in the Blank, but is now married to Joe Smith.'"

They both laughed.

"Don't worry," Mary said. "It'll just be the three of us, plus Anthony—and of course anybody you might feel like inviting."

Gillian's head tilted. "As in, am I dating anyone? The answer to that is no."

"What about Ben?"

"Please. He's a kid."

"About your age, I'd say." Gillian wasn't biting, and Mary dropped the idea. "Do you mind if I get a drink of water?"

"Let me find a clean glass."

Gillian was still dressed in her hip-hugging pants and short top. When she reached for a glass, Mary saw that she had a tattoo on her lower spine. It was a delicate, circular design in black.

"Is that real?" she asked. "Or part of the costume?"

Gillian glanced over her shoulder. "Another remnant of my rebellious youth. Ice?"

Mary shook her head, accepted the glass, and walked to the sink. She filled it and took a long drink. "What I could never figure out," she said, holding up the glass for inspection, "is why Minneapolis water is so good, and St. Paul water so bad. I mean, the two cities are right next to each other."

Gillian smiled and settled herself on the arm of the old green couch. "It's one of life's mysteries." Her feet were bare, her face free of makeup. She looked about seventeen. "You know, I have another tattoo here—" She pulled down the neckline of her top to reveal a small red rose on the curve of her breast. "Isn't that funny?" She laughed again, but this time the sound was broken, frightened, and confused. "A rose. Can you believe it? It feels like a brand, like I've been branded by Gavin. Branded by a rapist and murderer. He was with me when I got it."

She ran her fingers through her hair, pulling the blond locks from her forehead and then dropping them where they fell back into their perfect cut. "It's so weird to think of the threads that tie everything together, threads that connect through layers and layers of time. When I got this tattoo, I was ignorant of the future and how a rose would figure into it. But the connection was already there, even though I couldn't see it. Nothing is freestanding."

"This might be hard for you to believe, but I'm sorry the killer turned out to be Gavin," Mary said. "And I'm sorry for everything that bastard has put you through."

"He always wanted me, and now I wonder if that's what this was all about. Was he pretending those girls were me? Is that where the rose came into play? You were right about him all along. I just refused to see it. I was clinging to my youth, and the memories of that youth—the youth before he killed Fiona. I just don't think I wanted to face it, or didn't want to believe that Gavin murdered her, because if he did . . . then I was also responsible."

"Why do you think that?" Mary asked cautiously, not sure she wanted to hear Gillian's answer.

"I was jealous of Fiona. You know that. I complained about her to Gavin." She bit her lip, looked up at the ceiling, then down at the floor. "I even said I wanted to kill her. That Gavin and I should kill her."

It was what Mary had always suspected. But now that Gillian had finally come clean, her confession didn't hurt the way Mary had expected it to hurt. It no longer carried with it the weight of a horrendous betrayal. Instead, it signified the loss of childhood innocence.

"The only person responsible for Gavin is Gavin," Mary told her.

"No. He was so impressionable. And he was infatuated with me. I should have known he would do whatever it took to make me happy. Even kill somebody."

"Gillian, you were a child. A *child*."

She shook her head. "We talked about it just once, but I should have known."

Everybody had spiteful feelings at one time or another. How could Gillian know that those feelings, planted in the wrong mind, could be transformed so horribly? For her sister's sake, Mary moved on to another subject, one that had been bothering her ever since Gillian had brought it up. "Are you going to tell me what Gavin did to you the other day?"

"What? Oh, that." Gillian had apparently already dismissed it. "He kissed me. Not a nice kiss. A mauling kind of kiss."

"That bastard," Mary said, even though she was relieved to find it had been just a kiss. It could have been much worse.

"It doesn't matter. It seems irrelevant now. The mauling is nothing compared to everything else he's done. I feel like such a fool. You were on target when you said I wanted to be a cop because I thought I could somehow make things right."

"You have to accept the past and move on."

Gillian looked at her in disbelief. "I can't believe you're saying that. I can't believe *you*, of all people, are telling me that."

"I'm being a hypocrite, I know, but it's the best advice to give. I'm not saying I took it myself. I tried, but for some reason I've never been able to let it go. I'm just like Mrs. Portman, who sits in that dark tomb of a house, that shrine to a daughter who's never coming back."

She must have sounded pretty forlorn, because Gillian—always the demonstrative one—got to her feet and put an arm around her, her head on her shoulder. Mary stiffened, then relaxed. The contact was comforting. "We're a bit of a mess, aren't we?" Gillian said.

"I didn't realize how much of one until I came back here." After a moment's hesitation, Mary put her hand over Gillian's. "The past has hooks that reach into infinity, into yesterday and today and the future."

"Like a fucking rose tattoo," Gillian said.

"Yeah. Like a fucking rose tattoo."

In the cage in the corner of the room, Birdie woke up. "Hel-lo, hel-lo," he said, bobbing his head.

Chapter 23

Blythe loved parties. When the girls were little, she baked cakes and lit candles, and was sure to commemorate every occasion that presented itself. Because life was to be celebrated, and you never knew how long the good times would last so you had to embrace them.

After Fiona was killed, Blythe tried not to think about the young girl's death too deeply. Though she ached for Mary and saw her daughter change, she tried not to allow it to darken her own aura. After all, someone had to remain optimistic. They couldn't all drag themselves through the days, bemoaning the unfairness and ugliness of life. With hindsight, she realized now that ignoring what had been going on around her hadn't helped—it had only made things worse.

But Mary was home, and her daughters were speaking to each other again, and maybe they would be able to spend Christmas together for the first time in years. True, Gillian was suffering, but Blythe would be there for her. She would help her get past the pain.

It was time to celebrate.

She made a sinfully chocolate cake from a prize-winning recipe she'd gotten from a little café in St.

Paul. It was moist and full of gooey layers, just the kind of decadence required for the ultimate party.

She'd baked bread and prepared a tossed salad. Her special lasagna was in the oven. Wine waited to be opened. Lights were turned down, and candlelight reflected off glass.

The doorbell rang.

"Mary!" she shouted. "Will you get it?"

She heard Mary's footsteps on the stairs. It made her think of the old days, when they were a family.

They could be a family again. Couldn't they?

She heard a male voice. Anthony? Such a nice man. And so *good-looking.* One voice was joined by another, announcing the arrival of Gillian.

In a flurry of cold air, they burst into the kitchen. Anthony handed her a bottle of wine. Gillian inhaled, praising the odors coming from the oven.

Nothing about Blythe's place was formal. They ate in the dining area connected to the kitchen. Wine and conversation flowed, along with laughter. As if by unspoken agreement, they didn't mention the recent case or Gavin Hitchcock.

When Blythe brought out her masterpiece of a cake, everyone applauded, then sighed. Mary and Gillian, both chocolate addicts, closed their eyes and almost purred. The meal had lasted over an hour, but it was done with much too quickly.

"I have something else planned," Blythe said as Anthony and Mary cleared the table.

Mary put a hand to her stomach. "No more food—please."

"Pot throwing."

At Blythe's announcement, Mary and Gillian exchanged a conspiratorial look. They'd been getting along extremely well all evening, Anthony had noticed. "Pot throwing?" he asked, drawing a blank.

"As in pottery and a potter's wheel." Gillian got to her feet and rubbed her hands together. "This will be fun."

Anthony quickly made up an excuse, horrified at the thought of an artistic endeavor, especially one that involved clay. "I'm going to have to get back to the hotel. I haven't packed."

"Packing won't take you all night," Mary said, immediately seeing through his ruse. He was surprised she was encouraging such a leap. But then he noticed the way she was smiling at him—obviously amused by the idea of putting him in an uncomfortable situation. Or could it be that she'd simply had too much to drink?

He rather liked the idea of witnessing this more relaxed side of his partner. He smiled back. "Sounds like fun."

Blythe's shop was located off the kitchen in what used to be the garage. Shelves were lined with bowls and pots in various stages of production. Some were drying. Some had recently been removed from the kiln and were awaiting glaze. Others were ready to be fired, and many had already been glazed, fired, and were now cooling.

Blythe had two electric wheels and one manual treadle machine. "I propose a contest," Mary said. "The best pot wins."

"I'd have to guess that you've done this before," Anthony said. "So a contest hardly seems fair."

"Mary *has* done it before," Gillian declared, "but she's horrible at it."

Mary couldn't get mad, especially when Gillian looked so adorable in a pair of snug red plaid pants and a fuzzy black top. Earlier she'd claimed she was going to at least get some good out of her new clothes. "I am pretty bad," Mary admitted.

Anthony eyed his partner with a slight smile. "In that case, I'll accept the challenge."

Mary was drunk. She'd realized it as soon as she'd gotten up from the table. She'd been mildly drunk only a few times in her life, and hadn't enjoyed it at all. She liked being in control. But now she was thinking that being a little out of control was more fun than she'd remembered.

She sat down at the wheel with her piece of clay. Was she going to make a total idiot out of herself? She didn't even care.

"Ten minutes," Gillian said. "Let's see what you can both make in ten minutes."

"I don't even know what in the hell I'm doing," Anthony said as Blythe put a canvas apron over his head.

"I'll show you." She gave him a quick five-minute lesson; then they were off.

Mary's glob of clay immediately got off balance and she had to start over. She shot a quick look at Anthony. He had his wheel on low, meticulously working the clay.

"More water," Blythe said.

"Mom! Don't coach him!"

"I can coach him if I want to. He's never done it before."

"Your daughter can't stand to lose," Anthony said.

"*I* can't stand to lose? What about you?"

When the time was up, Mary's small bowl was thin and distorted on one side, thick on the other. "Another minute and it would have gone flying across the room," she said wryly. Anthony's, on the other hand, while unfinished and unexceptional, was on its way to becoming an actual coffee cup.

Then it was Gillian's turn.

At one time Gillian had been fairly adept at the

wheel, but apparently she was out of practice. She immediately began having such a hard time that Mary started laughing and couldn't stop.

"Oh, Gillian!" she gasped.

Mary looked up to catch Anthony watching her with a disconcerting expression on his face. When he retained eye contact, she broke away, confused.

Ten minutes later, Gillian was slapping her rejected piece of clay, starting over again for the third time.

"Anthony wins, hands down," Blythe said.

Anthony and Gillian decided they needed more practice and played around a little longer, Blythe and Mary gathering close, coaching them and laughing. Finally Blythe took the seat and they watched as she quickly created a beautiful vase, removed it from the wheel, and put it aside to dry.

"That's why you're the artist and I'm an FBI agent," Anthony said, smiling.

"You're too sweet."

Was her mother flirting with Anthony? Mary wondered. No, surely not. Or was Anthony flirting with her mother? She'd called him sweet and he hadn't batted an eye.

The party didn't break up until almost midnight.

"Do you need a ride to the airport tomorrow?" Mary asked Anthony.

"No, thanks. I have to drop off my rental car there anyway. Can I talk to you a minute?"

"I'll grab my coat and join you outside. I could use some fresh air."

"I'll glaze your coffee cup so Mary can give it to you," Blythe promised.

Anthony shook hands with Gillian, then surprised Mary by giving Blythe a quick kiss on the cheek. "Thanks for dinner. I had a good time."

Mary walked with him to the street where his car

was parked. "Your mother's nice," he said, pausing near the curb.

She crossed her arms at her waist. "You didn't have to kiss her."

"Jealous? She called me sweet. That deserved a kiss."

"Deserved? That makes you sound awfully special."

"Why bring it up?"

"It just seemed . . . I don't know." She paused. "Out of character."

"Really? Then I guess you don't know me very well."

His delivery was teasing, but the truth behind his words stung. In some ways she knew him intimately. She could read every nuance of his expression, and often knew what he was going to say before he said it. When he wasn't around, she could hear his voice in her head, calmly offering theories. But in other ways, he was more of a mystery to her than he'd ever been.

She managed to shrug off his comment, not wanting it to spoil a wonderful evening. "I'm glad you came to Minneapolis."

"What about you? How's it been for you, being here?"

"I'm glad I came too."

"It looks as if you and Gillian are getting along. Maybe it'll be easier for you to come back now."

His insight surprised her. "I think it will." Cold air blew down her collar. She pulled her jacket tighter. "What did you want to talk to me about?"

He leaned against the car in what she read as feigned unconcern. "You *are* coming back, aren't you? To Virginia?"

"Of course I am. How could you think otherwise?"

"I don't know. I thought you might be starting to

like it here. And I know Elliot is in the market for a profiler."

She tipped her head. "Now I'm beginning to wonder if *you're* jealous."

"Do you think that's possible?" he asked slowly, his voice smooth.

"Of course not," she said, suddenly flustered. "I don't know why I said it."

"Maybe you're a little drunk.".

"Maybe."

He pushed away from the car and took her gently by both arms. He leaned close. . . . And then his lips touched hers—just a brush before veering to the right to plant a soft kiss on her cheek.

That millisecond of contact sent an electrical sensation along her skin, down her jaw, up to her scalp. Her breath caught, and heat suffused her body.

"That's so you don't feel slighted." And then he was pulling away, casually telling her good-bye.

She had to stop him. He couldn't leave just yet. "Anthony—wait."

He paused, his hand on the car door. Light from the Victorian-style street lamp fell over him, lending a film noir quality to the moment. As she looked at the contrasting shadows that made up his face, she suddenly became aware of the passage of time. Of weeks and months and years. She thought about all the unspokens, and how important it was to let the people you care about know how you felt. . . . But how could you do that when you weren't sure yourself?

"Mary?" Anthony asked. In his face, she saw a hint of the same pain and panic she'd witnessed in those slow-motion minutes after she'd been shot. "Is it your arm?"

"No. No, I'm fine," she said slowly.

Mary had been so sure of herself for so many years.

The ground she'd stood on had seemed so solid. Now it was shifting under her, slipping away, taking Anthony with it. Was he seeing someone new? she wondered.

"I wanted to tell you to be careful," she said. "And that I'll see you soon."

His worry vanished. He flashed her a smile and got in his car. She stood on the curb and watched as he drove away, watched as the red taillights disappeared around the corner.

"He likes you." Gillian had silently appeared on the sidewalk, just beyond Mary's shoulder.

"Anthony?"

"Who else?"

"I think he sometimes finds me amusing."

"He likes you. More than likes you."

Was Gillian right? Was that what Anthony's hot-cold and sometimes unreadable behavior was rooted in? The very idea of Anthony liking her was foreign and exotic and made Mary's heart hammer in a strangely frightening and exhilarating way. A case of arrested development? "What would make you say something like that?"

"I saw the way he was looking at you when you weren't watching."

Mary tried to wave off the idea. "He's constantly criticizing me and pointing out my faults." This was like something Gillian would have started when they were younger. "Remember that time you told me the cute boy down the block had a crush on me?" Mary asked. "So I wrote him some embarrassingly mushy note and had you give it to him. Do you remember how that turned out? He didn't even know who I was."

Gillian clapped her hands together, then threw back her head and laughed in delight—showing a flash of

the charming brat Mary used to know. And in that
outfit, with that hair, she looked like a teenager. "I
completely forgot about that stupid note!" She doubled over. "That was *so* funny!"

Mary laughed along with her, and when she finally
stopped her stomach muscles hurt from the unfamiliar
workout. *It's the alcohol,* she told herself. There was
a good reason she never drank—it skewed her perspective. Laughing her ass off, brought to her knees
by a kiss and some wine. And it hadn't even been a
real kiss. What would a real kiss have done? she wondered as she took Gillian's arm. "Come on. Let's go
harass Mom."

Together they returned to the house.

Chapter 24

Two days later, Mary was in the bedroom of her mother's house, typing up the final pages of her report, when her mobile phone rang. It was Elliot.

"Just got a call from Homicide," he said in a breathless, excited voice. "One of their guys is at a darkroom in Seward. Guess whose name is in their guest book?"

"Hitchcock?"

"Right. The date would fit too. He was there in late October."

She grabbed a pen and a piece of paper. "What's the address?"

"Take 35 West north, get off on Cedar, east on Franklin. It's two blocks south of the co-op. I'll meet you there."

She hung up and turned off her laptop. She slipped on her gun, grabbed her phone and coat, and ran down the stairs and out the door.

Seward was a neighborhood of Minneapolis located north of Powderhorn and just south of the West Bank campus of U of M. It was one of those places like Frogtown in St. Paul, where the crime rate was still higher than city officials and police liked, but was improving.

Mary didn't have any trouble finding the photo lab.

Three police cars were out front, plus Elliot's silver Taurus. She turned onto a side street and parked near a two-story Victorian with a chain-link fence and a yard that had been run bald by the German shepherd that was barking at her.

She locked her car with the remote, then hurried around the block to the photo lab. Inside the door and to the right was a coffee shop. Directly in front of her, curved cement steps led upstairs to a counter where Elliot stood talking to a young man of about eighteen. Elliot made introductions—the kid was a volunteer who worked there in exchange for free lab time.

On the counter in front of them was the sign-in book, open to the page with Hitchcock's name, date, and time of arrival and departure. "I wanted you to see it before we bagged it up," Elliot explained. "We'll send a photocopy to our handwriting expert. The rest will be checked for fingerprints."

"I doubt there will be anything left of Hitchcock's," Mary said.

"I doubt it too." Elliot slid the book into an evidence bag, stuck on a chain of evidence sticker, then signed and dated it. "Now for the fun part."

He led the way down a hall and through a narrow red door to a myriad of rooms and a winding, haunted-house-type maze that was meant to keep light from the developing and enlargement areas without the hassle of doors.

The overhead white lights were on, and police personnel were sifting through boxes of poor-quality photos that had been abandoned by patrons. With gloved hands, two women held strips of developed negatives to the light. Others went through trash containers.

"Ever taken a darkroom class?" Elliot asked.

"No."

"When it's dark in here, and there's nothing on but the red lights, it can be hard to keep track of all your prints and negatives. Especially if there are a lot of people using the lab at one time. It was a full house the day Hitchcock was here. One person for every enlarger."

"But wouldn't the others in the room have noticed his photos?"

"Not necessarily. He may have only made a contact sheet. The photos would have been too small for anyone to see. Or he could have kept his paper upside-down in the developing bath. And if he was only taking pictures of half-nude girls, maybe nobody would think anything of it anyway. You know how artists are. The body is a work of art and all that."

Mary nodded, thinking darkly of Sebastian Tate. "What about fingerprints?"

"Crime lab says it's been too long and too much traffic through here to bother."

"Okay, where do you need me?"

One of the women working with the negatives offered her a strip. "This is the most tedious job," she said apologetically. "Here—" She handed her a small magnifier. "This helps."

Mary took a seat near a lamp, turned it on, and got busy. "Family vacation to Disney World." She groaned. "Why would somebody want black-and-whites of a vacation to Disney World?"

"People do weird things," Elliot said. "As you well know."

"Right."

It didn't take her long to go through the strip of thirty-six. There was the castle. There was the ever annoying It's a Small World.

"What are you smiling about?" Elliot asked, sitting across from her, a negative strip in his hand.

"I was thinking about a trip we took to Disney World. Gillian must have gone on Mr. Toad's Wild Ride six times."

"I heard they closed that," Elliot said, his voice distracted as he concentrated on his own negatives.

"No!" Mary couldn't believe it.

"Not exciting enough or something."

"Closed Mr. Toad's Wild Ride? That's sacrilegious!"

Others got into the conversation, the way people do when working on something monotonous. One person admitted she thought it was past time for the ride to go, and two others agreed.

"Gillian will be devastated." Mary marked the negative strip with a small piece of white tape to show it had been examined. She hung it back up in the drying closet and pulled out another strip.

"I think I may have found something," said one of the investigators who'd been sifting through the trash. He held up a piece of a negative with a pair of tweezers. He moved closer to the light. "It's a woman, anyway. At least partially nude."

"Let's get a print."

They shut off the white lights and turned on the red overheads. Elliot set the negative up in the enlarger. "Anybody see any paper around?" he asked, opening drawers.

"Here—" Someone handed him a black package. "Feels like glossy."

"That'll be fine. Just so it's not fiber, or something that takes too long to develop." He opened the light-safe sleeve, slid out a contact sheet and placed it in the holder, glass on top. "I'm just going to guess on the time. Six seconds is middle of the road and should give us a readable image." He flipped the toggle switch on the timed light. When it automatically clicked off, he lifted the glass, carried the blank white paper to the solution area, and slid it into the developing tray. The group crowded around as the image slowly materialized.

It turned out to be a close-up of a woman from her navel to her thighs, nude, pubic hair exposed. After waiting a minute and a half, Elliot picked up the eight-by-ten with wooden tongs, dropped it into the adjoining stop bath, and then followed with the rinse.

"Turn the lights back on, and let's keep looking," he said. "Maybe we can find the other pieces."

Four hours later, they'd gone through the trash in the entire building, plus the Dumpster in the alley. Elliot called the research department and explained the situation. "I need you to find the name of the landfill where Gabe's Garbage takes their trash. Then get some people out there to go through it if it's in any way feasible."

The person on the other end must not have liked the sound of that.

"I don't know," Elliot said with obvious irritation. "Get some protective gear from the toxic waste crew or something. Listen, on NPR I heard about a guy who flew back home, found out where his trash had been taken, went to the landfill, and rescued his son's teddy bear, so I know it can be done." With that, he hung up.

"What about a trip to Holly Lindstrom's?" Mary asked. "She should be home from school by now."

"You read my mind. And what about your sister? It sounds like she and Holly got along pretty well. Maybe we should pick her up on the way."

"I'll give her a call."

"You can leave your car here," Elliot said as they left the building. "We'll get it later."

Mary got in touch with Gillian, catching her at

home. Since her apartment was only a few miles away, they swung by and picked her up.

Gillian was waiting at the door. As soon as Elliot pulled into the driveway, she locked her house and hurried to the car, quickly sliding into the backseat. "I called Holly," she said breathlessly, slamming the door as Elliot backed up. "She's home. I told her we'd be there in a half an hour. Where's the photo?"

Mary passed it over the seat, and Gillian settled back to examine it. After a few moments, she said, "There's no way of knowing if it's her, is there?"

"That's why we're hoping Holly can shed some light on the mystery," Mary said. "I know she said he took photos of her."

"We can get a specialist to blow up the print," Elliot said. "If you look closely at the top and bottom edge, you can see a sliver of fabric. Maybe we can find a match."

"I sent the negative to the lab. They're going to do everything they can to it."

"You said Hitchcock's name was on the sign-in book?" Gillian asked.

"Late October," Elliot told her, stopping at the metered light on the access ramp to 35W. "Rush hour," he moaned.

They had to wait through four cars; then he was accessing the freeway, heading to the south Minneapolis neighborhood where Holly lived.

"Do you mind if I speak to her by myself?" Gillian asked. "Poor kid. She was pretty upset when I called her. She's trying to put this behind her, and now I'm going to show her a nude picture that might be of her."

"We were thinking it would be better if you talked to her alone," Mary said. "It will be embarrassing enough for her without having an audience. Put it in here." Mary handed her a large manila envelope. Gillian slid the print inside.

Traffic was stop and go. Because of rush hour, it took them longer to reach Holly's than Gillian had thought. They were ten minutes late by the time she knocked on the door.

Holly answered. She and Gillian embraced; then Gillian took a step back, her hands on Holly's arms. "Are your parents home from work?"

Holly shook her head. "Not yet."

"Would you like to wait until they get back?"

"No! I was all worried they'd get home before you got here. I don't want them to see it. Not now, anyway. And what if it's not even me? Then they wouldn't have to see it at all."

"Okay. Are you ready? Here—let's go sit down on the couch."

They moved over to the couch, sitting side by side. Gillian handed Holly the envelope.

Holly opened the package and slipped the photo out, leaving one end still inside the envelope in case she had to quickly hide it.

She stared at it for a long time.

"Well?" Gillian asked.

"I don't know."

"Is there a chance that it *could* be you?"

"Well . . . yeah. Yeah, it could be. But I don't know. I mean, it's somebody's crotch. It could be *anybody's* crotch."

"Look at it carefully and ask yourself if there's anything about it that tells you it *can't* be you."

She continued to stare at it, then finally shoved it back inside the envelope. "No."

"Okay," Gillian said. "That's all we wanted to know."

Holly handed the photo over. "I suppose that's

going to be passed around all over the place," she said uneasily.

"It's evidence. Some experts are going to enlarge it so they can compare the fabric in the photo to the clothes you were wearing the night you were found."

"Enlarge it? Oh my God. Do they have to?" Holly began to nervously jiggle her knee.

"They aren't going to be looking at you—or whoever it is. And it might not be you at all. They're going to be looking at the fabric. That's all they'll care about."

"Most of them, sure. But there's always going to be somebody in the bunch who'll make a joke out of it."

Unfortunately, that was true.

Her knee moved faster. "They'll blow it up to the size of a billboard and slap it on a wall. Or it will end up on one of those games where you guess what the enlarged object is. Is this a Brillo pad magnified a hundred times? Is it an extreme close up of a moon rock? No, it's Holly Lindstrom's crotch!"

Gillian laughed, and a moment later Holly joined her, a little manic at first, but then she began to calm down. "Hey—how would you like to come to my place this weekend?" Gillian asked.

"You mean, stay over?"

"Yeah. We can rent some comedies or whatever. We can hang out and talk."

"Yeah, cool!"

They quickly made their plans, and then Gillian was joining Elliot and Mary in the car.

"Well?" Elliot asked as he backed out of the driveway.

"She doesn't know," Gillian said. "But there's nothing about the photo that ruled her out either. And believe me, she was looking because she didn't want it to have anything to do with her."

"That's all we could have expected," Mary said. "Either a no, or a it's possible. I had an idea while we were sitting here. Take me back to my car and the photo lab. I want to talk to the kid at the check-in desk. I started thinking about a woman I used to know who hated to pay for trash pickup, so she would bag up her garbage and drive behind grocery and discount stores and toss it in their Dumpsters."

"But the photo lab has a Dumpster," Elliot said, weaving in and out of traffic.

"Yeah, but did you notice how much garbage they had?"

School was out, and people had gotten off work. There weren't any empty parking spaces near the building, so Elliot dropped Mary off; then he and Gillian circled the block in search of parking.

Mary found the same young man inside at the counter.

"Does anybody ever take any trash away from here to dispose of somewhere else?" she asked.

"We have a Dumpster in back."

"Suppose it was full. Would anyone take a few bags home to throw away in their own waste container? Or maybe even throw it away in another store's container in order to save an extra pickup fee?"

She must have hit on something, because he looked a little worried.

"Can you get in a lot of trouble for that?" he asked.

She held his gaze. "We aren't concerned with trash being dumped in the wrong place. We want to find something that may have ended up in that trash and we need your help."

He shifted uncomfortably, looking away. "We used to leave the extra stuff bagged up beside the Dumpster, but we got in trouble for that. And we used to just not take it out, but we got in trouble for that too.

The owner told us to make it fit no matter what, but that's a hassle, and sometimes it just won't fit, you know?"

"Where would it have been taken?"

He gave her a weak shrug. "There's a bar about two blocks from here. And a grocery store on Oak Street. Oh, and a school. I forgot about the school."

"What about this week and last week?"

"Hey, lemme call somebody."

He hunched over the phone and dialed a number, hiding the buttons so she couldn't see. "It's me," he said into the receiver. "You know that trash you took out a few days ago? Where'd you dump it? Okay. No, just somebody looking for something." He hung up. "The bar," he said.

"Thanks."

Mary was leaving the building when she met Elliot and Gillian heading in. "Some trash was dumped at the bar down the street," she said.

They piled in Elliot's car and headed down the block. The place the kid had told them about turned out to be a little neighborhood bar called Catfish. Behind the building, in the alley, was a Dumpster overflowing with trash.

"Luckily we don't need a search warrant," Elliot said, standing in front of the huge metal container with his hands on his hips. "Once garbage hits the alley, it's public property."

Mary eyed the black bags. "I'm going to go in and tell the bartender all the same."

When she stepped into the dark building, several of the men at the bar looked boldly at her. One flash of her badge had them all staring straight back down into their drinks.

"You can have all the trash you want," the bartender said.

They didn't have to go far to find the two bags that belonged to the photo lab. But they continued through the refuse, digging all the way to the bottom to make sure they had everything. Then, since it was getting dark, they took their booty back to the lab to examine it in the light. The investigative team had dispersed, leaving two members to finish up. Those two, a man and a woman, helped sift through the bags of trash.

Gillian found three pieces of a negative. She held them to the light and was able to make out a female form.

"I have something," she announced.

Everyone rushed to her side.

"Rather than trying to hold the negative together," Elliot said, excited again, "let's enlarge each piece separately, then put those pieces together."

"I'll do one while you do one," Gillian said, taking a section over to an enlarger. "Could somebody get the lights?"

"I'll do the third piece," the man from the investigative team said.

Mary headed for the door. "I'll get the photo from the car."

"You'll need these." Elliot tossed her his keys.

All three sections went into the developing bath at the same time. As everyone watched, the broken images slowly appeared, each eight-by-ten sheet blank except for a strip that was the image left by the torn negative. After the final rinse, the lights were turned on and the pieces were cut with scissors, then put together like a puzzle along with the original photo.

It was of a woman, or girl, lying on the ground, panties around her knees. Gillian pressed a hand to her mouth. Even though the girl's face was turned away, she could see it was Holly.

This should get Gavin a life sentence.

She didn't know how long she stared at it before she heard the dead silence of the room. She looked up. Mary was watching her with compassion in her eyes, and the sympathy and understanding she saw there had her suddenly feeling dangerously close to tears. Slowly, she nodded.

"Okay," Elliot said quietly to everybody in the room. "We've got what we were looking for."

Chapter 25

He was tired of being lonely. That's all.

He wanted somebody to take care of. He wanted somebody to adore.

That evening, as he'd done so many evenings, he drove to Holly Lindstrom's house and parked a block away. The street was crowded and narrow, with vehicles wedged tightly down both sides. Good. That way his car wasn't conspicuous.

The media had a knack for leaking information the cops didn't want reaching public ears, and one of the things going around was that investigators were looking for more physical evidence. What kind of evidence? He heard they were hoping to find photos that had been taken of Holly Lindstrom, so he'd supplied them. He'd gone to a photo lab, found a line that had been left empty in the sign-up book, written in Hitchcock's name, and then left the torn negative for someone to find. And they'd found it. Just like he'd hoped they would, and now nobody was looking for him, and nobody was watching Holly anymore.

He perked up as a little red car pulled into her driveway. Mazda? he wondered. It was hard to tell. So many cars looked alike nowadays.

Someone got out and hurried to the door.

She was back!

What happened to her Mustang? Oh, it didn't matter. She was back! Back!

The front door opened, and he saw Holly's blond head. He heard a feminine laugh. Then the two of them scampered from the house, got in the little red car, and drove away.

He turned the ignition key, put his car in gear, and followed.

At Intercontinental Video, Gillian and Holly discovered they both had an affinity for old movies. They ended up renting four because there was a special going on, and they loaded up on popcorn, soda, and black licorice. At Gillian's apartment, Holly carried in her pillow and backpack while Gillian grabbed the supplies.

"Oh, wow! You have a bird!" Holly dropped her things and ran to the cage.

"Hello," she said.

Birdie stared at her.

"Does he talk?" Holly asked, glancing over her shoulder, then back at the bird.

"Once he starts he doesn't shut up. He's just getting used to you right now."

"He's *so* cool."

Gillian walked over and poked her finger at the bird. "I've had him since I was eight. We guessed he was about twelve then, but parrots can live eighty years or more."

"Oh, man. I don't know if I'd want to spend eighty years in a cage. Do you ever let him out?"

"Quite a bit, but he seems to prefer the cage. I think he feels safe in there. Maybe because I lost him once. I let him loose in the house and he got out a window I'd forgotten to close. He was gone about twenty-four hours, and when my sister and I found him and brought him home, he wouldn't leave his cage for two weeks."

They made microwave popcorn and poured cola over ice. Gillian grabbed some blankets and a pillow from upstairs. Knowing Holly's penchant for darkness, she lit a couple of candles, turned off the lights, and settled in front of the TV.

Holly had already popped in *Sabrina*. It was the original, with Audrey Hepburn. They discussed Audrey Hepburn's clothes and style and long neck, and temporarily forgot about Gavin Hitchcock.

When the movie was over, they got into their pajamas and opened the futon for Holly. Gillian covered Birdie's cage, then stretched out on the couch and hit the PLAY button on the remote to watch movie number two.

"This is one of my favorites," she said as the opening credits for *Harvey* began to roll.

"Jimmy Stewart was so cool."

"Did you see *Rear Window*?"

"I love that movie! Did you see the digitally remastered version when it was at Oak Street Cinema?"

"Yeah!"

"No way! Me too! And even though I'd seen it maybe five times on TV, I swear my mouth was hanging open, it was so awesome to finally see it on a movie screen. Wouldn't it have been cool to have lived then, and dressed like Grace Kelly? When she came in with that net thing on her hat, and she raised her arms like this and folded it back away from her face. That was too cool."

The opening scene began. They fell silent and directed their attention to the TV screen.

Even though the movie was one she loved, Gillian began to drift off. The last three nights—nights in which she'd been unable to sleep—were catching up with her.

One time she woke to see that Holly was watching the third movie. It was a more recent release, something Gillian didn't think looked very good. The candles had burned down and gone out by themselves, and the room was dark except for a blue glow coming from the television.

Holly glanced over at her and smiled. "Go to sleep, silly!" she said, seeing how hard it was for Gillian to stay awake. Gillian let out a sleep-drugged laugh and closed her eyes.

Holly turned back to the movie. It was boring and hard to follow, but she finished watching it anyway. That's how she was. She could never stop reading a book halfway through, no matter how bad it was, and she could never stop watching a movie.

When it was over, she rewound the tape and put it back in the case. Leaving the television tuned to MTV, she turned down the volume and settled back on the futon, pulling the blanket to her chin. She always liked to have something on when she was going to sleep—the radio or TV. It didn't matter. Just sound to fill the silence.

As soon as she fell asleep, she began to dream. And the dreams were all mixed up. Gillian and Jimmy Stewart were there, and a rabbit in a birdcage. Suddenly Gillian turned into Grace Kelly. Over her face was black netting. "You look like a movie star," Holly told her in the dream.

Gillian was walking toward her, her footsteps light. Holly felt pressure on her shoulder, turning her around, turning her over.

She smelled adhesive.

Suddenly a hand pressed a wide band of tape across her lips, extending from cheek to cheek, almost to her ears. She felt hot breath on her skin while something cold and metallic was shoved into her neck.

Gillian came awake with a start to see a silhouetted figure backlit by the flickering glow of the TV. The man wore a dark, bulky jacket and a ski mask over his face. Standing, his arm clamped around her stomach, was Holly. Her mouth was sealed, her eyes large and terrified.

She made a sound deep in her throat—a scream halted by the tape.

"Please—" Gillian slowly sat up, swinging her feet to the floor, struggling to keep her voice calm. "Don't hurt her."

How is this happening?

He shifted slightly. Something caught in the flickering light. A gun. Her own gun was upstairs. *Too far away.*

"Lie down on the floor," he told her. "Hurry. Now! Or I'll kill her." His voice was neither deep nor high-pitched, and he didn't sound especially agitated—not a good sign. Some of the most horrendous killers in history remained calm and emotionally detached throughout their attacks of violence.

Gillian dropped to her knees. He lashed out with a booted foot, kicking her in the back of the head. The impact sent her sprawling, her chin smacking wood. She didn't feel anything. He shoved Holly facedown into the futon. "Stay there. Don't move."

He knelt above Gillian, wrenched her arms behind her, and wrapped her wrists with duct tape. He tore off another piece. Before he could silence her with it, knowing this was her last chance, she rolled to her back, her arms and hands crushed beneath her.

Two thoughts raced through her mind simultaneously. *This is the Lucia Killer.*

Gavin is in jail.

She tried to remember everything she'd learned about the killer, his likes and dislikes and what he wanted in a victim. Her sister's words came back to her. *You fit the victimology.*

"Take me," she said, looking up at him, adrenaline and fear pumping through her veins. "Don't take her, take me."

The shabby ski mask stared at her.

"That's what you're here for, isn't it?" Gillian asked. "You've come for Holly?"

Inside the oval holes, eyes blinked. Seemingly curious, he reached down and fiddled with her hair, rubbing it between his gloved fingers.

On TV, a psychic was telling people to call for a free reading: "I know you're lonely," the psychic said. "I can help you find your perfect soul mate."

The psychic's words seemed to be Gillian's cue. "Holly isn't right for you. And the others—they weren't right for you either." *Don't lay it on too thick. He might not believe you. You might make him mad.* "But I've studied you—enough to know we're a lot alike. We're both—"

"Stop talking."

He slapped the tape over Gillian's mouth, then jerked her to her feet, pulling her against him. His next words were a startling revelation. "I came for you," he whispered against her cheek, the wool of his mask rubbing her skin, his breath lifting her hair in puffs. "You're the one I've been watching. You're the one I want."

Tate? she wondered. Was the Lucia Killer Sebastian Tate after all? The height was right. Was the voice? She didn't know. Couldn't remember.

He shoved her away from him, then pressed the tip of the gun to the back of Holly's head.

Even though her mouth was sealed, Gillian let out an anguished cry. *NO!*

He paused and looked at her.

NO! Don't do it! she begged him with her eyes. *Please. Don't do it!*

Inside the ski mask, he didn't seem fully human. Still, he pulled the gun away from Holly's head, turning it on Gillian.

He shoved Holly's face against the pillow until she began to struggle. He let her up long enough to take a breath, then forced her down again. "Stay there for fifteen minutes," he commanded. "You hear me?"

She nodded. Her entire body trembled, muffled whimpers coming from her throat.

"A full fifteen minutes."

She nodded again.

He hustled Gillian in front of him, shoving her out the door into the dark night and down the sidewalk. For a moment, she thought of making a run for it, but discarded the idea. With her hands behind her back and her mouth covered, he'd quickly overtake her. And in his anger, what would he do? Kill her and abduct Holly? Kill them both?

He opened the trunk of his car. Gillian stared in horror at the dark, gaping hole. No. She couldn't get in there. She could already smell it—a cloying, rotten corpse odor. This was not a trunk but the death pit that had held the bodies of the murdered girls. Of Bambi, April, Justine, and Charlotte.

Reason vanished. She was a terrified animal fighting for her life. She tensed, struggling to keep her feet on the ground, pushing against him, a panic-filled keening coming from her throat.

In one smooth motion, he lifted and pushed her forward, slamming the trunk lid behind her.

Chapter 26

Gillian struggled for breath, fear sending her heart rate several notches higher, her chest rising and falling in accelerated panic.

Had Holly gotten up as soon as they left and called the police? If so, cops would be swarming all over looking for her right now.

And the guy. The guy driving the car. *Not Gavin.* Definitely not Gavin. Was it Tate? What the hell was going on?

Bile rose in her throat. She thought about Charlotte Henning choking to death on her own vomit.

Calm down.

She forced her muscles to relax and started counting to regulate her breathing.

Don't think. Don't think about anything but staying calm.

Holly waited until she was sure fifteen minutes had passed.

Then she waited another ten.

With her mouth and wrists taped, she struggled to her feet, shoving her forehead against the couch as she pushed herself upright.

After repeated tries, using her elbow and the side

of her bound arm, she was finally able to get the doorknob unlocked and turned. In her socks and sleep T-
shirt, she ran across the frost-covered yard into the
street.

Every part of her wanted to scream at the top of
her lungs, but the only sound that came out was a
muffled roar from deep in her throat.

The street was deserted. Two blocks away were
some college hangouts—Chinese restaurants, cafés,
bars, and bookstores. Even though it was early morning and nothing would be open, she ran in that direction, unmindful of the near-freezing temperatures.

She heard a car in the distance, heard it slow, heard
it turn.

Was it him, coming back?

She wanted to jump behind a mailbox and hide. But
Gillian was in trouble. She forced herself to remain in
the center of the street. The car came at her, then,
at the last minute swerved, honking the horn as it
disappeared into the darkness.

She turned and hurried back in the direction she'd
come, running to the porch of the first house she saw,
using her elbow to ring the doorbell. She rang it and
rang it and rang it until an angry man jerked the
door open.

"What the hell's going—?" He stopped. "Oh my
God. Judy. Come here!" he shouted behind him.
"Judy!"

Holly jumped up and down and shook her head.
Take off the tape. Take off the tape!

"Hold still," he said, "an' I'll pull that off. This'll
hurt."

I don't care! Just do it! Do it!

He ripped off the tape. At first she felt no pain;
then fire spread across her face. She began shouting.
"Call the police! Call the police!"

By that time his wife had shown up and joined her husband in his horrified reaction. "Oh, you poor dear. You poor thing." She pulled her into the warmth of the house. "Her hands are taped, John. Get a knife. Hurry!"

"No! Call the police!" Holly shouted. "You have to call the police—NOW!"

"Okay, honey. We will. Let's get you loose first."

She was about ready to kick somebody when the husband handed his wife a knife. "You cut her loose. I'll call."

While the guy dialed 911, his wife worked on Holly's hands. As soon as the tape dropped away, Holly pounced for the phone. She tried to grab it from the man, but her fingers were numb. He held it to her ear while she composed herself enough to tell the dispatcher what had happened.

Gillian lost all sense of time. It seemed that she'd been in the trunk for at least an hour and a half, but she was in no state to confirm such an opinion. That didn't keep her from trying to figure out how far from Minneapolis a ninety-minute drive could take her. Going south, they could be all the way to Iowa. Going east, into Wisconsin, past Eau Claire.

The last thirty minutes had been spent bouncing over a rough road made of gravel or dirt, judging from the dust drifting in the cracks. There had been several turns, several times when she thought they were at their destination, only to feel the weight of the car shift as they rounded another corner before accelerating again.

They went up a steep hill to eventually level out, slow, then stop.

The engine was shut off.

She heard a car door.

She listened to footfalls approach. Heard the key in the lock.

The trunk opened.

Mary had been in the business long enough to know a call that came before sunrise was never good. But having a case that was all but settled left her thinking the ringing phone had to be Anthony, calling too early from the East Coast, maybe with a new case that required her immediate attention. When she realized it was Elliot Senatra on the other end of the line, she was doubly puzzled.

"I have some bad news."

He sounded upset. She immediately ran through a short list of the people she cared most about: her mother, who was in the house with her; Gillian; and Anthony. She latched on to the last name. Had something happened to Anthony?

"Gillian has been abducted."

She pushed herself up in bed, thinking she must have misunderstood. "Say that again."

"Gillian's been abducted." He told her that Holly had spent the night with her sister, and someone had broken into the apartment. "Holly swears it's the same guy who kidnapped her."

"Where are you now?"

"I'm on my way to your sister's. Wakefield's already on the scene."

"Where's Holly?"

"She's been taken down to the station to get her statement."

"I'll be there as quickly as I can."

She hung up.

Shit. Oh, shit.

She opened her mobile phone and punched number one. As soon as Anthony answered, she began blathering, trying to tell him what she knew in one sentence. She stopped and took a breath, realizing she was close to tears, close to flipping out. "I'm not thinking straight," she said, her throat tight. "Christ. This is bad, Anthony. Really bad." The phone call had taken her back to another time when she'd felt hopeless, the time Fiona had been killed. She pressed her lips together, then asked, "Will you come?"

"I'm on my way."

She fought off a fresh wave of tears. "When?"

"Soon. Today. This afternoon, if possible."

"Thanks."

She disconnected, then went to give her mother the news.

Blythe was already standing in the hallway. "I heard," she said before Mary could say anything. "Where? When?"

Blythe followed her back to the bedroom.

"Someone broke into her apartment." Mary began throwing on clothes—a pair of jeans. A shirt. A sweater. "About an hour ago. Holly Lindstrom was there. She thinks it's the same guy who abducted her."

"I don't understand. I thought Gavin Hitchcock did it. Isn't he in custody?" She covered her mouth with one hand, eyes large with shock and disbelief. "What about the photo? What about the girl he tied to his bed?"

"I don't know." Mary strapped on her gun. "Maybe I was too anxious to find Hitchcock guilty," she said miserably.

"Where are you going?"

"Gillian's apartment. After that, I'm going to talk to Holly."

"I'm coming with you."

Mary didn't like the thought of her mother being at the scene of the crime, but she also knew she had every right to be there. "The police will probably want to take our statements."

Mary drove too fast through streets that were beginning to show signs of life even though the sun wasn't yet up. They rode in silence until Blythe broke down.

"I can't believe this is happening again. What's wrong with this world?" she said, her voice choked with tears. She shook her head. "After Fiona died, I should have moved. I thought about it, but I didn't want to leave here. And the law of averages was on our side. It's like when I know you're going to be flying, and I worry about the plane crashing, then I hear about a crash somewhere else, I think, Okay, there's the one plane crash. Now I can relax because I know your plane isn't going to crash. And then I feel guilty. Because of all the people on the plane, but I can't help feeling a little less worried for you. Oh God. I'm babbling."

"That's okay."

Mary turned down the street that led to Gillian's apartment. As she spotted the crime van, her stomach dropped. Blythe was right. This couldn't be happening.

They had to park two blocks away. Yellow crime-scene tape was strung around the front yard, all the way out past the sidewalk.

"It looks like somebody's been murdered here," Blythe said.

"Nobody's been murdered," Mary reassured her. "They've cordoned everything off so no evidence is destroyed."

A police officer stopped them before they got to the yellow tape. Mary flashed her ID. "We're also the mother and sister of the victim."

They were allowed to pass.

Wakefield met them at the door. The loss of Gillian had left its mark on him too. "He cut the window with a glass cutter, removed the glass, and unlocked the lock."

"Any leads?"

"We're working on fingerprints, but so far the ones we've lifted are all small. Women's, most likely. This asshole's too smart to go without gloves."

"Anybody see or hear anything?"

"We have officers canvassing the neighborhood, but so far nothing. People aren't too cooperative this time of the morning."

"What about Sebastian Tate?"

"His roommates don't know where he is. Say he hasn't been home in two days, but we've got every cop in the state looking for him."

Inside the apartment, technicians were dusting for prints and collecting evidence. A couple of detectives stood with tablets in hand, making notes and taking the statements of the first officers on the scene.

Senatra separated himself long enough to give Mary's arm a comforting squeeze and tell Blythe how sorry he was. Then he got back to work.

"What about Holly?" Mary asked Wakefield. "You said she thinks it's the same guy."

"She seemed sure of it. If it is, it means he followed her here. Then, for some reason he took Gillian instead. Holly claims she ran for help as soon as the kidnapper left with your sister. The first officers on the scene were here within two minutes of the 911 call. At that time, six patrol units surrounded the area, but didn't find anybody."

"Did Holly have a description of the car?"

He shook his head. "Which makes me wonder how quickly she really went for help."

"Is she still at the station?"

"Let me check." He called the police station, then nodded to Mary. "Don't let her go," he said into the phone. "I have an FBI agent here who wants to talk to her."

Leaving Blythe with Wakefield and Senatra, Mary hurried back to her car and headed downtown to City Hall and the police station.

She immediately found inconsistencies in Holly's story. Sometimes in cases in which somebody was left behind, or someone escaped uninjured, guilt played a part in their account of what happened. Mary suspected that's what was going on with Holly. Mary also suspected that the time between the kidnapper's departure and the time Holly actually went for help was longer than the "minute at the most" Holly was describing.

"Would you mind if I spoke to her alone?" Mary asked Holly's parents.

"Our daughter's been through an awful lot," Mrs. Lindstrom said. "We'd really like to take her home now."

"It's okay," Holly said, looking up. She was dressed in jeans and a yellow sweatshirt. Her eyes were swollen from crying, and there were raw areas on her cheeks where the tape she was bound with had ripped the skin away.

When they were alone, Mary said, "I know this is hard for you, but you need to tell me exactly what happened in just the way you remember. You may have information you think isn't important, but sometimes it's the things that seem unimportant that help solve a case," she added gently. "And sometimes it's the little things that don't seem important—things like time—that can send investigators in the wrong direction. Gillian is my sister. I want her back as quickly as possible."

Mary pulled out a chair and sat down on the same side of the table with Holly. "Do you know that most victims of home invasion don't call the police as soon as their assailant leaves? In most cases, the assailant will tell them not to call—and they don't. They might be in shock, and most of them are afraid he'll come back, or afraid that he hasn't really left. It's impossible to think straight in that kind of situation. You're running strictly on survival mode, and that mode is telling you to lie low and not make a sound. So, Holly . . . if you didn't go for help right away, nobody will blame you. Nobody will think poorly of you for doing what your natural instincts were telling you to do."

Holly stared at her pop can, turning it in her hands.

"You waited to go for help, didn't you?"

"He told me to wait fifteen minutes."

"I'll bet you waited longer, just to be sure."

Holly continued to stare at the can, as if finding it the most interesting thing in the room. "I think maybe I did."

"How much longer, would you say?"

"Five minutes. Maybe ten."

"Thanks, Holly. I appreciate your honesty." Mary called Wakefield and updated him on the time element.

"No need to have these guys beating the bushes around here," he said. "Sorry, Mary. That means he's gone."

Chapter 27

He'd blindfolded her—something Gillian knew killers did to depersonalize, disorient, and control their victims.

Fear heightened her senses as the trunk lid groaned open.

She smelled his nervous sweat, heard his rapid breathing; she smelled the rubber of the spare tire beside her, and the heavy dark stench of burnt engine oil. She felt his fingers wrap around her arm.

He pulled her from the trunk. Her legs, unprotected in cotton pajama pants, dragged across the metal latch, scraping her shinbone.

He shoved her forward, a hand to her back, one on her arm. She turned her head, listening to the echoes of his steps, feeling cold cement under her bare feet.

They were inside a building.

A garage?

Without warning, she was lifted into the air. She felt the thud of her weight against his chest, heard him strain as he carried her up a short series of steps. The way she was being held compressed her lungs, making it hard to breathe.

Had they parked in a garage attached to a house?

If so, that would explain how he got his victims inside without being noticed.

He shoved her down on something hard—a wooden chair. Deftly, he taped her legs to the chair legs, the sound of ripping tape as big in her head as a tree being hit by lightning.

Even though she couldn't see anything, she had the oddest feeling that she was viewing the scene from a distance, from a safe location far away. And suddenly it struck her as funny, hysterical. She almost expected her abductor to start saying things like, "I been lookin' fer a gal like you. Pa's gonna be mighty happy."

Instead he said, "I'm going to remove the tape from your mouth, but if you scream, if you make any kind of noise at all, I'll hit you—then I'll put the tape back on your mouth. Do you hear me?"

Had she heard a hint of a drawl, or was it just her imagination?

The hysteria was building. She couldn't get the hillbilly movie out of her head. If he removed the tape, she was afraid she might laugh.

"Do you understand?"

Frantically, Gillian shook her head. *Don't take off the tape. I might laugh. I don't think you'll like it if I laugh.*

He repeated his earlier warning, then removed the tape in one swift jerk. The stinging pain halted the initial threat of laughter, but then bubbles started to rebuild.

She'd once heard about an innocent woman who'd been convicted of a crime because she couldn't stop laughing on the witness stand. The jurors had mistaken her hysteria for delight over what she'd done.

Gillian held it as long as she could, but finally the laughter exploded. She felt as if she were watching herself from far away, watching as she threw back her head, sucking in lungfuls of air as she laughed, unable to stop herself. She was like one of those ridiculous laughing boxes.

"What are you doing?"

She'd hoped to be more mature and professional about this. She'd hoped, when the time was right, to say intelligent, understanding, sympathetic things that would weaken his defenses so he would see her as a person, maybe see her as someone he could talk to, eventually confide in. In one scenario, she'd imagined talking him into turning himself in. Instead, she was laughing her ass off.

The blow came out of the darkness, striking her in the side of the face, knocking her and the chair to the floor. She tasted blood.

She heard the tear of tape, smelled the glue as he slapped a fresh piece over her mouth. Leaving her lying on the floor, he kicked the chair once, twice. Behind the blindfold, she squeezed her eyes shut, bracing herself for another blow. It didn't come. Instead, she heard his heavy footsteps as he walked away.

She'd laughed at him. *Laughed* at him.

The stairs were narrow, and his shoulders barely fit as he took the winding flight to the second story. Years ago, the small wooden steps had been painted mint green. They were still in good shape. The wallpaper, with its huge red flowers, had yellowed, though. Near the ceiling were drip marks where winter ice dams had caused water damage.

He loved the house. He felt safe in the house.

But at the moment it gave him no comfort. He felt sick to his stomach, sick and confused.

He'd thought she was the one until she laughed at him.

Upstairs, the hallway floor was made of thin strips of varnished oak that had also yellowed over the years. In the center of the floor was a tacked-down runner of wool carpet. The walls were covered with the same wallpaper as the narrow stairway. Flowers everywhere.

Four empty bedrooms lined the hall. There were another two downstairs. His sister told him that the house had been a stagecoach stop, and she'd even pointed to a couple of holes in the wall where she said somebody had been shot and killed. She knew the entire story, even the names of the people involved, and she used to tell it to him whenever he asked.

Historians referred to it as the Poplar Grove Massacre. He never knew how it could be a massacre when only two people got killed, but that's what they called it.

He went to the last bedroom, the floorboards creaking under his boots. The door always stuck. As he pushed, it made a shimmying sound, then creaked open.

The room looked the way it had the day his sister left. The bed was covered with a white chenille spread. Next to it was a matching walnut dresser and mirror. There was floral wallpaper here too, and bowls of dried rosebuds. At the vanity was her brush, comb, and mirror set lying neatly at an angle. What would she think when she came home and saw everything unchanged? Would she laugh and say he was foolishly sentimental?

If she laughed, it would be a tender, loving laugh, not the laugh of the girl downstairs, not a cruel laugh.

In the closet, he slid hangers along the large wooden dowel, going through the dresses she'd left behind. "All terribly outdated, I'm afraid," she'd told him once. "I don't know why I keep them."

But she kept everything. That's how she was. He'd

once read an article about a woman who never threw anything out. Her house was so full of junk that you couldn't get through it without crawling. He'd shown the article to his sister, telling her that's what was going to happen to her if she didn't watch out. But he really hadn't minded. He loved her idiosyncrasies.

Some of the dresses were really costumes, left over from the days when she'd been part of a vaudevillian-type act that spent summers traveling from one small town to another.

He was searching for something sedate, because after all, clothes made the woman. He found a pink dress. The top looked almost like a man's shirt, but the bottom half was full and long. He pulled it out, then found an apron to go over it.

He wasn't anxious to see the girl again—she'd been mean to him. But he didn't have time to waste hiding upstairs. He had to make things happen. Before leaving the room, he debated about undergarments, finally deciding on a slip and pair of hose. Downstairs, he found the girl where he'd left her—lying on her side, unable to move.

He lifted her upright, settling the chair legs firmly on the floor.

She was going to be the one, he told himself. She *had* to be the one, even if he had to shove her into the mold. But still he hesitated when it came time to take off her blindfold so he could dress her. At the last minute, he pulled his ski mask over his head.

He didn't want her to see his face yet. That way their relationship would remain impersonal.

He removed her blindfold.

For a moment, she kept her eyes squeezed tightly shut, as if expecting him to hit her again.

"I'll hit you only when you do something wrong," he explained. "If you disobey, you get punished."

She opened her eyes.

It was the first time he'd gotten a really close look at her.

She was perfect.

Small-boned and delicate, with eyes as blue as delphiniums. Of course, right now those eyes were bloodshot and red-rimmed, but that was understandable. He was sure she would look much better when she was cleaned up and rested.

"Let's try the tape again. What do you think?"

She nodded.

He jerked off the tape.

She flinched and gasped, then pressed her lips together.

It seemed she could be trained.

He was sorry to see that the tape left red marks on her skin. He was sorrier to see that her mouth was swollen, her cheek discolored from his blow, chin bruised. He brushed away the guilt, turned and filled a glass with water. With his back to her, he opened a brown prescription bottle and added a few drops of liquid to the water. It was a cocktail of his own invention, pentobarbital mixed with morphine. To that he added three green drops of mint flavoring. He returned to the girl and lifted the water to her lips.

Gillian took two small swallows before noticing the bitterness. She pulled back, remembered the drugs that had been found in the blood of two of the victims. "I have to go to the bathroom," she told him. Maybe she could make herself throw up.

He led her down a hall into a small, windowless room. "I really shouldn't undo your hands," he said, "because you haven't earned my trust. But let's say this will be another test."

He pulled a pocketknife from his brown canvas pants, flicked open a blade, and sliced the tape, freeing her hands. Then he shoved her into the bathroom and locked the door from the outside.

She used the toilet, then looked at her reflection in the mirror above the sink. Her face was bruised, her lip swollen. She kept staring. She was trying to recall something important she'd planned to do when the room began to move and the floor began to slant. She grabbed the edge of the white porcelain sink. It dissolved under her hands, and she collapsed.

The key turned in the lock. The door opened. She felt his hands under her armpits. With her feet and legs trailing behind like dead weight, he dragged her across the floor.

Six hours after receiving Mary's call, Anthony arrived at the Minneapolis–St. Paul International Airport. Luckily a couple of rookie NCAVC agents had been eager to do the fieldwork on his newly assigned Utah infant abduction case. They would stay in contact, faxing him information as they received it.

Immediately upon landing, he called Mary to let her know he was in town. "Where are you now?" he asked, heading down the escalator to pick up his checked luggage.

"At Gillian's house." She gave him the address and directions.

"I'll be there as soon as I can." He folded his phone and slipped it into the pocket of his black trench coat, retrieved his luggage from the carousel, and cut over to the car rental counter.

The heavy afternoon traffic hadn't yet hit. He was able to get on 35W without any trouble. He headed north, toward downtown Minneapolis, the U of M, and Dinkytown.

He had a problem with the one-way streets and ended up finding the address after two wrong turns.

Cars were parked in front of the house. The yard was surrounded by yellow crime-scene tape. Beyond the tape were clusters of people, reporters, video camera technicians, some just hanging around, taking in the sights.

The day was brilliantly sunny, about fifty degrees. When he stepped into the street, the crisp air was welcome after the stuffiness of the car. His stomach growled, but he ignored it as he edged through the mob of people, flashing his ID when necessary.

"Ooh, FBI," a black girl said, pausing between each letter and batting her eyes in mock admiration. She had a hundred-dollar braided hairdo and fifty-dollar, mile-long, curved red fingernails. "Lookie. FBI."

Her lack of respect didn't make him mad. Quite the contrary. He admired her don't-take-shit attitude. She would never be a victim.

"Excuse me, ladies." He squeezed past while they continued to check him out.

In the yard, a team of workers had established a string grid and were going over every square inch, raking and vacuuming the grass for anything that may have dropped from the kidnapper. Another officer was crouched on the ground, making a cast of a footprint.

Anthony found Mary inside. She was wearing jeans, a white shirt with untucked tails, and a gray sweater. Her hair hadn't been brushed, and she wasn't wearing any makeup. As soon as she saw him, she hurried over.

He grasped both her cold hands and rubbed them between his.

"Anthony—thank you so much for coming."

It was unsettling, seeing her in the role of the victim's family member. A battle was going on inside her between professional FBI agent and hurt, bewildered sister. The bewildered sister was winning. He wanted to put his arms around her. Instead, he released her hands and asked, "Have they found anything?"

"Fibers that they've taken to the lab. They were navy blue, like the others. Officers are going door to door, conducting interviews. A couple of witnesses identified a photo of Tate, saying they saw him hanging around on more than one occasion. They found some minute bits of mud on the carpet that they're sending to the University of Minnesota's agricultural campus to see if anyone there can determine where the mud came from."

"Fingerprints?"

"All over the place. They lifted one set that didn't match anybody we know of who's been here. Those are being fed to databases right now."

"What about the footprint outside?"

"Left by a work boot. They think it might belong to a man. Any man. Maybe our man. You know how that is. This house is next to a college campus. A lot of traffic goes through the yard."

"Where's your mom?"

"Home. Agents and police are there tapping the phone and setting up recording equipment in case he tries to call."

"He won't."

"I told them that, but we have to do something. They're also going to tap Gillian's phone."

Exhaustion was written on her pale, drawn face, and he asked, "When did you last eat?"

"I don't know. Yesterday, I guess. I haven't even thought about it."

"Let's go down the street and get something. You can fill me in at the same time."

"I don't think I even brushed my hair."

He smoothed out a couple of strands. "You look fine."

They were leaving when Ben came bursting in. "Is it true? Did he take Gillian?"

"Yes," Mary told him.

"Oh, man!" Ben put both hands to his head. "I can't believe it! I fucking can't believe it! This can't be happening! Shit! Oh, shit!"

"Calm down," Anthony told him.

"Calm down! How can you say that? How can you both stand there looking so . . . so *not busy*? When you know as well as I do what is happening right now! She's being tortured! Her fucking eyes are being cut out! Do something! You have to do something!"

Mary's face turned ashen, and Anthony thought she might pass out. Before Ben could do any more damage, Anthony grabbed him roughly by the arm and steered him out the door, practically throwing him down the steps. "In your present mental state, you have no business being here," he said coldly. "You aren't helping anybody."

"Neither are you! How could this happen? You said the guy was in jail! You said everybody was safe. That Gillian was safe. Well, you were wrong! Wrong!"

"Hitchcock confessed," Anthony said. "He fit the profile. Evidence pointed to him."

"You people are supposed to know more than the rest of us!"

"You're overreacting."

"Overreacting? You're *underreacting*." He began to cry. "She's dead! You know it and I know it! She's already dead!" Sobbing, he turned and ran.

The door slammed, and Mary came to stand beside Anthony on the porch. "Should somebody go after him?" Her voice sounded tight, as if she might fall apart any second. He'd never seen Mary cry. He didn't want to.

In the distance, two blocks away, Ben was still running. "Let him go," Anthony said angrily. "Let him run himself into exhaustion."

"He was just saying what everybody else is thinking."

"Well, he's wrong." Anthony turned so he could see her face. *Don't cry. Please don't cry.* "About Gillian. You know that, don't you?"

Mary pressed trembling fingers to her mouth. Tears filled her eyes.

Anthony put his arms around her and pulled her close. He wanted to say they would find her, and when they did she would be okay. But that would be a foolish promise to make. Mary, more than anybody, knew things could get bad. Really bad.

He pressed his lips against her hair, against her head. She was almost his height, but she was so frail, so vulnerable. "Come on." With his arm around her, they walked down the sidewalk.

The café wasn't crowded, and Anthony ordered sandwiches for both of them. As they waited for their food to arrive, Mary composed herself enough to fill him in on what she knew.

"Gillian was able to talk him out of killing Holly," Anthony said. "Which means she has some influence and control over him."

"I know. I keep telling myself that."

When her food arrived, she grimaced. She wasn't sure if she could get any of it down, and even less sure she could keep it down.

"What we have working for us is Gillian," Anthony said. "She read the profile. She studied him. She knows him. She also knows who he wants her to be. She can be his ideal woman. She can be perfect for him. She's going into this armed with knowledge the other girls didn't have, and I think her chances of coming away are good."

"That's what I've been thinking, but I needed to hear you say it."

Anthony waited until she looked up and met his gaze. "You probably still see her as your little sister, but I saw a young, capable, smart woman who can stand up to this guy."

Mary nodded, her expression strained. Then she pulled out her phone and entered a speed-dial number. "Mom? Anthony's here with me. He has something to tell you." She handed the phone to him. "Tell her what you just told me."

Chapter 28

The whir of a shutter woke her.

The man in the ski mask loomed above her, a camera in his hand while the lamp beside the bed cast tepid light into the room. As she watched, he adjusted the aperture and took another shot. There was no flash—he must have been using fast film and a slow shutter speed.

Gillian's head throbbed. A rotten taste filled her mouth. She shifted her weight—and realized she was tied to the bed by her wrists. A second ago she'd been in the bathroom. . . . How had she gotten from there to here?

Confused, she looked down . . . and the feeling was one of total disconnection—like looking at someone else's body.

She was decked out in a pink shirtwaist dress with a flowered apron—the kind of apron she remembered old ladies wearing when she was little, the kind that crossed and tied in back. On her legs were thick black hose, on her feet a pair of clunky black shoes.

A sound escaped her—a sound she couldn't believe she'd made. It was a whimper, coming from deep in her chest.

He looked over the camera. From behind the ski

mask, two cold eyes watched her. He was tall—probably over six feet. He wore a plaid shirt with tails that hung out. On his legs were brown canvas pants. The ski mask was gray with a red stripe—ratty, stretched out, and snagged.

He continued taking pictures, posing her, turning her in different directions.

Finally he untied her. "Put your hands like this." He demonstrated.

Her arms were asleep. She couldn't lift them.

He sighed and placed her hands on her hips, then stepped back and took a shot. Apparently finished for the time being, he put down the camera and asked, "Are you hungry?"

The thought of food made her stomach lurch, but she nodded. Anything to move to another scenario.

"Come into the kitchen." He motioned for her to follow.

She swung her legs over the side of the bed, then sat and waited for the room to stop spinning. When it did, she got to her feet.

The shoes were too small. Her toes were crushed, but she managed to wobble to the kitchen, dropping into the chair he pulled out.

The table had been intimately set for two. Place mats and cloth napkins had been arrayed, along with a single tapered candle and a red rose. So that no one could see in, the windows had been covered with floral wallpaper.

In front of her was a bowl of tomato soup and a glass of milk. His setting was empty.

Slowly, she pulled her napkin to her lap, unfolding it. She reached for the spoon. Fingers still wooden, she accidentally dropped it on the floor, where it landed with a clatter. She flinched, afraid he would hit her.

So this is how it happens, she thought. *It's easy.*

Without conscious thought, she was already doing all she could to keep from making him angry, all she could to keep from being punished. In a few short hours, the person known as Gillian had vanished, replaced by someone who existed on an instinctual level.

He picked up the spoon and placed it next to her bowl. He reached for her, and she drew away. But he merely caught her arm and began rubbing it. His palms were as rough as sandpaper, those of someone who worked outside. She'd never felt Tate's hands, but she couldn't imagine that he'd done much physical labor in his life. He grabbed her other arm and did the same. "Better?" he asked.

She nodded.

"Good."

He sat down across from her. She picked up the spoon again, and this time didn't drop it.

The salty soup stung her lips and the inside of her mouth. She forced herself to swallow, forced herself to take another bite.

"My name is Mason."

What's that rattling sound? Like dice?

While he talked, he kept one hand buried deep in the pocket of his pants.

Dice. He has dice in his pocket. Dice that he kept nervously fiddling with as he watched her eat.

"What's your name?" he asked.

Was this a test? she wondered. Was she supposed to answer or keep quiet?

"You can speak."

She was at a disadvantage since she couldn't read his face, but he sounded pleased.

"I give you permission."

"Gillian." Her voice came out a rough croak. She cleared her throat and tried once more. "My name is Gillian."

"Gillian."

That rattling again.

"Mason and Gillian. I like that."

Wouldn't he already have known her name? Wouldn't he have heard it on the news? Yes, he was testing her to see if she told the truth.

Blythe must be out of her mind with worry. And Mary. What was Mary doing? She'd be pissed at her for getting herself into such a mess. What would Mary do if she were here? Gillian wondered. If she were sitting across the table from a killer?

"Eat some more," Mason demanded.

It was hard to think of him as someone with a name. The mask over his face made him seem inhuman.

While he watched, she ate a little more soup and drank some of the milk. The numb, thick-lipped feeling started coming over her once more. She was staring into her bowl, watching the tiny bubbles of orange oil gather at the edges, when he said something.

Hmm? She lifted her head. It was heavy. Her whole body was heavy, and she realized she'd been drugged again.

"Are you finished?"

She nodded, her eyelids weighted.

"Would you like to dance?"

She suddenly imagined him doing the twist in the middle of the kitchen. She started to giggle, but at the last moment was able to turn it into a hiccup.

Her feet were bound in the crippling shoes, and she stumbled as he led her to the adjoining living room. He left her standing in the middle of a round, floral, latch-hook rug. *Beam me up, Scotty.*

He fiddled around in the corner, then came back and put one hand at her lower spine, her right around his waist. With the other, he grasped her free hand, poised in what she guessed was going to become a waltz.

The music started.

It was Britney Spears singing, "Oops! . . . I Did It Again."

Maybe the drugs were a good thing. She might have laughed for real if she weren't so fucked up. And it certainly took the edge off her fear.

He dragged her around in the cramped shoes, her head lolling from side to side.

Oops, I did it again.

She wasn't a very good dancer, he thought, looking down at her through the annoying edge of the ski mask. And at the moment, she wasn't very pretty. Her eyes were half-closed, and her mouth was hanging open. But he liked her. At least he thought so. It was hard to tell because she hadn't really said much, but at least she hadn't lied to him. She hadn't tried to tell him she was somebody else.

He knew who she was: Gillian Cantrell. He knew she was a cop assigned to the case—a BCA agent. The media had let that slip last night. The police department and the FBI had been hoping to keep her occupation a secret. They must have been afraid he'd panic and kill her if he found out who she was. On one channel, a Minneapolis detective named John Wakefield had been interviewed, and he'd berated the news people for not being able to keep their mouths shut. He'd waved his arm at the camera, saying, "All for a story. You're nothing but a bunch of sharks."

The song ended, and he stopped.

"Mason?"

The *s* was slurred. Her eyes were closed. He'd given her too much dope. It was hard to know how much to give a person. She ate more of the soup than he'd thought she would, and the drugs seemed to hit her harder than they had the other girls.

"I gotta sit down."

He dragged her to the couch and propped her in the corner. He should have carried her into the bedroom, but he wanted her to sit with him awhile. He pulled up a chair so he was close to her.

"Do you have a boyfriend?" he asked.

She shook her head.

"That's good."

"Would you like a boyfriend?"

"Not . . . r-really."

He laughed at her honesty.

"What do you do for a living?"

She frowned. "Huh?"

Playing for time, he noted. "What do you do?"

She pretended to be sleeping. That made him mad. He grabbed her arm and squeezed. "Do you want me to hit you again?"

"N . . . no."

"I have a place where I take girls who are bad. It's a special place I've made. Do you want me to take you there?"

"No."

"Then tell me what you do."

Her eyes opened. Beyond the drug-laden haze was lucidity and the core of who she was. "W-why are you . . . askin' me somethin' . . . you already know?"

He was caught off guard. Was she talking back? Was this something she should be punished for? She hadn't lied to him. He decided it was funny, and he laughed. "I like you!" he said, delighted. She was fading again. He shook her arm, not wanting their conversation to end. "Don't go to sleep. Let's talk some more."

She was lolling in the corner of the couch. Her posture was bad, but he felt this wasn't the time to scold her for it. "I want to talk," he repeated. "Those other girls were stupid. They weren't interesting to talk to at all. But I think you might be. Do you like to read?"

Gillian struggled to stay awake. She'd been a reader her entire life. There had even been a time when she'd tried her hand at writing. "Blake," she said, not expecting to produce the right answer, but hoping it would open up the conversation.

"Blake? You read Blake? He's overrated."

"Joyce," was her next offer. This was like playing the child's game of hotter and colder.

"Well . . ." Warmer.

Then "Proust."

She heard him inhale and knew she was hot.

"You've read Proust?"

"Not everything. I read *Swann's Way* and *In a Budding Grove*."

"Really? I've never met anybody who's read Proust."

He'd apparently been hanging around with the wrong people. She used to belong to a Proust group that met every other Thursday at a coffee shop on the U campus.

"I've read the entire seven volumes," he announced proudly.

A diehard. Even in her exalted group, she didn't know of many who'd read all seven. "That's . . . amazing."

"More than once. Maybe five or six times."

Five or six times? She felt a black wave of sorrow wash over her. Once was admirable; five or six times was impossible to fathom. It was an obsession beyond obsession and a total lack of social interaction rolled into one. It spoke of delusion and a life that existed completely within the boundaries of fiction.

"This is fantastic! We were meant for each other!"

Mason was ecstatic. "I must do something. Share something of myself with you."

He was already sharing enough, she thought, shoving herself up a little higher, her hand sinking into the plush couch.

All at once, he pulled off the ski mask.

There was nothing monstrous about him. Nor was he handsome in the way the witness from Canary Falls had stated. Something she would later notice was that he had a face that, when you really examined it, seemed unfinished. There was a haziness to his features, an undefined quality, as if he'd been erased a little. He was the last copy before the printer decided too much quality was being lost. He was one of her mother's pots before the detail and glaze were added.

He was no one she knew. None of the suspects on the police department's list. No one they were watching or looking for.

"This is something rare."

Mary, Anthony, and Elliot stood in the lab of Dr. Henry Joseph Ling, Professor of Horticulture at the University of Minnesota. He was a leading authority on roses, and held patents on many varieties that were currently being tested at the Minnesota Landscape Arboretum. "This rose petal, the one found with the raped college student, is a garden-variety rose. But this one—" He pointed to the microscope. "This is something unique."

Anthony bent and looked through the lens.

"Unique? How?" Mary asked.

"The coloring. The veining. The ruffled edge. It's a hybrid that I've never seen before, and I thought I was familiar with all the work being done by hybridizers in the Midwest."

"Are you saying it can't be purchased at a floral shop?"

"I'm not sure it can be purchased anywhere, period."

"Would you care to speculate as to where this may have come from?" Anthony asked.

"A private collection, perhaps. But even at that, I've seen most of the roses in private collections. People who are grafting on their own aren't usually doing it for their exclusive enjoyment. They do it for competition. They love the challenge, and they want people to know when they've developed something earth shattering. That's what it's all about. One-upmanship, not to mention money and fame."

"Thank you, Professor."

"Delighted."

Once they were outside, Elliot called the research department. "I need you to get the names of anybody and everybody in Minnesota, Wisconsin, and Iowa, who grows—that's not the right word—*produces* roses. I don't know. They graft them or something. They create completely new varieties. They're horticulturists, but the technique they use has some certain name. Propagating. Yeah, that's it. And the people who do it are called hybridizers. Yeah, that's a real word. The guy we're looking for might not belong to any organizations, but he'd be buying supplies and whatever it takes to do that kind of thing. He'd have a greenhouse and all that rose kind of stuff. This is connected to the Gillian Cantrell case, so put a priority on it." He ended the call and looked from Anthony to Mary, his hands on his hips. "So we got a guy who grows roses and owns a navy blue blanket."

"There aren't that many people who would fall into the rose-growing category, plus fit our profile," Anthony said. "I suggest we get this information to the media with a tip line people can call."

"Done." Elliot was pulling out his phone when it rang. "Senatra." He listened intently. "Send it to the crime lab. We'll be there in half an hour." He disconnected and looked from Anthony to Mary. "A manila envelope just arrived at the FBI office addressed to Special Agent Mary Cantrell. No return address."

The crime lab technician balanced the manila envelope between a gloved forefinger and thumb.

"Get any prints?" Anthony asked.

"We managed to lift a couple of blurry whorls, but nothing good enough to try to match." The technician was a perky middle-aged woman with straight dark hair and a knee-length lab coat. She ran her fingers along the edges. "I don't feel anything that makes me concerned about a detonation device." She took several flash photos of the envelope. "Now we'll open it."

She put on goggles. Everybody else stepped back several feet. Using a small, scalpel-like tool, she carefully sliced open one end. Then, very slowly, she slid out the protective cardboard, lifting the top piece away to reveal an eight-by-ten black-and-white of a woman in an old-fashioned dress and apron.

Gillian.

Her eyes were half-closed, the pupils large and glassy.

Nobody moved. Nobody said anything. Mary forced herself to say the words no one else would voice. "Is she alive?"

Her question was followed by a long silence. Finally Anthony said, "It's impossible to say." He looked at her, and she could read the compassion in his eyes. "Let's get a copy and take it to a medical examiner," he said.

"Do you know her?" the technician asked.

Mary pulled her gaze away from Anthony. "She's my sister."

"Oh. I'm so sorry."

The technician made a copy; then all three of them piled into Elliot's car and headed for the ME's office.

Elliot had called ahead, and their buddy Dr. Phillips was waiting when they arrived at the morgue.

"Can't say," he announced after he'd examined the picture. If he recognized Gillian from the Charlotte Henning autopsy, he didn't mention it.

"Care to make a guess?"

"Everything about the body looks alive."

With a magnifying glass, he went over the photo as he talked. "No lividity, no discoloration. Eyes look wet. Not a gnat, not a fly. Not a single sign of an insect. No outward signs of postmortem. But that's speculation. I deal in absolutes. I can't responsibly tell you the subject in the photo is alive. She may have been killed seconds before this picture was taken."

"What about the body itself?" Mary asked. "Can you determine anything from the way she's posed?"

"I've seen people as limp as rags that I thought were dead but weren't. And I once saw a dead guy who seemed so animated I would have sworn he was alive. You can't always be sure. Especially from a photo. Bring me the body—then I'll let you know." He handed the photo back to Anthony.

"Dipshit," Elliot said as they stepped from the building into the weak sunlight.

Chapter 29

Mason hummed to himself as he packed his lunch to take with him to the commercial greenhouse where he worked. He hadn't felt this good since . . . since, well, since his sister had been home. But his life was turning around. Jo was coming to visit soon, and he had a girl, just like she'd always wanted. A girl who read Proust.

"I worry about you," Jo had told him once. "I'd feel better leaving here if you had somebody. What about that nice Lauren who works at Dr. DeLong's office?"

"She isn't my type," he'd said, closing the book he'd been reading. Dostoyevsky's *The Idiot.*

"What kind of girl *is* your type?"

"I don't know." He'd looked at her light hair, her blue eyes, her sweet face. "Maybe somebody kinda like you."

She'd laughed. "Oh, Mason. You're so sweet, but you don't want a girlfriend like me."

"Why not?"

"You shouldn't limit yourself in that way. There are so many different kinds of people in the world."

In the dark of the kitchen, he replaced the lid on

the mayonnaise jar and put the container back in the refrigerator. A minute ago, he'd been blissfully happy. Now a deep, unreasoning sorrow pressed down on him, coming out of nowhere. A moment ago, the world had seemed a promising place. Now bleakness stretched out before him as far as he could see.

The girl, he thought despairingly, exhaustion washing over him. Did he have enough energy to deal with her today? Earlier, he'd been so happy knowing she was in the house. Now taking care of her seemed more than he could cope with. Before, everything had been sharp and well defined. Now his thoughts were fuzzy, with sloppy, disturbing edges that couldn't be repaired.

This life is an illusion, he thought, mentally quoting Graham Morris. The words often gave him comfort in times like these.

The girl. He had to deal with the girl. He had to do something with her while he went to work. Normally, spending the day among acres of roses brought him comfort. How could it today if he spent all the time worrying about *her*?

Last night he'd left her tied to the bed, her mouth covered with tape in case she woke up and decided to start screaming. He could leave her there. Not even look in the room. He could leave for work and forget about her for eight hours.

It all seemed so hard. It all suddenly seemed stupid. That was perhaps his biggest fault—allowing an idea to carry him away so that he jumped into new situations without giving them enough thought.

Wearily, he made his way to the bedroom.

She was awake. Her eyes were open, and she was watching him. Even though she was wearing his sister's clothes, she was just a girl.

There was nothing special about her.

She reads Proust. How many people do you know who read Proust?

None.

True, but that didn't mean she *understood* it. Lots of people read books and listened to music they didn't understand or care to understand. It didn't mean she could spend hours discussing Proust.

You haven't given her a chance.

She'd disappointed him, just like the others.

What was he going to do with her?

When he was little, he'd read a book about a dog, and suddenly he wanted one. His sister took him to a kennel, where they bought a mutt. He'd wanted a real dog like a collie or Labrador retriever, but Jo insisted on getting one from the pound. "To save him from being put to sleep," she'd explained. She'd spent her life caring for strays of all kinds, so he couldn't speak against the very thing that defined who she was.

The dog was an ugly, pathetic thing, with big brown eyes and soft hair, and the most irritatingly timid nature. If Mason as much as frowned, it would tuck its tail between its legs and piddle all over the floor.

Mason knew nothing about dogs except what he'd learned from television, books, and movies. It turned out that those dogs—the kind with leading roles on screen—were lies. He'd expected the mutt to be smarter, to be able to communicate with him and understand everything he said. At the very least, it should have been able to entertain itself.

The dog was an annoyance. A horrible, time-consuming annoyance. It had to be taken outside when it wasn't convenient, and it chewed up the furniture. Worse, it chewed on Mason's books.

It constantly wanted to play. It constantly wanted attention, and didn't like to be left alone even for ten minutes. It was a pathetic, useless creature that took and took and took, and never gave anything back except for ruined books and stained carpet.

Jo adored the pathetic creature, the way she seemed to adore all pathetic creatures. "We're all made by God," she'd say, smiling. She would toss sticks to it and pet it, talking to it in her soft, quiet voice. When she did so, the dog would actually calm down and mind, at least a little.

"Isn't he wonderful?" she'd sometimes say. "Isn't he adorable?"

The more Jo liked it, the more Mason hated it. Stupid dog. Stupid, worthless dog. Eating and shitting, eating and shitting.

Mason tried to lose it. He took it miles from home. Then, when it wasn't looking, Mason ran away. But the dog—Seymour was its name—found its way home. Which meant it wasn't as stupid as Mason thought. But that was just instinct, Mason had argued with himself when the dog had arrived panting and happy on the doorstep. Turtles had instinct. Salmon had instinct. Worms had instinct.

The girl on the bed was making Mason feel the way he'd felt toward Seymour. She was an irritant that was creeping under his skin. Someone who'd lured him with promises of being more than she was. She'd tricked him into thinking she was the prize, that once he found her, his life would be complete and the happiness that had eluded him for so long would be within his grasp.

But nothing had changed. Right now he was sad. It was an old, familiar sadness that was like a smothering blanket.

He would feed her and put her away for the day. And later he would think about what to do.

When he got so sick of the dog that he couldn't

stand it anymore, Mason—in order to save his sanity and his place in the household—was forced to take drastic measures he hadn't wanted to take. But it had been Seymour's fault. If Seymour had lived up to his expectations, nothing would have happened.

One day Seymour disappeared. "Up and disappeared," the locals would have said. But he and Jo weren't locals; they'd moved in when an uncle left Jo the house in his will, plus enough money to live on for several years. Mason and Jo had moved there from Louisiana, driving all the way in an old station wagon packed with their belongings. "A new beginning," Jo had called it.

But the people in the nearby town had never really let them in. Mason hadn't cared. "They can all go to hell," he'd told Jo. She'd been hurt by their rejection. Fifteen years later she gave up and decided it was time to go. When she left, only a handful of neighbors stopped to tell her good-bye.

Mason had stayed. He had his roses, and his roses were a part of him. He couldn't leave.

When Seymour vanished, he and Jo searched the area surrounding the sprawling farmhouse. They checked the outbuildings and the barn. They looked along the pond and stream that ran through the property. Then they got in the car and drove, going door to door, asking if anyone had seen a cute little brown dog.

No one had.

"He's gone," Mason told Jo after a week had passed.

"Where did he go?" she asked, sobbing in her handkerchief. "Why did he want to leave us?"

"Maybe he followed some other dogs," Mason suggested. "Or maybe he followed a car down the road. You know how he was, always chasing anything that moved."

Mason and Jo had clung together that evening, crying in the darkness. "Don't feel too sad about him," Mason had said. "He was faithless. He was a faithless mongrel."

With the dog gone, a heavy burden lifted from Mason. He never forgot the lesson he'd learned from Seymour. Life was full of disappointments, and nothing was what it looked like from the outside.

He let the girl named Gillian go to the bathroom; then he made her walk downstairs. He shoved her along in front of him, down the aged wooden steps into the stone basement with its dirt floor. The smell of dampness and earth hit him, and again he thought of Seymour.

The bare lightbulbs that lit the way from room to room were dim.

They wound along to finally come to the door with the chipped green paint. He reached around the girl, opened it, and then gave her a push.

Gillian stumbled forward, her heart hammering. The room was no wider than six feet across, each side lined with wooden shelves. On one of the shelves was a thin gray mattress and pillow. Attached to the shelf supports were handcuffs. In the back of the room, lying horizontally on the ground like a coffin, was a mustard-colored refrigerator. Dangling above her head, covered with cobwebs, was a bare, low-watt lightbulb.

He spun her around and yanked the tape from her mouth.

She didn't respond to the pain. "Mason, please, let's talk. I want to talk to you—" When she talked to him, he changed.

"I'm going to work," he said.

He pulled a wrapped sandwich out of his sweatshirt pocket and put on the mattress. Out of his other pocket came a jar of water. He put that next to the sandwich. "If you scream, nobody will hear you. But I don't want you to scream. If I come home and hear you screaming, I'll have to discipline you. I'll have to hurt you. If you're bad, you'll be punished. If you're good, you'll be rewarded."

"Mason, please—"

He turned and left, shutting the door behind him. She heard the jingle of metal as he locked the lock, then muffled footsteps as he walked away. A minute later the light above her head went out, plunging her into darkness.

Trying to keep her fear tamped down, she felt her way to the door and ran her hands across the rough wood. There was no handle on the inside. She pushed, then threw her weight against it. Solid, with no movement. She threw herself at it again and again until her shoulder ached.

She expected her eyes to adjust to the dark, expected the room to eventually lighten, but that didn't happen. It remained as dark as it had been when Mason turned off the light.

She thought about prisoners who'd been secluded in dark holes for months, sometimes years. If they hadn't been crazy to begin with, they were when they got out.

He was coming back, she told herself. He'd just put her down there while he was at work. Yet she couldn't keep from wondering, _What if he never returns?_—either intentionally or unintentionally. He could be in a car wreck. He could be killed. Nobody would know where she was.

Every instinct told her to scream as loudly as she could.

What if he hasn't really left?

What if he's upstairs, listening, waiting to see if you've disobeyed?

What if he's standing right on the other side of the door?

She rapped lightly on the door. "Mason?" she whispered. "Are you out there?" She paused, listening for an answer.

Silence.

Left alone in the dark with just her thoughts, she felt fear begin to grow.

He was different this morning.

He didn't like me this morning.

Even though he was a kidnapper and a killer, he seemed to be in awe of women in his own weird, twisted way. But this morning he'd been all business, hardly looking at her. She'd sensed disappointment in him. What had she done wrong? What had set him off?

Was he riding the downside of a manic episode? Now that the thrill of the capture was over, had the high evaporated, leaving him deflated and depressed?

She crossed her arms at her waist and pressed them to her empty stomach. It hurt. Her stomach hurt. She remembered the sandwich he'd dropped on the bed, along with the jar of water.

She couldn't inspect it with her eyes, couldn't examine it for bugs or anything else he may have decided to put inside. Even if she could see, she wouldn't be able to tell if he'd laced it with anything from rat poison to some kind of drug that would knock her out for the rest of the day.

Maybe that would be a good idea.

No, she decided, thinking of lying down on the filthy mattress, virtually unconscious for hours while roaches nibbled away at her. No, she couldn't make herself eat the sandwich or drink the water.

How much time had passed?

Two hours?

Five minutes?

Impossible to tell.

She had to focus her mind on something solid. Think about getting out. Think about what she would say to Mason when he returned to convince him never to put her here again. Think about not doing anything wrong. Think about being good.

But thoughts of Mason's return increased her anxiety and made her more aware of the slow passing of time. She had to dwell on something else, had to think of something nice.

A picnic in the park.

Fried chicken.

No, can't think about food.

Still standing, she leaned her back against the door and closed her eyes. "Swimming," she whispered to herself. She'd always loved to swim. When she was in high school, she used to force the air from her lungs. Airless, her body lost all buoyancy and she would let herself sink to the bottom of the deep end. She would lie there, looking up at the surface from her skewed perspective. When her lungs could wait no longer for air, she'd fold herself, then push against the pool bottom, shooting up to the surface, flying into the sparkling light, feeling exhilarated because she'd flirted with death.

"What are you doing?" Mary would shout in a frantic voice from the edge of the pool.

"Pretending to be dead."

"Don't scare me like that! I was ready to dive in and pull you out!"

Mary rescued people. It was what she did.

Gillian used to be brave. She used to be tough. She used to be scared of nothing. But that was all a facade. A teenage facade.

Fear is a terrible thing. An awful, horrible thing.

Maybe the *most* terrible, awful, horrible thing. It made you rearrange yourself, made you willing to compromise all principles. Made you desperately want to please a sick man.

Mary pulled up in front of Gavin Hitchcock's house, turned off the ignition, and got out of the car. After Gillian's abduction and Holly's statement, Gavin's confession had been tossed out and he'd been released on bail, the rape charge still standing. Now Mary was after reassurance and information. Sometimes killers worked in pairs, and she needed to be absolutely certain Gavin wasn't in some way connected to the recent murders—and possibly to her sister's abduction.

He answered the door dressed in jeans and a flannel shirt, his hair clipped close to his head, his face clean-shaved, his eyes dark-rimmed and hostile. Evidence of his overdose clung to him. He was pale and thin, and he looked as if he'd dropped thirty pounds since the day Mary had seen him at the auto repair shop.

"What do you want?" He chose a pose of intimidation, chest out, one bent arm high on the doorframe, fingers dangling.

"May I come in?"

He stared at her a moment, then dropped his arm and backed up to let her pass. "Have you heard anything about Gillian?" he asked, his tone warring between resentment of Mary and desire for news of her sister.

Mary sat down on the couch. His house was clean and tidy, very different from the last time she'd been there.

He remained standing. "What do you want?"

"You love Gillian, don't you?" she asked, trying to establish a foundation for the questions that would follow.

"That's no big secret."

"And you'd like us to find her, wouldn't you?"

"Of course I would." He became animated, angry at the implication that he might not want Gillian to be found. "I'm going crazy here. If I find out who did this to her, I'll kill him." He began to pace. "I don't care if I go to prison for the rest of my life." He jabbed a finger in her direction. "I want that son of a bitch dead. If I find out he did anything to hurt Gillian—" He stopped, and his voice cracked. Emotions and energy spent, he collapsed into a chair and buried his face in his hands. When he looked up, his eyes were red. "She has to be okay," he said hoarsely. "She has to be okay."

Mary had never before seen a lack of sympathy as a handicap, but she wasn't sure anymore. "If you can't feel what they feel, how can you begin to understand them and what they might do next?" Anthony had once argued when she'd accused him of giving criminals too much soul.

"Gavin—I have to know if you had anything to do with the recent murders."

He frowned in concentration, and she could see the confusion on his face. "I have epilepsy, you know," he told her. "Sometimes I have fits and pass out, and when I wake up I can't remember what happened."

"Do you have any memory of any of the girls? Of ever seeing them? Talking to them?"

He thought about it, then slowly shook his head. "No. Nothing."

"But you said you murdered them." Her voice was low, conversational, inquisitive. "You confessed. Why would you confess to something you have no memory of?"

"There was that Cammie chick, who said I raped

her. And I remember having a knife in my hand. I remember thinkin' about killing her."

"Thinking and doing are two different things."

"I know, I know." He picked up a plastic red lighter from the table and began nervously fiddling with it. Flicking it on and off, staring at the flame. "But then there was Gillian."

"Gillian?"

"Looking at me the way she was. Like I made her sick. Like I was some kind of monster. So I thought I must have killed them."

"Now what do you think?"

"I don't know." He tossed down the lighter. "My head is a mess. I can't even remember raping that college girl, but I must have done that too. I mean, I tied her up."

"Did she ask to be tied to the bed?"

"Oh, Christ." He looked at the ceiling, then rubbed his face again, clearly uncomfortable. "I think maybe she was passed out when I did it."

Mary was convinced he was in no way connected to the murders and Gillian's abduction. She didn't know about the rape. That would be for the court to decide. But now his innocence in the recent homicides brought up the other question, the main question, the question that had informed part of her life. She leaned forward, elbows on her knees. "Gavin, I have to know if you killed Fiona Portman." Her voice took on a softer, pleading quality. "You can tell the truth," she reasoned. "You've already served your time."

"You'd like for me to say yes, wouldn't you? Because then it would be over. You could quit thinking about it. But the truth is, it will never be over. Not for you. Not for me. Because I don't know if I killed her." Gavin rarely made eye contact, but he regarded her steadily as he said, "You maybe didn't know this, but Fiona used to meet me in the woods behind her house for sex."

A few weeks ago, Mary wouldn't have believed what he was saying. She sat up a little straighter, bracing herself. "No, I didn't know that."

"She didn't want you to. She wanted you to think of her as the sweet neighbor kid."

Fiona was electric and charismatic. She drew people to her, and in a way, she cast spells on them.

"She told me not to tell anybody about us," Gavin said. "She didn't want anybody to know that she was hangin' around with me. If I saw her in the hallway at school, I was supposed to act like I hardly knew her. I could say hi—something like that, because if I acted like she wasn't there that would have seemed weird."

"Didn't that bother you?"

He shrugged and pursed his lips. "I didn't think about it too much. I was just glad she wanted something to do with me at all. And the sex." He spread his arms. "How could a guy turn down sex?"

"How did you plan your meetings?" she asked.

"I didn't have a phone, so sometimes I'd call her from a pay phone, and if her mom answered, I'd pretend I had the wrong number. But usually she'd write me notes and hand them to me, saying they were from somebody else so nobody would know she was writing to me. The notes were always the same, telling me to meet her in the tree house in the woods behind her house."

Mary remembered the strange feeling of déjà vu she'd had at the high school in Canary Falls. In it, Fiona had been passing a note to Gavin. Now it made sense.

"Here I was, fucking the smartest, hottest, most

popular girl in school, and nobody knew about it. I kind of got off on it being a secret. It made it seem dangerous in a cool way. Something nobody else in the world knew about." He frowned. "Until her mother caught us."

"Abigail Portman caught you with Fiona?"

"Yeah," he said vaguely, as if struggling to remember. "We were in the tree house goin' at it, and her mother just pops in."

"Then what happened?"

"I pulled up my pants and got the hell out of there."

"Gavin, do you remember if that was the night Fiona died?"

He concentrated, trying to pull up the memory, then shook his head. "Everything's a jumble. Whenever I have fits, things get mixed up. Time gets weird. It's hard to separate my thoughts from reality."

Had Gavin Hitchcock killed Fiona, or had he been a convenient scapegoat? A victim of circumstance? Had Gillian been right about him all along? "Try to remember. Did you have a fit the night Abigail Portman caught you with Fiona?"

"Was it the same day?" he asked himself, perplexed. He finally had to give up and let it go. He couldn't remember. "All I know is that the day she died, I woke up in the woods a few feet from her. At first I thought she was asleep. Then I saw all the blood and knew she was dead. So I ran. I ran like hell. People saw me, saw the blood, and called the police. When they showed up to arrest me, I wasn't surprised. I still had Fiona's blood on me, and I thought maybe I did do it. I used to get weird ideas. I used to imagine killing people, and cutting them up. I fantasized about it, and drew sick pictures of guys with their arms cut off. Explosions with body parts flying through the air. Stuff like that. So I figured I probably did kill her.

But Gillian never thought so, and finally I began to wonder too. And now I don't know. Sometimes I think I didn't do it. But if I didn't do it, who did?"

Who did? His question echoed in her mind. And if Gavin was innocent, that meant someone had gone free while he served time for a crime he didn't commit. . . .

"I have to go," she said, getting to her feet. "Thanks for talking to me."

He stood, nervously rubbing his palms against his jeans. "Will you call me?" He swallowed, fear in his eyes. "When you find her?" *No matter how you find her?* were the unspoken words neither of them wanted to hear.

"Yes." Mary held out her hand.

He stared, puzzled and suspicious before finally shaking with a surprisingly firm grip. "Don't forget to call."

"I won't."

Outside, Mary was sliding into the car when her phone rang. It was Anthony. "Research just got back to us with a list of rose propagators," he told her.

"I'll be right there."

Chapter 30

The light above Gillian's head came on. She squinted against the blinding glare.

She'd spent the first three hours of solitary confinement standing with her back to the door. When her legs couldn't hold her up any longer, she'd felt around in the darkness to gingerly settle on the edge of the mattress, where she'd been ever since. She heard the rattle of metal; then the wooden door opened, shimmying against the cement threshold. She got to her feet in preparation for Mason's arrival.

In the short time she'd been with him, her old life had taken on a hazy, unreal quality. She remembered Blythe and Mary and Gavin, but they didn't seem as solid and substantial as Mason and this house.

In the back of her mind, she reasoned that the distance was brought about by drugs, lack of food, and fear, but that knowledge didn't make her other life seem any more real.

She searched Mason's face, looking for signs of his earlier impatience and lack of interest. His expression was blank, unreadable.

"I'm glad you're back," she said cautiously.

"Have you been good?"

"Very good."

"You didn't eat?" He picked up the sandwich from the mattress. "You didn't drink the water?"

"I forgot."

His lips curled. "Don't lie to me. I hate lies."

"Okay, I didn't forget," she said, quickly changing her story. Why had she said something that was so obviously untrue? She had to be more careful. "I was afraid you may have put something in it that would make me go to sleep, and I didn't want to lie down on the mattress. I was afraid to go to sleep here in the dark."

He tossed the sandwich to the floor. Then he took her by the arm and pulled her behind him, out of the room, through the winding basement, and up the stairs to the kitchen. He told her she could use the bathroom, and she hurried down the hall, shutting the door behind her.

In the bathroom by herself, she tried to gauge what his mood had been. Not much better than this morning. She was going to have to do something, come up with something that might impress him. *Be* somebody he wanted to keep. Because if he didn't want to keep her . . .

She splashed water on her face and was shocked by her reflection in the mirror above the sink. She looked like a junkie.

He was waiting for her outside the door. "Come on."

He led her into the kitchen, where he began frying pork chops in a skillet on the stove. "Can I help with something?" she asked, forcing herself to become a part of the surreal domestic scene. She had to act as if nothing odd was going on.

"Cut the potatoes for potato salad." He motioned toward the sink, where she found a pan of boiled potatoes along with a knife.

She picked up a peeled potato. By allowing her to use the knife he demonstrated the control he felt he had over her. It would be foolish to try to stab him. Odds were against her, and an attack would infuriate him—possibly enough to kill her.

"I love potato salad." She began cutting the potato into small squares, trying desperately to come up with harmless conversation. "Potato salad and baked beans. They just go together, don't you think?" Nothing intellectual, but it was all she could produce at the moment.

"I guess so."

Engage him. Make him answer questions. "What about apple pie? Do you like apple pie?"

"Yeah."

"Made with Jonathan apples. Maybe a few Golden Delicious thrown in, but mostly Jonathans."

"My sister used to bake pies." Upon mention of his sister, his voice suddenly became infused with life.

Small talk. Small talk was good. "Really? What kind?"

"Cherry. We have a cherry tree in the backyard. She was always baking cherry pies. And blackberry, when they were in season. She made a lot of apple pies too."

"I'd like to bake an apple pie for you," she ventured. "Would you let me do that?"

"No." The flash of elevated mood drained from him. "It wouldn't be right."

That had been careless of her. He apparently revered his sister. He wouldn't want Gillian trying to take her place. "How about a cake? Is your birthday anytime soon? I could bake you a cake."

He turned and stared. He had the strange eyes that murderers sometimes had—flat, dark, opaque.

Had she said something wrong?

"My sister is coming home soon."

Home? Does home mean what I think it means? Her heart began to hammer. "She's coming here?" *Stay calm,* she told herself. *Don't let him see your interest.*

"Tomorrow."

Tomorrow! She could hold out one more day. Of course she could hold out one more day. His sister would make him release her, maybe even make him go to the police. "We should have a party," Gillian said. "With cake and ice cream."

He smiled. He actually smiled.

Relief washed through her, and her muscles relaxed.

"You could put her name on the cake." Before her eyes, he transformed again, suddenly turning timid and shy.

"Yes! Welcome home . . . What's your sister's name?"

"Jo."

"Welcome home, Jo."

They ate their meal of pork chops and potato salad. Gillian's stomach had shrunk, and she couldn't eat much, but Mason didn't seem to notice. Nor did he seem to notice that she didn't drink any of the wine, only water from the same pitcher he used.

Tomorrow. She would be good. She would be good. She would be *so* good.

When they were done eating, he led her to the bedroom and dressed her in a low-cut, tight red dress.

I'm like his Barbie doll.

In the living room, he sat her down on the ottoman. He knelt behind her and began touching her hair, brushing it until she closed her eyes and exhaustion washed over her. She felt him putting makeup on her face, her cheeks, her lips. When he was done, he lit candles, turned off the lamp, and pulled out a book, settling on the floor at her feet.

"Shall I read to you?" he asked. "Would you like that?"

"Yes. Very much."

He chose the last paragraph in the overture of *Swann's Way*. It was perhaps Proust's most beautifully written passage about memory and the madeleine.

The paragraph was long and mesmerizing, wrapping the reader in bittersweet poignancy. Mason made it halfway through before he began to sob. The book dropped to his lap, and he buried his face in his hands.

"Here—" Gillian picked up the heavy volume. It automatically fell open to the page he'd been reading. In a soft voice she finished the paragraph for him, reading about the Japanese paper, the flower gardens, the whole of Combray springing up from a single cup of tea. When she was finished, she quietly closed the book and sat in silence. Out of seven volumes, he'd picked her favorite passage.

His sobs subsided, and he pressed his lips to her bare knee, hesitated, and then kissed her flesh again. "You're so beautiful. I want to take pictures of you," he whispered, looking up at her from his position on the floor. The flatness had left his eyes, as if his tears had momentarily cleansed them. "Would you mind?"

She didn't think she'd been drugged, but she felt strange and floaty and exceedingly calm.

He posed her, taking photo after photo. Some demure, some provocative.

"I have a lot of pictures," he said when he was finished. "Would you like to see them?"

"Yes."

He pulled her to her feet and led her from the room.

"I don't want to go back there," she said when she saw where they were heading. She tried to twist away, but he was too strong.

"Only for a little while."

Her feet were bare, and the steps were rough. The dirt floor, when they reached the basement, was damp and cold as they wound through the catacomb-like structure.

"Entrez," he said with a flourish, pushing her into a room she'd never seen before.

In front of her was a wall of photos. Several were of Holly lying on the ground, half-nude—all variations of the cut-up negative they'd found in the trash.

Gillian moved to the next wall. April Ellison. Wearing a red dress, posed provocatively. A breast showing here, a thigh there. Various parts of her body were also enlarged. In several photos, she had no eyes. Just bloody raw pits where the eyes had been.

She turned to an unfinished wall. Photos of her. *Oh, God.* It was disturbing to see herself lying in bed, unconscious and in various stages of undress. There were several of her breast with its rose tattoo.

"Here are my favorites."

He led her in the next display.

In front of her was a collage, eight-by-tens of body parts that went from ceiling to floor. At first they seemed random, but when he pulled her back, she was able to see that the enlargements made up an entire picture—of a girl lying in a bathtub. She was naked, and she was posed, her eyes open, flat, and dead. Very, very dead.

Gillian had always imagined that Charlotte Henning's death had been an accident, and that when Mason found her dead he'd quickly taken her body and dumped it in the river. Instead, he'd played with it. He'd made her pose for him even in death. And then he created this eight-feet-tall monument to the murder, a shrine to himself.

The sight of the photos made her insides curdle, made her feel sick to her stomach.

He was watching her. He'd jammed his hand into his pocket and was rattling the dice as he waited nervously in anticipation.

She quickly tried to pull on a blank mask, but it was too late. Nothing she now did or said could erase the horror and revulsion he'd seen in her face.

"Bitch!"

He grabbed her and dragged her through the passageway to the room where she'd spent the day. Adrenaline shot through her and she fought him, trying to wrench free, but her lessons in self-defense evaporated before his rage.

She gripped the doorjamb, her bare feet planted on the floor. She couldn't go back in there. He shoved. She stumbled forward.

He followed. He wrapped his hands around her throat and began to squeeze. Her breath was cut off. In survival mode, forgetting every technique she'd learned, she grabbed his wrists and tried to free herself. Suddenly he let her go, and she dropped to her knees, coughing.

"Close your eyes and hold out your hand," he commanded.

Wheezing, tears running down her cheeks, she did as he said.

He placed two small objects in her palm and closed her fingers over them. "A little gift for you, since you liked my photos so well."

She heard the door slam. The lock slid home.

On her knees, she opened her hand.

Lying in her palm were two shriveled blue eyeballs.

Chapter 31

Mason had been looking forward to this day for so long that he couldn't believe it was actually here. So engrossed was he in the anticipation of meeting his sister that he forgot to watch his speed. He glanced down—the speedometer had crept above sixty. He let up on the accelerator.

He'd allowed Gillian out of the basement long enough to bake a cake. She'd done a decent job, he had to admit. At least she was good for something.

She'd broken his heart, that's what she'd done. Reacting that way to his photographs. His photos were a part of him, they were a part of who he was, and up until that point everything had been going so well.

She'd hurt him. Hurt him deeply.

Girls were worthless. That was the bottom line. He would have to tell Jo that he was never going to find the right girl for him because the right girl didn't exist. They were good only for baking cakes and having babies, and he didn't want any kids and he could order a cake from the bakery.

Girls were deceitful. So full of lies. They were packages that looked enticing, alluring from the outside, but when you opened them up they were full of maggots.

Except for Jo. Jo fell into a completely different

category. She was a saint. She was perfect. She was beautiful inside and out.

When at last she stood before him, he was so glad to see her that he lifted her into the air and hugged her. She laughed, not in the mean way Gillian had laughed, but in delight and joy. She loved him. She'd always loved him, and oh, how he could bask in the warmth of that love.

On the way home he talked her ear off, telling her everything that had been going on while she'd been gone, telling her about his roses and how he'd taken good care of the house. He yakked and yakked and yakked.

Should he mention Gillian? he wondered when the conversation reached a lull. Should he even let Jo meet someone he wasn't going to keep? Someone who might disappear the way Seymour disappeared?

But it would be good to demonstrate to Jo that at least he'd made an effort to find a mate. That he'd kept his promise to her and that he'd been serious about it even though it hadn't worked out.

Was it anybody's fault that neither of them had known he was simply destined to be a bachelor? What was wrong with that, anyway? *What is wrong with that?*

Maybe Jo would extend her visit. Maybe once she was back, once she saw the house, she would want to stay longer. To hell with the people in town who'd snubbed her. She didn't need anybody else. Neither of them needed anybody else. Not as long as they had each other.

When they got home Jo went to her bedroom, saying she wanted to lie down awhile.

That was okay. It gave Mason time to get things ready for her party. While she was resting, he set the table.

Three places.

He decided to allow Gillian to participate. At times she could conduct herself with propriety, and surely with his sister gracing the house Gillian would be on her best behavior.

He got out the china and silverware. He put party favors at each setting. In the refrigerator was soft-serve ice cream from Dairy Queen—Jo's favorite after homemade. When he was little, she used to make homemade ice cream. He would turn the crank until he thought his arm would fall off. Jo always said the hand-cranked kind was the only kind to make if you were going to the trouble. Mason liked being able to do something, and the machine wasn't noisy like the electric ones. Those could send a person running out of the house.

He lit candles for atmosphere and put on a record—Mahler's arrangement of Schubert's Quartet in D Minor, "Death and the Maiden." Then he went to see if Jo was awake. . . .

Music woke her.

It drifted into the basement and oozed through the stone walls. Gillian sat up in the blackness. She had no idea if it was day or night, no idea how much time had passed since she'd visited Mason's photo gallery. He'd allowed her upstairs once since then. That had been to bake a cake for his sister's welcome-home party.

The light above her head came on. A moment later Mason unlocked the door and threw it open. He was dressed in a black suit with sleeves that were too short. His hair was wet and combed back off a white fore-head. "Party time!" he announced with puppylike enthusiasm. "How do you look?" He pulled her under the light and examined her.

She hadn't eaten since the pork chop dinner, and she'd been using the corner of the room as a toilet, but his mind was too caught up in other thoughts for him to find fault with her. "Come on," he said in a bubbly voice, swinging her arm.

"What time is it?" she asked, stumbling along behind him.

"Late. We have to hurry."

"I'd like to know the time."

He checked his watch. "Six-thirty."

"In the evening?"

"In the morning."

The exertion caused sweat to break out over her body, and the stone walls swam. "Mason—just a minute." She leaned her face against the clammy wall and closed her eyes, afraid she was going to pass out.

"Come on." He tugged at her arm. "My sister's waiting."

His sister. Gillian had momentarily forgotten about his sister. His sister. Her time in hell was almost over.

The knowledge of potential freedom gave her strength. She pulled in some deep breaths, then continued after him, hardly noticing when she smacked her toe into a step, tearing the nail at the root.

Upstairs, candles burned everywhere. The music was something classical. Through the doorway she could see the kitchen table, see the candles and cake and roses, the wineglasses shimmering. Sitting with her back to her was a small blond-haired woman wearing a dark dress.

Thank God. She was here. Finally here! Until that point, Gillian hadn't been sure she was real, afraid Mason was just making her up. Gillian felt close to tears as relief and gratitude rushed through her.

Rather than waiting for Mason to make introductions, she took the initiative. "Hi. I'm Gillian Cantrell," she said, moving forward into the room, swinging around to face the woman in the chair, her hand extended.

The floor shifted.

Behind her, the basement door slammed shut. A vacuum sucked the air from the room.

Sitting in front of her, hands folded demurely on her lap, eyes closed, face bearing undertaker's makeup, was a dead woman.

Denial, confusion, and disbelief fluttered in Gillian's brain.

A corpse.

No!

Her mind struggled with the presentation. *NO!* Not real. Not happening. A dream. A nightmare.

"This is my sister, Jo Von Bryant," Mason said, proudly striding in behind her, pulling out a chair so Gillian could take a seat at the table, across from Jo.

"Sit down," Mason commanded, a familiar irritation creeping into his voice.

With jerky movements, Gillian sat, her hands in her lap, her eyes focusing on the cake in the center of the table. WELCOME HOME, JO.

Jo, the dead woman. Jo, the corpse.

Even though Gillian wasn't looking at her, she may as well have been. She could see her anyway. Such was the persistence of memory. She could see the way the shiny, transparent skin of her face stretched across the bridge of a narrow nose. Her mouth had been a round black pit, as if she'd died while crying out in pain.

Had Mason killed her?

Make this go away. Make this all go away.

Gillian unfolded her napkin and spread it on her lap. She cleared her throat. "H-how long have you been gone?" she asked.

"A year," Mason said, slicing a knife through the cake. "A year today."

Where had she been all of this time? In the house? In one of the rooms upstairs?

A smell emanated from her, not a rotten smell, but something Gillian associated with funeral parlors.

Embalming fluid.

As her mind raced and then screeched to a stop, Mason continued to cut and serve the cake. He hummed as he scooped ice cream onto three plates and finally took a seat between Gillian and his sister.

"Bon appétit."

With a shaking hand, Gillian lifted the heavy silver fork. She sliced into the cake.

It was white cake with white frosting because Mason had told her that was his sister's favorite.

She raised the fork to her mouth. The bite of cake quivered there, just beyond her lips. She inhaled. The scent of embalming fluid filled her nostrils.

She dropped her fork with a clatter of metal on china and pushed from the table, getting to her feet and spinning around, her back to Mason and his dead sister. She gripped the edge of the sink, wondering if she was going to throw up, wondering if she had anything *to* throw up.

Had he killed her?

The question was caught in a loop in her head.

Had he killed her and preserved her to bring her out on special occasions? Did he have other bodies around? Was the fucking house full of bodies?

As she stood there, her mind reached a saturation point. A removed, out-of-body feeling came over her.

So what if she's dead?

What is death anyway?

Was the body sitting there any different from a leaf that had fallen from a tree and blown into the house?

Any different from a dry, faded flower? Any different from her own body, except that her own body had blood pumping through it?

"Aren't you going to join us?" Mason asked.

She could tell he was angry, but didn't want to show it in front of his sister. Which meant his sister, dead though she was, might still prove Gillian's ally.

Gillian turned around, her hands clenched together. She forced herself to look at the woman.

Not that bad, she told herself now that the initial shock was over.

Her hair, her light blond hair, shimmered softly in the candlelight. Just an empty vessel that had once held life, she told herself. "Your sister is beautiful," she whispered to Mason.

He nodded. Without getting up, he reached for Gillian, taking her hand, leading her in a semicircle back to her chair, where she sat down, lifted her fork, and took a bite of cake.

Outside, in the distance, she heard the sound of car tires moving over gravel. Mason jumped to his feet and ran to a living room window. A second later he was flying around the kitchen, blowing out candles.

Chapter 32

The true story of Josephine Von Bryant's life was one Mason cherished every bit as much as his adored fiction. One of his favorite ways to pass the time was to listen to his sister's tales.

"Start when you were ten years old," he used to beg her, because that was when she really began the search for her true self.

At ten, Josephine decided she wanted to dedicate her life to God. Their parents found her devotion frightening, so obsessed was she with living a humble existence. At one point, she shaved her head and slept on the hard floor. She starved herself, and when she couldn't find any stores that carried the hair shirts she'd heard and read about in catechism class, she bought a wool sweater from the church's store for the poor and wore it against her bare skin through summer and winter until her mother stripped it from her and burned it.

Her obsession with faith worried her parents so much that they removed her from Catholic school and put her in a private, all-girls institution. At first the other students made fun of her, calling her a freak to her face, but then she began developing signs of stigmata. The first spot started out as a blister on her palm. A week later, on the opposite side of her hand, blood began to ooze. Her classmates were fascinated, and soon Josephine had a group of faithful followers who couldn't get enough of her biblical stories of lust, suffering, and devotion.

Even though she scratched herself until she bled and kept the wounds from healing by continually picking and stabbing at them, Josephine convinced herself they were real.

By the time Josephine hit puberty, she'd grown bored with religion. Her psychologist helped her to realize it wasn't religion that had brought about her obsession with living a cloistered life, but a fear of men. She had no childhood memories of suffering at the hands of any man, so she could only guess that her fear was genetic. She became a lesbian for a while, but grew tired of that even more quickly than religion.

When their parents died unexpectedly, leaving Mason in her care, she suddenly found a new calling.

Mason.

She adored him.

Nine-year-old Mason came into her charge at a vulnerable time. He would watch her as she moved about a room, never letting his eyes waver, afraid she might leave and not come back. He would follow her to the bathroom and wait outside the door, sometimes curling up on the floor while she bathed.

Jo got a job with a traveling acting troupe, but after two years decided it wasn't the life for Mason. When an uncle died, leaving them an estate in Minnesota, they moved into the farmhouse a week after the paperwork was finished.

"This is it," Josephine said, standing in the front yard, looking up at the two-story house. "Our home."

Jo threw herself into their new life with the same enthusiasm she'd shown for religion, but no matter how hard she tried, she often lamented that it never seemed quite real to her.

Sometimes as she moved through her day, washing clothes, hanging them on the line to dry, baking pies, canning vegetables, she said she felt that she was living someone else's life. Not a bad life, by any means, she'd told Mason. Just not her life.

Was there a lack of sincerity in the way she approached things? she'd asked her brother. How did a person know when she had it right? She thought she had it right when she shaved her head and wore a wool sweater. Now she looked back on those days with embarrassment. She thought she had it right when she decided to become a lesbian. She and her partner went to gatherings where they spoke up for women's rights. She never wore a dress and didn't take any shit from anyone, especially a man.

But that had all been playing at life, experimenting and experiencing what it meant to be human. It hadn't been who she was.

Then she was diagnosed with terminal cancer.

This, she told Mason. *This is real.*

Their last year together was spent reading a translation of the entire seven-volume set of Proust's *Remembrance of Things Past,* because that was something Jo had always promised herself she would do. They spent evenings listening to music and just talking quietly.

But there came a time when Jo was much too blunt, when she came right out and told Mason that she wouldn't always be there for him, that she would be leaving one day and he would never see her again. They had to make plans.

Her biggest concern was that he'd be lonely. "You need to meet girls," she would say to him as she lay in bed at night with Mason in a chair nearby. "When I'm gone, you need to get busy. Find someone. There's somebody out there for you. Somebody who will love and adore you. But you won't find her here, sitting at home or piddling around with your roses. You've got to go out and find her. Promise me you'll do that? Promise me you won't just hide here, being sad?"

He wouldn't listen. Anytime she brought up the subject of her impending death, he shut out her blunt and awful words. "We can move," he told her. "We can go somewhere else. I know you've never liked it here. I know those women in town have been mean to you."

"Moving won't change anything," she said sadly. "Mason, I'm dying."

He refused to believe her. He was twenty-seven, but he reverted back to his childhood.

Jo enlisted the help of a hospice, but they knew only about death; they didn't know about helping the living. She contacted the local church. It wasn't Catholic, but she didn't think that mattered. The minister came to visit. Mason kicked him out, telling him to get the hell off their property.

Her doctor had ordered plenty of heavy-duty drugs to keep the pain at bay. Those drugs eventually sent her into a sleep from which she never awakened. . . .

Someone else may have thought she was just sleeping, but as soon as Mason saw her, he knew something was wrong. The essence he knew of as Jo wasn't there.

He didn't call anybody for two days.

He kept thinking maybe something would happen. Maybe he would step into the bedroom and she'd be sitting there, smiling at him. He kept vigil. Several times throughout the day he would leave the room, then return in order to give her the chance to come back, to start over.

She never woke up.

He didn't know a body could go bad so quickly.

She began to smell. He heard a buzzing at the window near the bed, and when he pulled back the curtain he saw what had to be thousands of flies clustered on the glass, piled up where the wooden frame met metal, trying to squeeze in the small cracks.

They were the shiny kind of flies, fat-bodied black ones he associated with the dead rabbits and squirrels he sometimes came across. Behind him, he heard more buzzing. He swung around. The sheet that covered Jo seemed to be moving. He lifted it. A rotten smell hit him in the face. At the same time, a cloud of flies swarmed him, going for his mouth and nose. He ran from the room, picked up the phone, and dialed 911.

It would end up being one of those calls paramedics talked about over beers whenever stories were being shared.

All they knew as they headed for the secluded farmhouse was that the patient was an elderly woman who was thought to be dead.

The smell hit them before they reached the door. Hands held to their mouths weren't enough. They had to retreat and pull out carbon filter masks.

The door was covered with flies. They opened it, shaking them loose. A black cloud unfurled and then immediately settled back down, sticking to the flesh, biting.

Inside the house a man stood wringing his hands, his eyes red. "She's in there," he said, pointing to a room off the living room. "I think she might be dead."

The paramedics looked at each other but didn't say anything. In the bedroom they glanced at the body, which had passed out of rigor long ago. "I ain't driving back with that in the van," one said to the other. "We'll never get the smell outta there."

In the ambulance, they put in a call to the coroner's

office, which sent a plain truck with a topper—the vehicle used for the stinky cases. Without lingering, they whisked the body away to the mortuary, where it was pumped with four times the recommended amount of embalming fluid.

The mortician had a bad habit of shorting his clients when it came to such things, but in this case cheating wasn't even an option.

Laid out in the casket, her cheeks rosy, wearing a dress with a brooch at the throat, she waited. She didn't have many visitors, and the ones who came did so out of morbid curiosity.

Mason stayed with her morning and night until the mortician had to pry him away, telling him it was time to let her go, time to bury her.

"NO!" Mason had screamed. "NO!"

When Sheriff David Vance got the call telling him a grave at Poplar Grove Cemetery had been vandalized, he immediately thought of a group of kids that had gone around last year, digging up old graves and carrying bones around with them in their backpacks. They hadn't meant any harm. They'd just been inquisitive.

But when David reached the cemetery and saw that an entire body had been stolen, he dismissed his earlier assessment and recalled the story told to him by Harvey Blake, the local mortician.

He called him. "Harvey, you remember that kid you were telling me about last year? The one who didn't want to bury his sister?"

"Yeah."

"What was her name?" he asked, staring at the headstone.

"Von Bryant. Josephine Von Bryant."

"You remember the kid's name?"

"Uh . . . Mason. Mason, that's it."

"Thanks, Harvey." After hanging up, David asked the first officer on the scene if the crime lab was on its way.

"Should be here any minute."

"I'm going to let you handle it from this end," he said. "I've got a stop to make."

It was a small county, and he'd heard about the woman and kid who had moved in years ago. People said they were strange, but that's how it was in rural settings. Nobody liked anybody new. He felt sorry for outsiders who moved into the area. They always came excited about the beauty. Almost every one of them left within a few years, moving back to where they came from or to a place with influx and a higher population. The Von Bryants stayed on.

He knocked on the door. Nobody answered. The windowless garage was shut; he couldn't see whether a car was inside or not. He walked around the property. The sky was dark. A storm was blowing in, bringing wind and rain that was supposed to turn to snow. He hoped the lakes froze early this year. He'd spent the summer building a new fishing house, and he was anxious to get it set up.

The farm was a nice little place. He remembered when old Samuel Griffin had lived there. Sam had died while feeding his hogs, and the hogs ate him. Nothing left for anybody to find but bones.

Hogs were weird that way. Especially in a feedlot situation. He knew a guy who'd just slipped and fallen. Before he could get up, a hog bit off his ear.

There was no sign of activity. Maybe it was better this way. Take him by surprise with a search warrant. That was if his suspicions were enough for a search warrant. He'd made some bad calls in the past, and the judge was getting reluctant to spit warrants out the way she used to. Damn woman.

From a crack in the living room drapes, Mason watched the police car drive away, smoke from the rapidly blown-out candles burning his throat. The girl—Gillian—was lying on the floor, unconscious from a blow to the head. Her fault. She shouldn't have tried to run for the door.

He'd known the police would come. He just hadn't thought it would be so soon.

Chapter 33

Anthony sat hunched over a desk in the corner of Elliot Senatra's office, going over the matches they'd come up with from the list of rose propagators. They'd narrowed it down to twenty-three men, not a figure Anthony was happy with, but they couldn't risk dismissing the remotest possibility. Mary, who Anthony didn't think had slept in days, was on the phone with Detective Wakefield. Time was their enemy, and she was desperately trying to pull together forty-six people in order to simultaneously send teams to the twenty-three remaining addresses.

The door flew open, and Elliot stuck his head inside. "A grave in Poplar Grove's been robbed," he announced. "And get this—the missing body belongs to Josephine Von Bryant."

Von Bryant. One of the names on the propagator list.

"Does she have a husband?" Mary asked. "Or a son?"

Elliot smiled broadly. "A brother. Mason Von Bryant."

The rental car flew down the country road, gravel and mud hitting the undercarriage.

"The turn should be coming up on the left." Mary leaned forward in the passenger seat. It was raining hard, and the rapidly clicking wipers could barely keep up.

Mason Von Bryant's house was located on the top of a hill, with an unobstructed view of the half-mile lane leading to it and the connecting highway. When planning their strategy, they'd decided it would be too risky for a parade of patrol cars to approach the house. Instead, Mary and Anthony were going in and would call for backup when needed. Parked along the highway two miles away was Elliot, along with four BCA agents, four police officers, six members of the SWAT team, and an ambulance. Even though it wasn't his jurisdiction, John Wakefield was also on hand.

"There it is." Anthony slowed and then turned the car onto a road with a PRIVATE PROPERTY sign. The narrow lane was deeply rutted, and he was forced to slow down.

He pulled up behind the garage and shut off the engine. Then he radioed Elliot and the waiting team to let them know they'd arrived.

He and Mary opened their doors and stepped out. Wind caught their raincoats, whipping them about their legs. Hunching their shoulders, they ran for the house and the overhang above the front door.

Anthony tried the doorbell, then knocked. When no one answered, he jiggled the knob. It was unlocked.

He looked at Mary with raised eyebrows. They withdrew their weapons from their shoulder holsters. She nodded, and he pushed open the door. With guns drawn and pointed skyward, they entered cautiously.

It was an old house. Wind shifted a curtain and crept into a crevice around the sash, sounding like breath being blown across the curved glass lip of a soda bottle.

Immediately in front of them was the kitchen where a table had been set with wineglasses and a cake. In a vase were red roses.

Seated at the table, her back to Mary, was a woman. Mary inched forward, slowly approaching her while Anthony kept his eyes on the living room and hallway.

Mary had come expecting to find Mason Von Bryant's dead sister, so she wasn't surprised to discover that the woman seated at the table was a frozen-faced corpse, an untouched glass of wine and slice of cake in front of her. The ice cream had melted, dripping to the floor to dry in a congealed puddle.

Was every traumatic event in her life going to feature cake? Mary wondered.

The body neither shocked nor frightened her.

She motioned to Anthony, and they scoured the lower story of the house, quickly and efficiently checking the living room, dining room, two bedrooms, and bath. Then they climbed the narrow, twisted stairs.

The ornate railing was covered with glossy, chipped white paint, the stair steps with a wool runner. The walls were smothered with overwhelming floral wallpaper, yellowed and stained with age. The house smelled like mildew and rotten wood.

In the doorway of the first bedroom, Anthony paused and tensed. Behind him, Mary looked over his shoulder. Reclining in a narrow twin bed, pillows at his back, dressed in light blue pajamas, was a man she assumed was Mason Von Bryant. He watched passively with emotionless eyes.

There was no dismissing the emptiness there. She'd seen it before. That kind of emptiness belonged to killers, to mass murderers. To people without souls or conscience.

Where is Gillian?
Is she still alive?

Those were the two questions foremost in her mind. If the case hadn't involved her sister, Mary would have said he'd most likely killed her the first or second day. But this was Gillian they were talking about, and Mary couldn't face the possibility that her sister was dead.

Beside her, Anthony sensed Mary's fear and apprehension, sensed the way she struggled with the scene as presented to them. These situations always fit a pattern, and her years of experience would be telling her that her sister was dead. Right now Mary was probably clinging to the few cases that fell outside the norm. *Let this be one of those,* he prayed, all the while afraid such prayers were useless. Gillian was dead. That's what his gut was telling him.

Both their weapons were trained on the man in the bed. Anthony pulled out his ID and introduced himself and Mary. "Are you Mason Von Bryant?"

"As a matter of fact, I am."

"Where's Gillian?" Mary asked, her voice neutral.

"Aren't beds the greatest?" Von Bryant asked, acting as if they had come to visit him. "I always feel safe in my bed."

Anthony remained focused on the man, watching for the smallest flicker of movement that would indicate a weapon. "Put up your hands."

Von Bryant slowly lifted his hands and held them high. "I always wanted to do that," he said, smiling.

He was like a kid, Anthony realized. Like some thirteen-year-old kid. In a matter of seconds, Anthony went from anger to pity. And now, peripherally, he took note of the surroundings.

The room was done in cartoon animal wallpaper. Black-and-white photos covered one wall. A glance told him they were of Mason Von Bryant and variations of the woman downstairs. On the bed was a big stuffed bear and a purple elephant. Shelves held model cars, toy rockets, and arrowheads—all lined up neatly in rows. The sheets on the twin bed were faded and worn, but not so worn that Anthony couldn't make out characters from the 1977 *Star Wars* movie.

Jesus.

It was the saddest fucking thing he'd ever seen.

How did this happen? How did people get so messed up, so twisted around in their heads? The poor guy. Poor kid.

"Where's Gillian?" Mary repeated.

"I'm not afraid of dying," Von Bryant stated.

"We don't want you to die," Anthony said carefully.

"This isn't real. None of it's real, so it doesn't matter."

"Mason, this *is* real."

"I've always felt safe in my bed."

"You *are* safe."

"No place is really safe, is it? Don't you know that? No place. Not even this bed."

"That's not true," Anthony lied.

Mason cocked his head to one side. "Listen to the rain. Doesn't it sound peaceful? The way it's hitting the roof like that?"

Mary made a little choking sound deep in her throat, a sob that she tried to stop but couldn't. *She knows*, Anthony thought. *She knows Gillian is dead.*

"Where's Gillian?" she suddenly shouted, extending her gun with both hands and taking a step toward the bed. "Where's my sister?" She was half-sobbing now, the gun trembling.

Anthony put a hand out to stop her and comfort her. "Careful," he warned.

"Everything sucks," Mason said.

Anthony could kinda see where he was coming

from. Sometimes he thought it was just him and the business he was in. When you deal with evil every day, you tended to think life sucked.

"I understand," Anthony said.

"You?" Mason asked sarcastically. "*You* understand? Are you saying you understand what it's like to be me? Nobody knows what it's like to be me. Can I put my arms down? They're getting tired."

"Go ahead, but keep them above the sheets."

Mason lowered his arms.

"I don't know what it's like to be you," Anthony said. "But I know what it's like to be human. I know what it's like to wonder where this is all heading, and why. The world is a hard place to live in. That's all I'm saying. It's a hard place to deal with."

"I can't relate to you in any way."

"I don't expect you to."

"With your suit and tie and city haircut. You don't have any right to tell me the world is hard. You're the kind of person that makes it hard. Good-looking, efficient bastards like you make the rest of us look bad, make the rest of us look like shit."

"I'm sorry."

"It's too late."

"What do you mean, too late?" Anthony asked. Too late for Gillian? Or too late for Von Bryant?

Up until that point, Mason's movements had been slow and slothlike. Suddenly he acted with agile speed, pulling a handgun from under the sheets. But instead of turning it on Anthony or Mary, he turned it in his direction.

"He's going to kill himself!" Mary screamed.

She lunged. Before she made contact, his weapon discharged. The sound was deafening in the cramped room. The pressure of the expanding gases from the single bullet caused the bones of Von Bryant's skull to separate along the suture lines. Like a deflated balloon, his face caved in on itself.

"No!" She grabbed fistfuls of his pajama top. "No! You son of a bitch! NO!"

"Mary, he's dead!" Anthony tried to pull her back, but nothing registered. "He's dead! Let him go!"

His words finally sank in. She released him. With her sleeve, she wiped away the blood that flecked her face. "We need to search this place." She ran to the closet and jerked open the door. "We have to find Gillian!"

Anthony radioed Elliot. "Von Bryant's dead."

"What about Gillian?"

"We're still looking. Check the garage and outbuildings, plus the area surrounding the house."

"We're on our way."

Chapter 34

She was suffocating.

Had Mason known the holes he'd drilled in the refrigerator wouldn't be enough to keep her supplied with air? That would be something he would do, something gutless. Why not just kill her outright? Shoot her, or give her an overdose of his nasty drugs? Instead, he put her away. He shut the door and didn't plan to open it again. Forget about her. Pretend she didn't exist.

It was possible her body would never be found. Her poor mother would keep looking, year after year, waiting for news. And all the while Gillian would be here, stuffed in a fucking refrigerator.

She'd tried to be good. She'd even talked to his dead sister. But it hadn't been enough. No woman would have been enough for him, because no woman could live up to the woman who was already dead.

She'd been naïve enough to think she could get through to him. How idiotic. How childish of her. She wasn't a negotiator. She hadn't been trained to talk someone into giving up. And now, in this eleventh hour, she could admit that after all these years, she was still trying to prove herself to Mary.

*　　*　　*

The basement was cold and damp, the floor was dirt, the walls wound around like catacombs.

"Gillian!" Mary shouted. "Gillian!"

She and Anthony hurried through the cramped space, ducking under wooden beams, their shoulders rubbing against stone and cement. One pass, and they found Mason's darkroom. No sign of Gillian.

Mary quickly looked around, her gaze moving over the photos plastered to the walls. There was Holly. Charlotte Henning. April Ellison. Underneath some of April's photos was a neatly printed word: BITCH.

"Anthony—look." Mary stood in front of an enlarger. Visible in the compartment below the lens were the notched edges of a negative strip. "He must have been developing these."

Anthony immediately fell into action. "Shut off the overhead." He flicked on a red light screwed into a nearby socket.

Mary looked frantically around the room, running her hands across stone and cement block walls. "I can't find a switch!" She grabbed a broom and swung at the dangling bulb, breaking it like a piñata, glass shattering to the floor.

"See if you can locate developing solution," he said urgently. "It should be there somewhere near those trays." He turned on the enlarger light and bent close. "These could be Gillian, but I can't say for sure."

Mary found a jug labeled DEVELOPING SOLUTION and poured it into a plastic tray.

Anthony flicked off the light, then slipped a contact sheet under the metal frame, quickly setting it up for an eight-by-ten. "Here we go." He pushed the timer button. The light clicked on for eight seconds, then off. He pulled out the contact sheet, hurried to the table, and dropped it in the solution.

"Stop bath," he said, looking around.

"Here." Mary handed him a brown bottle.

He poured a small amount into another tray and then added water. "We don't need anything else," he said. "We're not going for quality here. Watch the paper. When the photo is clear, pull it out and put it in the stop bath." He hurried back to the enlarger to make another print from a different negative.

As Mary watched, an image slowly appeared.

A woman.

Dressed in an off-the-shoulder evening gown.

Lying inside something.

A box?

Coffin?

Mary pressed a hand to her mouth.

It was a woman stuffed inside a refrigerator. Both doors were open. A notch had been cut in the freezer compartment, just large enough for a neck; her head filled the freezer, her body the lower section.

"It's Gillian," Mary said, unable to take her eyes from the photo.

Anthony returned to slide in another contact sheet. Using his bare hands, he pulled out the developed print and dropped it in the stop bath.

"Is she alive in the photo?" he asked.

"Yes." Her answer came on one tight, exhaled breath.

Standing opposite each other, they stared at the developing tray, waiting for the second image to appear.

It was a close-up of Gillian's face framed by the freezer. "She's alive in this one too," Anthony said.

Mary spun around, pulling a flashlight from her pocket as she went. Hurrying back through the stone maze, she trained the light on the dirt floor, then the steps that led to the kitchen.

Upstairs, she dived for the refrigerator, jerking it open.

Packed with food.

She slammed the door and ran back to the basement, where Anthony stood bathed in red light, three eight-by-tens spread out in front of him. "There has to be another refrigerator somewhere," she said breathlessly.

He pulled out his flashlight and trained the beam on the developed photos. "We need a clue to the location."

How long could a person remain alive in a refrigerator? Minutes? An hour?

Mary grabbed the photos, one after the other. "This one." She pointed. "Right here," she said, her voice rising. "Isn't that a stone wall?"

Anthony looked closer. "You're right." He was already moving. "Let's check the barn and outbuildings," he shouted over his shoulder. "They probably have stone foundations."

Halfway up the stairs, Mary stopped. Could they have missed something in their initial perusal of the basement? "Go on," she said, hurrying back downstairs. "I'm looking here once more."

He cleared the rest of the steps, taking them two and three at a time. She heard his feet pounding above her head. From outside came the sound of voices. Elliot and his team had arrived.

She and Anthony had gone through the basement quickly the first time. Now, while her heart pounded in her head, she forced herself to move methodically, training her flashlight on every crack and crevice.

Cobwebs. Mildew. Dripping water, falling and running across the ground. A door she'd checked before. She opened it again, shining the flashlight on canning jars of green and yellow beans. She directed the beam down. On the dirt floor was a footprint. A bare footprint. Small enough to be a woman's.

She stepped inside the cramped, smothering room and discovered something that hadn't been apparent from the doorway. The room appeared to be a rectangle about five feet deep. But once inside she saw that it was L-shaped, with the short length of the L turning to the left. At the end of that turn was a small padlocked door.

It was insanity to shoot a gun in such a tight space. She would never have graduated from the Academy if she'd done something so stupid during training.

Mary drew her gun, took aim, and then turned her face away as she squeezed the trigger.

She smelled burnt gunpowder. Her ears rang. When she looked back, the lock had shattered. She grabbed it, hot metal searing her fingers. Ignoring the pain, she jerked the lock loose. It dropped to the dirt floor with a soft thud. She lifted the metal hinge and shoved open the door.

A torture chamber.

A filthy mattress tossed across wooden slats. Handcuffs attached to a framework that made up the bed. She put a hand to her nose. The smell was bad, not like death, but more like an outhouse.

Something caught in her hair. She stepped back to see a shattered bulb dangling in front of her face. She moved the flashlight beam around to the back of the deep, narrow, suffocating space. There, lying on the ground like a coffin, was a refrigerator.

She bolted across the room, shoved open both doors, and shined her flashlight inside.

Visions of another time flooded her brain. Fiona. Dead. Murdered. Blood. Flies. And empty eyes. Those empty eyes . . .

Gillian was dead.

Her lips were blue, her skin, in contrast to the red

satin gown, transparent. Red rose petals had been scattered—they clung to her white flesh.

The flashlight fell from her fingers as Mary dropped to her knees.

Too late. Too late.

She wasn't strong enough to lift Gillian from the tomb, so she leaned over, squeezed open her blue lips, and blew into her lungs.

What are you doing? Do you think you can wake the dead?

She blew another breath, then another, the panic she'd kept at bay until that point rising within her. She could feel the frightened wings beating against her heart, feel a helpless fear coming over her that threatened to shut off her mind completely.

It was a sensation she recalled from her youth.

Make it stop. Make it stop.

She blew another breath. And another.

Waking the dead.

A clatter behind her told her Anthony was there. His flashlight beam careened around the room. "I heard a gunshot. Oh, Christ," he said, spotting Gillian.

Now that Anthony had arrived, she broke down. "She's dead, Anthony!" she sobbed in disbelief. "She's dead!"

Together they lifted her from the refrigerator, the jagged edges of the freezer cutting into the sides of Gillian's neck. Blood beaded.

They put her on the floor, where Anthony placed two fingers against her carotid artery. "A pulse!" He turned to her. On his face was the most amazing mixture of incredulity and happiness. "She's breathing shallowly, but she's breathing!"

"I can't believe it." Mary fell to her knees beside

him, an arm across his shoulders. "I can't believe she's still alive." Then she began to cry.

Sunlight hit Gillian full in the face, blinding her.

Was she dead? Was that the bright light they were always talking about?

A dark spot moved across the brightness. Her father? Grandmother?

"Gillian?"

She recognized Mary's voice.

"You're not dead, are you?" she asked, then realized nobody could hear her. She lifted a hand to her face. Something plastic. An oxygen mask.

"Here—" Someone removed the mask.

Gillian's eyes began to adjust to the brightness. The shadow that was Mary became more distinct until she could see her sister smiling at her. The smile was a smile from the past, from a time when they were young and the world was full of promise. She felt air move across her skin, and realized she was outside.

Birds were singing madly, the way they did after a rain.

Chapter 35

Gillian stood at the window of her apartment, watching for her sister. After being kept overnight at the hospital for observation, she'd spent the last twenty-four hours taking it easy and receiving visitors, including Holly, Ben, Wakefield, and Gavin. Nobody had wanted her to stay by herself, but she'd insisted upon it. The visits were nice, but highly emotional and draining. She needed time alone.

Then her mother, in true Blythe fashion, couldn't wait any longer to celebrate Gillian's return from the dead.

A car pulled up to the curb. Mary, bundled in a long wool coat, hat, gloves, and scarf, hurried across the yard, her body bent into the wind. Winter had finally arrived. Snow had blown in the night before, and the temperature had dropped to the teens.

"You'll need a hat," Mary told her, stepping inside, bringing the cold with her. Gillian pulled on a lime green stocking cap and dug a matching scarf from the closet. "I knit these last winter," she said. "Remember when we learned to knit? Mrs. Portman taught us."

"After school. I also remember we used to make some fantastic snowmen," Mary said, tying the scarf around Gillian's neck and giving the cap an extra tug.

"And snow women." Gillian emphasized the word *women*. They both laughed. You didn't have a feminist mother without snowmen of both sexes.

"We'll do that again, won't we?" Gillian searched Mary's face for affirmation and found it. "Play in the snow?" Suddenly she felt brittle and fragile and dangerously close to tears.

"Soon," Mary said. "Very soon." She gave her a gentle hug. "Come on."

In the car, Gillian stared through the windshield. "I was so out of it when I was there." She felt no need to explain *there*. At Mason's. Mary would know. Mary would understand. "I keep trying to remember exactly what happened, but I can't. I recall snatches of conversation, and snapshot images. I know some questions have no answers, but I keep asking myself, *Why?*"

"Loss can be a catalyst for many things," her sister said. "Unfortunately, Mason was unable to cope with the death of his sister."

"You probably think it's best if I just let it go, quit trying to remember, but I have an overpowering need to put those days together into some kind of perspective."

"That sense of unreality could be a protective mechanism. Abused children often have no memories of the abuse. Even adults have been known to subconsciously block out traumatic events."

He's still there, Gillian thought.

In my head.

For the rest of her life, she would be connected to Mason whether she wanted to be or not. It was out of her control.

He'd been buried in Poplar Grove Cemetery, next to his sister. The siblings would spend eternity together—or at least a few hundred years. Gillian had been told that both Josephine's and Mason's graves would be covered with cement to discourage any possible grave robbers. For some reason, people tended to dig up the graves of murderers. Sometimes such desecrations were committed by family members of victims who had been killed. Sometimes they were done by people who had an unhealthy curiosity about such crimes and were looking for souvenirs.

In the cellar room where Gillian had been kept, the crime scene team found the dehydrated eyeballs Mason had given her, plus an unearthed, mummified dog.

It was over.

The house was no longer considered a crime scene. All the evidence had been collected, photos confiscated, the building sealed. In six months, maybe a year, if no living relative could be found, a cleanup team would come. They would strip it of everything. Personal belongings would be bagged and taken to the dump. Later men would come and board up the windows and nail KEEP OUT signs to the doors.

The roses in Mason's private greenhouse had been promised to the U of M horticultural department. When students arrived to pick them up, they found that high wind had peeled back the plastic from the roof and freezing temperatures had killed the delicate plants, turning their leaves a withered black.

Better that way, Gillian had thought when Detective Wakefield told her.

Mary stopped the car in front of her mother's house. Darkness had fallen. The snow had stopped. She could see lights and hear laughter coming from inside. The feeling took her back to her childhood, reminding her of short winter days when she would come home to find the house full of light and people and energy.

She and Gillian could barely squeeze in the front door. The living room was packed with people Mary vaguely recognized—most of them her mother's friends. Music was playing, and Blythe was floating around with a bottle of champagne, refilling glasses as they emptied.

"Hello, sweetheart," Blythe said. "You remember Freddie, don't you?"

Mary looked at the short man with the red silk shirt and black glasses and struggled to recall him. Before she could answer, Blythe stuck a heavy plate in her hand and sailed off with Gillian in tow. Freddie smiled, handed her a fork and napkin, and trotted after Blythe's trail of exotic perfume.

After Fiona died, Mary began feeling resentful toward her mother. Not toward Blythe herself, but what she was doing with her life. She'd felt that any kind of art was a ridiculous waste of time. What good was music, and parties, and laughter? Innocent children were being killed. The time to laugh was over. Done with. You could laugh as long as you didn't know how bad the world was, but how could people keep laughing once they knew? Kids were out there dying. What good did a piece of baked clay do?

It kept the soul alive.

I've wasted so many years.

Not wasted, she told herself. *How can it be a waste? I've stopped murderers in their tracks. I've rescued kidnapped children.*

But through all that, had she really lived? She'd been shut off. Numb. Harboring a deep hatred, a deep darkness of spirit.

She directed her gaze to the plate in her hand—it contained a slice of white cake with white frosting. She looked up and saw Anthony staring at her from across the room, a champagne glass in his hand.

He smiled at her. It was the kind of smile that

passed between people who knew each other's deepest secrets.

She smiled back.

Anthony watched as she crossed the room. On the way, she put down the plate and grabbed a glass of champagne. "I thought you were going back to Virginia this morning," she said, taking a sip and looking at him over the edge of the glass.

"I was, but you know how persuasive your mother can be. I'm leaving first thing tomorrow instead. How about you?"

"Late tomorrow evening. I have a few things I need to finish up here."

He let out a slow breath, realizing that after what had happened with Gillian, he'd half expected her to say she wasn't coming back at all.

"I need to talk to you in private." She put down her glass, took his hand, and pulled him through the kitchen into her mother's pottery studio, shutting the door behind them.

A nightlight covered in blue glass bathed them in a velvet hue. From beyond the closed door came the sound of laughter and muffled voices. Sounds of life. It was one of those poetic, crystalline moments he recognized as two-thirds magic, one-third reality.

"I talked to Gavin Hitchcock."

Business. Spell broken.

Anthony took a swallow of champagne and waited. It was always business with Mary.

"I think Gillian might be right. I think it's possible Gavin Hitchcock didn't murder Fiona."

"Really?" He had trouble being as interested as he should have been.

"I'm going to suggest that Elliot get permission to reopen the case. Oh, look—your cup. It's been glazed."

She picked up a shrunken, misshapen cup in the most godawful yellow he'd ever seen. He didn't recognize it. "Are you sure that's mine?"

"Of course it's yours." She turned it around.

He didn't think he could have made something so ugly, but wasn't in the mood to argue. Instead he said, "I had a nice time that night."

"Me too." She smiled. "Remember when you kissed me?"

"Vaguely."

"I was drunk."

"I suspected as much."

"But I'm not drunk now."

"What are you getting at?"

She put the cup back on the shelf, then took his champagne glass from his hand, and set it beside the cup. "Ever since then I've been wondering if it was the alcohol that made it seem so nice."

Mary was someone who required a good three feet of personal space. Now she was standing absurdly close. An invitation if he'd ever seen one. *Mary, Mary, quite contrary*. "Are you suggesting a test?"

"It might answer some questions."

"And you're always looking for answers, aren't you?" He put his hands lightly and impersonally on her arms, then thought, *What the hell,* and pulled her snugly against him.

He could feel her chest rising and falling against his. And he thought it would be a cruel world to bring them together like this only to have her tell him she felt nothing, that it had been the alcohol after all. He'd better make the kiss an artistic masterpiece. What was he thinking? He glanced at the yellow cup, then back to Mary. He was no artist.

So he just kissed her. Lips to lips, breath to breath.

When she finally opened her eyes, he asked, "Fireworks?"

"Sparklers."

He would have been disappointed, except that her breathing was funny, and he could feel her heart thundering against his. As always, she would give him only so much. It was a game they played. She was tormenting him, and he liked it. Their time would come. However long it took, he would wait for her.

Chapter 36

Abigail Portman picked her way through the darkening woods. The weather had taken a warm turn the way it often did in early November, and much of yesterday's snow had melted. She'd read in the paper that the Cantrell girl had been found alive. That wasn't the news she wanted to hear. She'd wished she'd died, because it made her feel better to know other people were suffering, that other people's lives were as miserable as hers.

When she reached the memorial, she removed the dead roses and replaced them with a fresh bouquet. Then she straightened and stood in silence, staring at the white cross. . . .

She and Fiona had fought the morning of her death.

That's what people always talked about after a loved one died. The trivial argument they'd had beforehand. Maybe an argument over a messy room, or milk that had been left out of the refrigerator.

In their case it had been about sex.

Abigail recalled the folded note she'd found that had fallen from Fiona's coat pocket. She'd pretended it was a list, or maybe something she herself had dropped. But she'd known it was Fiona's, and she'd been curious. Not in a sneaky way, but in an oh-what-fun way. A we-share-everything way.

Fiona won't mind. We're best friends.

She opened the note, fully expecting to find some light chatter from Mary Cantrell or someone else Fiona hung around with. Instead, it was a note from a boy—or a male anyway. The fact that it was written on lined paper and had been folded into a small square made her think it must be someone from school, but that didn't really have to be the case.

It had been a shock to find that her daughter was a slut.

The note outlined every disgusting thing the person had done to her daughter, and outlined every disgusting thing Fiona had done back, wondering when they could meet again. The word *fuck* appeared again and again. *Fuck.* In a house that had never as much as allowed the word *damn.*

For a short time, Abigail's mind shut down, refusing to believe what she was reading. It was a joke. A stupid, sick game.

"What are you doing?"

The unfolded note, on wide-ruled paper torn from a spiral notebook, was still in Abigail's hand. Fiona stood in the doorway, dressed in a cute plaid skirt, kneesocks, and dark sweater. Her hair was shiny and straight, falling from a middle part. She looked so sweet and innocent that Abigail wanted to give her another chance. Maybe this was something this boy did to hurt good girls.

"Are you reading my note?"

Fiona crossed the room and snatched the paper from her mother, her face contorted with rage. "That's mine!"

There was no respect in a single cell of her body. Only rage. This wasn't her daughter. This was a stranger. A vicious, hateful stranger.

Where had the other girl gone? Abigail's daughter?

The girl she babied and worshiped and spoiled? The girl who got everything she wanted and more? Had she ever been there? Or was she someone Abigail had made up? Someone she'd created in her own mind, bestowing false traits on the person standing in front of her?

She thought about the mother and daughter day they'd shared a year ago. They'd gone out to eat at Café Noir on Hennepin. Over crepes, they'd had a timid discussion about boys and sex, with Abigail nervous but dead set on getting through the conversation. The subject had come up in the past, before Fiona had even started her period, and Abigail thought it would be good to have a refresher, this time going into things a little deeper. She knew Fiona wasn't having sex, and wanted to reassure her that a girl didn't need to have sex to be popular with the boys.

"I've gotten you something." She slid a small, wrapped box across the table.

Fiona unwrapped it, then opened the black velvet case inside.

"It's a promise ring," Abigail explained. "All the kids are getting them. It's a statement that lets people know you plan to remain a virgin until you marry."

Fiona smiled and slipped the ring on her wedding finger. At the time, the smile had seemed sincere, but now Abigail felt it had been a sly smile, a mocking smile.

"Thanks," Fiona said, examining the ring. "What a cute idea."

Now Abigail could see that the word *cute* had been issued in a mocking way too. Fiona had been making fun of her for years, and Abigail hadn't even known it.

Parents were blind. She'd often said so herself, but she'd been talking about other people. She'd ridiculed parents who didn't have a clue about their children, but she'd never thought she could be one of them. She and Fiona had a special bond, a special relationship. They could tell each other anything.

Their relationship had been a lie.

Fiona was wearing the ring now.

Had she laughed about it to the boy who'd written the note?

"Why didn't you tell me you had a boyfriend?" Abigail asked.

"I'm going to be late for school."

"How long has this kind of thing been going on?"

"You don't really want to know. Just forget it. Forget all about it. This is my birthday, remember? My *birthday*."

Even though their district had a perfectly acceptable bus system, Abigail had always taken her daughter to school. She had to be the best mom she could be.

"I want to know. As soon as you tell me," Abigail said woodenly, "I'll take you."

"This note?" Fiona shook the wrinkled paper. "This note isn't from a boyfriend. I don't have a boyfriend. I don't *want* a boyfriend. This is from a guy who is dumb but good when it comes to fucking. There. Is that what you wanted to hear? Do you feel better now?"

Abigail was afraid she might throw up. Like a robot, she went to the kitchen and got a drink of water. Then she came back, put on her shoes, and drove Fiona to school.

"Don't forget Mary," Fiona said when Abigail flew past the Cantrell house.

She braked, backed up, and honked. Did Mary know? she wondered. Was Mary a friend of the bitch or the sweet girl?

Brown-haired Mary came running across the lawn and threw herself into the backseat, laughing and breathless. "I thought you guys were going to forget me! Happy birthday, Fiona!" She reached over the back of the front seat and tugged playfully at Fiona's hair. "Sixteen! Finally!" Mary herself was seventeen. She'd started school late.

Was this all an act, part of the charade?

Abigail blocked out their chatter, driving but unaware of turning corners or obeying traffic lights. She must have done okay, because nobody ridiculed her. She let the girls out near the front of the school.

"Bye, Mrs. Portman!" Mary said, giving her a wave as she ducked to see inside the car. "Thanks for the ride!" The girls spun away, latching arms, laughing, and falling into each other as they skipped up the wide walk.

Abigail wanted to go home and crawl into bed, pull the covers up over her head. Her husband was out of town, but it would do no good to talk to him. They had grown apart years ago. A man with no personality, he was the ghost who occasionally showed up at their home. Tonight, if he thought about it, he would call his daughter and wish her a happy birthday, saying he was sorry he couldn't be there. Now Abigail wondered if he'd ever really wanted to be there.

She wished she'd never read the note. She wished she'd picked it up and slipped it back into Fiona's pocket. And now, even though she *had* read it, she guessed that Fiona would be perfectly willing to continue as if this morning had never happened.

People did that all the time. That's how they got through their days. But no, Abigail thought with anguish. Not when things had been so perfect. She could never forget, never go back.

It was over. The life she'd known was over because her daughter *was* her life. She'd read dozens of child-rearing books, so adamant had she been about doing things right. In almost every one they'd warned against getting too wrapped up in your child. *Don't give up an important goal for your child. Don't give up a dream job for your child. Don't give up a once-in-a-lifetime trip to Africa for your child.*

She'd laughed about that, and she'd secretly looked down upon Blythe Cantrell, who was always busy with her pottery and her art friends and her causes. *What kind of life is that for a child? When the mother is never there when her children get home from school?*

Abigail's one and only goal had been to be a good mother.

Not a birthday had gone by without Abigail planning a lavish party. Today was no exception. She'd intended to bake a cake herself—she hated it when people didn't bake birthday cakes for their loved ones. What kind of message did that send? But she didn't think she could pull herself together enough to bake a cake. And in years past the message had meant nothing to Fiona, so she went to the grocery store and picked up a large white sheet cake.

Last year she'd decorated Fiona's cake with tiny records and a tiny record player even though she knew most kids didn't play records anymore. Fiona had hugged her and called it adorable. Had she really thought it stupid? Probably.

"Is this for a special occasion? Would you like anything written on it?" the man behind the counter asked.

"Happy Birthday, Fiona."

"Fiona. Great name. Is this for a kid? An adult? What color would you like the lettering?"

"It's for my daughter. She's sixteen today."

"Sixteen. Wow. I remember sixteen. That was a wonderful age."

"Yes," Abigail numbly agreed.

She took the cake home and spent the rest of the day decorating for the party when all the while it seemed she was preparing for a funeral.

She picked up Fiona and Mary after school, dropping Mary off at her house. "See you at the party!" Fiona shouted after her.

"What do you think of the cake?" Abigail asked once they were inside their own house.

Fiona shrugged. "From a store, huh?" She stuck her finger in the frosting, scooping off a glob to pop in her mouth. "Good."

"Better than my cakes?" Abigail challenged, wondering what Fiona would say, what part she would play.

With her head tipped, she gave it some thought. "I don't know. Maybe a little." She turned and ran upstairs.

When she came back down a half hour later, she was wearing a dress Abigail had never seen. It was low-cut, showing cleavage, and the hem was so short her panties would show if she wasn't careful.

"You aren't wearing that dress for the party."

"Who says?"

"I say."

"It's my birthday. I should be able to wear what I want on my birthday." Angry, she flounced across the living room to the front door.

"And you certainly aren't going outside with that on."

Fiona smiled sweetly, opened the door, and left.

Abigail went to the window and watched as Fiona headed into the woods behind the house. She watched her disappear.

Abigail paced the kitchen, waiting for her to return. Waiting, waiting. Finally, unable to stand it any longer, she went after her.

A narrow path led deep into the woods to the tree house. Abigail was almost there when she stopped. Sounds came from the small wooden structure. Laughing and moaning, wild thrashing. Sounds of sex.

Fiona. And a boy. She was using the innocent tree house as a place to meet boys.

Anger rushed hot through her veins, blurring her vision, clenching her hands into fists. She strode across the ground, trampling wildflowers, her feet ripping through vines. She climbed up the ladder. Using a strength she didn't know she had, she grasped two branches and pulled herself up so she stood on the floor of the house. In one corner, on a filthy blanket, was her daughter, her dress around her waist. Between her knees knelt a boy—or a man—with stringy brown hair. Strewn around the room were empty beer cans and whiskey bottles.

"What are you doing!" she screamed.

The male looked at her over his shoulder, his mouth dropping open, his face turning red. Gavin Hitchcock. A foster kid who'd been kicked out of school more than once and who'd even been in jail.

He scrambled away, pulling up his pants as he went.

"Come on. We're going home," Abigail told Fiona. "You're having a party, remember?"

Fiona found her panties and put them on. Then she planted a big kiss on Hitchcock's greasy mouth. "Later," she said. She descended the ladder.

"I can't believe you followed me," she said as she watched her mother struggle to make it down the last few rungs.

Abigail dropped to the ground. She came to stand directly in front of her daughter, lifted her hand, and slapped her. "Whore."

Fiona's face became enraged, and she shoved her mother with two hands, pushing her into the leaf-covered forest floor. Then she turned and moved rapidly away.

Abigail was on her feet, running after her daughter. In her hand was a big rock—how had it gotten there? She had no memory of picking it up.

She swung, striking Fiona in the side of the head, knocking her down. Fiona stared at her in shocked disbelief. Abigail swung again and again.

She felt hands on her. "You're hurting her! Stop it! Stop!"

It was the boy—Gavin Hitchcock. He struggled to pull the rock from her hands.

She was all-powerful. She was the one in control of her daughter's life. She shoved Hitchcock away and struck Fiona again. Behind her, she heard sobbing intermingled with mumbling, begging, whimpering. Then silence. When she turned to look, the boy was unconscious, his mouth hanging open and edged with slobber.

She walked back toward the house. On the way, she washed the blood off the stone and off her hands, then left the stone in the streambed. At home, she took a shower and changed. She greeted the children when they arrived with gifts in their hands. When they asked about Fiona, she told them she was upstairs getting ready. And when she didn't show up, Abigail cut the cake and served it. When Fiona still hadn't arrived, the children ran shrieking and screaming and laughing through the woods, obliterating all footprints and clues as they looked for her.

Mary Cantrell found Fiona.

Abigail never intended to incriminate Gavin Hitchcock, but a gift was a gift. His prints were everywhere, in the tree house, on the beer cans and whiskey bottles. His semen was found inside Fiona, her blood on his clothes. What sealed the case was Gavin's own testimony. He said he didn't remember what happened to Fiona that night—which, to the jury and everybody else, was an admission of guilt.

And he *was* guilty, Abigail had told herself. He'd lured her daughter out there. He'd traded alcohol for sex. It was as much his fault as anybody's. And then, when he all but confessed, it seemed like something that was meant to be. She herself had been treated unfairly. Gavin Hitchcock going to prison for the crime seemed to even things out a little.

As the years passed, she occasionally felt guilty about Hitchcock, but never enough to publicly confess to killing her own daughter.

And it hadn't been her daughter. Not really. It had been some demon that had taken over her daughter's body. She'd *saved* Fiona.

Her grief was real. She mourned the loss of her daughter every day. She missed her with a pain that never subsided.

"I thought you might be the one bringing the roses."

She turned from where she was kneeling to see Mary Cantrell standing behind her. Abigail wearily shoved herself to her feet and stood facing Mary, searching her face for clues. Did she know?

"Why did you tell me you never come here?" Mary asked.

Abigail shrugged. "I don't know. I really don't. I do things I don't understand."

"So do I." Mary's voice was neutral but not unkind. "Mind if I walk back with you?"

They fell into step beside each other. For a moment, she wanted to blurt out everything. She suddenly had the overwhelming urge to tell Mary about Fiona and Gavin, about the sex and alcohol and how Fiona had hurt and humiliated her. But at the last moment, she stopped herself. What had she been thinking? Mary was an FBI agent. She wouldn't understand; she wouldn't feel sympathy for her—and sympathy was what she craved. And she didn't want Mary to know about the bad Fiona. Mary believed in the innocent, pure Fiona, and her naïve endorsement put the old Fiona that much closer to the truth. Abigail needed to keep only good memories of her daughter alive. *Your secret's safe with me, sweetheart. Safe with me.*

"I suppose you heard that we found Gillian," Mary said.

"Yes, I did. What a relief."

"That was nice of you to send the food and cards to Mom."

"I wanted to."

Mary paused, and Abigail looked up at her. She was such a tall girl—with such sad eyes. Green, weren't they? So somber. When she was little, she was always laughing. Now, dressed in her black city clothes, she looked like a priest who'd just heard the confession of every inmate on death row. Did she carry a gun? Had *she* ever killed anybody? She had a nice, full mouth, but she wasn't nearly as pretty as Fiona. No girls were as pretty as Fiona.

"I wanted to tell you that I'm sorry. Not sorry we found Gillian, but sorry things couldn't have turned out the same for you."

Abigail reached out and gave Mary's hand a comforting squeeze. "I'm just glad she's okay."

When they reached the Portman house, Abigail told her good-bye and went inside.

Mary stood in the street, in front of the Portman house for a long time. Then she pulled out her mobile phone and called Elliot. When he answered, she said, "I know who really killed Fiona Portman."

"Who?"

"Her mother. Abigail Portman. I think if you question her, she'll confess."

Mary disconnected and walked slowly home, to the place where Gillian and Blythe were waiting for her to join them for supper before taking her to the airport. To her mother's house, where a light was burning.

Savannah medical examiner John Casper believed in what some scientists termed the cluster effect. Toss a bunch of anything down—seeds, flower petals, cards—and they always grouped together. Same thing with dead bodies. They never came one at a time but in bunches. The latest bunch had been exceptionally large, with doctors and assistants working overtime to process an unusually high volume that had left their cold storage filled to capacity. They were almost caught up, with people heading home complaining of headaches from lack of sleep and too many hours spent inhaling formalin fumes.

"Have you looked outside?" Willy Claxton, the one remaining assistant asked, hovering nervously in the doorway of the main office just off the autopsy suites. "A bad storm is blowing in from the islands. They been talking about it on the radio."

John pushed his paperwork aside and leaned back, chair creaking. Even in the isolation of the morgue, the air and his head had that heavy feeling that came with a dramatic drop in barometric pressure. "Why don't you go on home? Before it hits."

"What about the last body?"

John glanced through the decedent's file. "Pretty straightforward. Looks like a heart attack victim."

John stood and stretched. He'd been there for more than twelve hours. His joints ached, and his skin had that prickly, tight feeling that came with too little sleep. "Help me get him on the table, and you can take off."

Willy wheeled the body from the cold unit, then pushed it into an autopsy suite. The room smelled strongly of the disinfectant used between examinations. He locked the wheels, then the two men heaved the corpse from the gurney to the stainless steel table. John noticed that the zipper on the body bag hadn't been pulled tight—there was a gap of about two inches.

"Thanks, man," Willy said, snapping off his gloves and tossing them in the biohazard bin. "I need to get home. My wife's afraid of storms."

John nodded, allowing the man his dignity. Everybody knew Willy grew uneasy when darkness came. A lot of people were like that. Even some of the other medical examiners. John found it interesting that modern man still suffered from ancient fears left over from a period in history when humans lived in the open and darkness was a real threat. It wasn't the darkness that would get you, it was the people in that darkness. You didn't work in a morgue without coming away with that lesson well learned. Homicides had doubled this year, and the city was feeling just as uneasy as Willy.

After Willy left, John suited up in a gown, a mask, goggles, and latex gloves, then put on some tunes. Had to have autopsy tunes.

He unzipped the bag and leaned back, waiting for the stink to hit him.

Nothing.

Sometimes bodies didn't smell. But then again, when you worked around dead people as long as John had, your olfactories shut down. The brain finally decided, Hey, I've smelled that before. Smelled that a lot. No cause for alarm.

John spoke into the Dictaphone: "Decedent's name: Truman Harrison. No middle initial. Body belongs to a fifty-one-year-old African-American male with a history of heart disease."

He photographed the body, then removed and bagged the clothing—not easy without an assistant. He examined the cadaver externally, surprised to find no outward signs of rigor mortis or livor mortis. The guy must not have been dead very long before being put on ice. And he chewed the hell out of his fingernails, John noted, lifting a hand to examine it more closely.

Outside, the storm was raging, but the autopsy suite within the heart of the morgue was silent. John had almost forgotten about the weather until the unmistakable sound of a nearby lightning strike penetrated the thick walls, rattling glass containers in nearby cupboards. The room plunged into darkness. Seconds later, John heard the emergency generators kick in, and the lights flickered on.

Everything under control.

John continued with the autopsy. He placed a rubber block under the cadaver's neck, then positioned the scalpel for the Y incision, beginning at the right shoulder below the collarbone. One inch in to the cut, the dead body let a long sigh.

The scalpel slipped from John's fingers, clattering to the stainless steel exam table. He stared at the dead man's face, searching for signs of life. A decaying body rapidly formed gas, and it wasn't unusual for a dead person to appear to exhale. Some bodies even moved as the gas shifted around looking for an escape route.

"Jesus." John let out a nervous laugh. He'd had bodies move before, but it was always unnerving.

He retrieved the scalpel and poised his hand to continue with the incision. He was shaking. "Shit. What a fucking baby. Calm down. It was just a little gas, that's all." Too late, he remembered the Dictaphone. With his slipper-covered foot, he shut it off with the remote switch, then stood there breathing hard. The downdraft fan was humming.

He tossed the scalpel on the instrument tray, then picked up the dead man's wrist and felt for a pulse.

Nothing.

He felt the carotid artery in his neck.

Nothing.

He pulled out a miniature flashlight and checked his pupils. Nothing.

In the adjoining scrub room, he rummaged through the cabinets until he found a stethoscope. Why anybody would have a stethoscope in a morgue was beyond him, but it had been there since his first day. Back in the autopsy suite, feeling foolish and glad nobody else was there, he turned off the downdraft fan and placed the stethoscope against the dead man's chest. Was that something? A faint sound? A gentle *lub . . . lub?* Or was it his own heart beating frantically in his head?

He pulled the stethoscope from his ears, then began another search, finally finding what he was looking for. A mirror. Round, eight inches in diameter. With a paper towel, he rubbed it clean, making sure there were no smudges or fingerprints on the glass, then held it to the dead man's mouth and nose.

Primitive, but effective.

Keeping his eye on the clock, he waited a full minute before lifting it away.

On the surface of the mirror were three condensation marks—two small, one large—marks that gradually vanished as John stared at them in horror and disbelief.

HUSH

Anne Frasier

"INTENSE...This is far and away the best serial killer story I have read in a very long time."
—Jayne Ann Krentz

"CHILLING...Don't read this book if you are home alone."
—Lisa Gardner

Criminal profiler Ivy Dunlap is an expert at unraveling the psyches of the most dangerous men alive. She understands the killer instinct. But even Ivy has her limits. And the Madonna Murderer will test them...

0-451-41031-9

To order call: 1-800-788-6262

ONYX

A KISS GONE BAD

Jeff Abbott

"A BREAKTHROUGH NOVEL."
—*New York Times* bestselling author Sharyn McCrumb

"Rocks big time...pure, white-knuckle suspense. I read it in one sitting."
—*New York Times* bestselling author Harlan Coben

A death rocks the Gulf Coast town of Port Leo, Texas. Was it suicide, fueled by a family tragedy? Or did an obsessed killer use the dead man as a pawn in a twisted game? Beach-bum-turned judge Whit Mosley must risk everything to find out.

"Exciting, shrewd and beautifully crafted...A book worth including on any year's best list."
—*Chicago Tribune*

0-451-41010-6

To order call: 1-800-788-6262

S425/Abbott